T0292947

Occupational Risk Control

Derek Viner's name is synonymous with the study and practice of engineering approaches to health and safety. In this highly readable and instructive book he draws on his enviable wealth of experience, taking the reader on a journey from the foundations of accident theory through the measurement, control and management of risk using practical, down-to-earth examples to de-mystify and simplify the subject and dispel common misconceptions.

Steve Cowley,
SafeWork Solutions

By totally unpacking the subject, Derek Viner has not only provoked the reader into exploring areas of risk mythology but also probed areas for those who are non-safety aware. The book poses questions that you may not have thought about before. It not only poses the questions but the writer gives well-reasoned and suitably researched answers. Encompassing areas outside the OHS parameters allows the reader to consider and explore from the broadest of perspectives. Those on the path of becoming part of the OHS profession will be able to use the book as an ideal reference to add to their portfolio of knowledge.

John Lacey, Vice President,
Institution of Occupational Safety and Health (IOSH), UK

This book has something for everybody from the experienced OHS professional to professionals from other disciplines who have a role in understanding and managing risk. Viner uses an easy story-telling style to take the reader on a journey. ... The book is a good read and a major contribution to the "science of risk" ensuring that the social influences and practical context are also considered.

Pam Pryor, Registrar,
Australian OHS Education Accreditation Board

This work is dedicated to the 2,950,000 people annually who lose their lives due to their work, and to the families and loved ones who experience their loss and carry their memory each day.

Occupational Risk Control

Predicting and Preventing the Unwanted

DEREK VINER

Routledge
Taylor & Francis Group

LONDON AND NEW YORK

First published 2015 by Gower Publishing

2 Park Square, Milton Park, Abingdon, Oxfordshire OX14 4RN
52 Vanderbilt Avenue, New York, NY 10017

Routledge is an imprint of the Taylor & Francis Group, an informa business

First issued in paperback 2019

Gower Applied Business Research
Our programme provides leaders, practitioners, scholars and researchers with thought provoking, cutting edge books that combine conceptual insights, interdisciplinary rigour and practical relevance in key areas of business and management.

British Library Cataloguing in Publication Data
A catalogue record for this book is available from the British Library

Library of Congress Cataloging-in-Publication Data
Viner, Derek.
 Occupational risk control : predicting and preventing the unwanted / by Derek Viner.
    pages cm
 Includes bibliographical references and index.
  ISBN 978-1-4724-1970-5 (hardback) -- ISBN 978-1-4724-1971-2 (ebook) -- ISBN 978-1-4724-1972-9 (epub) 1. Industrial safety. 2. Risk assessment. I. Title.
  T55.V533 2015
  363.1--dc23
                                                                              2014039147

ISBN 13: 978-1-4724-1970-5 (hbk)
ISBN 13: 978-0-367-87923-5 (pbk)

Contents

List of Figures

List of Tables

About the Author

Derek Viner is a consulting risk engineer and management consultant in risk control, whose career has spanned the period from the late 1970s to the present. During this time he has been instrumental in developing the academic disciplines of accident phenomenology and risk philosophy through his continuous involvement with post-graduate courses in risk and safety. Derek's second book, *Accident Analysis and Risk Control*, published in 1991 has been described as something that should be compulsory reading for all engineers.

Foreword

Despite more than a century of effort by governments and industry to prevent accidents, in 2014 they continue to occur in epidemic proportions. Given the acclaimed benefits of years of science and technological development to society, it is a travesty that the failure to effectively manage risk continues to cause untold misery and loss. Despite technical advances, lives are still being cut short or irreversibly affected, and the loved ones of those killed and injured are left to cope with their memories and loss. At the national level, in the so-called developed countries at least, the failure to effectively manage risk costs billions of dollars annually. For example in Australia, the annual direct cost of accidents is approaching A$80 billion or around 8 percent of the country's gross domestic product. There is no evidence to suggest that this is atypical of other nations in the Western world, and by the year 2020 some 10 percent of the wealth generated by global industry and society will be wasted because of the institutionalised lack of effective management of risk.

Albert Einstein is credited with saying 'It is insanity to keep doing the same thing over and over again and expect different results', yet the corollary of this, that if you do different things you'll get different results, seems to be equally inappropriate to illustrate what has been the case in the supposed modern approaches to addressing the unabated accident phenomenon.

The last 50 years or so has seen a plethora of attempts to focus attention on different aspects of the problem. There have been continuous attempts to legislate the problem away. First by prescribing specific solutions to known failure types, the prescriptive approach, which seems not to work because the law writers can't keep up with the unrelenting advance of technology. Secondly, by enshrining in law the obligation of those in control of risk to ensure safe outcomes, the so-called performance-based approach where the methods required are not prescribed but the 'safe' outcome target is set. The former approach is the basis of safety laws in the USA, and the latter that of the Westminster-derivative systems of law. However, while the legislation is just a starting point, a comparison of accident occurrence data between the USA and the Westminster countries suggests that both approaches have been equally unsuccessful in stemming the tide of accidents, failures and losses. In fact, it seems the legislative model is somewhat irrelevant and the actual solution must lie elsewhere.

There has also been a continuous effort to address the problem with an emphasis on apportioning the blame for accidents to individuals and then taking legal action against them. Too often, those directly involved in accidents, such as the driver of the vehicle, the pilot of the aircraft or the operator of the machine, are the ones that are blamed. Most of what is expected of people in almost all industrial settings is prescribed in rules and procedures and it is usually easy to identify where actual methods and behaviours that led to an accident deviated from the expected prescribed methods and behaviours. As long as there have been accidents there has been litigation against those thought to be responsible, either to recover damages or to apportion penalties. Stemming from the almost innate human need to find someone responsible for their loss, this derivative of the Common Law has also been found wanting as an effective prevention measure.

In the latter years of the 20th century there was a shift in emphasis away from the errors and violations of those 'at the coal face' to the notion of the organisational accident, where the underlying errors and decisions of management were deemed to be equally culpable. The need to blame was satisfied with a different target.

The reality is that accidents are a complex phenomenon. There is a popular adage that no accidents are caused by a single factor, and while this is indeed true it is equally unhelpful because in reality even the apparently simplest accidents are the result of intricate relationships between the processes, systems, technologies, environment and people. Singling out one aspect for attention and treatment, as seems often to have been done in the past, is at best unhelpful and at worst reduces the effectiveness of prevention efforts.

The accident epidemic continues unabated despite the plethora of fashionable approaches offered as panaceas over the years. While it could be argued that there needs to be a dramatic change in approach across industry and society, in actuality it would seem more pertinent to suggest instead a need to rediscover the basic principles in the underpinning science of risk and turn away from a safety practice that is reduced to the simple application of a risk assessment matrix, which delivers often dubious outcomes.

There is a clear need to use risk management approaches which maximise the success of people in the systems and provide operating environments, systems and processes that are error tolerant. System designs need to ensure that there is sufficient redundancy to deliver reliable and safe outcomes even when human performance is suboptimal.

This book will serve to place accident prevention attention on the underpinning science of risk and reliability. Beginning with a comprehensive description of the accident phenomenon and the history of attempts at understanding and mitigation, *Occupational Risk Control* offers a pragmatic and thorough description of the concepts, methods and principles of risk. Central to the tenets offered is the notion that it is energy that causes the harm when accidents occur and therefore effective accident prevention, in other words the effective control of risk, must involve the effective control of the energies present in the organisational systems and occupational environments in which people operate. Clear annunciation of these principles also dispels some of the myths and commonly held misconceptions surrounding risk, where weaknesses in control systems are often mistaken for hazards, with resultant loss of efficacy of risk management efforts.

This book should be read by everyone with responsibility for effectively managing risk. It should be a mandatory text for risk management and safety professionals, academics and students alike. It provides insights into effective control of risk across all industries and all aspects of human endeavour.

Associate Professor Geoff Dell, PhD
Discipline Leader, Accident Investigation and Forensics
Central Queensland University, Australia
and
Principal, Protocol Safety Management Pty Ltd

Preface

There is much that brings complexity to the study of risk and the practice of its management. Each different type of risk requires a different understanding of its origins and how to control it. Even the same type of risk may be found in very different technologies and very different circumstances that greatly influence it. In addition, the essential uncertainty of various aspects of risk, particularly where and when we may suffer from it, result in an extraordinary complexity in our personal and societal responses to it. The enormous range of this uncertainty brings within the scope of investigation matters whose effects are as varied in consequence as routinely experienced machinery breakdown and infrequent catastrophe. Our ability to harness the powers of nature in the service of industry and society has grown rapidly, especially since World War Two, and far more rapidly than our understanding of risk and its management. The punctuation of the historical record with high profile disasters continues apparently little influenced by our efforts, as anyone with access to world news knows.

Various strands of theory and research have the potential to contribute to a better understanding and capability, from statistics and reliability mathematics to the study of psychology and human factors and failure analysis and prediction tools. However, it is generally true that developments in these disparate areas have proceeded in parallel and it is further evidence of the complexity of this field of study that each can be accommodated without apparent overlap. There has also been little development in the way in which society as a whole responds to significant events, and in parts of the English speaking world at least no real thought has been given to how laws might be framed to allow society to better learn how to control risk.

It is not all bad news, however, as one thing that can be said to have changed dramatically for the better in modern times is the amount of effort and good intention devoted to this field. This has given rise to a rapid growth in both undergraduate and graduate courses of study and to a somewhat unsatisfied need for useful texts to support these studies. There is a particular need to present a view of risk and its management that sketches the overall character of the subject and that is founded on essential underlying principles that have stood and will stand the test of time. These principles should be relevant to the whole wide scope of pure risk and accommodate complexity, whatever its source. Such a text should also ensure that the new generation of aspiring risk engineers, advisers and managers is able to learn from the costly lessons of the past. It is hoped that the present work satisfies all or many of these needs. Much insight can be gained from practical examples, but a book can become unwieldy if it contains too many of them. Consequently, a number of examples are to be found on the associated web site, to which the reader is invited.

This book is the distillation of 40 years of experience in teaching and practising the management of risk, beginning in the mid 1970s when the author was given the task of establishing a postgraduate course in occupational hazard management. It quickly became apparent that the prominent practitioners of the time shared very little by way of terminology or methods and that there was also little material suited to inclusion in a course of study at that academic level. What there was had been widely ignored in favour of ideas from the 1930s. Industrial safety was a behaviour-oriented sub-professional activity supported less by research or theory than by beliefs. At the gathering of the first group of students admitted to the course, one asked: 'What makes you think you can teach us anything?' Subsequent experience made it clear that teachers learn from students and students learn from teachers. In my case, the teacher took himself out into the real world, which is where the great majority of my work has been over the years. Consulting work was punctuated by the need to conduct lectures in the subjects of accident phenomenology and risk philosophy and to absorb the implications of hundreds of case studies submitted by students as the subject matter of their assignment work. It was also punctuated by periodic assignments as an expert witness, which provided an opportunity to see both the good and bad influences of the operation of the law and insurance companies.

A scientific education equips one less to understand the peculiarities of human behaviour in industry than to recognise the risk problems that people seemed so unable to perceive for themselves. Ideas of fault and blame appear to be both innate and virtually immoveable and people are ready and even grateful to return to them after a period of discomfort experiencing the more rational (and perhaps therefore frightening?) world to which the underlying principles direct attention.

The need is to uncover a theoretical basis for understanding risk that is in accordance with the idea apparently credited to Einstein (but understood and approved of by many scientists) that everything should be made as simple as possible, but not simpler. From a good and simple theory comes the opportunity to understand complexity for what it is – the interaction of the real world with the principles which govern it. The temptation to enter the world of correlative statistical analysis of circumstances trusting that, with luck that can later be disguised as brilliance, deeper analysis will uncover the real meaning of an accident has been resisted. It almost certainly will not. For the same reasons, the student and practitioner of the subject should develop a healthy caution towards the fads and fashions that periodically sweep through this field in the form of models and methods.

With these admissions made public, the content of the book will be no surprise: exploration of complexity, with its point of connection with underlying principles hopefully always made evident. Wherever extraneous complexity exposes itself (for example decision theory, human error theory, present net value, the details of reliability mathematics) the choice has been to exclude it, in the belief that it can always be studied at another place and time and from a more qualified teacher. Because of the still pervasive acceptance of accident theory, including the need to find causes, a chapter is included that explicitly explains the theory and the results of adopting it. Where appropriate, attention is drawn to the links with the principles that are given a more thorough explanation in the book.

Every idea and guiding principle contained here has demonstrated its practical value in understanding real problems, given birth often in moments of the need to understand or to explain. The occupational scope of these testing grounds has included heavy engineering (integrated steel plants, open and deep mines, the power industry, fabrication and construction, petrochemical), manufacturing, paper, fish farming and forestry, food processing, universities, hospitality, as well as local and national government departments (regulators, ports and harbours, water, roads and traffic). The cultural scope has included very large and very small industries, well- and not so well-managed ones, large bureaucracies and industries in developing as well as developed nations.

At all times, the emphasis is on the development of preventive capability. Very little emphasis is given to reactive methods, including accident investigation. If one understands the processes of damage and loss well, no special understanding is required to conduct an accident investigation, unless it be unravelling bent metal (in which case theory is not of much assistance), or seeking someone to blame or prosecute (which has little social or practical value).

The underlying physical principles on which risk can be understood can be applied no matter what the organisation, industry or culture. Understanding management structures and capabilities is a completely different problem. Risk management requires a special set of capabilities not necessarily found in day to day management. As one manager said: 'I can understand every aspect of managing this company, from sales to production and industrial relations. Why is it I cannot understand safety management?' In the early days of the author's career as an aerodynamicist there was a sign in the aerodynamics design office, which said: Simplicate and add lightness. Therein lies the task for risk advisers. Not being skilled in management theory, nor in individual and group psychology, the author cannot claim to offer much in the way of theoretical insight into this fundamental need. It is, however, a fact that risk management is a specific rather than a general task. No matter what the culture is, what needs to be done remains the same. The method of getting it done needs to be suited to the ability of the organisation and the people presently occupying positions – it will still need to be done long after they have moved on, so the task belongs to the organisation, not the individuals currently on watch.

We cannot afford to be too prescriptive about how the tasks are done or the objectives achieved, as this may be uncomfortable for the affected manager, whose abilities and ideas must be respected. We can inform and educate, listen carefully to the reasons for lack of progress and then think of ways in which the goal can be achieved within that framework, or capabilities developed that will eventually lead to the goal being reached.

In all this work, it is very important to distinguish between the management of operational risks and risks of a more general nature. Operational risks are those that arise in the specific processes of the organisation and if badly managed may lead to highly significant adverse consequences. Health and safety practitioners are experienced with general risks but their methods may be, and in many cases are, unsuited to the management of operational risks (and, regrettably, possibly also to understanding general risks). It is unsettling to see the effective and embedded practices to manage operational risks in the commercial aviation industry being threatened by general safety management methods of unproven value.

This book is written as a contribution to other practitioners, academics and students as well as to industry professionals including other engineers, scientists and managers in the hope that it makes even a small (although a large one would be better) contribution to reduction in the numbers of people killed by their employment, which will have amounted to about 55 worldwide since you began reading this preface.

Further information about this book and its subject matter can be found at www.derekviner.com.

Derek Viner
Devizes

Acknowledgements

In the course of a few working decades one gains so much from so many people that it is hardly possible to remember them all. No experience or wisdom is gained without opportunity being made available, nor without the hospitality shown by those who freely expose the innermost workings of their organisations, nor without the contributions and questions of students, nor the discussions with colleagues, nor without family support. And so I would like to thank all those countless employees at all levels with whom I have spent thousands of hours, as well as probably thousands of students whose contributions, insights and challenges have also been invaluable. At the risk of unintended omission, for which I apologise, for opportunity, trust, debate, correction and humour I would like to thank: Alan Bruce, John Butler, Cheryle Burns, John Carlton, Ron Cordingley, Dr Steve Cowley, Dr Geoff Dell, Captain S.M. Divekar, Dr Jack Harvey, Gary James, John Lacey, Pam Pryor, the late P.K. Roy, David Skegg, Somboon Thagoolsawat, Dr Yogeswara Thotad. For family support and love, without which effort has little purpose, I say thank you to my daughter Emily and son Rishi and their families and last but not least my late wife Bess.

Glossary:
Definitions Reduce Confusion

Accident	An unplanned, unexpected and unwanted event that gives rise to injury, damage or loss, usually occurring over a short period of time.
Accident Type 1	An aspect of *Error* in which a person who is aware of the correct action needed but performs an action unintentionally which has adverse effects.
Accident Type 2	An aspect of *Error* in which a person who is unaware of the correct action needed but performs an action unintentionally which has adverse effects.
Accidental	Something that happened unintentionally.
Action failure	The post hoc assessment that an action by a person was not what it should have been or an action that differed from a defined standard. Also called 'active failure'. See also *Error*.
Asset	Something of value to a Risk agent. This term is used in risk theory to describe anything that may sustain a *Consequence* of an *Occurrence*.
Audit plan	A formal plan for checking the implementation of risk control measures nominated in a *Risk register*.
Barrier	That which stands between and prevents access or progress. Used as a form of risk control with powered machinery, edges (gravitational potential energy), electrical energy and radiant energy (including noise, heat and ionising radiation) in all of which cases the purpose is to prevent a susceptible object (e.g. a person) proceeding past a point at which risk is considered to be unacceptable. A barrier may be passive (always present) or active (present when the susceptible object approaches the *Damaging energy space*). The term is also used in modern versions of *Accident* theory and in the use of Bow-tie models, in which usage it is a synonym for *Control measure*.
Best available technology	A term derived from legal expectations that risk *Control measures* will be the best that is available, typically when the *Likely Worst Consequence* is very significant.

Best practical technology	A term derived from legal expectations that risk *Control measures* will be the best that is practicable, typically when the *Likely Worst Consequence* is relatively moderate in *Severity* and implying that considerations of cost and functional inconvenience may be taken into account.
Blame	The finding of fault or responsibility for something that has gone wrong: lawyers, the police, public enquiries and members of the public want to find a person to blame afterwards. See also *Scapegoat*.
Boolean algebra	A form of algebra that enables the probability of an event to be calculated where that event is brought about by various logical possibilities described by algebraic operators such as AND, OR, NOR (not OR), NAND (not AND). It is widely used in *Quantified risk analysis*.
Bow-tie diagram	A simplified form of risk analysis diagram showing *Mechanism* and *Outcome/Consequence* options without the use of rigorous analysis or logic diagrams.
Breakdown	A maintenance engineering term, meaning that the equipment in question is no longer able to perform its function.
Burn-in	A maintenance engineering term, synonymous with *Infant mortality* and meaning that equipment has failed due to some manufacturing or installation defect.
Captive key	An *Interlock* method in which a cative key is only released when required conditions are met and can then be used to open a *Guard* to enter a *Damaging Energy Space (DES)*. Until the key is returned to capture, the DES cannot be energised.
Cause	In the context of a 'cause–effect' view of the universe, that which produces an effect. Cause–effect thinking gives rise to qualifying terms such as contributory, necessary, root, etc. causes. Accident theory depends on the idea that prevention results from the removal of cause(s).
Cause analysis	Any of a number of methods of understanding Cause, including those that make use of logic diagrams used in *Risk Analysis* (*Fault Tree* and *Event Analysis*). Cause analysis is distinguished by the allowance of judgemental terms such as 'insufficient', 'less than adequate' etc. which have no place in risk analysis.
Cause – contributory	A cause that has some influence on *necessary* and *sufficient causes*, such that its removal changes the character of these causes or their effect in some way.
Cause – necessary	The cause in question always and only creates the specified effect.

Cause – proximate	The cause most closely associated with the effect in time.
Cause – root	In a sequence of 'cause–effect' happenings, this is the first 'cause', the one that started the whole sequence. See also *Root cause analysis*.
Cause – sufficient	The cause in question is one way the specified effect can be brought about, but not the only way.
Cause – ultimate	The cause at the very start of the cause–effect process that created the effect, the furthest back in time from the effect. Accident theorists like to call this the root cause).
Chance	A colloquial term which is a synonym for *Probability*.
Chemical bonding energy	When substances join together to form a new chemical substance, energy is involved in the creation of the chemical bonds that form at an atomic or molecular level. Energy is also involved when a substance changes state from solid to liquid to gas, for example. When the bond is changed energy may be released (an exothermic reaction) or absorbed (an endothermic reaction).
Circumstance	A Circumstance is something subject to fairly regular and recognisable change, for example the weather. Used in Risk theory to assist in understanding *Risk factors*.
Collision	A term used when a mobile object hits either another mobile object or a stationary feature of its operating environment. The force of the collision creates damage as the energy of the object(s) is absorbed in structural *Strain energy*. Collision types can be categorised on the basis of one or both objects moving and the direction of approach (e.g. from one side, overtaking, approaching head on).
Combustion	The process of oxidation of a substance that has the characteristics of *Fire*, namely flames and radiant heat.
Concluding (*Condition* and *Circumstance*)	A *Condition* or *Circumstance* that is influential in determining *Outcome* pathways of an *Occurrence* or the *Consequences*.
Condition	A Condition is something that is fixed or that changes sufficiently slowly (if at all) for the fact of change to be unrecognisable.
Condition monitoring	A maintenance strategy to monitor the health of an item of equipment so that it may be allowed to operate for as long as possible and its subsequent maintenance planned at a convenient time.
Conflict	In *Collision* theory, a conflict arises if the speed vector of a moving object, such as a vehicle, will result in a collision with either another moving object or a stationary object if corrective action is not taken.

Conflict of interest	The conflict that exists between the motivation to gain a commercial or personal advantage and the moral or ethical need to control *Risk*.
Consequence	The unwanted, negative or adverse result of the *Occurrence* process. Consequences are of three general types: *Injury, Damage* and *Loss*.
Consequence Value	The value of the *Consequence* of a *Risk* to a Risk agent. This may be measured in terms of monetary value, or by a word scale.
Consequence Value – likely least	Any *Risk* can give rise to a range of possible *Consequence Values*. The likely least such value is the smallest *Consequence* that would be noticeable or the smallest value at which an *Occurrence* may be reported. Abbreviated as LLC.
Consequence Value – likely worst	Any *Risk* can give rise to a range of possible *Consequence Values*. The possible worst Consequence Value is often distinctly different from the likely worst Consequence Value. A synonym for this in use in the insurance industry is 'worst probable loss'. Abbreviated as LWC.
Contributory factor	A factor that in some way supports or could support the existence of a process that could lead to *Damage*. It contributes to the presence of the process or to its *Likelihood*, or contributes to the *Consequence* or its *Consequence Value*. The meaning is very similar to if not identical to that of a *contributory cause* in cause–effect language.
Control – active	A *Control measure* that is put in place or activated following the detection of a process that could lead to *Damage*. Examples include water sprinklers, intruder alarms, presence-sensing devices used in machinery.
Control – administrative	A *Control measure* of an administrative nature, the purpose of which is to support and provide the foundation for risk controls of a more physical or procedural nature.
Control – passive	A *Control measure* that is put in place in anticipation of a possible future *Damage* process that requires no activation to make it work if the process does occur. Examples include: fire hardness in buildings through the use of materials that significantly slow the progress of *Fires*, such as concrete floors and wall; fixed *Guards* on machinery.
Control measure	Anything whose purpose is to make a process that could lead to *Injury, Damage* or *Loss* less likely to occur or less damaging if it did occur.
Control mode	The mode of control of an item of equipment or a system. This may be manual, semi-automatic or automatic. A maintenance mode may be provided that allows restricted energisation for the purpose of trouble-shooting or adjustment.

Control system	A control system detects the state of performance of a system and compares this against a pre-determined desired state, making any required adjustments to track the desired state as accurately as possible. See also *Controller*.
Controllable	A term used in common law in discussions to establish whether Injury or Damage arose from Negligence. If the process that gave rise to the injury or damage is considered to not be reasonably controllable, then it is unlikely that the person or organisation would be considered negligent.
Controller	This term is used to describe a function whose purpose is to keep a system at a required state, for example hot water at a desired temperature, a vehicle on a particular track. The malfunction of a controller is one possible *Mechanism* of an *Event*.
	A controller consists of an input mechanism (that detects the relevant state, such a temperature or track of the vehicle), a processing mechanism, that compares the detected state with the desired state (e.g. the actual temperature vs the detected temperature) and an output mechanism that is able to change the state of the system, for example by increasing the temperature if that is what is needed.
	A controller may be a human being or a mechanism (e.g. a thermostat, a computer).
Corrosion	An oxidation process that usually proceeds slowly. The term is usually applied to metals and refers to the commonly seen rust when steel or iron corrodes.
Criticality	The extent to which the functioning of an item of equipment is critical to the proper or safe operation of a system.
Damage	An unwanted change to the desirable qualities of an *Asset*. Damage is one form of *Consequence*.
Damage threshold	The intensity of *Energy* at which *Damage* will begin to be experienced.
Damages	The monetary penalty imposed by a court of law on a person or organisation found to be *Negligent*. Payable to the injured party as a recompense for the *Injury* or *Damage* caused and even as a punishment for this.
Damaging energy space	The actual volume in space in which *Injury* or *Damage* to an *Asset* is possible if the space is energised. Examples include the volume between the closing faces of a press, the line in space through which a high-powered laser beam can pass, the volume around an electrical conductor within which an arc can form if a person or other object is introduced.

Danger

In colloquial speech this implies the source of possible *Injury* or *Damage*, (as in the phrase 'the presence of danger') or the *Likelihood* of it (as in the phrase 'immediate danger'). The term is not in regular use by scientists working in this field.

Danger tag

A tag attached to an item of equipment to indicate that operation, entry or use is prohibited due to failure or incomplete precautions.

Dangerous

An unacceptably high level of *Risk*. See *Risk – acceptable*.
In colloquial speech this term may be used simply to mean that *Injury* or *Damage* is immediately possible, for example when approaching a cliff edge, or driving at high speed on a winding road.

Demand

A type of *Exposure*, suited to use with equipment that is occasionally subject to a demand to perform, for example an alarm system.

Disease

When some aspect of the body of an animal or plant is not functioning as intended, it is said to be diseased. Generally this term is not used if the reason for the malfunction is a result of a *short-term Energy transfer* (which tends to create an acute *Injury*) or even a *multiple repetitive Energy transfer,* for the same reason. The International Classification of Diseases is the authoritative guide to the names of diseases.

Duty of care

A legal construct, derived from common law and defined in Statute law and applied to those in responsibility in organisations or who have the power to design equipment, for example.

Electromagnetic field

Static electrical charges are surrounded by an electric field that is detectable at a distance from the particle. Accelerating electrical charges (for example an alternating electric current) are also surrounded by a magnetic field, which is also detectable at a distance. The electromagnetic field (EMF) has the property of being able to transmit energy away from the source of the field, in a manner approximately analogous to vibration being transmitted through an elastic medium. On encountering a suitable material, this EMF may in turn create induced alternating currents and charges. The frequency of the EMF is the same as the frequency of the source alternating current. The EMF frequency range is very large and includes radio waves and microwaves.

Emergency stop

Also called an E-stop. A control whose sole purpose is the emergency shutdown of the powered equipment on which it is installed. An emergency stop has as its primary objective rapid and complete de-energisation of the equipment in order to minimise the potential for *Damage* or *Injury*. Ordinary stop functions bring equipment to a de-energised state in an orderly manner and usually in a longer time period.

Enabling (*Condition* and *Circumstance*)	These affect the *Likelihood* of *Mechanisms* for which *Prerequisites* already exist.
Endogenous	A term used to describe the situation in which a risk is taken by a *Risk agent* by their own decision.
Energy	Energy is the ability to do *Work*, if a suitable means can be found to convert the source of energy into a physical device able to move a *Force*. All forms of energy are interchangeable, for example heat energy can be made to increase *Kinetic energy* or *Gravitational potential energy,* and vice versa. *Chemical bonding energy* can be transformed in to heat, light, sound, pressure energy and kinetic energy, which is what happens when there is a chemical explosion.
Energy – stored	Energy, typically in equipment, that is stored, typically in the form of pressure, charge, heat and gravitational potential energy.
Energy conservation	The law of conservation of *Energy* states that whenever a process results in a change of the form of energy, the overall energy is conserved during the process. For example, if an *Explosion* occurs the energy released from broken chemical bonds in the explosive substance will equal the energy imparted to the effects of the explosion, such as the heat wave, the pressure (shock) wave, noise, light and *Flying objects*.
Energy damage	*Damage* is a term used to indicate that the structure of something has been materially modified for the worse – distorted, torn apart, punctured, etc. Such modification can only be achieved by the application of *Energy* in *Intensities* that the strength of the object is unable to resist.
Energy damage model	The name given to the model of the process of *Energy damage* described in this text.
Energy intensity	Energy intensity is the amount of *Energy* per unit area of the surface through which the energy flows. For example, energy in the form of radiant heat will flow outwards from a point source of heat and the surface through which it flows is the surface of a sphere. As the distance from the point source becomes greater the energy intensity decreases proportionately with the increase in surface area of the sphere.
Energy radiation	Energy radiation is a term used to indicate that *Energy* from a source is able to move (radiate) through space. Energy radiation in the broadest sense is what happens during the *Outcome* pathway in Risk theory. See also *Energy transfer mechanism*.
Energy transfer mechanism	The physical means that enables the released *Energy* to reach a *Recipient*.

Energy transfer, multiple repetitive	*Energy* transfer that occurs repeatedly. For example, building workers exposed to impact noise from hammers and nail guns, production workers exposed to bursts of fumes from a process, e.g. when moulds are broken in metal casting operations.
Energy transfer, short term	An *Energy* transfer occurs once and over a short period of time. For example, a car crash, a person falls and hits the floor, an *Explosion* occurs and flings debris violently. Colloquially referred to as an *Accident*.
Equitable	A situation in which a person is exposed to *Risk* but is able to balance the imposition of the risk with the direct benefits they receive from that exposure.
Ergonomics	The study of people at work. As an academic discipline, it attracts physiologists, psychologists, engineers and others. See also *Human factors*.
Error	The post hoc assessment that an action by a person was not what it should have been or an action that differed from a defined standard. A synonym for *Action failure*. Also called 'active failure'.
Error Type 1	An *Action Failure* in which a person knows what is required and has the intention of complying but does not do so.
Error Type 2	An *Action Failure* in which a person is not aware of what is required and by chance acts in an inappropriate way.
Event	Defined here as the point in time when control is lost over the potentially damaging (or *Loss* inducing) effects of a *Hazard* or *Threat*.
Event analysis	The analysis of *Outcomes* using formal logic diagrams to map all possible pathways that can result from an *Event* and create *Consequences*.
Event tree	The name of the logic diagram used to analyse *Outcome* pathways. Named because of the similarity of its appearance to the branches of a tree.
Exogenous	A term used to describe the situation in which a risk is externally imposed on a *Risk agent*.
Explosion	An oxidation process that releases *Chemical bonding energy* at a very rapid rate, one which is faster than the propagation rate of the flames.

Exposure	The number of occasions per year in which the situation exists within which an *Occurrence* could occur. For example, a person is exposed to the potential for *Injury* from a car crash when riding in a car. The number of times a year that a person does ride in a car is their Exposure. Where it is routine for the damaging *Energy* to be released (for example noise, fumes) and the situation always exists during the working day, Exposure is the product of the *Energy intensity* experienced by the *Recipient* and the time period for which this occurs.
Fail-safe	A desired attribute of any item of equipment or process. If the item fails, then it does so in a manner that is non-injurious and non-damaging. See also *Soft landing*.
Failure – command	Failure that is 'commanded' by either an automatic control system or by the intervention of a person. For example: the controlling computer signals a valve to close when it should be open; a person switches an item of equipment off, when it is the wrong item of equipment or the action should have been to turn the equipment on.
Failure – common mode	A mode of failure that is common to more than one item of equipment in a *Fault Tree Analysis*.
Failure – primary	*Failure* of an item of equipment under loads for which it is designed. For example, a crane boom fails when it picks up a load within its design capacity.
Failure – secondary	*Failure* of an item of equipment under loads or conditions for which it is not designed. For example, an electrical circuit is subject to a large voltage when lightning strikes the circuit, a crane tries to pick up a load in excess of its design load.
Failure (of equipment)	When an item of equipment no longer performs the role that is expected of it and for which it is designed.
Failure mode and effect (criticality) analysis (FME(C)A)	The way in which an item of equipment can fail is identified and the effect of the type of *Failure* is explored. For example, a pump may fail to deliver the required volume flow and the effect of this on the process is considered, or the pump may stop altogether or it may even allow reverse flow. These are three possible modes of failure. The criticality of the failure mode for the process outcomes may also be assessed.
Fault tree analysis	A method for determining how a *Top Event* might occur. The method takes its name from the shape of the logic diagram that is used, which is similar to the roots of a tree, splitting as the analysis proceeds from the 'trunk' of the *Event* being analysed.

Fire

A relatively rapid exothermic chemical reaction (faster than corrosion and slower than explosion) characterised by the use of an oxidizing agent (often oxygen in air).

Flying object

A flying object is one possible source of *Kinetic energy*. It is projected into space in some way but does not have its own on-board power source and is not capable of being controlled once launched. For example, a stone flicked up by a powered grass mower, a golf ball hit by a golfer.

Force

Anything that is able to change the velocity of a *Mass* is called a force. The sources of force are many and include: gravity; electromagnetic attraction or repulsion; fluid dynamic forces (wind, aerodynamics, water flow); *Pressure*; buoyancy.

Frequency

The product of *Probability* and *Exposure*. It is a measure of the rate per unit of time at which *Occurrences* or *Consequences* occur.
In physics and in the most common uses of the term, frequency is a term used to describe the number of cycles per second of any wave form, given the name Hertz (Hz). This is used, for example, with pressure waves, electromagnetic waves, gravity waves.
In statistics, the relative frequency with which a particular value of a variable is found or expected to be found in a sample.

Frequency rate

The number of cases of *Injuries* that have occurred in a given number of man-hours of *Exposure*, for example 35 cases per million man-hours. Various terms are derived from this, for example: lost-time injury frequency rate (LTIFR); medical treatment frequency rate (MTFR). The denominator, typically either a million or 100,000 man-hours, is defined by convention in the country in which the figures are published.
See also *Hazard rate*.

Gravitational potential energy

A *Mass* in a gravitational acceleration field experiences a *Force* known as *Weight*. This mass can be made to move vertically 'against' the field by a force that opposes the weight. Since the point of application of this force moves a distance, then *Work* is done by the force. The total amount of work that is done to raise the mass from the start to the finishing elevation is known as the change in gravitational potential energy of the mass. It has this name because if the force did not continue to support the mass it would fall back to its starting point and in doing so would gain *Kinetic energy* equal to the work done on it in the first place.

Gravity-energised waves

Waves on the surface of a liquid primarily involve vertical movement of the liquid and exist due to gravity and in consequence of a vertical disturbance of the liquid surface. Waves can transmit a lot of *Energy* in this way. In appropriate circumstances, for example a boat bobbing up and down next to a jetty, this movement can produce *Damage* and *Injury*.

Guard	A device fitted to a powered machine, the purpose of which is to prevent a person from being injured in the *Damaging energy space*. A guard may be either active or passive.
Harm	A term that encompasses the meaning of *Injury* and *Damage* at least, and possibly also *Loss*.
Hazard	The proposed meaning in this text is a source of potentially damaging *Energy*. In this case, the energy form of interest is the form the energy has immediately before control is or could be lost.
	In common usage, a hazard is any feature of the physical, organisational and/or behavioural environment that contributes to the process of *Injury* or *Damage*, as in the common definition 'anything that may cause harm'.
Hazard and operability analysis (HAZOP)	A design tool initially developed to make petrochemical plant more robust in the face of component *Failure* and less likely to experience *Explosions*, leaks and *Fires*. In recent years, the concept of HAZOP has been adopted in other industries, for example the construction industry in looking at improving the safe design of constructions.
Hazard control	That which maintains control over the potentially damaging properties of an *Energy* source.
Hazard control failure mechanism	The reason for the failure of a *Hazard control*, how the failure occurs.
Hazard management standard	A synonym for *Risk control standard*.
Hazardous	This term is essentially synonymous with the term *Hazard*, although its use often conveys a suggestion of a situation being *Unsafe* or of high *Risk*.
Hierarchy of control	A statement of the preferred order in which *Hazard controls* should be selected. This is typically based on design change as the most preferred and behavioural control measures as the least preferred.
Human error	See *Error* and *Action failure*.
Human factors	The scientific study of those characteristics of people that are relevant to understanding how they respond to the world around them, most particularly the artificial world of the workplace, the built environment, domestic and transport technology, etc. Scientists who are interested in this work may come from fields such as physiology, psychology and engineering. See also *Ergonomics*.
Ill health	A general state of lack of full health, mostly applied to humans. 'Health' implies that all biological systems are functioning as intended.

Illness — The presence of a *Disease*.

Incidence — The number of cases of interest per denominator of *Exposure*. For example, car accidents per 100,000 cars.

Incident — A synonym of *Accident*, or an *Occurrence* in which no adverse *Consequence* has occurred (for which also see *Near miss* and *Null outcome*).

Incidental — A possible class of *Mechanism*. For example, when paint is being sprayed, the release of particles of possibly toxic material is incidental to the wanted task of painting something.

Injury — Damage which is experienced by the body of a mammal.

Intensity (energy) — See *Energy intensity*.

Interlock — A term used in relation to powered equipment to indicate that the way in which the equipment is able to function is dependent on the state of some aspect of the equipment. For example, a gate may be interlocked with the controls of a machine to prevent the machine operating if the gate has been opened. Interlocks may be of present for functional reasons as well as for safety reasons. The design and installation requirements for safety interlocks are different from those of functional interlocks.

Ionising radiation — Radioactive substances emit subatomic particles. These high-*Energy* particles are able to interact with other substances they encounter in such a way as to move electrons from their orbits, or 'ionise' them. Hence the stream of emitted particles is known as ionising radiation. This effect can also be brought about by some very high frequencies of *Electromagnetic field*, which is also then known as ionising 'radiation', although it is not a radiation as such.

Isolation — The stopping of all incoming energy sources and the removal of all stored energy sources in an item of equipment. The required standard to which this is done is determined by the degree of *Risk* in the event that the isolation fails.

Joule — The joule (J) is a unit of *Work* or *Energy*.

Kinetic energy — Kinetic energy (KE) is *Energy* evident in the form of the speed of a body with a *Mass*. It can be in a linear form or a rotational form.
Linear KE is equal to $\frac{1}{2}mv^2$, where m is the mass of the object (kg) and v its speed in metres per second (m/s).
Rotational KE is equal to $\frac{1}{2}I\omega^2$, where I is the rotational moment of inertia of the mass (kgm^2) and ω the rotational speed in radians per second (rad/s).

Since speed is always measured in relation to a reference state, KE is a relative measure too. To increase speed linearly, a *Force* must be applied to the mass. As the point of application of the force moves, *Work* is done by it. In the absence of any resistance, the work done is equal to the increase in KE that results. To increase speed of rotation, a torque must be applied to the mass.

Latent failure
An inadequacy in the coverage or management of *Risk control* measures that is typically discovered after an accident has occurred and which has been present for some time, but unrecognised.

Liability
A state of being responsible for something adverse because of a contractual obligation or a legal requirement.

Likelihood
A colloquial term, which is properly a synonym for *Probability*.

Loss
The reduction in the monetary value of an *Asset*.
The unwanted emotional or physical absence of a loved one or item of value, for example due to death or to theft respectively.

Loss rate
The annual average amount of money required to pay for the cost of adverse *Consequences* when they arise. Loss rate is equal to the product of the *Frequency* of the *Loss* and its *Severity*.
See also *Risk*.

Lost time injury frequency rate
See *Frequency rate*.

Mass
That property of matter that resists a change in its velocity. In order to change the velocity of a mass, a *Force* needs to be applied. Newton's law provides the relationship $f = ma$, where f is the force, m the mass and a the acceleration.

Maximum probable loss
A term used by insurance companies to indicate the likely worst *Consequence Value* (LWC).

Mean time between failure or loss
The mean value of the interval between experiences of either Failure or *Loss*. A statistical parameter that may enable the *Probability* of the failure or losses to be calculated.

Mechanical energy, flowing
See also *Power*. When a constant movement is made to occur in the presence of resistance, it can be inferred (see, for example, the entries on *Mass* and *Kinetic energy*) that *Work* is being done continuously by some source of motive *Power*. For example, as long as a circular saw is driven by a motor, any quantity of material may be cut. If the motor is stopped, however, there is a limit to the amount of wood that may be cut before the saw blade stops as its kinetic energy is diminished to zero. When the motor is running, it is not the kinetic energy that is cutting the wood, but the 'flowing mechanical energy'.

Mechanism of Event	The means by which control is lost of the potentially damaging properties of the *Energy* source or non-energy *Threat*.
Metastable	A stable state of a system that may readily become unstable state. For example standing on ice.
Mitigation	In common use this means to make something less serious. It has become used in *Risk management* to mean any measure to reduce a *Risk* and is now synonym for *Risk control*.
Near miss	See *Null Consequence*.
Negligence	A legal concept applied to the behaviour of a person who did not do what a reasonable person should have done in the circumstances. What a reasonable person arguably should have done depends on the foreseeability of the need to act and the availability of reasonable opportunities for action.
Newton	The unit of *Force* in SI units is named after Sir Isaac Newton, the 17th-century English mathematician and scientist famous (amongst other things) for his elucidation of the laws governing motion. Abbreviated as N.
Null Consequence	An *Outcome* that proceeds down a preferred route which does not lead to any adverse *Consequence*. Popularly known as a *Near miss* and a *Soft landing*.
Null Outcome	A brief *Outcome* that is rapidly terminated. Popularly known as a *Near miss*.
Occurrence	The process leading to adverse *Consequences*. The process is described by *Time Zone 2* of the *Time Sequence Model* and involves *Energy* or non-energy *Threats*.
On demand	One form of *Exposure* measure relevant in situations in which there is a periodic requirement, for example the operation of standby pumps and generators, of automated valves or a periodic need to perform a task.
Opportunity for improvement	A self-explanatory quality management system term, identified by *Risk control* measure reviews, audits, insights and *Incidents*.
Organisational failures	Failure to meet defined *Hazard management standards/Risk control standards*.
Outcome	That part of the *Occurrence* subsequent to the *Event* and which ends when adverse *Consequences* are experienced.
Outcome analysis	A synonym for *Event analysis*.

Performance shaping factors	Any factor that influences the existence and *Probability* of *Action failure* (*Error*) in a given situation.
Permit to work	A Permit to Work (PTW) is issued in industrial plant as an indication that the place, time and method of proposed maintenance work is acceptable. A PTW is issued in accordance with a defined PTW procedure and subject to an approved method of work being followed.
Potential energy	Any form of *Energy* that has the potential to do *Work* given a suitable mechanical arrangement. Examples include: *Gravitational potential energy*; *Strain energy*; electrical potential energy (volt).
Power	Power is the rate at which *Energy* is produced or used. Its units are energy per second, for example joules/second. The common unit of power is the watt.
Prerequisite	A Prerequisite is any feature of the everyday environment (i.e. *Time Zone 1* of the *Time Sequence Model*) that makes *Event Mechanisms* possible.
Pressure	The pressure in a volume of fluid is equal to the *Energy* stored in the fluid per unit volume as a result of the *Work* done to achieve this state.
Prevention	An effort made to improve a situation before the situation has had the opportunity to bring about some adverse effect. Also called 'proactive efforts'.
Probability	The proportion of trials that produce a given result. Probability is a number that lies between 0 and 1, where 0 means impossible and 1 mean certain.
Psychosocial stressors	A *Stressor* that is of psychological or social origins.
Purposeful	A possible form of division of a *Mechanism*. For example demolition, warfare.
Quantified risk analysis (QRA)	A formal *Risk analysis* using *Fault tree analysis* and *Event trees* that includes estimates of *Probabilities*. The result can be a numeric estimate of the *Risk* itself, measured as units of currency per unit of time, e.g. £ per year.
Quantified risk estimation (QRE)	A direct estimation of the magnitude of *Risk* using *Incident* data or judgement.
Reactive	A reactive action to control a *Risk*. Basing risk control efforts on insights arising from *Incidents*.

Reasonable	A legal term. A reasonable person is one who possesses a normal awareness of the potential for *Injury*, for example, and of the way in which the potential could be minimised and who displays a normal conscientiousness and concern for the welfare of his fellow man by ensuring that the risk is minimised (or the *Risk controls* optimised).
Recipient	The *Asset* that receives the *Energy* transferred during the *Energy damage* process or which suffers *Loss* in a non-energy *Damage* process.
Reliability	Reliability is defined as one minus the *Probability* of failure. It may be applied to any item of equipment as well as to the action of people.
Risk	The uncertainty that an adverse *Consequence* (of a given size) will occur. The relationship between *Frequency* and *Consequence Value* that is characteristic of a situation in which adverse consequences could occur. In everyday speech, a synonym for chance or *Probability*, as in 'there is a risk of a thunderstorm'.
Risk – acceptable	A *Risk* is acceptable if it satisfies one or more of a number of criteria: the control measures on the risk satisfy legal (statutory) requirements; the standard of control measures satisfies moral requirements, where these exist; risk agents feel comfortable about the risk, that is subjectively accept it, assuming that knowledge of the risk is not hidden from them; further improvements in *Risk control* come at such a cost that the benefit:cost ratio is very small and the cost is seen as an inappropriate expenditure that could be put to better use in some other proposal.
Risk – critical	A general Risk, the most likely worst *Consequence Value* of which is a fatality or multiple fatality or its equivalent (quadriplegia, comatose patient, etc.) or the equivalent in terms of *Damage* to the environment, equipment, production processes or commercial processes.
Risk – general	A *Risk* that arises from *Energy* (or *Threat*) *Exposures* in circumstances that aren't unusual and that require control measures largely common in all industries with a similar risk type. For example, electricity reticulated at domestic supply voltages.
Risk – voluntary	A situation in which a *Risk agent* voluntarily exposes themselves to a Risk, for example choosing recreational activities in which fatalities could occur, such as mountain climbing.
Risk – operational	*Energy* (or *Threat*) exists in significant and unusual quantities and in circumstances closely associated with the function of the organisation, so there is a potential for *Loss* to have a highly significant adverse effect on the organisation, possibly even threatening its existence.
Risk – pure	A Risk that can only give rise to adverse and unwanted *Consequences*.

Risk – reference	A *Risk* that is used for comparison purposes in a *Risk assessment* process is called a reference risk. For example, a risk being assessed could be shown to be no different from another that the community has previously found quite acceptable.
Risk – residual	A term used to convey the idea that after changes have been made to improve the control measures over a *Risk*, there remains some risk, the residual risk.
Risk – speculative	A *Risk* that can give rise to both adverse and desirable *Consequences* is regarded as a speculative risk. For example, investment decisions could give rise to increased wealth as well as to *Losses*.
Risk – tolerable	An assumed level *Risk* that a *Risk agent* is able to tolerate.
Risk acceptance	Risk acceptance is one possible result of a *Risk evaluation* and, as the name suggests, means deciding the *Risk* is acceptable without the need for further control measures.
Risk analysis	A structured analysis of all possible ways in which a defined process leading to adverse *Consequences* could occur. *Risk* analysis provides a means of synthesising estimates of the *Frequency* and value of the associated adverse *Consequences*.
Risk assessment	The process of identifying *Risks*, determining their significance and deciding what, if anything, needs to be done about their control. In common usage, a synonym for *Risk evaluation*.
Risk assessment – preliminary	An assessment made at the outset of a project, the purpose of which is to understand the major classes of Risk to which the project will be exposed and will be present in the result of the project (for example factory, building, item of equipment).
Risk aversion	Risk aversion is one possible result of *Risk evaluation* and is the decision made to reduce the *Risk* by use of some *Risk reduction* changes (that is, *Risk control* improvements) or to avoid *Exposure* to the risk altogether; see *Risk avoidance*.
Risk avoidance	Risk avoidance is one *Risk aversion* strategy. As its name suggests, *Risk* avoidance means either removing the origin of the risk (the *Energy* source if it is capable of *Damage*) or *Exposure* to this. Risk avoidance is a decision made as a result of a *Risk evaluation*.
Risk Classes	In this text, Risk is classed in two ways: Classes A and B for distinguishing the nature of risk control measures (Chapter 7) and Classes 0, I, IIa, IIb for distinguishing the needs of risk evaluation (Chapter 8).

Risk control – systemic	An approach to *Risk control* that goes beyond the boundaries of organisations within which *Risk* exists to include educators, regulators, suppliers and similar in a conscious and organised manner, the prime purpose of which is the control and minimisation of risk.
Risk control	A *Risk* control is anything that influences either the *Consequence Value* or the *Frequency* of the Consequence Value through any one or more of the following: the *Probability* of a *Mechanism*; the probability of an *Outcome*; the probability of a *Consequence* type and value; *Exposure* to the situation within which the Consequence could occur. Where risk controls already exist, they may be recognised by the fact that their removal would result in an increase in any of the above. *Risk mitigation* and *Risk reduction* are synonyms.
Risk control standard	The standard to which a *Risk* is to be managed, including physical and organisational control measures. A synonym for *Hazard management standard*.
Risk diagram	A graphical representation of the relationship between *Frequency* and *Consequence Value* for a given *Risk*, using logarithmic scales.
Risk engineer	An engineer well-grounded in *Risk* theory, who is able to use formal analytical techniques to understand risk, is knowledgeable about rules and regulations relevant to risk in their area of practice and who is able to make appropriate use of sources of *Probability* data to estimate the size of risk.
Risk estimation	The process of estimating the *Frequency* and *Consequence Value* of a *Risk*. These numbers are estimated, as it is virtually impossible to determine them in an objective manner.
Risk evaluation	The process of comparing the benefits and detriments of experiencing a *Risk* with the benefits and detriments of doing something to change the risk.
Risk factor	Anything that is able to affect the *Frequency* (and hence *Probability* and *Exposure*) or *Consequence Value* of a *Risk*.
Risk Group	In this text (Chapter 5), Risk is grouped by significance to the organisation as Group 1 Operational risks, Group 2 Critical general risks, Group 3 Non-critical general risks, Group 4 Welfare and quality of life risks.
Risk identification	Risk identification is any process used to recognise that a *Risk* exists and describe it in detail that is useful for the process of *Risk assessment*.
Risk management	The organised process of identifying *Risks*, determining their significance, deciding what control measures are needed, maintaining those measures over time and periodically ensuring standards of

control remain adequate in the light of changing legal and community standards and expectations and technology.

Risk management plan | A statement of the policy, objectives and strategies that underpin *Risk management* activities.

Risk management system | A process to manage Risk set up within an organisation. See also *Systemic risk control.*

Risk mitigation | See *Risk control.*

Risk ranking | Ranking the significance of a number of *Risks* in a *Risk register*. This may be based on both the estimated size of the risk and other variables relevant to its significance.

Risk reduction | See *Risk control.*

Risk register | A register of all identified *Risks* and *Liabilities* used as the basis of a *Risk management* programme.

Risk-taking behaviour | Behaviour that results in an increased level of *Risk* (or decreased level of *Risk control*) for reasons of personal or organisational gain. The gain may be material (increased profits, awards) or psychological (peer group approval) or even simply personal satisfaction. For example: by reducing investment in equipment renewal, maintenance and training, an organisation may improve its apparent profitability, in the short term at least, but in fact be increasing the financial and even *Injury* and *Damage* risks associated with its operation; groups of young men are known to engage in risky activities such as street car racing, vandalism and so on, with status rewards going to those who expose themselves to more risk than the others; base jumpers and other examples of extreme sports appear to be attractive to people because of the personal satisfaction they gain in overcoming their fears.

Risky shift | When the opinion leaders in a group of people gain or retain their position in the group by *Risk-taking behaviour* that becomes increasingly more extreme, the norms of the group may shift towards that extreme behaviour. This is known as risky shift, a shift in the normal and accepted values of the members of the group towards increasingly risky behaviour.

Root cause analysis | An analysis whose purpose is to uncover the original *Cause* of something, usually an '*Accident*'. Root cause analysis is based on the repetitive asking and answering of the question 'Why?'. For example: Why did the plane hit the mountain? (the pilots descended below lowest safe altitude); Why did they do this (overload in the cockpit); Why? (poor weather); Why were they flying in poor weather? etc. A root cause is found when it is not possible to explore the question further.

Safe

An acceptable level of *Risk*. See *Risk – acceptable*.
Implied meanings derived from various legislative statements include a zero level of risk; not being injured.

Safeguard

A term normally used in the context of powered industrial equipment, a safeguard is something whose purpose is to prevent a person accessing a danger point (*Damaging energy space*). It may be a physical fixed *Guard*, or an *Interlocked* guard, but it is generally not used to describe a procedure or rule.

Safety – Intrinsic

Something is intrinsically safe if it has been designed with levels of energy that are incapable of injury at any time or has been designed for minimal levels of energy while access is possible.
The term is also used for electrical equipment that is enclosed to prevent it being a source of ignition in situations in which flammable or explosive atmospheres may exist.

Safety integrity level (SIL)

In the context of powered industrial equipment, safety in operation is dependent on the functioning of various *Safeguards*, including devices *Interlocked* with programmable logic controllers. As these are used for safety purposes, it is important that they have adequate *Reliability* in operation. Just how reliable is considered acceptable is determined by use of an accepted *Risk assessment* tool. Depending on how severe the effect of a *Failure* in the safeguard is, the required safety integrity level of the equipment can be determined. The SIL is brought about both by how the interlock system is designed and the quality of equipment used to make it work. The method of determining a required SIL is specified in various international standards.

Safety management system

An organised and systematic manner of managing safety in an organisation.

Scapegoat

A term that has its origins in a Hebrew religious practice. There is an often-observed propensity for people to want to find some person they can consider to blame, and then punish, for a calamity. This person is the scapegoat. This propensity is easily observed today in both developed and undeveloped societies. In the latter, the experience may include punishment meted out by a mob; in the former it is done in a more respectable manner through the law courts, but the underlying primitive need appears similar. In the arena of public *Risk* (road, rail, etc.), examples abound of calamities occurring, the person most immediately involved being found 'guilty' (basically of just being a person on the scene), while the responsible government department quietly improves the design, maintenance or operational problem that allowed the *Damage* to occur, while trying to ensure their neglect is not seen as such.

Severity	A term synonymous with *Consequence Value*. Severity is often indicated by use of a word-value scale, such as 'minor, major, disastrous, catastrophic'.
Soft landing	A term used by *Risk engineers*, usually about an industrial process plant, to mean that if something goes wrong the system has been designed to shut itself down in a manner that does the least *Damage* to the equipment and the process.
Space transfer mechanism	The means by which *Energy* is able to travel through space.
Space-time coincidence	All *Collisions* between mobile objects arise because of this. Two mobile objects, A and B, will collide if they are in the same point in space at the same time. All that is required for this to occur is for the projected movement pathways of A and B to cross each other at the same time. A potential space-time coincidence occurs if the projection shows this to be possible unless avoiding action is taken by one or both objects. An actual space-time coincidence occurs when no change in direction or speed of either object occurs. 'Dancing behaviour' occurs before the coincidence point if the objects perform mutually cancelling avoidance manoeuvres.
Strain (mechanical)	The unit change in length of an elastic material when subject to the application of a tensile or compressive *Force*. If the change in length is Δl and the unit length of the gauge on which this measurement is taken is l, then the strain is $\Delta l / l$. Strain is a dimensionless number.
Strain energy	When a *Stress* is applied to an elastic solid, a *Strain* results. The presence of strain means that the point of application of the stress has moved a distance (equal to the change in length of the solid) and has consequently done *Work*. The work done is stored in the solid as strain energy and it will be released when the stress is removed and the solid returns to its original length. This principle can be applied both in linear geometry (stretching a wire, for example) and in torsional geometry (twisting a wire, for example).
Stress (mechanical)	Stress arises in a structure when a *Force* is applied. It is defined as the force per unit area of the cross section of the structure that resists the stress. For example, if a metal rod of cross sectional area A is used to support a *Weight* of W, the stress in the rod at any point in its length is W/A. The stress in this example is a simple linear stress and is constant across the cross section of the rod. If a torque is applied to a rod, such that the rod tends to twist, then the resulting effect in the cross section of the rod is a torsional stress. The units of stress are the same as those of *Pressure*, namely pascals.

Stress reaction (human)	When a person is exposed to a *Stressor* of any sort, a stress reaction can occur. Stress reactions can themselves be psychological (e.g. emotional effects) or physical (e.g. raised blood pressure, increased adrenaline). Stress reactions are not directly related to the stressor that gives rise to them. For example, a psychological stressor can give rise to physical stress reactions, and a physical stressor to psychological stress reactions.
Stressor	A term used in the social and physiological sciences to indicate anything that results in a *Stress reaction* in a person. Stressors can be of these different types: psychological, sociological, workload, physical.
Thermal energy	When the temperature of a substance rises, it has absorbed *Energy* in such a way that the heat content of the substance has increased. Heat flows from hot (high temperature) to cold (low temperature), that is, thermal energy flows from places of high energy to places of low energy. Thermal energy flows by any of these mechanisms: conduction; radiation; convection.
Threat	A source of potential *Loss*.
Threat and Vulnerability Model	The name given to the model of the process of non-energy direct *Loss* described in this text.
Threat control	That which maintains control over the potentially *Loss*-inducing properties of a *Threat*.
Time Sequence Model	The Time Sequence Model is the name given in this text to the time-based model of the process which leads to *Damage*, *Injury* or *Loss*.
Time Zone 1	In the *Time Sequence Model*, the period for which the potential for an *Occurrence* exists due to the presence of the *Energy* or *Threat* in the technology or practices of the organisation. The day-to-day character of the organisation out of which an *Occurrence* can develop.
Time Zone 2	In the *Time Sequence Model*, the period in which a *Mechanism* begins and the complete *Occurrence* unfolds, up until the development of *Consequences*.
Time Zone 3	In the *Time Sequence Model*, the period in which adverse *Consequences* develop and are responded to up to the time when all responses (for example repair, rehabilitation, recovery and including all legal ramifications) are finalised.
Top Event	The name used in *Fault tree analysis* for the event being analysed.
Total cost of risk	The sum of the investment made in efforts to prevent *Damage* or *Loss* and the cost of reacting when damage or loss do occur.

Toxic	A substance is regarded as toxic if it has an adverse effect on the functioning of an exposed biological system. As far as people are concerned, *Exposure* can be by ingestion (swallowing), inhalation (breathing in vapours, fumes, etc.) or contact (e.g. with the skin).
Trial	A statistical term to indicate one count of the situation in which something could occur, for example one toss of a coin in which the coin could come to rest heads up or heads down. See *Probability* and also *Exposure*.
Uncertainty	In *Risk* theory, the term is a synonym for chance and for *Probability*. In everyday use, it means that state of not being certain with respect to an outcome of some sort.
Unsafe	An unacceptable level of *Risk*. See *Dangerous*. In common use, a situation is often suddenly considered to be unsafe if an *Occurrence* has taken place, even if people were quite unconcerned by it immediately before the occurrence.
Unsafe act	A term immortalised by Heinrich, unsafe act refers to the actions of a person such as 'standing under suspended loads, starting machinery without warning, horseplay, and removal of safeguards'. An unsafe act is one possible *Cause* of an *Accident*. Heinrich's research suggested to him that 88% of all accidents were caused by unsafe acts.
Unsafe condition	A term immortalised by Heinrich, unsafe condition refers to 'mechanical or physical hazards such as unguarded gears, unguarded points of operation, absence of rail guards, and insufficient light'. An unsafe condition is one possible *Cause* of an *Accident*. Heinrich's research suggested to him that 10% of all accidents were caused by unsafe conditions.
Vulnerability pathway	The way in which an *Asset* may experience *Loss* as the result of a *Threat*.
Watt	The watt is a unit of *Power*, being the rate at which *Work* is done or *Energy* expended. The units are joules per second (J/s). The unit is named after the Scottish engineer James Watt, whose work on steam engines in the 18th and 19th centuries brought him fame.
Weight	Weight is the name given to the *Force* that is exerted on a *Mass* when it is in the earth's gravitational acceleration field. The standard acceleration due to earth's gravity is 9.81 m/s^2 or 32.2 ft/s^2. A mass of 1 kg has a weight of 9.81 N (newtons), and a mass of 1 lbm a weight of 32.2 lbf.
Work	In the field of mechanics, work is the name given to the product of *Force* and the distance moved by the point of application of the force. If a force of 1 lb moves a distance of 1 ft, the work done is 1 ftlb. A force of 1 N (newton) moving a distance of 1 m does work equal to 1 Nm.

Workload

Workload refers to the work done by a person. Workload can be of three different types: physical, in which the muscles do *Work* in the sense used in mechanics; mental, such as doing mental arithmetic; perceptual, for example judging closing distances and speeds, steering a vehicle. In this role a person is modelled as a *Controller*.

Workload results in various physiological changes, most notably an increase in heart rate, and results eventually in fatigue.

Abbreviations

ALARP	As low as reasonably practical
DES	Damaging energy space
EA	Event analysis
EDM	Energy damage model
EFTO	Engine failure on take-off
FME(C)A	Failure mode effect (and criticality) analysis
FTA	Fault tree analysis
HAZOP	Hazard and operability study
HCR	Human cognitive reliability
HRA	Human reliability analysis
ILS	Instrument landing system
ISO	International Standards Organisation
LLC	Likely least consequence
LTIFR	Lost-time injury frequency rate
LWC	Likely worst consequence
MPL	Maximum probable loss
MTBF	Mean time between failures
OED	*Oxford English Dictionary*
OFI	Opportunity for improvement
OSHA	Occupational Safety and Health Administration (US)
PLC	Programmable logic controller
QRA	Quantified risk analysis
QRE	Quantified risk estimation
RMS	Risk management system
SI	International system of units
TCOR	Total cost of risk
THERP	Technique for human error rate prediction
TQM	Total quality management
TSM	Time sequence model
TVM	Threat and vulnerability model
VOR	VHF omnidirectional radio

1

History:
The Historical Origins of
the Management of Risks

Introduction

There was once a time when the survival of individuals was threatened only by exposure to extreme weather, wild animals, hostile groups, disease and hazardous environments. Early technology created new ways in which people could be hurt: fires for the smelting of metals and the production of pottery and glass; primitive weapons with increased speed and sharp points to increase the intensity of energy at the point of application to the skin; boats with which to explore the sea beyond the safe havens close to the shore. In some parts of the world, population centres became possible as farming and the specialisation of work drew people away from nomadic hunting and gathering. With this came the diseases that attend dense populations in unhygienic conditions and the ever-present chance of fire in buildings made from wood.

Technological change became dramatic with the industrial revolution, which began in the mid 18th century in the United Kingdom and spread rapidly to other developed nations. This revolution was chiefly made possible by the development of steam power, but also harnessing power by water and wind turbines. The resulting processes of mass production exposed workers to the power of rotating and reciprocating machinery, the chemicals used in various processes and levels of noise and atmospheric pollution never before seen.

The rate of growth of industrial technology would have seemed astonishing then, but even more significant changes took place in the 20th century, picking up pace in the period between World Wars One and Two and exploding in the period after 1945 and the Vietnam War. The industrial technology we now know and its reach into every facet of our lives, from food to medical treatment, transport, war, recreation, communication and touching even the health of the planet is unprecedented in its nature and its effect. Industrial countries with the longest experience of technology, meaning those of the Western world, have only 260 years of experience in managing the effects, and the greatest effects by far have arisen only in the last 65 or so years. Currently developing industrial societies have been doing so only in this last 65 years at the most and in significant cases, for example India and China, the greatest part of this is in the last 30 years. Not all parts of the world have undergone these changes and even today we can meet peoples who retain the culture of the hunter-gatherer or small-scale farmer.

It is useful to recognise this history as we study the science and psychology of risk, if only for the purpose of understanding how people today respond to the need to manage these artificial risks. We can learn much about the origins of our attitudes by looking at those of peoples who have not participated in this technology journey, as well as by knowing something of the history of our own society's attempts to manage the adverse effects of it through legal and other means.

For many years our natural desire to reduce the incidence of injury and illness has been frustrated by the difficulty of formulating a coherent philosophy of the problem. This has not been helped by the widely held belief that 'safety' is, after all, just common sense. Our individual and collective ability to be wise after an event is nothing short of astonishing and we appear to experience no disquiet as a result of contemplating, if we ever do, why we were not so wise before the event. As growing industrialisation led to demand for industrial practitioners of applied science (in various branches derived from chemistry and physics), manual skills, accountancy, law and eventually even in management, there has been one area, namely safety, in which the need for specialisation has been ignored for the large part of the industrial revolution journey. Everyone has a personal skill, originating in the warnings of parents from the very earliest days, in negotiating the common hazards of modern life: how to dodge cars on a road; use stairs; manage household electricity and cleaning chemicals; and so on. How easy it must be for us to just assume that this mindset is all we need to manage safety in a modern complex industry, or even for the planet. There is a subtle trap in this extrapolation from personal to industrial. Our personal understanding is that it is we ourselves who are responsible for crossing the road safely, we cannot rely on some kindly person to help us. We extrapolate this view to the bigger picture of industry and the planet at our peril as it is far too simple. Yet extrapolate it we do.

From the earliest times of the industrial revolution in the United Kingdom, the law of employment began with the idea that an employee accepted the risk of their employment by agreeing to work and was therefore responsible for doing something that brought about injury to themselves. The injured person was, by definition, to blame for their injury.

Societal Attitudes to Injury and Disease

Historians have documented the social response to disease of the European cultures of the 14th century onwards, showing how disease was seen as retribution from God, imposed selectively to punish improper behaviour (Nohl, 1926). As faulty personal behaviour was seen as a causal factor, control strategies were developed which attempted to minimise such behaviour by the imposition of social punishments, some of which are summarised in Table 1.1. It is true that other control strategies documented by Nohl included the quarantine of sick people, suggesting a coexisting belief that disease could also be transmitted from one person to another. Nevertheless, faulty personal behaviour was seen as a significant reason for the disease.

There is some reason to believe that pre-scientific societies draw little distinction between injury and disease. In such societies, supernatural forces are believed to be responsible for any phenomenon for which no obvious cause exists. People with the power to understand or influence these supernatural forces become powerful within the community. Anecdotal information records that in Africa witch doctors have been known to be employed as safety officers on mines. Their role was to seek mercy from the supernatural forces to ensure the safety of miners at the beginning of a shift. I have been told that in some of the isolated areas of Papua New Guinea, injury, like disease, is seen as being a reflection of personal fault or disability of the stricken individual. I am also aware of individual cases in our own society where a serious injury resulting from an accident has led to the affected individual losing image, status and self-confidence as a result of the personally held belief that the accident in some way is evidence of a personal failing.

Table 1.1 **Plague regulations in Europe**

Speyer 1347	A strict prohibition against gambling in churchyards
Council of Turnai	All concubines to be expelled or married
	Sundays to be strictly observed
	Manufacture, sale and use of dice to be completely suppressed (dice factories turned to making rosary beads!)
Rouen 1507	No gambling, cursing, drinking or excesses

Source: Nohl (1926).

Since that pre-scientific time in Europe, medical science has developed an understanding of the causation of diseases based on the existence of microbiological organisms acting as vectors. Despite this scientific fact the social response to disease is not uncommonly affected by our perception of the role of behaviour in exposing ourselves to the vectors. The AIDS situation is a recent example in which religion and attitudes to sexuality have played dominant roles in community attitudes and control strategies.

During the industrial revolution the relationship of work with disease and injury attracted attention due to the squalid and dangerous conditions, the use of children and the visual evidence of maiming which became so prevalent on the streets of the great industrial centres. An interesting review of the period is to be found in Wigglesworth (1978). In England the first attempt to regulate these conditions was the Morals of Apprentices Act of 1802 which aimed to provide a basic standard of life for the numerous poor and parentless children from workhouses who were used in industry. A legislative framework of the 'prescribe, police and punish' type developed from 1837 onwards (Eddington, 2006). In 1833, the first Factories Act was passed and the first four factory inspectors appointed to enforce it (HSE, n.d.). These inspectors recognised the need to fence the ubiquitous dangerous machinery to prevent serious maiming and deaths resulting from their use, with the result that in 1844 a revision of the Act created the first legislative requirement to guard machines. However, these requirements were resisted by employers on the basis that accidents were a natural part of work and that they could not be held responsible for the acts of their employees. The result was the development of a trio of mostly short-lived legal doctrines, namely:

1. Voluntary assumption of risk in which it was held that injury and health risks were inherent in the processes of industry and that when seeking employment in a particular industry the employee had in effect accepted that they would be exposed to the risks in that industry. Thus, the more common the injury in that industry the easier for the employer to invoke this doctrine in their defence.
2. Common employment, which held that an employer could not be held responsible if an injury to one employee was due to the negligent actions of another employee.
3. Contributory negligence, which held that employees had a duty to look after themselves and could be held negligent for not keeping a look out, or for some other personal failing.

Of these, only the last remains a feature of the common law to be found in many countries. An excellent documentation of occupational case histories covering the modern period in Europe is to be found in Weindling (1985). One such of particular interest is of the Welsh slate industry, which had a history from the 17th century to the late 1930s. In 1933 a study of tuberculosis 'black spots' indicated that the death rate per thousand population was 0.724 in England and Wales on average. In the slate quarrying districts of Wales it rose to 2.052 in one area and 1.718 in another.

In 1882 the tubercle bacillus was discovered by Robert Koch, showing that the disease had a physical basis similar to others. In the 19th century it had otherwise been generally regarded as an inherited disease of the poor. A link between the disease and exposure to the slate industry was suspected in the late 19th century and a government study in 1926 showed that the slate dust contained up to 50 percent quartz (silicon dioxide) which irritated the lung, causing a build-up of tissue. The conclusion was that this silicosis predisposed the miners to tuberculosis. The study also concluded that the miners' tuberculosis was not less infectious than that of the public generally (as had been believed) and that consequently the miners were an important source of infection.

Interestingly, the medical practitioners of the area disagreed with these conclusions, with one even claiming that slate dust, far from being a problem, was beneficial to health. The more general view amongst medical practitioners of the cause of the high incidence was influenced by the perception of the time that tuberculosis was a social disease associated with poor hygiene conditions. However, the majority of their attention was focused on a number of other personal factors, particularly those listed in Table 1.2 (Bryder in Weindling 1985). The quarry owners also disagreed with the results of the study, although for different reasons, suggesting that slate dust was probably no more harmful than road dust and that the prevalence of tuberculosis in Wales may well be a coincidence. The owners warned that if all sorts of fantastic rules and regulations, incurring considerable expense, were foisted upon employers, the time would come when their business would not be worth continuing.

Table 1.2   Medical community perception of the causes of tuberculosis in Wales

Sanitary conditions	Race
Heredity	Intermarriage
Language (unusual cadences)	Fatalism
Diet	Religious principles
Kissing	Insufficient sleep, fresh air, exercise
Ignorance and carelessness	Attitude (tuberculosis was regarded as a disgrace not a disease)

All this discussion continued despite the discovery of the bacillus in 1882. It is noteworthy that the medical opinions of the time (apart from those of the medical scientists who researched the problem) conformed with the fault of the victim doctrine and the case study shows that the majority of the preventive effort was directed towards influencing these perceived behavioural causes of the disease. The most commonly advocated social solution to the problem was the education of housewives. This is despite the fact that regulations had been passed under the British Factories Act in 1864 and 1867 requiring the containment of dust at source. However, little was done to allay dust hazards even by the 1930s. Sadly, even the union was not active in promoting change because of the fear of unemployment if additional cost burdens were placed on the industry. At an individual level there was fear of unemployment if the disease was diagnosed, to prevent infection of others.

It seems that little change had occurred in society since the times of the great plagues, with social solutions being advocated even in the face of scientific knowledge indicating the need for engineering strategies. In 1986, in the *New Scientist* magazine, an almost exact parallel was reported in the wooden furniture industry around High Wycombe, England (*New Scientist*, 1986). Here the high incidence of nasal cancer has, on scientific evidence, been linked to exposure to some wood dusts. The factory owners were reportedly fighting hard to avoid having to provide respiratory protection to the employees, also on the grounds of excessive financial hardship. It was not reported what, if any, social causal factors were being implicated to remove the blame from the employers on to the workers affected.

The Birth and Growth of Organised Occupational Safety

In the USA, according to the National Society for the Study of Education (1926), 'There was certainly no organised safety movement before 1910'. This date marks the time when, according to this source:

> A few far-sighted employers began to realize that accidents were wasteful, that they interrupted production and that it was expensive to break in new men. They began to study their accidents, asking not 'whose fault was it' but 'how could it have been prevented'. They concluded that, even though legally it might be negligence for a workman to put his hand into unguarded gears, nevertheless the simplest way to prevent such an accident was to guard the gears ... They began to study every industrial operation from the standpoint of the safety of the workman, as well as of speed and economy of production, and of quality of the product.

Also according to this source, the first safety organisations began to be formed from this time, involving a safety committee of executives responsible for the direction of the safety programme, a safety engineer or director to carry out the work and committees of foremen and workers to report problems and suggest improvements. After guarding powered machinery (being the most obvious hallmark of the industrial revolution) they discovered that still some accidents remained and attacked these by education and promotion, emphasising the serious effects of an accident on the economic health of the organisation and the workman's family.

In the 1920s in the USA, workmen's compensation laws were also enacted, resulting in a direct charge on industry for injury to their workers leading to a greater interest in the safety movement in industry and, it is reported (National Society for the Study of Education, 1926, p. 7), even insurance companies became less interested in fighting claims and more in helping their insured to prevent them.

Also reported by this same source (p. 8) is the role of legislation. In the USA at that time, the role of labour departments was the enforcement of guarding legislation, but 'this policy never produced results in accident prevention' and it was replaced 'in the more progressive state departments' by a role of encouragement and assistance to industry and workers. No doubt this early attention to the guarding of machinery was a necessary outcome of the industrial revolution, essentially characterised, as it was, by the provision of previously unknown powered machinery.

By the early 1970s, however, the US Department of Labor formed the Occupational Safety and Health Administration (OSHA), which is today known for the publication of numerous prescriptive standards for the management of specific hazards as well as the general duties of employers to 'keep their workplace free of recognized hazards' (OSHA, 2012). In the USA, a full circle has been experienced, from prescription (of guards on machines) to organisational and consultative processes to prescription again, in the space of 50 years. It is interesting to note that the enlightened approach of consultation, adopted in the USA by the mid 1920s, took 50 years to be adopted across the Atlantic Ocean in the United Kingdom. It was only in 1974 that the Health and Safety at Work etc. Act of that date, arising from the 1972 report of Lord Robens (1972) into workplace health and safety, replaced the emphasis of government instrumentalities on inspection and the enforcement of prescriptive and hazard-specific regulations with providing for a process of consultation between employees and employers and setting up a commission (to determine strategy) and executive (to implement the strategy). The Act defined in detail the duty of care of employers to make sure their workplace was safe 'as far as is reasonably practical'.

We now have the interesting spectacle of these two influential English-speaking developed economies each making use of different overall strategies for the management of occupational safety and health; one with prescriptive statements of the minutiae of risk control and the other supportive of the efforts of those exposed to the risks. As with all simplifications, it is entirely possible that the brevity of this comparison ignores the complexity these two jurisdictions have developed since the origins of their systems, but it is sufficient for the present purposes of sketching the history of this discipline.

Those of us who recall the decades of 1970–1990 are aware of the general state of industrial safety at that time outside the USA. Safety officers were typically appointed from amongst foremen and workers, had a position with little support (possibly due to lack of understanding) from senior managers and had a role that chiefly involved promoting 'safety' by means of posters and running training courses for workers. The prevailing view was that accidents were caused chiefly by unsafe worker behaviour and that there was value in exhorting those at risk to be more careful. This is well reflected in a commonly held view amongst safety officers at the end of the 1970s that safety could adequately be defined as 'a state of mind'. I recall, from that time, two main points of discussion amongst thinking safety officers. The first was, does showing workers distressing images of people who had been severely injured have a positive or negative effect on the subsequent behaviour of workers? The second was, should we be talking about the cause of accidents or the causation of accidents (implying the possibility of more than one cause)? Should we use the term incident as more inclusive than accident? It was felt to be very important to convey to workers that accidents were indeed caused and did not just happen spontaneously. This view was held quite passionately by thought leaders well into the 1980s.

The Work of Heinrich

The best-known and documented early attempt to apply the scientific method to this field was that of Heinrich (1959) during the early 1930s. His text was a result of experiences with injury prevention work while employed as an engineer with an insurance company in the United States of America.

Table 1.3   Heinrich's list of unsafe acts and conditions

Unsafe acts of persons	Unsafe mechanical or physical conditions
1. Operating without clearance, failure to secure or warn	1. Inadequately guarded, guards of improper height, strength, mesh, etc.
2. Operating or working at unsafe speed	2. Unguarded, absence of required guards
3. Making safety devices inoperative	3. Defective, rough, sharp, slippery, decayed, cracked, etc.
4. Using unsafe equipment, or equipment unsafely	4. Unsafely designed machines, tools, etc.
5. Unsafe loading, placing, mixing, combining, etc.	5. Unsafely arranged, poor housekeeping, congestion, blocked exits, etc.
6. Taking unsafe position or posture	6. Inadequately lighted, sources of glare, etc.
7. Working on moving or dangerous equipment	7. Inadequately ventilated, impure air source, etc.
8. Distracting, teasing, abusing, startling, etc.	8. Unsafely clothed, no goggles, gloves or masks, wearing high heels, etc.
9. Failure to use safety attire or personal protective devices	9. Unsafe processes, mechanical, chemical, electrical, nuclear, etc.

Heinrich undertook a study of 12,000 cases found at random in insurance company files and a further 63,000 cases from the records of factories. The conduct of such a study in the days before computers must have required nothing short of monumental organisation and an extraordinary amount of time. Actuarial records and engineering reports were consulted and employers cooperated in the study. Only one possible cause (the cause judged to be of major importance) was assigned to each case – either unsafe acts of persons or unsafe mechanical or physical condition (see Table 1.3). He discovered that at first sight, 25 percent of these cases would normally (but improperly) be seen as due to 'defective or dangerous physical or mechanical conditions'. However, on closer inspection the main cause of many of these was seen as 'man failure'. This judgement reduced the number ascribed to unsafe mechanical or physical conditions to a mere 10 percent. The protocol for making this judgement is not recorded. As he says (Heinrich, 1959, p. 21), 'personal judgement may lead to error, but it is defensible and necessary and in the majority of cases results in fair conclusions'.

An overall conclusion was reached that 98 percent of all the cases were of a preventable kind with 50 percent being practically preventable. Of all cases, 88 percent were caused by unsafe acts of persons and only 10 percent by unsafe mechanical or physical conditions. The remaining 2 percent were judged to be unpreventable (acts of God) and so excluded from the counting at this point.

Heinrich refers to two other large studies. One was conducted by the National Safety Council (of the USA) and the other was of cases reported to the State of Pennsylvania. These two studies allowed both unsafe acts and unsafe mechanical conditions to be ascribed as causes to accidents, not just one of these as in Heinrich's study. The results were unsafe acts 87 percent and 82.6 percent respectively and unsafe mechanical conditions 78 percent and 89 percent respectively.

Heinrich's purpose was to formulate an understanding of the factors and processes involved in accidental injury causation. He concluded that 'man-failures' (of knowledge, attitude, fitness or ability) actually caused or permitted these unsafe acts and unsafe mechanical or physical conditions, which themselves caused accidents. This he presented in the form of a model showing a linear series of interconnected causal factors. The causal (if/then) link between the factors was demonstrated by illustrating them as dominoes so lined up that if one fell over it would knock down the adjacent one which in turn would knock down the next and so on. This well-known domino model proposes a sequential ordering of five features of accidents, as follows:

Domino 1: Ancestry and social environment.

If people are born with and/or are socialised to develop faulty personal
characteristics such as recklessness, stubbornness, avariciousness, etc.
then

Domino 2: Fault of person results.

Either inherited or acquired, faults such as recklessness, violent temper, nervousness,
excitability, inconsiderateness, ignorance of unsafe practices, etc. are proximate reasons
for committing unsafe acts or for the existence of mechanical or physical hazards,
and

Domino 3: Unsafe act and/or mechanical or physical hazard will result.

Unsafe acts including standing under suspended loads, starting machinery without warning,
horseplay, removal of safeguards and mechanical or physical hazards which include
unguarded gears, unguarded points of operation, absence of rail guards, insufficient light,

resulting directly in

Domino 4: Accidents,

which are events such as falls of persons, striking of persons by flying objects, etc.
which cause

Domino 5: Injury

such as fractures, lacerations, etc.

It is evident from the model that if you wish to stop injuries happening (prevent Domino 5 falling with the others) then accidents must be stopped (Domino 4 stopped from falling with the others) by removing their cause, i.e. preventing unsafe acts and/or conditions by removing Domino 3.

Heinrich is also well known for the way in which he drew attention to the fact that the seriousness of the injury resulting from an accident was often a matter of pure chance and that a large number of relatively minor injuries (or even no injury) would generally occur before a major injury from an accident of the same type. He describes a detailed study of case records and the difficulty of finding cases which actually provided the information being sought – how many previous no-injury or injury accidents had occurred in the same circumstances. Cases were not used for various reasons: injury because of a mechanical defect in a machine; cases where employees were assigned to work for which their temperament or ability did not suit them (how this was decided is not explained). Eventually, over 5,000 cases were selected with what was judged to be adequate information. The study concluded that for every accident producing a major injury there are 29 minor injuries and 300 no-injury accidents (incidents). It was assumed that there were an unknown but presumably much larger number (thousands or hundreds of thousands) of unsafe acts and conditions that may have existed before any of these happened. Heinrich concluded that injury prevention relied on the prevention of these unsafe acts and conditions. These ratios were presented in the form of a triangle with the one major injury at the top and the multitude of unsafe acts and conditions at the base. A later chapter in this book discusses risk, which is what Heinrich was really observing in these statistics.

Heinrich is almost exclusively known for two things: this so-called triangle of the foundations of a major injury and his 88 percent unsafe acts/10 percent unsafe conditions statement. There are some lesser known but perhaps more important points he made too. A very much less well-known fact is that he also said this (p. 19):

> *The most ardent supporters, including the author, of the belief that man-failure accident causes are predominant are, nevertheless, firmly convinced that mechanical guarding and correction of mechanical and physical hazards are fundamental and first requirements of a complete safety program.*
>
> *They believe, and act on the belief, that safety begins with safe tools, safe machines, safe processes, and safe environment.*
>
> *This attitude is not at all inconsistent with the emphasis placed herein on the importance of man failures as a causative factor, and is more readily visualised when one considers 'corrective action'.*
>
> *In the same breath it can be truthfully said that although man failure causes the most accidents, mechanical guarding and engineering revision are nevertheless important factors in preventing the most accidents.*

Heinrich understood the difference between 'cause' (of which there is a longer discussion in Chapter 2) and prevention. This statement has been far less recognised over the years than the image of the removal of 'cause' in the domino image. For very many people, it is counterintuitive to suggest that injury is not the consequence of the victim behaving in some way (the cause of the injury) which runs counter to an assumed code of good behaviour, the details of which become crystal clear to all after the event. Indeed, the inability to see otherwise seems almost innate, so common and hard to displace is it. The difference between perceived cause and effective prevention is one of the most important distinctions that can be understood.

Heinrich was also at pains to point out that the needs of accident prevention were exactly analogous to those of production. Management and supervision could employ the same tactics for both. Indeed Heinrich mentions a 1928 study by the American Engineering Council which used an interesting technique to determine if safe factories also enjoyed good productivity. They found the results shown in Table 1.4.

Table 1.4   Results of research by the American Engineering Council in 1928

Companies in which:	Numbers of employees
Production is increasing and accidents decreasing	845,631
Production is increasing and accidents increasing	72,200
Production is decreasing and accidents decreasing	7754
Production is decreasing and accidents decreasing	7377

Heinrich's ideas, selectively interpreted to emphasise unsafe acts as the predominant cause of accidents, continues to be a major influence in the design of accident prevention programmes, accident investigation methods and the collection of cause data from injuries to support safety programmes. Accident prevention programmes are still based on the encouragement of (often unspecified) safe behaviour through the use of posters and films. Unsafe act auditing has been promoted in the petrochemical industry (Brown, 1988) and enthusiastically adopted by many industries since then and to this day.

Heinrich's domino model has its origin in two ideas strongly rooted in our communal psyche. The first is that cause–effect logic is a satisfactory means of understanding the world around us. This simple idea is a comfortable fit with a clockwork mechanistic view of the universe. The second, which is so deeply rooted in our collective psyche, is the need to find a cause so that blame may be apportioned and retribution sought. These may be sufficient to explain why the basic ideas he propounded have endured for so long.

The Era of Organised Management Practices

To properly understand how approaches to occupational risk control have developed over the years, it is helpful to also understand something of the development of industrial management practices, particularly as these are apparently indistinguishable from the needs of safety management, as Heinrich and the American Engineering Council pointed out. The end of World War Two marked the start of a new world order in political, social and industrial ways. Wars, it seems, always produce a revolution in technology which is harnessed for civilian purposes when the war ends. The need to rebuild civilian production and the economy created the opportunity to do things better than before.

As a proto-baby-boomer, my own experience of the management of industry begins in the mid 1970s. The decade of the 1960s introduced industry to problem-solving techniques: how to rationally approach a problem, be it production inefficiencies or safety. These provided a useful structure to how a problem (poor quality, low productivity, damage, injury) might be objectively described and its origins explored so that proposed improvements could be identified in a logical manner. Ishikawa (1968) made popular the so-called 'fish-bone' diagram. Imagine the spine of a fish with numerous ribs branching off it. The name of the problem is put where the head of the fish would be. A subject heading is then assigned to each rib, for example equipment maintenance, work methods, supervision, etc. Analysis of the origins of the problem required thought to be given to how each one of these subjects contributed to the problem and by inference where changes might be made to avoid or reduce the significance of the problem. Each rib bone then sprouted the main headings or ideas that arose from this analysis.

By the 1980s another approach, typically promoted under the banner of total quality management (TQM, which grew from the work of Deming (1986) and his lesser-known co-workers), was popular in industry in North America and shortly after in the whole industrial world, some considerable time after being successfully adopted by the industry that emerged in Japan after World War Two. Deming's contribution was a formulation of the organisational and statistical basis of the development of improvements to production processes. By the formation of teams of relevant people (production people, technicians and engineers, for example), suitably educated in the process of improvement which he formulated, production problems (causing delays, quality problems) could be analysed and solved. As numerous small improvements were made in this way, the experience of problems could be expected to diminish in frequency and significance. After a time, a revolutionary understanding might be reached that would lead to a step change in productivity and quality.

Deming's process improvement teams would have found it unnecessary to distinguish between productivity and quality problems. If the early associations made in the USA proved correct, one might assume, therefore, that safety improvements would, or could, form a natural part of the work of these teams. That this was so was proved to my satisfaction when, in the mid 1980s, I was asked by a large and well-managed factory, part of a much larger group, to provide them with an approach to the management of safety that would take them through to the year 2000. At the time, they were in the early stages of introducing these process improvement teams as part of their TQM programme. Following a substantial investigation into the hazards and culture of the company, I recommended that they could do no better than include hazard identification and hazard management standards into the work of the process improvement teams. It was only around 2005 that I returned to the site for other reasons. There was visible evidence that the recommendations were still being followed. The current Chief Executive Officer told me that on implementation of these recommendations and over the next few years the severity of injuries 'dropped through the floor' (as he put it) and the need to be seen to be doing something about safety obliged them to implement a behavioural safety programme aimed at the most minor of injuries, while retaining the TQM-based control process that had been recommended.

TQM was followed by the creation of international quality management standards derived over many decades from roots in the USA military and the British Standards Institution. First published in 1987, the International Standards Organisation (ISO) Standard 9000 series defined the functions and processes of a quality assurance programme. In the year 2000, a completely revised standard, ISO9001, defined (quality) management as a process of maintenance and improvement of management practices, not dissimilar to the intent of TQM (based on a cycle of continuous improvement) but with a broad emphasis on management practices. Later, an environmental management standard series numbered ISO14000 was developed by making relatively minor changes to ISO9001. When the ISO proposed a similar series applicable to occupational health and safety it did not receive support and it was an independent group of interested parties (the Occupational Health and Safety Advisory Services project group) promoted by the British Standards Institution which eventually designed the OHSAS 18000 series. Over time this became more closely aligned to the ISO9001 and ISO14001 series to facilitate mutual use within user organisations. The implementation of each of these standards is designed to be externally audited and certified and the display of a certificate by the user organisation gives suppliers and customers a degree of confidence in their management practices. The similarity of each of these standards is evidence that both safety (or risk) and environmental management are quality of life and quality of management concerns. Without certain management abilities it will not be possible to also manage these qualities.

The era of externally certified management systems introduced by these standards has the positive effects of ensuring, or at least encouraging, enduring management attention to quality, an organisational ability to learn from its mistakes and the creation of a corporate memory. Most of these attributes, which are so significant for effective risk management, were lacking from pre-certification era companies. Over time, however, there is a tendency for organisations to see that the satisfaction of an auditor's needs is sufficient: the emphasis is on managing process rather than hazards. Hazard management standards are not, in fact, mentioned in these standards. There are also organisations that have departed the world of certified management practices owing to 'audit fatigue' and clerical overload, despite current efforts to merge quality, environment and safety management standards.

Science and the Modern Understanding of Safety

The modern era, arguably the period from the 1960s to the present, has seen the beginnings of a groundswell of involvement of researchers from many disciplines as occupational and road injuries, the risk from nuclear power plants and the petrochemical industry became of greater concern to the public. Psychologists, physicians and engineers made significant contributions, many of the details of which are developed in later chapters.

The most significant step was the conceptual leap made by a group of researchers in the USA looking at the problem of injury from road accidents. One member of the group was J.J. Gibson (1961), a psychologist who made a notable contribution to perceptual psychology during World War Two. He was the first of the group to publish a formulation of the idea that energy is required to produce damage (or injury), although the idea first arose in group discussions[1] as they tackled the road accident problem. He wrote: 'Man ... adapts ... and responds ... to the flux of energies which surround him – gravitational and mechanical, radiant, thermal, and chemical. Some ... provide stimuli for his sense organs; others induce physiological adjustments; still others produce injury'. Gibson saw dangers as facts of the natural and artificial environment. He excluded consideration of infection as a special danger with its own well-understood characteristics, and also starvation for the same reason, saying: 'we are primarily concerned with safety, and, in ordinary speech, this is distinguished from health and nutrition'. From this standpoint Gibson classified dangers as shown in Table 1.5.

---

1   Personal discussions with David Klein.

Table 1.5   Gibson's classification of 'danger'

Mechanical energy:

- active impact, e.g. due to falling (vertical motion) or colliding (horizontal motion)
- passive impact, e.g. due to being struck by an object in either vertical or horizontal motion
- interference with breathing, e.g. through 'encountering the wrong medium'
- tool and machine forces
- machine failures, e.g. tyres blowing out, flywheel failures
- animal forces, e.g. due to biting and clawing
- weapon-induced forces

Thermal energy:

- extreme or prolonged heat gain or loss

Radiant energy:

- e.g. ultraviolet, atomic radiation

Chemical energy:

- i.e. poisons

Electrical energy:

- e.g. lightning and reticulated electricity

In Gibson's view accidents occurred either because of a misperception of danger or because of an inappropriate reaction to a perceived danger: a 100 percent unsafe act, one could say. Gibson's paper contains an interesting discussion of the perception of danger. Perception can fail because of inadequate external stimulus or because the stimulus is not registered by the individual. Reaction may be inadequate because of inhibition (e.g. due to fear) or lack of skill. It is not only a matter of having good reflexes or quick reaction time.

Gibson observed that the word 'accident':

> ... refers to a makeshift concept with a hodgepodge of legal, medical and statistical overtones. Defined as a harmful encounter with the environment, a danger not averted, an accident is a psychological phenomenon, subject to prediction and control. But defined as an unpredictable event, it is by definition uncontrollable.

Gibson saw the work of safety as a matter of understanding the 'ecology of dangers' and the natural or artificial signs of danger as well as the psychology of the perceptions and reactions aroused by these signs. In his view, danger does not automatically give rise to a chance of injury (which he calls also a risk) because of the possibility of skilled human intervention in the process necessary to allow the danger to create an injury. As an example, the presence of a cliff as a danger does not create a risk for a person who can see it and consciously keep themselves away from the edge.

Other members of this research group, Haddon, Suchman and Klein (1964), drew attention to the way in which society distinguishes between disease processes and accidents, often in situations in which there are substantially identical injury or damage processes involved. Haddon (1973) drew attention to the fact that:

An important landmark is reached in the evolution of a scientific field when classification of its subject matter is based on the relevant fundamental processes involved rather than on descriptions of the appearances of the phenomena of interest.

He goes on to give examples from geology, zoology and medicine. A child inadvertently swallowing a polio virus would not be thought of as having experienced an accident, as distinct from the same child ingesting a harmful toxin, say from the garden shed. The distinction is seen as being unnecessary, particularly when these authors note that few if any accident-prevention measures then (and perhaps now, too) in use lack parallels in the prevention of disease.

Until quite recent times in the industrialised world, and to this day in other parts, the prevalence of extra-rational (act of God) or moral beliefs (a punishment for poor moral conduct) about accident causation amongst otherwise rational people was or is noteworthy. Such beliefs clearly act as a barrier to effective research and prevention.

The basic medical model of disease as a process giving rise to different possible types of damage (symptoms) seems to be capable of easy transference (Haddon 1987; Wigglesworth, 1972) and lead to a definition of injury as: 'A unit of bodily damage resulting from the transference to the body of amounts of energy in excess of the injury threshold or from interference with normal body energy exchanges (as in suffocation)'.

The process is the transference of energy.

Haddon's publication of 10 countermeasure strategies based on the energy damage concept demonstrated the practical potential of this concept. These strategies, with some minor paraphrasing for brevity and clarity, are:

1. Prevent the marshalling of the energy in the first place (for example don't concentrate uranium, don't climb the ladder, don't use compressed gases).
2. Reduce the amount of energy marshalled (for example limit the quantity of flammable materials in a single storage, reduce the height you need to climb, reduce the pressure or volume of gases).
3. Prevent the release of the energy (for example everything that might be done to prevent flammable liquids escaping from containment).
4. Modify the rate of spatial distribution of the release of the energy from its source (release the energy more slowly, for example make it most likely that liquid leaks will be through very small holes, arrest the fall of a person so that they come to a halt slowly).
5. Separate, in space or in time, the energy being released from the susceptible structure (for example stand away from an X-ray machine when triggering the beam, use a bomb disposal robot rather than people to do the job).
6. Separation of the susceptible structure from the energy by means of a barrier (for example surround an explosives magazine with a massive earth wall).
7. Modify the contact surface through which the energy impinges on the susceptible structure. (Stated more generally, this captures the idea that the intensity with which energy impinges on a susceptible structure will determine whether it results in damage. Intensity is the measure of the amount of energy per unit area of contact surface. For example, a sharp knife cuts more deeply than a blunt one.)
8. Strengthen the susceptible structure (more generally, enable the susceptible structure to be exposed to greater energy intensity before damage occurs, for example by using body armour, hearing protection, etc.).
9. Detect and counteract the damage that occurs (for example, detect burning materials and suppress the fire).
10. Repair the damage.

The significance of energy in accidents was recognised also in the influential work of Johnson (1973). Here 'unwanted energy flow' was seen as leading to an incident, which could in the presence of a person inadequately protected by barriers lead to an accident.

As a subject of scientific study, as Haddon pointed out, the field of safety has much in common with the sciences of biology and geology. Both of these sciences discovered the significance to their research of understanding underlying processes. The expression of knowledge in both sciences is in the understanding and classification of these processes rather than in the form of the mathematical expression of physical laws, which is particularly familiar to physicists and is the image of science carried by the general public. Regrettably, the message of energy damage has had no significant effect on the design or conduct of safety programmes in industry or on the efforts of researchers. The message of the need to understand process has similarly had no effect on the design of standards for the classification of accidents by government agencies and standards bodies. The mere fact that this is where classifications are developed says much itself. It is impossible to imagine geologists and biologists accepting that a government or standards agency should be the custodian of the essence of their knowledge. It is an indication of the paucity of research into safety that there has not even been a debate on this, despite the undisputed evidence of inadequacy in existing classification systems.

Multiple Parallel Paths of Development

The emergence of the cold war from World War Two gave rise to the deployment of nuclear warhead ballistic missiles and the concurrent space race to the development of space exploration technology. These developments created a demand for analytical engineering techniques to better understand the ways in which adverse, instead of intended, outcomes could occur. The resulting tools (fault tree analysis (FTA) and event analysis (EA), described in Chapter 9) made use of logic diagrams to synthesise an understanding of how damaging processes could arise from the functional failure of components and to estimate the probabilities associated with these so that the final probability of the consequences of such adverse outcomes could be used to assess acceptability of the proposed design or mission. These damaging process logic models have since been widely adopted in the petrochemical industry and have more recently found application in the design of other complex technical systems, supported by failure mode and effect (and criticality) analysis (FME(C)A). These latter tools, as their names suggest, look to see what the functional effects on a system would be following individual component failure in each of the possible modes of failure. In the petrochemical industry, engineers developed a method for the review and operational hardening of a process design, known as the hazard and operability study (HAZOP). HAZOP studies pose challenges to a basic design by asking (using a suite of guide words) how it would cope with conditions very different from the design requirements, for example, with reverse flow or excess pressure. HAZOP has relatively recently been used in different industries, using different guide words, for the same purpose.

In the 1960s and 1970s, early days in the development of nuclear power, large petrochemical plants, the pharmaceutical industry and the car industry, the public became vocal in expressing concerns about risk decisions being made on their behalf by industry and government. Much social and theoretical research resulted, particularly in the USA, the aim of which was to better understand risk and how public perceptions of risk could be understood by governments. The results of that work are of great value in understanding how people respond to risks and the various situations in which greatly different perceptions exist. Rowe's (1977) seminal work

An Anatomy of Risk, of which much use is made in this book, is unique in providing a valuable logical derivation of terms and concepts.

Since at least World War Two, psychologists have been engaged in research to better understand how humans interact with the increasingly complex mechanised processes of industry, in such physical environments as aircraft cockpits, power station and petrochemical plant control rooms and the like. For example, J.J. Gibson studied the psychology of perception in an attempt to better understand what a pilot experienced when landing on the deck of an aircraft carrier. With early motivation from nuclear regulators and later with support from industry itself, a theory of error resulted, expressed most simply as a classification of error types and the circumstances relevant to them but including logic diagrams for the synthesis of estimated probabilities of the overall failure of complex tasks and of processes for predicting error probability in a task, all collectively named human reliability analysis (HRA). The field is characterised by the proposal of practical tools, for example technique for human error rate prediction (THERP; Swain and Guttman, 1985), human cognitive reliability (HCR; Hannaman, Spurgin and Lukic, 1984) and cognitive reliability and error analysis method (CREAM) (Hollnagel, 1998). The application of this work developed from typically process plant (power stations) to the more dynamic operational environment of commercial aviation.

During the majority of the period under review here, the field of occupational safety and health stagnated, making little progress from the point that prompted Waller and Klein (1973) to make the previously quoted remark that 'the field of injury control has for many years suffered from conceptual rigor mortis'. However, landmarks in the journey since that time (including Flixborough 1974, Three Mile Island 1979, Exxon Valdez 1984, Bhopal 1984, Piper Alpha 1988, Hillsborough Stadium 1989, Deepwater Horizon 2010, Fukushima 2011) have forced the pace of conceptual and legal change. The leadership in conceptual change has come from the human factors academic community and taken the form of better understanding of organisational behaviour, culture and dynamics; see, for example, and respectively, Reason (1977), Hudson et al. (2000) and Hollnagel (2012).

Legal changes arising from reaction to these disasters vary between the two available extremes of 'we'll tell you what to do' and 'you show us how you are doing it well', while legislators appear unable to envisage a purpose for legislation much beyond defining responsibility/culpability.

2

Accident Theory: Dominos and Triangles – Enduring Influences

Introduction

In Chapter 1 the view was introduced that the term accident is unsuited to scientific use. Gibson saw it as a makeshift concept burdened with legal and other overtones. Haddon noted the need for science to be based on an understanding of the fundamental processes involved rather than descriptions of the phenomena of interest (and by implication did not see accident theory as having this quality). As an example, botany no longer uses descriptive classifications of subject matter (for example bushes, trees, etc.) but classification structures that recognise the evolutionary processes that have given rise to what is being looked at today. Research in both biology and geology was stultified until process-based knowledge arose. Accident theory has given rise to descriptive classifications of accident types analogous to biologists describing bushes and trees. Arguably, research in the field is also stultified. Haddon, Suchman and Klein saw accident-based theory as supporting an unnecessary and unhelpful distinction between injury and disease. This first group to investigate safety in a scientific way looked at and discarded the domino-model-based industrial safety theory of the day: Waller and Klein dismissed the industrial safety field as being in state of conceptual rigor mortis. The dependence of accident theory on the essentially judgemental term 'unsafe' was also noted and criticised in Chapter 1. However, the unquestioning acceptance of cause–effect thinking (unsafe acts cause accidents cause injury) and the nourishment this gives to the deep need to apportion blame is not easily overcome by scientific argument.

Apart from being in colloquial use (where it would be expected to remain), the term accident is also in common use by industrial safety practitioners and even researchers. It is for these reasons alone that this chapter is devoted to a better critical understanding of cause–effect concepts and accident theory and the effect they have on industrial safety practices. A coherent theory, with scientific and practical attributes, is developed in later chapters.

A number of axioms arise from the adoption of this theory, the acceptance of which gives rise to the nature of accident prevention programmes and the way in which safety is thought about in industry. For these purposes, the Oxford Dictionary definition of 'accident' contains all the associations needed to understand the use of the term in accident theory:

1. An unfortunate incident that happens unexpectedly and unintentionally, typically resulting in damage or injury.
2. An event that happens by chance or that is without apparent or deliberate cause.
3. (In Aristotelian thought) a property of a thing which is not its essential nature.

The First Axiom – Accidents are Caused

An accident is a sudden coming together of unrecognisably small nuances of the normal flow of day-to-day, minute-to-minute happenings with an unexpected and sometimes savage effect. It has typically been hard for people to envisage that these shocking and apparently random happenings can be understood to have actually been caused by something amenable to investigation, rather than being simply evidence of the stochastic nature of the universe. I once read an accident report in which had been written, in response to the requirement to investigate in order to determine the cause(s), 'there was no cause – it was an accident'. In the mid 1970s the second sense of the *Oxford Dictionary* definition was a prevalent view, and a major message being promoted in industrial safety training programmes was that accidents were, in fact, caused and that by knowing this we could search for and remove the causes. It was thought to be of utmost importance that this truth be understood by the workforce. By associating the view that the world can be understood in cause–effect terms with the first sense of the dictionary definition, it is then conceptually possible to do what Heinrich had been promoting, namely to find the cause(s). This set of views is paramount in the world today. Every newspaper report of an accident will include the reassurance that officials are investigating its cause. We assume that by accumulating an understanding of causes we will know how to prevent such things in the future.

Accident Aetiology: Cause and Effect

The notion that cause–effect is a satisfactory way of understanding the workings of the world is pervasive amongst both the general public and some scientists. In the *Oxford Dictionary*, 'cause' is defined as 'a person or thing that gives rise to an action, phenomenon or condition'. The phrase 'giving rise to' implies a time relationship between the thing before and the thing after. We understand a world in which time goes forward and we understand that what we see now had its origins in aspects of the past without which it could not exist. The acknowledged first statement of this idea in Western philosophy is attributed to the Greek philosopher Lefkipos (c.450BC), who said that everything we experience is derived from preceding causes. In other words, in the flow of time what was observable is what is observable and if what is observable is not the same as what was observable then the difference has been caused in some way by a cause of some other kind acting in the past. While the absolute truth of this perspective can be argued philosophically, it is the possible narrowing of our understanding of the real features of the processes that give rise to damage and loss that is the justification for an investigation here of the real meaning of this perspective.

Various different types of causes have been proposed. Aristotle is known for drawing attention to four types: material, formal, efficient and final. Causes are popularly categorised as:

1. Necessary: the cause in question always and only creates the specified effect.
2. Sufficient: the cause in question is one way the specified effect can be brought about, but not the only way.
3. Contributory: A cause that is neither of the above but the presence of which has some influence on them, such that its removal changes the character of these causes or their effect in some way.

These three may each also be categorised as:

1. Proximate (being closest in time to the creation of the effect); or
2. Ultimate (being the very start of the cause–effect process that created the effect, the furthest back in time. Accident theorists like to call this the root cause.)

Implicit in this thinking is the idea that one cause produces an effect, which in turn may be a cause, of one type or another, of another effect, and so on, linking together in principle without limit.

The influential 18th-century philosopher David Hume (Millican, 2007) lived at a time when the newly discovered objective scientific method was producing results that disturbed some of mankind's beliefs about how the world worked. Hume is known for his writing on the subject of cause and effect thinking, much of it to illustrate that such perceived relationships owe more to our mind's ability to infer from correlation of observations than to any absolute existence of a cause–effect relationship. In more recent times, the philosopher Collingwood (1938) undertook a detailed investigation of the meaning actually being conveyed in speech by the word 'cause'. He considered that propositions of the type 'x causes y' are ambiguous and described three possible senses in which the phrase is used, as summarised in Table 2.1.

Table 2.1   Collingwood's three senses of meaning of the word 'cause'

Sense	'x causes y' used in speech to convey the idea of	Example
I	x makes us want to do y	Hot weather makes us want to swim
II	If we change x the effect will be y	I can prevent this if I do that
III	As a law of nature, x causes y	Force causes acceleration

Sense II is relevant to use in accident theory. As Collingwood says: 'the cause … is the handle, so to speak, by which we can manipulate it (i.e. the event or thing). If we want to produce or prevent such a thing, and cannot (do so) immediately …, we set about looking for its "cause"'.

Using Collingwood's example, if a car stops on a hill it is more helpful to identify the cause as being loose spark plug leads than the fact that the hill results in a greater power demand of the engine because of gravity. There is no particular value in seeking to list all the causes if the effect can be avoided by one change. In popular parlance, the search for the cause of cancer is indistinguishable from the search for a cure. There is little doubt that the origins of (many) cancers are to be found in our lifestyle, food and environmental pollution but the efforts made to reduce the adverse influence of these origins fail to capture the public imagination in the way that efforts to find a cure do. Cure implies we can remove or deactivate this cause and prevent cancer. As a corollary, an accident with no conceivable point of control has no cause, thereby fitting the 'act of God' category used by Heinrich (see Chapter 1).

Sense III is simply a convenient form of speech. It is convenient to talk about a force causing an acceleration when discussing dynamics but just as possible to talk about an acceleration causing a force. In reality, forces and acceleration coexist.

From a study of the aetiology of the word 'cause', Collingwood concluded that cause–effect terminology is but a metaphor whose literal meaning is the description of means to ends, so that if we express ourselves literally we will find that 'all this language about causation disappears … and (we) are left with a vocabulary in which all that is said is that we find certain means useful to certain ends'. He regarded 'the idea of causation' as simply a relic of animism (the basis, in his view, of Plato's perception of the world) foisted upon a science to which it is irrelevant.

This cause–effect thinking is very different from thinking based on understanding the process that produces the phenomenon of interest to us. A zoologist would find the idea that the species

Homo sapiens (human beings) was caused by either orang-utans or chimpanzees either amusing or ridiculous. At best one can say that cause–effect is a linguistic convenience, but at worst its entanglement with our deep need to have an explanation for otherwise mysterious happenings is a barrier to achieving a scientific understanding of the processes leading to damage and loss. As noted in Chapter 1, there is much anecdotal evidence that tribal societies attempt to prevent what we call accidents by appealing to local deities for protection through the use of ritual and sacrifice. As a corollary, injury is interpreted after the event as evidence that the injured person has been punished by these deities (spirits) for some transgression of a moral code; that they are to blame in some way for their misfortune. Mysterious natural processes, such as thunder and lightning, the weather and the presence of disease in man and in crops were similarly interpreted as acts of the gods and, depending on their manifestation, as possibly an expression of anger at human behaviour or of the desire of the gods for human sacrifice. Modern civilised people may dismiss these as mere superstitions but are seldom conscious that the vestiges of the need to explain the inexplicable remain and are felt deeply when an accident happens. We seek someone to blame and rather than forming mobs to attack the scapegoat (a phenomenon still evident in some societies) we codify this in our laws of negligence and punishment and seek retribution (a scapegoat) in this way. For evidence of this deep need, we need look no further than accounts in the press of people's reactions to disasters. At the time of writing, an explosion and fire in a coal mine in Turkey killed many hundreds of miners. The Turkish prime minister is reported (*The Times*, 2014) to have promised that the investigation would include the 'smallest detail' and that 'no negligence will be ignored'. While mobs may jump to conclusions based on flimsy insight, in the practice of the law the generally normal behaviour of those involved is subject to retrospective scrutiny upon which judgement is made with the assistance of simple statutory statements of responsibility: if there is an accident, then it is evidence that someone has not met their responsibility. A statement of cause is no more than a retrospective judgement of convenience. As Heinrich made clear, his choice of unsafe act or unsafe condition as cause was intrinsically based on judgement.

One last problem with the acceptance of cause–effect thinking is that it is not helpful in predicting the future: if orang-utans cause human beings, what do human beings cause? Why is it that orang-utans do not always cause human beings? Describing human beings as being caused in this way does nothing to promote investigation of the process that is involved. Research only progresses when the process is investigated.

The Second Axiom – Unsafe Acts and Conditions Cause Accidents

Heinrich's popular exploitation of the domino effect to illustrate his formulation of this idea was described in Chapter 1. The cause(s) of accidents are to be found in the physical conditions of the workplace and in the way in which at-risk people behave in the workplace. In Heinrich's case, this idea could account for 98 percent of all the cases he studied. In the view of the (US) National Safety Council and the State of Pennsylvania, they accounted for between 80 percent and 90 percent of all cases studied. Clearly all three sources recognised that there were other causes that could not be explained as unsafe acts or conditions. I have seen no discussion over the years on these mystery causes.

A practical problem with the search for unsafe acts and conditions is that what is unsafe to one person may be quite acceptable normal behaviour or conditions to another. Further, what is unsafe to one person at one time may become safe to the same person at another time when the influences of understanding, need or skill have changed. The very common belief in the existence of unsafe acts and conditions and the search for them during accident investigations cannot be said to provide support for the fact that they objectively exist. We see what we wish to and name it according to a convention.

The role people play in many workplaces is both complex and varied and includes handling multiple tasks, responding to circumstances and using judgement to make decisions, often opportunistically. The significance of the immediate behaviour of people in a workplace can vary from minimal, where routine tasks are completed each and every day and determined by virtually unvarying process and equipment (for example making cheese, canning vegetables), to of great significance, where operator response to unique circumstances is continuous (for example flying an aeroplane). Close to the latter extreme is chemical process plant and power station operation. Somewhere in the middle is the operation of an integrated steel plant and of a mine, since while much of the operation is fixed there is much room for variation in the way people work the processes.

In any case, the effective control of what may be seen as undesired human behaviour may well require design, administrative and management practice change. At some point, all accidents in the artificial environment of industry and commerce are due to human involvement, as even unsafe conditions must have been created by or allowed to exist by someone.

The very high proportion of unsafe acts judged to be the cause of accidents is possibly due to vagaries of behaviour of those closely associated in space and time to the accident, which may well be more apparent as well as more frequent than the occurrence of physical changes to equipment or awareness of previously unseen aspects of equipment design. The latter are more likely to be due to gradual degradation or original design intent than to any sudden and dramatic or noticeable failure. Statistics on human and equipment failure (Gertman and Blackman, 1994) indicate that humans are in many situations orders of magnitude more likely to fail than equipment. In other situations (routine and repetitive learned actions), the reliability of humans is on a par with that of machinery. In either case, if a person does something unexpected or which later becomes part of a process of injury, is this evidence of a failure on their part or evidence that a human being is not an infallible machine? The expectation of perfection is unrealistic.

The Third Axiom – Unsafe Acts and Conditions are Not Sufficient Causes of Accidents

It would be hard to argue that what are commonly put forward as the causes of accidents are what invariably and unconditionally precede an accident of the type in question. They are mostly neither necessary nor sufficient causes. This suggests, if the cause classifications offered previously are to be used, that generally identified unsafe acts and unsafe conditions are contributory proximate causes.

This axiom is supported by Heinrich's observation that there may be many hundreds of thousands of unsafe acts or conditions for every accident. That is, not all accidents made possible by these unsafe acts or conditions actually occurred in the time interval of interest.

People in a workplace may behave in various ways that an outsider could feel is unsafe. Day after day, perhaps year after year, their behaviour does not lead to an accident. Being familiar with the work and not sharing the views of the outsider, to them the situation is not unsafe. Moreover, they may behave like this in the presence of what some might see as an unsafe condition and so also not form the view that the condition is unsafe. Unsafe is fundamentally a value judgement. Prior to an accident everything is felt to be safe. Retrospectively, it is judged to be unsafe.

As an example, consider an open-topped sump tank at a blast furnace, which collects very hot water used to cool hot slag from the iron-making process. Open concrete drains direct the water to this sump, access to which is limited only by a removable post and chain barrier, which is commonly not in place as it obstructs access by equipment for the purpose of periodically cleaning out the fine slag particles that find their way into the sump. The open drains and the accessible sump tank exist for many, many years before, one day, a person falls into one of the drains and suffers burns that lead to his death a few days later. At the time this happened it was dark and the area was, not surprisingly, enveloped in steam. People are present in the area when water is flowing and the channels are open because of the need to control the flow through the drains and react to the accumulation of silt. Depending on our point of view, we may see these conditions and method of work as unsafe conditions and acts. But what was it that led to a man's death on this occasion but not on the numerous other occasions that had occurred in the preceding years? This set of conditions and practices occur, in round figures, 500 times a year and have been doing so for about 30 years.

If we insist on using this term, clearly some other cause needs to be identified, that has the properties of being present (proximate) immediately before the man fell into the drain.

Heinrich does not offer an explanation or description of what these trigger causes might be. So, if these unsafe acts (in this case people close to the drains) and conditions (the open drains and steam) as causes do not produce predictable effects, what is this missing type of cause?

The Fourth Axiom – Removal of Cause(s) Prevents Accidents

Inconsistent though it may be with the prior axiom, Heinrich's drawing of the domino model places an emphasis on this axiom by showing the 'Unsafe Act and Condition' domino being removed.[1] If the cause(s) of the accident are removed, then the accident itself will not occur and then nor will the injury or damage. Heinrich also strongly expressed the different view that while causes are mostly unsafe acts, there is a need to direct our attention to the change of workplaces as the necessary corrective or preventive action. Heinrich believed strongly in the need for engineering design as the means of removing unsafe acts from the causal sequence. Quite how he reconciled this with his other views that 88 percent of all accidents were caused by unsafe acts and that the removal of causes prevents accidents is unclear. Perhaps it is unwise to subject this theory in general to too much logical scrutiny as inconsistencies are not hard to find.

The Fifth Axiom – There are More Minor Injury Cases Than Major

Heinrich's research concluded that for every major injury there were some 29 minor injuries and 300 no-injury accidents. Subsequent to this, Frank Bird and others (Bird and Germain, 1986) are reported to have studied over 1.75 million accidents and looked at the ratios of fatalities to serious accidents, other accidents and incidents. By any standard, the study of Bird et al. was a major one, involving large numbers of participating companies and thousands of hours spent interviewing people to establish the ratio of incidents to accidents. An incident was defined as an accident that did not result in injury. Bird concluded that the ratios of these cases were 1 fatality to 10 serious accidents (injuries) to 30 minor accidents (injuries) to 600 incidents (no injury). These ratios are typically shown as triangles (accident triangles), but are shown in graphical form in Figures 2.1 and 2.2, as this is a form consistent with the understanding of risk presented later, in Chapter 6.

---

1   As a web search will quickly make evident.

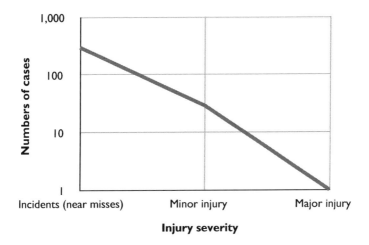

Figure 2.1   **Heinrich – the more serious the injury the less common it is**

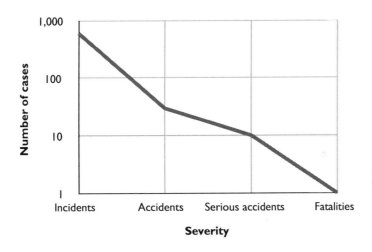

Figure 2.2   **Bird – serious injuries occur in smaller numbers than major ones**

A very similar representation of the distribution of accident consequences in the USA in 1968 is shown in Figure 6.3. Adherents to accident theory are keen to deduce that if the relatively large number of incidents can be reduced in number then the number of serious and fatal cases will reduce in number also. This logic is carried further and applied also to the much larger number of unsafe acts and conditions that underlie the incidents. This deduction relies on the normally unstated and unrecognised proviso that the incidents being reduced must be related to the processes that give rise to the serious and fatal cases. An example will serve to illustrate this. Incidents involving people slipping on stairs may be easy to recognise and report. In the circumstances in which they are observed, they may be precursors to a lost-time injury at most. However, the stairs may belong to a petrochemical plant with the potential for a major release of hydrocarbon gas. The incidents relevant to gas release may be far less obvious and not reported, as well as entirely unrelated to slips on stairs.

There is no point in seeing the accident triangle as anything other than a collection of triangles relevant to specific damage processes, such as one for electricity, one for falls, another for gas release and so on. The generic way in which the accident triangle is reported and accidents understood obscures this fact as it conveys the implied assumption that all unsafe acts and conditions and all incidents are all indicative of the causes of serious injury and fatality. When the fallacy of this view is not understood, the measures of success of a safety programme, such as lost-time injury frequency rate (LTIFR), are misunderstood as an indication of the overall safety of the plant. In petrochemical plants this can lead and has led to tragic results.

Modern Variations

As mentioned in Chapter 1, Johnson (1973) incorporated 'unwanted energy flow' into accident theory by proposing that it directly created an 'incident' if barriers to the energy flow did not contain it, and the incident could then escalate into an 'accident' in the presence of a person as victim and in the absence of suitable protective barriers for the person.

In the late 1990s, Reason (1997) breathed new life into the theory of accidents and revived the barrier theme of Johnson, in the form of 'defences'. In this view, losses result from hazards when the 'defences' that normally stop this happening fail due to either latent (unsafe) conditions or active participation (unsafe acts). Unsafe acts are seen as arising from local workplace factors (effectively replacing Domino 2), which themselves are due to organisational factors (effectively replacing Domino 1). Unsafe conditions also arise from these organisational and local workplace factors but are called latent conditions, suggesting that they are present for long periods of time. Conditions are the physical representation of the workplace, its equipment, machinery and facilities and they do exist without rapid change over long periods of time. In another expression of the idea, Reason sees accidents as arising from errors and violations by the workplace team or person and allowed to happen because unsafe, latent conditions themselves arise because of management decisions and organisational processes. These unsafe conditions are seen as creating failures in the defences that would otherwise prevent the accident. At that time, Reason listed the types of defences as:

1. understanding and awareness
2. safe operating methods
3. alarms and warnings
4. response to recover to a safe state
5. response to contain the damage
6. escape and rescue.

So, to the extent that each of these types of defences exist and are relevant to a given case, latent (having been there for some time) or active failures (immediately before the accident) in them can lead to their inability to actually defend against the accident. In principle, either the accident (or the loss, depending on which expression of the model is being used) can be interrupted at each of these defences. For example, if (a) and (b) fail then the remainder might stop the damage occurring.

Reason's contribution to the accident model is the introduction of management decision-making and the way the organisation works rather than the social environment and the behaviour of the individual.

The idea that an organisation can live with characteristics that contribute to these unsafe acts and conditions then leads to the possibility that these characteristics can be looked for within an organisation with the hope that modification of them can minimise their worst effects. The idea was proposed that these latent and active failures could be termed 'pathogens'.

The failure of defences was illustrated by holes in physical defensive barriers and this gave rise to the idea that many latent holes may exist (defences are not perfect) but not line up from one defence to another. That is, the deficiency in one defence may not be aligned with (relevant to) the deficiency of another defence and so the accident could be stopped by any one defence, it only being when a set of holes lined up in all the defences that the accident occurred. In a picturesque manner, the defences are drawn as slices of the variety of Swiss cheese in which many air bubbles are found. The Swiss cheese model of defences preventing accidents has since been used widely, although seemingly often with little reference to the original model, with almost anything able to be seen as a line of defence.

The Effect of Accident Theory on Industrial Safety Practices

Accident statistics have traditionally been relied on as a measure and possibly the only measure of the success of the safety programme. The commonly used LTIFR is a proxy for the probability of injury of a lost-time severity in any one work hour. LTIFR is the number of lost-time injuries per hundred thousand (sometimes per million) man hours. What constitutes a lost-time injury is subject to legislative definition, which can and does vary between jurisdictions. For example, a case may be classified as lost time if the injured person does not return to work on the following shift. In a workers' compensation insurance company's files the cost of time lost, medical treatment, legal fees and so on is a practical measure of injury severity. Figure 2.3 is the result of analysis of a large number of closed workers' compensation claim files. The monetary values have been converted to the mid 2000s. The figure tells the same story as that of the previous two figures. Close to 90 percent of all the records are for claims with a final value of about £150. The truly significant cases (both in cost terms and presumably to the injured person) amounted to a little less than one percent of all the cases. The conclusion is that in any given organisation LTIFR is almost exclusively influenced by the relatively insignificant cases and is no indicator of the success of the organisation in managing the risk associated with hazards of high severity potential.

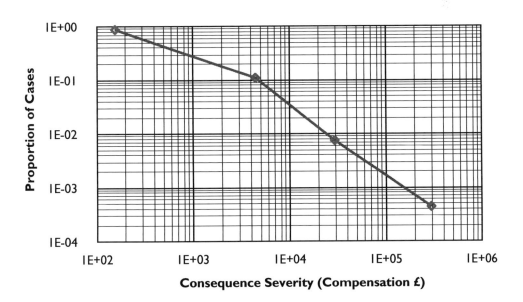

Figure 2.3   **The value of closed workers' compensation cases (N = 27,472)**

The discussion on the fifth axiom is relevant and the message is clear that LTIFR will not indicate the potential for a disaster. A low LTIFR can exist alongside a high potential for disaster, as has been demonstrated several times over the last 30 or more years. However, many managers believe strongly that LTIFR numbers give them a real indication of the health of their safety programme. A much-publicised desire to bring the LTIFR down may well lead to a culture of non-reporting as each accident is seen as evidence of failure by the workforce. The simple message is that the accidents that occur most commonly do not generally provide information about the accidents that will lead to significant and dramatic loss.

In conjunction with this belief in LTIFR, it is common for the most senior levels of management, including the board, to have a belief in the importance of being given information about relatively minor cases, for example spider bites and splinters. It seems there is a belief that if the board show interest in these little things then the sites will too. In fact, a perverse effect often accompanies such aspirations as sites fear having to report such things in much the same way that a schoolboy fears being reported to the headmaster for slovenly dress.

Because LTIFR is almost exclusively responsive to the large numbers of relatively minor injuries for which time off from work is to some degree discretionary, promotional programmes encourage workers not to have accidents. The implication is that workers are not averse to self-inflicted injury. Actually, the concern is more with the propensity to take time off work when an injury occurs; the payment incentive is an encouragement to stay at work when they have the discretion to do so, that is very minor injuries. Cohen (1977) was an early author who showed that LTIFR is very sensitive to the general climate in the organisation and since that time many papers have been written exploring the effect of organisational and management culture in detail. When working conditions are pleasant, the management climate encouraging and democratic, etc., then LTIFR is often also low. Of course, one cannot conclude from this that such things have anything directly to do with 'safety' at work.

Our propensity to blame people for accidents is reinforced by legal concepts of negligence. A lack of awareness of the no-blame nature of workers' compensation insurance commonly leads to the facts of a case being glossed over or radically altered to protect the income or job of the workmate who was injured. A very common supervisor response to the 'what action have you taken?' question on accident report or investigation forms is of the 'I have told her/him to take more care/be more aware of their surroundings/not act so hastily …' type. This is not surprising as the supervisor can often see little opportunity to change any other aspect of the work environment, such as equipment design (there is not enough money and probably no one to listen) or the way work is administered (the number and type of people doing the job, time pressures, etc.) and so these 'causes' are not seen as such.

Following naturally from the simple idea that over 80 percent of all accidents are caused by unsafe worker behaviour, the second significant feature of accident-theory-based safety programmes is that workers are encouraged to be safe through attitude modification training programmes and incentive schemes. Workgroups are rewarded for accident-free periods and individuals see messages that they are responsible for their own safety. Safety slogans are incorporated into company logos, clothing, letterheads and advertising. This focus on 'safety' attitude and consciousness, rather than directly on behaviour, is noteworthy. Psychologists tell us that attitude is not a good determinant of behaviour and that if we want behavioural outcomes we need to work directly on identifying and promoting the behaviour we want. For example, fining people for failing to wear seat belts in cars is likely to be more effective than exhorting them to do so by means of advertisements aimed at changing attitudes.

In the 1980s it was not uncommon for posters and training programmes to be the most obvious parts of a safety programme and for the main role of safety officers to be changing posters and selecting and organising training sessions. Taken to its extreme, this approach can lead to safety officers policing safety requirements and to safety departments bearing the responsibility for safety in the organisation, both of which I have seen many times.

In these circumstances it is common to observe a high value placed on the 'commitment' of senior management towards 'safety'. When pressed, they do not really understand what 'safety' means but do see that it is, in some hard to define manner, different from normal management functions. In the last 10 years, a form of cultural blanket has been thrown over some organisations with the idea of 'safety culture' being taken to the sort of extremes in which debate is seen as dissent: 'if you ain't with us you must be against us'. This can create the sort of political environment in which a totalitarian ruler would be comfortable. In one organisation, which exemplified this character, there was evidence of a sort of safety resistance movement, replete with clandestine graffiti and a shocking highly visible deliberate sabotage of the sacrosanct permit to work system exactly when risk consultants arrived on site for the first time. In another, on returning after some years, I was told a previously highly valued senior manager had to leave as he simply did not conform to the belief system.

It perhaps goes without saying, but should be said for completeness, that in organisations that accept accident theory, the investigation of accidents results in the expected conclusion that 80 percent or more of all cases may be simply attributed to either the fault of the victim or to some personal weakness. Also, there is a deeply held sense that as accidents are unanticipated, sudden, surprising and unwanted, they are also unpredictable. This belief is possibly the most destructive aspect of this theory as it leads to a strong resistance to the idea that accidents can be prevented. I well recall one manufacturing organisation to which I provided some advice in the form of a report on the various workstations making up the production process. My report was not received with enthusiasm and I did not continue working with them. Some two years later I was surprised to receive a call from the production manager with a request to come back. When walking down the corridor to the meeting, I met the human resources manager coming the other way. He had not expected to see me, but diverted me to his office where he retrieved my report from his filing cabinet and asked me how it was that I had accurately identified all of their current troublesome workers' compensation claim cases? He was incredulous and genuinely interested to know how this was done. As I said to him, the only uncertain aspect of it all was exactly when the various injuries would occur, otherwise it was all very predictable. It is simply not true that accidents are entirely unpredictable. The unpredictability resides only in the timing and location of them, not in the manner of their causation.

Summary

Cause-effect thinking has been subject to critical review for a very long time and in each case found wanting in objectivity and real meaning. When used to formulate a concept of accidents, it does little other than support the apparently innate belief that people are responsible for their own injury, possibly with the gods intervening. Accident theory, consequently, is popular despite its inadequacies. When subject to logical analysis, accident theory is found wanting in every aspect from cause modelling, the interpretation of accident triangles and the content of safety programmes. Its continued popularity amongst the managers of large and complex social, commercial and industrial undertakings is of concern both because of its inadequate substance and the support it lends to unhelpful beliefs and attitudes.

The Origins of Damage and Loss: Understanding the Processes

3

Introduction

The accident theory discussed in the previous chapter has one significant feature which betrays the fact that it is not based on a scientific and logical analysis. This is its reliance on the essentially judgemental term 'unsafe'. What is unsafe to one person may be a matter of normal daily experience to another. It is an easy judgement to make after an accident, but surprisingly hard to make before it. Heinrich admitted that it was an essentially judgemental process that enabled him to derive his much-quoted 88 percent unsafe act and 10 percent unsafe condition analysis of accident causes. No scientifically derived theory could rely on a concept so clearly founded in judgement and so ostentatiously lacking in meaningful definition. Notwithstanding its popularity and long life, his domino model lacks the requisite scientific substance. Other fields of enquiry have experienced the limitations of ideas not founded in the reality of the physical world. For example, alchemy gave way to chemistry, magic gave way to modern medicine and religious ritual was no longer needed to provide the courage to venture onto the oceans. Very little was learned about the nature of the physical universe by believing that it all revolved around the sun. Popular belief is no indicator of reality. Of course, scientists themselves can become so enamoured of their worldview that their belief in it is unshakeable. We are, after all, just human. Nevertheless, there are few who would argue that the scientific approach has not led to an extraordinary understanding of the workings of the universe from which society as a whole has derived great benefit.

The well-known essence of science is the application to the greatest possible extent of objectivity and logic. Objectivity may make itself evident in different ways. Some fields are readily described in the language of mathematics. For example, mechanics (statics and dynamics, applied to both solid bodies and fluids), electromagnetics, nuclear physics, astronomy and thermodynamics all use mathematics to express the laws of nature relevant to these fields of study. These laws include those governing the relationship between forces and acceleration, energy conservation, conservation of momentum, molecular forces and so on. In other fields of study this mathematical language is less applicable and knowledge is held in the written word or in diagrams, which are used to record the understanding that exists of the phenomenon of interest. These include the botanical, zoological and geological sciences. Plants, for example, can be described by their physical appearance: size, form of leaf, colour, existence of fruits, presence of flowers, etc., resulting in descriptive classifications. They may also be classified, as was discovered by Swedish biologist Carl von Linne (1707–1778), by how they came to be what is now seen, by the process that gave rise to them. Two plants with very similar appearances today may have reached this point by a very different evolutionary route. As pointed out in Chapter 1, each of the botanical, zoological and geological sciences has found that little is gained by the simple description of the phenomenon of interest, but much by understanding the processes which have given rise to what is being seen. The field with which this book is concerned is one that is more naturally adapted to the use of words than mathematics to express our understanding. Clearly we should respect the lessons of the botanical etc. sciences and concern ourselves with developing a process-based understanding of the phenomenon of damage and loss.

Until recent times, however, the reality is that the field has given rise to very few ideas that satisfy these requirements. The concepts described in the previous chapter, apart from lacking definition and objectivity, have led to no great progress in our understanding and practice (as is evident by the disasters that regularly occur), nor given rise to vibrant research. Waller and Klein (see Chapter 1) could well have been writing today when they commented on the lack of life in accident theory.

This chapter is concerned with the first of three features of the processes that give rise to Damage and Loss. The first is that damage always results from the application of energy to the damaged object or person. This is a fact of the physical universe and needs to be understood. Damage gives rise to loss because of the costs associated with recovery and lost opportunity. Loss also occurs in other ways, not associated with damage, for example theft or equipment malfunction. The second feature of these processes is that they take time to occur. Understanding the time structure assists in evaluating the practicality of possible control measures. The third feature (Chapter 4) is that damage and loss do not occur predictably – the processes are not deterministic. The uncertainty associated with this gives rise to our use of the term 'risk'. This set of features (see Table 3.1) will provide the basis for the structure of subsequent chapters where aspects of the theory and their application are presented in detail.

Table 3.1   The three features of Damage and Loss processes

1.	The process that gives rise to Damage necessarily includes energy. The process that gives rise to Loss only, involves a non-energy-based Threat.
2.	The process takes time to unfold.
3.	The process is uncertain.

Definitions, Scope and Principles

There are two distinct categories of risk. The first is what Rowe (1977) calls 'pure risk', in which the potential only for negative, adverse consequence exists. This is the case for all 'accidents' and also for all ill health. The second is speculative risk, in which the potential exists for positive and beneficial consequences, possibly as well as negative ones. Speculation occurs when buying a lottery ticket, for example, or buying shares in the hope that they will increase in value. A lottery ticket involves a known small outlay (loss) for a possible large gain. Share purchases involve the possibility of loss and gain of equal size. Speculative risk may also involve a strategic decision (for example in industry or in war) that could produce large gains but may also produce losses.

In all cases of risk, the process that gives rise to the consequences does not unfold in an entirely predictable way.

This text is concerned only with understanding pure risk. The analysis of pure risk may assist in understanding some aspects of speculative risk, but those involved totally in speculative risk have developed detailed specialised financial tools to do their work.

Consequences are the result of the process that gives rise to them and the term Occurrence is the name used in this text for this process. It is convenient to collectively call injury, damage and loss the types of Consequence(s) of the Occurrence. Damage can be defined in general terms as an unwanted change to the desirable qualities of anything we value (an Asset), be that tangible (such as injury to our bodies, damage to the environment, a production process or a piece of equipment, and so on) or intangible (such as reputation). Physical damage is, for example, the crushed body of our car, the broken casing of a pump, the cracking of a building after an earthquake and so on. Injury is usually a word used to describe damage to the body of a human or animal, although in law its use is sometimes more broad than that. Bodily injuries include fractures, cuts, burns, bruises, abrasions and so on. We can use the term Damage to include injury and where used in this text you may assume this is intended. Loss is a term with two clear meanings. One meaning is the reduction in the (usually) monetary value of an Asset such as occurs when the Asset is damaged or shares drop in value. The other meaning is the literal loss of an Asset that has been removed from us, as when a person dies, a robbery occurs, a species is lost, etc.

Each of these types of Consequence will have a Consequence Value. For example, the Consequence Value associated with injury may be indicated by descriptors such as permanent or temporary incapacity, fatality (and the numbers of people killed). The Consequence Value associated with damage to equipment may be expressed as the amount of money required to repair the equipment, and so on.

Some processes of interest give rise to Damage with Losses arising as a consequence of this. Other processes simply give rise to Losses directly, for example loss of money or of an item of value either through theft or fraud or not knowing where it has been stored. These Losses do not result from the presence of Damage. Hence, we can distinguish between two different types of processes of interest: those that give rise to Damage and those that do not. Physical damage necessarily requires an energy source, as work is always done in creating damage. This is the energy damage process. A model (the Energy Damage Model, EDM) is introduced to assist in understanding the energy aspect of Occurrences. Assets affected by energy can be thought of as Recipients of the energy transfer. In Occurrences that give rise to Loss only (with no damage), no energy is required and the process is made possible due to the existence of a (non-energy) Threat. For example, a burglar or a stock market crash are both Threats to our Assets. It will be seen that the EDM can easily be transformed into a threat loss model.

Some Damage processes occur intentionally. Consider, for example, environmental damage arising from steady discharge of a pollutant. Apart from some possible uncertainty arising from incomplete understanding of the totality of the effects of the pollutant or whether a fine will be levied for discharge in excess of licence provisions, there is no other uncertainty involved. Here, what experiences the Damage (the environment) has no formal standing or ability to express its needs. Consider, also, wanted Damage such as in demolition work. In warfare, while Damage is unwanted by those who experience it, its creation is intentional, as it is also with criminal assault.

The pioneering work of Gibson and Haddon in recognising the need for energy to create damage was introduced in Chapter 1. Gibson provided a simple classification of dangers by energy type and Haddon described the ten countermeasure strategies. In this chapter, the scope and application of the energy damage idea is examined in detail.

Energy is a term defined in physics as the potential to do work. Work itself is defined in physics as the product of a force and the distance through which the point of application of the force moves. In the international system of units (SI) force is measured in newtons and distance in metres. Hence, the unit of work is the newton metre (Nm). The English physicist James Joule was the first to recognise that all forms of energy were essentially interchangeable and the unit of energy and work is named after him: one joule (J) is the work done when a force of one newton moves a distance of one metre. The time rate at which work is done is the joule per second (J/s) and, by definition, this is called power. The name given to one joule per second is the watt, named after the Scottish engineer James Watt.

Energy can be experienced in many different forms, some of which are common and familiar and others less so. Table 3.2 is a list that illustrates this in more detail than Gibson's original listing (Table 1.5). Some of these energy forms are a matter of common experience in the natural environment. We know of the potential for a fall to injure us. We are aware that a falling tree branch or rock or avalanche can cause great damage. We fear being struck by lightning and know of the devastating effects of fire and disease. We are not aware of some forms, even though they may be all around us (for example nuclear particle radiation). In today's industrialised and developed world almost all of these energy forms exist in quantities and circumstances not found in the natural environment.

Table 3.2   A listing of common forms of energy

Energy form	Subform or description
'Potential energies'	• Gravitational energy, including weight effects and waves in liquid–gas interfaces • Structural strain energy • Stored energy in compressed fluids
Kinetic energy	• Energy stored in a body's mass due to its speed in linear or rotational motion
Mechanical power	• The rate of energy flow in machinery from the source of power to the point where the energy is absorbed in the action of the machine
Pressure waves in fluids and solids	• Noise (a pressure wave in fluids) • Acoustic shock wave (a wave travelling faster than the speed of sound) • Mechanical vibration in solids
Electrical energy	• Electrical potential energy (volts) • Electromagnetic fields • Electrostatic charge
Nuclear particle radiation	• Radiation of a nuclear origin (e.g. X-rays)
Thermal energy	• Solids, liquids, gases (including flames) • Ambient (atmospheric) condition
Chemical energy	• Molecular bonding energy released in oxidising reactions (e.g. corrosion, fire, explosion) • Modification to the chemical processes of the body (e.g. acute toxic and non-respirable conditions)
Microbiological 'energy'	• Viruses, bacteria, fungi
Muscle energy	• Attacks (purposeful) or inadvertent striking • Use of muscles for work

Note: Some of these exist within the body of a Recipient (self energy) and some outside the body (external energy).

The potential for damage depends on the intensity with which the energy is able to impinge on the Asset (person, environment, animal, object of value). Intensity is defined in physics as the amount of energy passing through a unit area. Its units are joules per square metre (J/m^2). Because the surface area through which energy from a source can pass is larger further from the source, the intensity diminishes with distance. Energy (heat) radiating from a room heater is more intense on the hand held close to it than away from it for this very reason. The skin has the ability to withstand a certain intensity of heat without suffering a burn. We can call this energy intensity the damage threshold. If the intensity is less than this damage threshold our experience of the heater will go from discomfort to pleasure as the intensity reduces.

The Occurrence process giving rise to Damage and Loss develops sequentially over time. It is true that some processes are very rapid and that others are very slow. While we may react differently to these (the rapid ones cause surprise) there is no essential difference between them. The time aspect of the process is called the time sequence, a model of which (the Time Sequence Model, TSM) is described below. The TSM and the EDM, in describing different aspects of the same thing, are interrelated.

The fact that we coexist with energy in these various forms and mostly find them beneficial is an indication of the fact that their use does not always lead to damage. When we switch on an electric light, we seldom receive a shock. We drive our cars at high speeds but seldom experience an accident. The simple fact that when energy exists it does not always create damage is sufficient for us to realise that the creation of damage is not deterministic but probabilistic. This probability is the origin of what we call Risk: the third feature being that Damage and Loss processes are inherently uncertain. This uncertainty is why we think of Risk as the distinguishing feature of this field of study. Uncertainty particularly affects our individual and collective emotional and managerial responses to these Occurrences and is consequently of great importance.

We can change the probability by well-intentioned design and/or behaviour, but the probability will always exist as long as an energy form in a quantity or an intensity which is able to exceed our damage threshold exists or a non-energy Threat exists able to produce Loss. The probability that this possibility leads to Damage or Loss is determined by the situation in which the energy source exists. As energy sources and non-energy Threats do not constantly generate Damage and Loss, the potential for them to do so is always under some form of control. It is also true that if something is possible it is only a matter of time before it occurs. It is easier to describe a possibility than it is to know when it will occur.

The Energy Damage Model

Gibson and Haddon drew attention to the fact of energy damage but did not expand on how the damage results. The process needs to be modelled in sufficient detail for its essential features to be understood and with sufficient simplicity for it to be of practical value to the researcher and practitioner. As is often the case in science, the simplest model is the most valuable as it does not unnecessarily constrain research and understanding while providing a basic framework in support of them.

Clearly an energy source is needed. The energy source itself is envisaged as being located somewhere, at a point in space. Each of the energy forms in Table 3.1 can be thought of in this way. The space occupied by the energy is the damaging energy space (DES).

Something able to sustain the Damage must also exist. In the EDM, this is shown as the Recipient of the Damage. Recipient is a synonym of Asset. As energy sources and Recipients are not always in the same place some means needs to exist to either take the energy to the

Damaging Energy Space

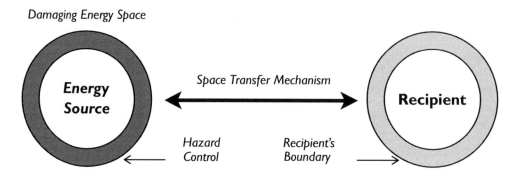

Figure 3.1   The Energy Damage Model

Recipient or the Recipient to the energy. This is the Space Transfer Mechanism. The double-headed arrow in Figure 3.1 illustrates the fact that movement can occur in both directions. There are a number of possible types of Space Transfer Mechanism and these are explained later. If the energy does reach the Recipient, then the damage threshold of the Recipient at the point of contact (the Recipient's boundary) must be exceeded (by the incident energy intensity) for damage to occur. The Recipient's boundary can be thought of as any part or quality of the Recipient which is sensitive to the form of energy involved. The Recipient's boundary is of many possible types and these are discussed later.

As the energy source is not continuously creating damage, it is clear that its ability to create Damage is normally under some form of control. For the purpose only of diagrammatic representation, this can be visualised as the energy being contained by the dark ring in Figure 3.1. The term 'Containment' is a literally appropriate way to describe the caging of a wild animal or the containment of a source of nuclear radiation or a hazardous fluid. A more suitable alternative to this term is possible if we define the Hazard as a source of potentially damaging energy. The containment ring is then what controls the potentially damaging properties of the energy source, in other words the Hazard Control. This has much to recommend it as an objective definition of the common term Hazard, capable of resulting in a limited and known number of Hazard types, which makes it possible to list (and therefore identify) Hazards uniquely and comprehensively. This cannot be said of a currently popular definition of the term as a source of potential harm. Anything from a twig on a tree to a politician can fall under the latter definition and it is not possible to list such hazards comprehensively and uniquely.

The nature of Hazard Control depends on the form of the energy. It is a fact of the universe that one energy form can and often does change into another. For example, the energy in flowing water can become electrical energy, electrical energy can become heat energy, chemical bonding energy of fuel can become the kinetic energy of a vehicle, etc. For this reason it is necessary to be precise in understanding the form of energy which is the source (Hazard). The form of the source of energy is necessarily described by the form it takes before control is lost over its potentially damaging properties. Energy form changes are common in real Occurrences:

1. When an object falls and the original gravitational potential energy is swapped for kinetic energy.
2. In a chemical explosion the source energy is the chemical bonding energy of the explosive materials. The propagating energies are thermal, electromagnetic (for example light), acoustic (air pressure) and kinetic (in the event that solid objects are flung outwards by the force of the explosion).

3. In a pressure explosion the source energy is the pressure of the fluid. The propagating energies are acoustic (air pressure) and kinetic (in the event that solid objects are flung outwards by the force of the explosion).

Each of these examples is of an energy form change occurring after the Hazard Control has failed.

Anything which conveys energy towards the Recipient or vice versa is a Space Transfer Mechanism, as the model shows a Recipient as being separate in space from the original energy source (Hazard). There are five different types of such Mechanisms.

1. Through a property of the medium between the source and the Recipient. Properties can include pressure, temperature and even gravity. Examples include temperature and pressure waves in a fluid, temperature and compression waves in solids, radiant heat (temperature flowing from a high source to lower temperatures in the surrounding medium). Waves occurring on the boundary between fluids of different densities, commonly a water/air boundary, result from a vertical disturbance of the surface and propagate away from the source of the disturbance, carrying with them the energy of the disturbance in the form of gravity waves.
2. Electromagnetic field disturbance, in which the energy of the disturbance radiates away from the source.
3. Mass transfer from the source, in which physical objects carry energies such as heat, kinetic energy and chemical energy and are given a motion away from the source energy. Examples include a flying particle from an explosion, a splash of chemical or hot metal, chemical fumes drifting from a source moved by buoyancy and air movement, steam escaping from a cracked pipe.
4. Nuclear particles from a radioactive source. This is a special case of type 3 above.
5. Movement of the Recipient towards the source or of the source itself towards the Recipient. The energy source or the Recipient or both may be mobile. Examples of mobile Recipients include people placing a part or all of their body in a DES. Examples of mobile energy sources naturally include cases where the source energy is kinetic, as with cars on a road. This could alternatively be thought of as a part of type 3 above. A wild animal escaping from containment in a cage is another example.

A Recipient is an alternative name for an Asset, one able to sustain Damage. Recipients of energy include people and animals, the environment (organisms, air, water), equipment (for example used for productive purposes) and buildings.

If an energy source can be considered hazardous it means a Recipient is able to be damaged by it. The boundary of the Recipient is a property of the Recipient's defences that is susceptible to the energy form. The strength of the boundary is indicated by its damage threshold in that above a certain intensity of energy (the damage threshold) the boundary will break down and fail to prevent damage. For example:

1. Human skin is, through its physical and chemical properties, able to resist certain intensities of radiation, heat, pressure, concentration of different chemicals and types of microbes and resist certain voltages before electrical current is able to flow into the body.
2. The ear is able to absorb certain amounts of sound pressure energy without damage.
3. Human organs such as the liver are able to process certain chemicals depending on the rate and total amount of absorption by the body.
4. People can inhale certain concentrations of carbon monoxide without permanent damage being done.

5. The bones and intervertebral discs in the spine can resist certain pressures before they fracture.
6. Muscles, tendons and ligaments can resist certain forces before they break.
7. Body organs can absorb certain levels of vibration before they break down.
8. Cars are able to resist impacts at certain speeds without structural damage.

In the previous section, Damage is defined 'in general terms as an unwanted change to the desirable qualities of anything we value'. The desirable qualities of the human body can perhaps be simply categorised as its physical, psychological and social attributes. It is considered that, in general, physical, psychological and sociological stimuli can each give rise to one or more physical, psychological and sociological effects on the body. For example, noise can lead to irritation and changes to respiration, etc. Stress from social interaction can give rise to psychological effects as well as physiological ones such as increased levels of adrenalin. As an engineer, of course, I have a very limited understanding of chronic illness and to a lesser extent also of injury, but the simple analysis that follows hopefully conveys something of the scope of Damage to people while not being too simple or inaccurate to be of use.

1. Physical attributes are obviously susceptible to, and hence able to be damaged by, either energy from outside (external) or from within the body. This damage can be due to:
    a) Direct overload of the physical defences of the structure of the body, a situation with which we are familiar and which we think of as an injury.
    b) An overload of the compensatory systems of the body (for example, thermal regulation, as the body is capable of functioning only within a narrow band of body core temperatures, when exposed to excessive high or low temperatures) and which typically we may not think of as injury, but perhaps as illness.
    c) An interruption to the normal processes that enable the body to function, such as respiration (for example lungs full of water or of carbon monoxide), blood flow, nerve function, digestion, etc. Depending on how these interruptions occur, we may not to think of these as injury. We tend not to think that a suffocated person has received an injury as such.
2. Psychological effects can be experienced from physical or psychological stimuli:
    a) Physical stimuli to the body such as chemicals, acceleration, heat, noise, electromagnetic radiation, etc. can result in various chronic (long term) and acute (short term) psychological conditions. Probably in all such cases we would refer to them as illnesses.
    b) Psychological stimuli can lead to physiological changes as well as psychological ones. Chronic exposure to the stimulus can lead to adverse effects from the chronic exposure to hormonal and other changes in the body. Again, these adverse effects would all probably be called illnesses.
3. Adverse social effects take the form of anti-social behaviour, withdrawal from society, lack of cooperation, etc. They are the social-level experiences of psychological state. We sometimes think of them as illnesses.

Environmental damage can also be of a chronic or acute type and can occur to animals, insects, microbiological organisms, the ground itself, to water and to air. Items of equipment, buildings and anything physical are thought of as having suffered damage typically when something sudden and unexpected has happened, for example a broken shaft on a pump, a tree falls on a building, a car hits another and so on. Slow processes also result in damage, for example corrosion or erosion on the impeller of a pump, rising damp affecting a building, corrosion of a car body, damage to paint through exposure to sunlight, etc.

The EDM makes it possible to identify and classify the types of control measures that can be used to avoid or reduce the probability of energy sources affecting Recipients. The origin of those in Table 3.3 will be self-evident from the portrayal of the EDM in Figure 3.1.

Table 3.3   EDM control measure strategies

Control measure type	Examples
1. Remove or replace the energy	Don't use chemical herbicides to kill weeds, use steam or natural acids like vinegar instead. In many cases in industry, it is only in the early stages of a design concept that this control measure can be considered.
2. Reduce the amount of energy	Use smaller quantities and/or more dilute herbicides. Here, too, it is mostly in the early stages of design that such a control measure can be considered.
3. Where one exists, ensure the Hazard Control Mechanism works to an acceptable level of reliability	Pay attention to the way herbicides are stored, mixed, transported and used. After basic process design decisions have been made, a multitude of practical control measures can be used, including equipment renewal, inspection and maintenance and preferred work methods all backed up by various administrative measures.
4. Remove or interrupt the Space Transfer Mechanism	Don't generate small spray particles when applying herbicides. Don't spray on windy days. Don't apply herbicides near pathways or waterways. In industry, this control measure type can commonly be seen in the provision of noise control barriers, fume extraction ventilation, blast barriers behind aircraft engine run-up bays, bunds to contain chemical spills, boundary controls such as locked gates and machine guards, road intersection controls such as traffic lights and intersection give way rules, and similar.
5. Strengthen the recipient's boundary – raise the damage threshold	Provide skin and respiratory protection to the person applying the pesticides. The use of personal protective equipment falls into this category: eye, ear, respiratory, skin and head protection. Essentially, these controls are similar to barriers but the difference is that they are fitted so close to the person being protected that it is simple to see them as fitting into this category. In a more literal sense, developing muscle strength and fitness to avoid muscle strain when carrying out physical tasks is clearly in this category.
6. Remove the Recipient from the presence of the energy source	Exclude people from the area in which pesticides have been applied. The automation of industrial processes falls into this category, for example on assembly production lines, in mining and mine ore hauling, etc.

The Special Case of Energy Source and Recipient Coexisting

This special case requires no Space Transfer Mechanism as the energy source is within the body of the Recipient. This occurs in a number of common situations as the human body is host to a number of energy forms:

1. Gravitational potential energy. This is the energy form involved in the common case of a person falling either onto the floor on which they are standing or onto lower levels if falling off a balcony, for example. It is also relevant to less common situations such as standing on a nail, rolling an ankle on uneven ground and any situation involving the simple application of body weight.
2. Kinetic energy. This is the energy form associated with speed and is relevant when a person walks or runs into an object or is flung around inside a vehicle during a sudden stop.
3. Muscle energy. Muscles are devices that convert food energy into force. These forces are used to do physical work and to maintain body posture. It is possible for muscles to generate sufficient force to injure themselves, joints and connecting tissue. Forceful movements of the body can also result in injurious interactions with the environment, for example knuckles hitting something when a spanner slips or a person standing up and hitting an unseen obstruction.
4. Chemical bonding energy. If you believe in spontaneous human combustion, this is the energy source involved.

Where the Recipient is a building, piece of equipment or some physical substance, it too is host to some or all the energy sources listed above for people. For example, one can readily imagine a piece of mobile hydraulically powered equipment falling down a slope, hitting an object, damaging itself through the power in the hydraulic rams or even burning. When a building burns, it is the last energy source listed above that is involved.

The Special Case of Mobile Energy Sources and Recipients

This special case is worth detailed attention because it is such a common situation in all aspects, industrial and public, of our modern life. There are three possible cases to consider:

* the Recipient is mobile but the energy source is not
* the energy source is mobile but the Recipient is not
* both Recipient and energy source are mobile.

Table 3.4 is a summary of how either passive or active controls can be used to avoid conflict between Recipient and the energy source in each of these three cases. Conflict, in a general sense, can be thought of as a space–time coincidence if the conflict arises purely because of random chance. For example, a car arrives at a railway level crossing at the same time that a train does or two cars approach an intersection such that they will collide unless something is done. We attempt to prevent such space–time coincidences by the provision of give way rules and the sequencing of traffic flow using traffic lights.

Table 3.4   Space–time coincidences and associated countermeasures

	Mobile energy, stationary Recipient	Mobile energy, mobile Recipient	Stationary energy, mobile Recipient
Passive controls			
Separation hardware and procedures	Divert or sequence the energy around the Recipient, e.g. traffic control cones direct traffic away from workers in the road	Diversion or sequence controls applied to both, e.g. stop signs, split-level road/rail intersections	Divert or sequence the Recipient around the energy, e.g. warning signs, access restrictions
Active controls			
Control over energy	Energy intrusion into the space of the Recipient activates a control mechanism or procedure, e.g. sprinkler systems, active gas extraction in mines, robot vehicles sense the presence of a Recipient	Intrusion of either into each other's space activates energy control mechanism or procedure, e.g. traffic flow rules	When intrusion is sensed, the space is de-energised, or, in order to gain access to the damaging energy space a procedure must be followed to de-energise the space, failing which access is denied
Use of a hardware barrier	Active use of a barrier to protect the Recipient, e.g. automatic fire doors, shield, security doors	Active barriers used by both, e.g. futuristic 'energy shields'	When intrusion is sensed, barriers are activated to prevent Recipient intrusion, e.g. security doors
Control over sequence and or direction	Over energy movement, e.g. active traffic light switching when a Recipient (other car or pedestrian) is detected	Over movement of both, e.g. combined press guard and stroke control, air traffic control, railway crossing lights	When a possible intrusion situation exists, warnings are given which require the Recipient to wait until the conflict is resolved

Collision theory describes the process involved when two mobile objects attempt to avoid each other, for example two ships, two aeroplanes, two cars or two pedestrians. There is the process of perception, recognition and response, all of which has to be timely and in the correct sense for a collision to be avoided. We have all had the experience of 'dancing behaviour' when confronted with another person walking towards us: we move one way and so do they, so we move the other and they do too. The reaction of each is out of phase and the result is we bump into one another. This can happen also with cars and with ships in sea lanes. The collision process of ships is characterised by slow closing speeds and also slow steering and speed change response. Large ships are not agile. The collision process of aeroplanes is characterised by high closing speeds and difficulty in observing each other so that avoiding action is often not possible.

The mobile Recipient, stationary energy source case is common in the occupational environment when we are concerned with the health and safety of people as Recipients. Many types of place may be off-limits because of the energy sources contained in them – examples include fixed machinery, aircraft engine test cells, electrical switchboards and power distribution rooms, rooms lit by high levels of ultraviolet light, rooms containing biological hazards, vessels containing non-respirable or toxic atmospheres and similar. Enclosures around radiating energies can for practical purposes be put into this category if the intent is that people should not enter the enclosure, which is there to prevent radiation into the Recipient's normal space. The technology for keeping people out of these areas is varied and can have much in common with the methods used in the security field to keep people away from valuables in bank vaults, for example. A detailed discussion of this technology is not the intent here but a brief overview of it is useful. Recipient exclusion mechanisms can be fixed, passive and physical barriers such as simple machine guards, locked doors, substantial fences and so on, or procedural barriers which require an active behavioural participation by the Recipient (complying with warning signs). Barriers can also be active if they sense the presence of a Recipient, and close access pathways as a result.

Mobile sources of energy are common in the form of vehicles and mobile plant and equipment. The source may contain significant amounts of kinetic energy, as does a road vehicle at speed, but this is not an essential feature. Mobile sources may also contain other forms of energy, such as:

- mechanical power in digging arms or cutting blades
- heat
- chemical energy, for example when people working in a vessel are deluged with a non-respirable or toxic substance
- gravitational potential energy, for example when a person is crushed under a moving vehicle
- a radiation source is on the object, for example when roadside workers are exposed to the noise of passing traffic.

Control over such processes involves avoiding the space–time coincidence between the Recipient and the mobile source. If the mobile source has the capacity to select its path, as does a vehicle, then control efforts are made to influence this to one which avoids the Recipient. If the source does not have this capacity then efforts are made to sequence the usage of the space by the Recipient. An example of this is the separation of people and rail vehicles, also the separation of road and rail routes.

Hazard Control Failure Mechanism

The failure Mechanism of the Hazard Control is the way in which the release of the potentially damaging capability of the energy source is brought about. In Table 3.5 these are divided into those occurring in the artificial environment of industry, commerce, transport and power and those in the natural environment of the earth and space.

In the artificial environment, failure Mechanisms can be categorised, following the suggestion of Rowe, as either purposeful, incidental or unintended. A purposeful Mechanism applies to cases in which there is an intention to release the energy to do damage. As an example, in military actions the chemical bonding energy in an explosive is normally carefully controlled, be it in the ammunition of guns or the content of bombs and shells. When needed, it is purposefully released to inflict damage on the enemy. Such releases can be legal or illegal. An example of a purposeful illegal Mechanism (using muscle energy) is the assault of a person by another. Incidental Mechanisms are to be found everywhere. Noise, heat, chemicals (insecticides, herbicides, pesticides, food additives of all types, plastics), fluids, fumes, vibration and electromagnetic field disturbances are routinely released from industrial processes, transport and communication equipment. It is typically these Mechanisms that attract the attention of people working to protect the environment and public health. Unintended Mechanisms of the two main types shown in the table are common in industry, commerce and transport. A Mechanism of this type may be a failure of an item of equipment, for example a valve leaks gas, brakes fail, a structure fails. It may also be a failure of the way in which the system is controlled, for example the control system signals a valve to open or a person opens it in error, a foot slips off a brake pedal, a heavy vehicle drives into the supporting structure of an overhead silo. Control systems may be automated or rely on human behaviour or be a combination of both. Obviously, an automated control system may fail because of a hardware or software failure. When the process control system relies on human behaviour the requirements are either in the form of defined procedures, expected learned behaviours or based on knowledge-based problem solving. Much can be written about these three options, particularly their reliability in different situations. Equipment failures and control system or procedural failures are what Heinrich called unsafe conditions and unsafe acts. It is typically these Mechanisms that attract the attention of people working to manage risk.

In the natural environment we are routinely exposed to the power of nature expressed in wind and rain storms, lightning, tidal surges, ultraviolet and ionising radiation. We are less commonly also exposed to events such as avalanches, landslips, floods, earthquakes, tidal waves (tsunami), fire and the massive electromagnetic field surges associated with solar flares, as well as the various ways in which animals (for example sharks, snakes), insects (poisonous bites and stings) and microbes (viruses and bacteria) adversely affect our lives.

Table 3.5   General types of failure Mechanisms for Hazard Controls

Hazard Control failure Mechanism types	Subtypes	Meanings, examples and further categories
In the artificial environment		
Purposeful acts	Legal	Warfare or policing, demolition
	Illegal	Criminal or terrorist activity
Incidental to the operation of a wanted process	Nil	e.g. fumes, noise, heat, vibration, electromagnetic fields
Unintentional	Physical failures of energy containment properties or devices	Failure of structures, components, insulation, etc. of primary, secondary or command failure types[†]
	Failure of system controlling function	Automated controller: Failure of equipment or software of primary, secondary or command failure types[†]
		Human controller: Failure using defined procedures, failure to conform with expected learned behaviours, failure to respond successfully to a novel situation using problem-solving based on knowledge. Numerous failure modes and reasons requiring a detailed understanding of human behaviour and capability.
In the natural environment		
Natural	Continuous release	UV, ionising radiation
	Intermittent and common release	Storms
	Intermittent but uncommon release	Avalanches, landslips, earthquakes, floods, tidal waves (tsunami), fire, solar flares, bites, stings, animal attacks

Notes: † Primary: under 'normal' loads or conditions, for which the equipment is designed. Secondary: under abnormal loads or conditions, for which the equipment is not designed. Command: made to behave this way by automatic systems or human action.

Energy Damage Duration Categories

The period of time over which energy damage takes place can be divided into three categories. The energy transfer can occur as a discrete and singular process. A single and short transfer of energy to the Recipient is typical of the class of Occurrences we like to call accidents. Most energy sources are capable of generating such discrete and singular energy bursts. For example, while we commonly associate noise-induced hearing loss with relatively continuous low-level exposure over a long period of time, it is also possible to sustain substantial hearing damage due to a single very high-level burst of acoustic energy in the form of a pressure shock wave following an explosion. Similarly, chemicals that are capable of producing a chronic condition after a long period of a low level of exposure are also capable of producing acute toxic results if a large quantity is absorbed over a short period of time. As an example, exposure to chlorine gas in 'large' quantities in a short period of time could prove fatal.

The possibility also exists of a succession of energy pulses, each of which is discrete but occurring in a multiple and repetitive fashion. Depending on the time scale of the repetitive transfers it may be difficult to distinguish these practically from a continuous low level of exposure. Typically, the energy level lies between that of the singular discrete and the continuous exposure. An example would be acoustic impact noise (hammering) where individual bursts of energy of a higher level than normally associated with continuous exposure exists, but they are at a much lower level than that associated with a single acoustic trauma such as occurring via a shock wave. Another example is exposure to puffs of vapour or dust from a process.

Table 3.6   Energy damage duration categories

Energy damage duration	Representative occurrences
Discrete – singular	
Duration of the order of one second or less, generally 'high' energy levels, typically what we call accidents	• falls • explosions • impacts/collisions • musculo-skeletal overload • acoustic trauma
Discrete – multiple and repetitive	
'Low' and 'medium' level discrete energy bursts absorbed on a large number of occasions	• acoustic energy absorption • multiple or repetitive musculo-skeletal loading • toxic substance exposures
Continuous	
'Low' energy levels, substantially constant over long periods of time (hours, days, years)	• acoustic energy absorption • ionising radiation bombardment • toxic substance exposure • musculo-skeletal postural strain

The last is where the energy damage takes place on a mostly continuous basis over a long period, typically involving relatively low levels of energy and often producing what would be regarded as chronic damage. For example, acoustic energy absorbed at relatively low levels over periods of several years is known to produce noise-induced hearing loss. The rate of damage is incremental in the nerve cells of the inner ear. Exposure to airborne toxic substances, such as vinyl chloride monomer, at low levels over a long period of time may lead to a chronic condition after

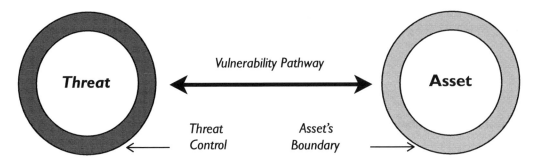

Figure 3.2   The Threat and Vulnerability Model

many years. Similarly, over a period of time a person who is forced to adopt an inefficient posture while working may suffer cumulative postural strain affecting the tendons, joints or muscles.

When No Energy Is Involved

An Occurrence that does not involve energy cannot produce a Consequence that includes Damage. Such Occurrences can only produce Loss, meaning a direct physical loss or loss of value, or directly of money itself. If energy in the EDM is replaced by Threat, the model becomes a Threat and Vulnerability Model (TVM) and energy would be seen as one type of Threat. A Threat may be defined as anything that is a source of potential Loss. Some 30 years ago it was common to talk of Threat and Vulnerability when discussing risks. Using these terms, the Recipient (asset) is Vulnerable to certain Threats. What is called here the Space Transfer Mechanism for an Energy can in more general terms be thought of as the Vulnerability Pathway that connects an Asset to the Threat. For example, a diamond ring is vulnerable because an open window makes it accessible to an opportunistic thief. See Figure 3.2.

Table 3.7   Non-energy Threats to Assets

Threat Control failure types	Subtypes	Meanings, examples and further categories
Influences of people	Actions with intended adverse effects)	Theft, fraud, corruption, collusion, sabotage, product contamination
		Espionage, counterfeiting
		Kidnapping, assassination
	Unintentional actions or actions with unintended effects	Failure to act, erroneous actions
	Loss of people	Strikes, loss of skill and knowledge
Failures of or in the system or process	Failure to conform to licence conditions	Due to actions or omissions, resulting for example in loss of operating licence
	Failure of something relied upon or expected	For example, a bank or investment vehicle fails, a new product cannot be developed, business model fails
	Loss of inputs	For example, money, raw materials, energy, labour
	Loss of output	For example, product or work in progress

	Failure of business process functions	For example, computer system unable to function as intended, production equipment breakdown or unable to be brought into service
	Of distribution of product or service	For example, distribution channels fail
Adverse external influences	Systemic adverse influences of the operating environment	For example, competition, loss of market, loss of revenue source, price reduction, economic or fiscal conditions, political or social ill will
	Random adverse influences of the operating environment	For example, volcano eruptions affecting income of an airline, effects of strikes, warfare
Liabilities	Derived from statutory or contractual requirements	For example, product liability

Non-energy-based Threats can be categorised as shown in Table 3.7. Threats to the function or role of the organisation can arise from criminal activities, functional failures, adverse external influences and liabilities. In the manufacturing industry functional failures mean the product fails to be produced and in the service industry the service can no longer be provided. For example:

- An organisation owning and managing a city freeway system, which includes a tunnel as a critical link, experiences a computer failure which means the tunnel exhaust fans cannot be run. The organisation finds it necessary to close the link, in case an emergency occurs within the tunnel. City traffic is chaotic for hours while the problem is diagnosed and the computer problem rectified.
- A car manufacturer, operating on the 'just in time' production principle, suffers production loss when a parts supplier goes out of business.
- An airline has its air operator's approval withdrawn because of a failure to comply with the conditions of the approval.
- A bank suffers large losses when a so-called rogue trader works outside the bank's procedures.
- A retail photograph printing business fails after the introduction of digital cameras and its services are no longer needed.
- Threats arising from the liabilities of the organisation towards others. For example, a miner and processor of asbestos is found liable for the sickness of thousands of people who have been exposed to its products as employees or members of the public.

If these Threats arise because of the actions of people, the actions (including inaction) can be categorised as intentional or unintentional and judged as criminal or negligent or otherwise according to social rules. If not directly involving people, these threats can be thought of as either failures of the function of something or failures of something that was expected or hoped for to actually happen, or systematic or random adverse influences over the commercial or technical environment to which the Asset is related.

Liabilities have the potential to adversely affect the reputation and financial health of the organisation. Examples include: building occupier's liabilities; contractual liabilities; directors' and company officers' liabilities; professional practice liabilities; liabilities arising from breach of statutory duties; product liabilities and liabilities arising from business arrangements, for example agencies, franchises. In our complex age, many legal liabilities arise and it is important to understand the details of these in the legal environment of the organisation.

Limitations and Complexities in the Use of the EDM

Some Damage is hard to conceive of as part of an energy process. Many diseases are the effects of microbiological organisms (bacteria, viruses, fungi). Can the way in which these interact with the healthy functioning of the body of an animal usefully be described as an energy damage process? Those with knowledge of the way in which symptoms occur are better able to explain the actual process involved and appear to find it easy to extend their understanding of the EDM to encompass this. As they say, these disease processes work on the cellular level of our body and interfere with the normal functioning of the body through changing the normal chemical processes, for which energy is a common currency.

Psychological stress may result from any form of stressor, either physical or psychological. If a person exhibits fearful behaviour as a result of exposure to an armed hold-up, is the problem largely an internal one due to the difficulty that the person experiences in trying to assimilate the upsetting experience or is the trauma externally imposed? In either case, is a form of energy really involved? Presumably a psychological stress state could be regarded as a neurological response to an external stressor of various subtle forms and transmitted to the Recipient through visual and auditory signals that use energy sources as the transfer medium. These energy sources do not really qualify as Hazards as it is not the level of energy that is a concern, but the way in which the information conveyed is assimilated by the Recipient.

When a person is exposed to an asphyxiating or non-respirable atmosphere the lack of oxygen in the lungs interrupts normal bodily chemical processes. It is true that these chemical processes involve an exchange of energy, but is this really an energy damage process as such?

It may be possible to add to this list, but this is sufficient to make the point that depending on one's background, some of the processes which lead to what have collectively been called damage to the body may be difficult to think of as arising from exposure to energy. This is an appropriate place to emphasise that what is actually important is an accurate understanding of the process leading to damage, rather than a clever attempt to fit this reality into the EDM, the TSM or any other model.

In many situations, multiple energy sources are present at the same place and time and in circumstances and conditions that link them inextricably. A person walking, running or cycling possesses both kinetic energy and gravitational potential energy. If they fall and injure themselves, which of these is the origin of injury? The answer is both. If a person on a motorcycle falls off and slides down the road, they may well suffer a broken arm bone from the fall (internal gravitational potential energy), massive grazing of the skin from sliding along the road surface (internal kinetic energy), quite possibly burns from contact with the hot exhaust pipe (thermal energy) and the handle bar could also hit them hard in the body and do damage to internal organs (external gravitational or kinetic energy). If the EDM is used as the basis of a classification of Occurrence types, a suitable convention is required to resolve any such ambiguities.

The Structure of the Occurrence Process – The Time Sequence Model

The second distinctive feature of the Occurrence process is that it develops sequentially in time – see Figure 3.3. No 'accident' happens in an instant, whether it be the simple fall of a box of eggs or a major disaster following oil spilling from an undersea wellhead. There is always a lead-up to things going wrong and always a development of the process until the final Consequences are apparent to all. The difference in these two examples is more to do with the complexity of the technology, the amount of energy involved and the magnitude of the Consequence Value than any other features. The structure of the process in both cases is identical.

As Damage processes necessarily involve the unwanted effects of energy sources, the time sequence structure must show how the energy damage process unfolds over time. The essence of this structure is very simple and it is an extremely powerful means of bringing clarity to all of the otherwise confusing and multifaceted appearances of accidents and their prevention. The anchor point of the process is the point in time when control is lost over the damaging properties of the energy source involved. When we read the report of a major accident we cannot help but notice the number of different things that happened one after the other, giving a sense that the accident developed ominously and inexorably over a period of time, as indeed they often do. Each 'thing' that happens at a point in time can, using normal English, be thought of as an event. The most significant event, however, is the point in time when control is lost over the potentially damaging properties of the energy source, in other words, when the Hazard Control fails. The great importance of this as an anchor point in the whole process can be conveyed by calling it the Event.

No Event happens mysteriously or spontaneously. It results from simple natural processes capable of being described in normal language and in accordance with the laws of the universe. This natural process is the Mechanism of the Event. A Hazard Control is what stops the Event happening and the Event Mechanism referred to here is the reason for the Hazard Control failing. Event Mechanisms arise because they can: all aspects of the normal everyday environment make this possible. Metals corrode, people act in certain ways, boxes of eggs get pushed by shopping bags being unpacked, etc., etc. These relevant features of the everyday environment that make Event Mechanisms possible are the Prerequisites for the Event Mechanism. The Prerequisites for an egg box falling off the bench are simply a bench and an egg box on the bench. So long as an egg box is on the bench, it is possible for it to fall off. Whether it will fall off the bench or not is much influenced by the conditions and circumstances of the situation. If the bench has a shiny polished surface then friction between the egg box and the bench top will be low, compared with a bench made of rough wood. The bench surface, whose condition does not vary with time, is an Enabling Condition in that it is above floor level and makes a gravitational potential energy event possible. If the bench top is full of shopping bags then the likelihood of the egg box being pushed without being seen is greater than otherwise. This, being something that comes and goes over time, is an Enabling Circumstance in that something is present that could push the box of eggs. Conditions and Circumstances are explained in more detail below. They may be called enabling because they enable the Event to occur. Without them, the egg box would stay on the bench top.

Prerequisites make Events possible: cars and roads means crashes are possible. Enabling Conditions and Circumstances provide the means of crash.

If an Event happens, then the damaging potential of the energy source has been unleashed and a process follows which eventually leads to Damage, unless interrupted. A quick-thinking person in the kitchen may catch the box of eggs before it hits the ground, or its fall may be interrupted when it hits the family cat. An automatic device on a wellhead may sense the excess flow of oil and shut a valve. In both cases, a response to the loss of control has directed the process to a non-damaging path.

In the EDM, this was described as the unfolding of the Space Transfer Mechanism, which is what is required to enable energy to reach a remote Recipient. However, we also saw that the Space Transfer Mechanism as such was not always needed (energy source and Recipient coexisting, for example, as in the case of the egg box). It is therefore not generally valid to call the process following the Event the Space Transfer Mechanism. Rather, the Space Transfer Mechanism is a possible part of what in general terms may be called the Outcome of the Event. The Outcome is the process that succeeds the Event and which leads to Damage or no Damage depending on how it unfolds. In the real world, many Outcomes do not result in Consequences and they are logically called Null Outcomes. A Null Outcome is one in which either the potentially damaging properties of the energy source are brought back into control, or by chance they fail to actually produce damage.

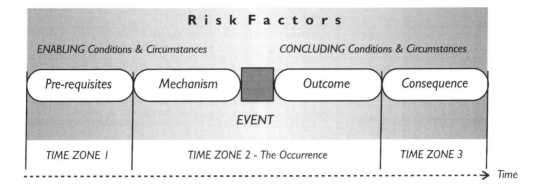

Figure 3.3   The Time Sequence Model

An example of the first case is a car skidding on a wet road but the driver manages to bring it back under control. An example of the second case is a brick falling off a platform but missing the people working underneath. Both cases tend to be called colloquially 'near misses'. They are discussed in more careful detail in Chapter 9.

While the general nature of an Outcome is determined by the nature of the Event, the exact way in which the process unfolds all the way into Time Zone 3 (see Figure 3.3) depends on the Concluding Conditions and Circumstances, which influence the way the Outcome process unfolds and concludes. For example, oil released from a sea-bed wellhead will follow water currents and its vertical movement will also be influenced by buoyancy effects, which together may direct the oil towards a particularly sensitive marine ecology. Exactly the same Event and Mechanism in a desert will also result in an uncontrolled oil flow but the influences of the environment are significantly different. Exactly what happens depends on the Conditions and Circumstances which influence the Outcome process.

The length of any time zone is very variable. The situation in which Event Mechanisms are possible may have been set up many years before a Mechanism occurs. In principle, the first time zone starts when the technology was first used. Entanglement in conveyor belts was not possible until powered conveyor belts were introduced for the first time, many decades ago. The opportunity to improve risk control exists from this very first moment of the technology, even if the particular conveyor system of interest is only a few months old.

From the initiation of the Event Mechanism to the end of the Outcome, a fall may take place in seconds. Other Event Mechanisms take months to develop to the Event (for example a fatigue crack in metal leading to structural failure). Similarly, the third time zone may take a number of years before it reaches a point of finalisation; a permanently disabling injury may still be developing Consequences of different types and values some years after the Event.

Conditions and Circumstances

Enabling and Concluding Conditions and Circumstances have a very significant effect on the particular nature of an Occurrence and Consequence. Collectively, they are commonly known as Risk Factors. For example, in the same organisation two falls (of people) could take place. The Mechanism of each could be a slip. One person slips on a small oil spill and breaks their wrist. The second person slips on a piece of construction plastic lying on an access route alongside a construction site and suffers internal injuries as a result of hitting upright concrete reinforcing rods. Most of the two processes are identical, but the critical differences arise from the Conditions within which each fall took place and the Circumstances present at the time.

Conditions are those features of the environment that change very slowly if at all over time. Any changes that do occur are quite probably unrecognisable except to someone visiting after being away for some time. Those of us who are parents are well aware of this experience as our children grow up: their appearance and behaviour changes imperceptibly to us but is instantly noticed by other family members who don't see them every week. This can apply to the type and condition of equipment as much as it does to the way in which work is performed. Over time a required method of work, for which no immediate benefit is apparent to those asked to work that way, will become less and less frequently complied with until after a few months it is no longer followed at all. A new person entering the workforce will not know it was ever needed. This slow drift from requirements has been imperceptible to the organisation. Equipment may originally have features provided as a result of careful consideration of design requirements, but which are slowly changed (for example signs obliterated by dirt or sunshine, guards removed from machinery) and the difference is not noticed. In principle, it is for these reasons that organisations implement routine inspections.

Circumstances are defined as those features of the environment that are subject to fairly regular and recognisable change. Change is more readily perceived if it occurs quickly and is essentially visible. Examples are the weather, breakdown of machinery and equipment, changes to orders or product requirements, being short-staffed on a particular day. Circumstances, being changes to the normal scene, are often highly noticeable, even though they may not be recognised as being of importance in the creation of or results of an Occurrence.

Time Zone 1: Yesterday, Here and Now

Time Zone 1 is the everyday world with which we are familiar. It requires some special effort to recognise Prerequisites and Enabling Conditions and Circumstances. The fact that day after day and year after year nothing much goes wrong lulls us into a sense of security and a belief that what we do is safe. It takes a shocking Occurrence for regulators, lawyers and an angry public to accuse us of being unsafe. Even moments before the Occurrence not one of these accusers would have known how to predict the Occurrence, yet immediately afterwards a flood of accusations arise. The task of prediction is not insurmountable but needs effort and intention. This is where prevention starts. Using accidents to inform us through the search for causes is reaction not prevention: given a long period of time and the ability to learn, it is possible for the lessons to be cumulatively learned and for Occurrences to reduce in frequency and severity but at considerable cost to victims and the community. Also, this learning requires the quality of discernment and the ability to remember, neither of which is present naturally in the majority of industrial or commercial organisations or in government. In an era of rapid technological change, do we have the time to depend on this method? Should life be a laboratory in which we all sacrifice something until scientists produce a statistically valid conclusion about what hazard is causing what disease? The answer to both questions is clearly no.

There are two main classes of approach to prevention work in this time zone. One is to formulate a model of general organisational (managerial) failures that relate to accidents. When actually in Time Zone 2, organisational failures, like unsafe acts, are evident through post hoc judgement: if only someone had done this, it would all have been prevented. In this sense, failure is used to indicate a control measure whose significance has become evident in retrospect. This is what regulators and lawyers do. Much has been written elsewhere on this approach and it can be likened to the use of a shotgun to hit a target. It is a more productive task to identify and draw attention to failures prior to an Occurrence. The most sensible way to define failure for this purpose is as not achieving a desired standard, just as it does in examinations. A statement of failure can only be made if the standard is explicit and known prior to the accident. With standards known, the organisation may be evaluated equally before and after an Occurrence. Without them it cannot be.

The technical requirement approach, based on the methods of risk engineering and the one explored here, is to direct attention to the specific predictable processes (there is a great deal that is predictable) that give rise to Damage and Loss and establish technically based Hazard (or Threat) management standards, also called Risk Control Standards. Where moral and ethical obligations arise, the desired standard is capable of being determined pre-Occurrence by applying the tests of negligence and common law or regulatory standards. Where no such obligations exist, it is reasonable for the organisation to assess possible control measures on an economic and opportunity basis. This approach can be likened to the use of a rifle to hit a target. These matters are discussed in Chapter 8.

The Prerequisites in the case of the egg box example were easy to identify. Damage to eggs from a fall (gravitational potential energy) is possible because the eggs are placed on the bench. Energy sources and non-energy Threats are always easy to identify and each gives rise to a possible Occurrence process that can readily be described. In the whole world and in any one industry there is a finite number of these, see Chapter 5, so the task is a practical one. The more varied Enabling Conditions and Circumstances are a product of the technology, processes and cultures of the type of industry, specific organisation and specific location. Both the technology and processes are amenable to being understood using the hazard management standards approach. Chapter 5 discusses these as Risk Factors and Chapter 9 is concerned with understanding Mechanisms (and Outcomes).

Culture, expressed at a national, industry, organisation and location level, is very variable but in the end the only features with significance to prevention work are whether it is supportive and capable. In one country and in one industry I experienced two diametrically opposed cultures. It might take a book to describe the differences but one was both disinterested and incapable of making any changes and the other engaged with the subject matter and endowed with excellent management capability readily able to make the necessary changes. In contrast to the former organisation, the latter learned quickly and well and within a very short time moved from being threatened with closure by the state government because of numerous fatalities to being given a national award for its safe operations. Chapter 11 expands on management capability and requirements. Given a supportive and capable organisation, it is the responsibility of the risk adviser to direct attention and efforts in an efficient and effective way. After all, everything that is truly preventative is done in Time Zone 1.

The starting point of Time Zone 1 is finite: it is when the technology or business process with which we are concerned existed for the first time. Mechanisms with electricity are irrelevant until electricity is first harnessed. Mechanisms with road vehicles are irrelevant until the first cars move on the roads. Mechanisms with computerised business processes in banks are irrelevant until such processes are introduced. The first Prerequisite is therefore that the energy source or Threat exists or a decision is made to use it in the processes for which it is to be used. This is an early design choice of the type of process. From this preliminary design stage, decisions will then be made as to how the system is to be controlled, either by people or by control systems. Next comes the decision about the type of equipment to be used. Capital costs are influenced by the quality of this equipment and pressures to use cheaper equipment will be felt subsequently by the operators, as they are faced with breakdowns and the need for more rapid replacement of equipment as it ages more rapidly than it might.

Once in operation, the way in which people use and maintain the equipment will have an influence on the likelihood for Mechanisms arising. This will depend on decisions made about staffing levels, qualifications and skills as much as on the transfer of design assumptions from the designer to the operators. However, by now and with little specific understanding of how any of this affects Mechanisms, operational managers will make decisions about maintenance, staffing and training expenditure as though this has no effect on risk, or at least with no explicit understanding of how it does. As there is no deterministic relationship between any of these and the next big accident, there is also no warning that all is not well, only the encouragement of those with an eye on the operating profit.

Evidently, Time Zone I is concerned with a number of features of the routine daily environment, not only today but also from the history of the technology and the individual site. These features can be categorised in various different ways, none of which is either correct or incorrect, but all of which can help to provide insight in different ways. This time zone can be viewed through different lenses.

One approach is based on a breakdown of the everyday world into categories and using these to draw attention to the management processes which influence them. For example:

1. *Physical conditions (equipment and facilities)*
    a) The original standards of design of the plant, the quality of construction and the quality of the original equipment installed.
        i.   The assumptions made by designers may include some which are critical to the future safety of the site. They need to have been communicated to those who operate the site and to have been included in formal operational protocols that are likely to survive the passage of time and changing managers.
        ii. The decisions made about original construction and equipment quality should influence the maintenance strategies (condition monitoring and replacement) adopted by the operators.
    b) Procurement practices for raw materials and consumables. That which is brought into the plant may be:
        i.   not what is intended or needed on the site;
        ii. incompatible with other things (for example substances, equipment) on the site;
        iii. in greater quantities or concentrations than the site was designed to handle;
        iv. of inappropriate quality, so that maintenance budgets in the future are adversely affected and calibration or inspection programmes are inadequate.
    c) Maintenance practices and equipment renewal history over the life of the site.
    d) The way in which site expansion and technology development is handled.
        i.   Incremental change requires well-managed engineering change control practices if the site's activities include engineered processes.
        ii. Major change needs to be managed as well as was the initial plant design.
2. *People and procedures (the way work is actually done)*   On any site there is usually a mixture of reliance on knowledge, learned skills (not only including the trades), experience and formal procedures (not always followed). When there is more work than time available, one can naturally expect short cuts and on-the-go changes to priorities. When contract labour is used, one can expect a low level of plant familiarity and the need for a greater degree of specification of how to do what in written work procedures. When unexpected situations arise a different approach is needed: someone with overall process knowledge is usually called on to apply that knowledge to decide how to manage the situation. This overall 'the way we do things around here' culture is influenced by:
    a) practices such as personnel selection, induction and task training;

     b)   how existing employees are selected for and inducted into positions in other parts of the organisation than those for which they were originally employed;

     c)   the presence and abilities of supervision or self-managed work groups;

     d)   the use of, or lack of, routine compliance checks on documented work procedures.

3. *The organisation* Hollnagel (1998) gives a useful classification of organisational styles into strategic, tactical, opportunistic and scrambled. These categories benefit from explanation, but are somewhat self-explanatory. From a management of risk perspective we need to aspire towards the strategic style. Risk management is really not possible in a chaotic organisation. Profitability, production pressures, the attitudes and capabilities of people and the culture of the industry all influence this. In addition, high rates of employee turnover, particularly managers, can very adversely affect the management of risk.

4. *The environment* (social, political, economic and physical)

     a)   The social and political environment can have a direct effect on risk, not just a background role influencing the previous three Time Zone 1 categories. Riot, kidnap, extortion, theft and violence are all possible.

     b)   The economic environment can give rise to risk in its own right if the organisation has vulnerable investments and we are concerned with Loss. It also has a significant background effect on the organisation and through that on the first two categories in this list.

     c)   The physical environment is the source of significant risks for many sites, through tidal waves, storms, lightning, earthquake, etc.

Hollnagel's approach is derived from trying to understand the origins of human error in work tasks. Not surprisingly, these are found to be based partly on the person, partly on the technological environment in which they work and partly on the organisational environment within which it all happens. Consequently his way of looking at the essential features of the workplace is as follows:

- organisation, of which relevant aspects are communication, training, approaches to maintenance, quality control and the design process, task allocation (who does what), social pressures, ambient conditions (of temperature, humidity, airflow), working conditions (amenable or not);
- technology, of which the relevant aspects are equipment failure (resulting in the need to respond), procedures (the formal expectations of how work is done), temporary and permanent equipment interface conditions, the so-called 'man–machine interface' of human factors engineering (also known as ergonomics);
- people, of which the relevant aspects are specific reactions to the demands of the tasks, planning, the influence of temporary circumstances, the influence of permanent conditions.

Reason (1997) sees the actions of people in the workplace as being due to the nature of the person and the team within which they work and the behaviour of these being affected by the conditions in the workplace itself, which are themselves created by management decisions and organisational processes. Together, these influences lead to things going wrong, such that if it were not for defences an accident is able to occur.

Table 3.8 summarises these ideas in one possible way, making use of ideas explored more thoroughly later, particularly in Chapters 7, 11 and 12.

Table 3.8   Risk control points in Time Zone 1

CONTROL POINTS ASSOCIATED WITH THE EQUIPMENT AND FACILITY DESIGN	
Design practices	Controls over the introduction of risks: original equipment design and the physical layout of the plant
Installation / commissioning practices	Controls over the introduction of risks: controls over risks imported in the as-built plant
Change management	Maintaining currency of the documentation of the as-built plant
Purchase / contracting practices	Controls over the introduction of risks: controls over risks associated with consumables and input resources, including labour
Inspection / maintenance practices	Controls over present risks: maintaining the reliability of design risk control measures
Equipment renewal practices	Controls over present risks: maintaining the reliability of design risk control measures
Design risk control reviews	Periodic reassessment of achieved design standards against current legal and good-practice requirements
CONTROL POINTS ASSOCIATED WITH WORK METHODS/PROCEDURES	
Work practices	Determining and documenting guidelines and requirements for the conduct of work: who needs what knowledge and skills? Where are defined work practices needed?
General and task-specific training practices	Maintaining currency of knowledge, skills and defined work practices amongst existing people
Inspection / maintenance practices	Establishing culturally suitable means of reinforcing and encouraging high levels of conformance with the above requirements over time
CONTROL POINTS ASSOCIATED WITH PEOPLE	
Skill and experience standards	Defining and recording significant requirements
Selection and induction practices, new and transferring employees	Ensuring new people understand and conform with work practice requirements, including limiting their role until role-specific induction is complete
ORGANISATIONAL SUPPORT FOR CONTROL POINTS	
Risk register	Development and maintenance of an inventory of risks
Hazard and Threat management standards (Risk Control Standards)	Developing and maintaining standards for risk register entries
Managing Organisational Failures	Processes to identify and respond to Organisational Failures to maintain risk control standards
Managing Action Failures	Processes to identify and respond to Action Failures to maintain risk control standards
Managing risk control improvement opportunities	Processes to record opportunities for improvement and make decisions at suitable levels of responsibility

Time Zone 2: The Occurrence

Arising from the fertile pastures of Time Zone 1 are the seeds of all the Events that are possible. The trick is to recognise them for what they are and arrest their growth. Fortunately, in principle this is not difficult, only complex, as each energy form (or non-energy Threat) needs to be treated differently because each has its own Mechanisms and each Mechanism has its own character. However, this simple fact is generally not recognised (by explicitly determining Hazard or Threat Management Standards), so that there is a gulf between the actual state of Time Zone 1 in most organisations and the desired state. There is little or no focus, no connection between the physical realities built into the production processes and the management practices that set the tone of day-to-day Time Zone 1 realities. This gap is the most outstanding deficiency in the modern management of risk. The truth is that managers in general (and risk managers in particular) have a poor understanding of what the origins of Mechanisms (the causes of accidents) are. The problem is apparently not solved by generic approaches to risk management practices, as many recent disasters in otherwise well-managed companies have made evident.

For example, the constraint of hazardous fluids in pipes and tanks depends on the structural integrity of the pipe and tank walls, their protection from impact or other external destructive forces, the way in which valves are operated and the fragility of pressure, temperature and level transmitter tappings. The structural integrity of the materials can be compromised by corrosion, cracking, embrittlement, etc. It is entirely feasible to recognise all the Mechanisms of interest. For each Mechanism a control can be implemented in Time Zone 1, such as periodic painting, etc. In Time Zone 2, condition inspections and wall thickness testing can be used to uncover the existence and rate of propagation of these known Mechanisms and the Mechanism can be interrupted at the appropriate time.

However, in some cases, Mechanisms arise rapidly and without warning. For example, a person inadvertently opens a valve that must remain closed. In an instant, an Event has occurred and the Outcome is under way. Alarms may sound in a control room and automatic shutdown may be initiated, leading to a halt to production, recovery and restart.

Where Mechanisms are fast and unpredictable, a preconsidered approach to the management of Outcomes is both indicated and essential, with automation being high on the list of preferences where significant energy sources are involved. Where Mechanisms are slow and predictable, there is time to build inspection practices into the work of the organisation or provide automated warning systems in the design with the aim of never having an Event – see Table 3.9.

Table 3.9   Risk control points in Time Zone 2

CONTROL POINTS ASSOCIATED WITH DEVELOPING MECHANISMS	
Detect and terminate developing Mechanisms	Inspection and maintenance practices directed at specific Mechanisms known to be amenable to this approach and associated with significant Consequence possibilities, for example condition monitoring
CONTROL POINTS ASSOCIATED WITH THE EVENT	
Develop strategies for Null Outcomes	Design strategies directed at specific Events known to be amenable to this approach and associated with significant Consequence possibilities, for example fire doors, acoustic and thermal insulation, shutdown capability
CONTROL POINTS ASSOCIATED WITH DEVELOPING OUTCOMES	
Develop strategies for Null Consequences or limited Consequences	Design strategies directed at specific Outcomes known to be amenable to this approach and associated with significant Consequence possibilities, for example extraction ventilation, emergency procedures

Time Zone 3: Damage and Loss

The end of the Outcome is the beginning of Damage and is when Time Zone 3 begins. As an example, when something falls, the Outcome path involves an increase in kinetic energy until the object hits the floor. This impact dissipates the kinetic energy in some way, often involving deformation of the object and noise. The actual point when Damage starts may not be easy to distinguish from the end of the Outcome but, if energy is involved in the Event, then the beginning of Time Zone 3 is when the energy starts to be absorbed by the Recipient, the evidence for which is the Damage that the Recipient displays immediately afterwards. Damage is discussed in some detail in the explanation of the EDM above.

It is easy to see that control measures in this Time Zone are based on limiting Damage, preparedness for it and recovery from it by rehabilitation, repair, reconstruction and replacement – see Table 3.10.

Table 3.10   Risk control points in Time Zone 3

CONTROL POINTS ASSOCIATED WITH DEVELOPING CONSEQUENCE	
Damage limitation	For example, seat belts and airbags in cars, sprinklers and fire separation in buildings
Emergency preparedness	Preconsidered planning for predictable emergency types
Rehabilitation, repair	Rapid rehabilitation and repair capability
Contingency planning	General planning for unpredictable emergencies, typically arising from external or otherwise uncontrollable risks, for example storms, attack

Loss Arising from the Production Process

One way in which pure Loss can arise is as a by-product of the production process – see Figure 3.4. Any productive process, whether for profit or not, makes use of a process for converting inputs into its product. By-products of this process can include waste, damage, injury and monetary Loss. Some of these will occur routinely due to process inefficiencies and others will arise because of failures of various types. This simple model can be applied to a typical industrial process or to a commercial process. The former rely on industrial hardware to turn raw materials into a product. The latter rely on computer-driven hardware or other physical facilities to support a service process. The industrial plant may suffer the breakdown of a critical item of equipment that stops production. The commercial plant may suffer breakdown of its production process when a computer system fails or when its people-based practices fail in some way. Even industrial processes rely heavily on management processes for their conduct. Examples include:

*   Failure of a management process to ensure that all aircraft airworthiness directives are carried out on time in an airline, resulting in noncompliance with the terms of its air operator's certificate, which is temporarily suspended.
*   Failure of a critical process vessel in a metallurgical plant, leading to an extensive shutdown and loss of production.

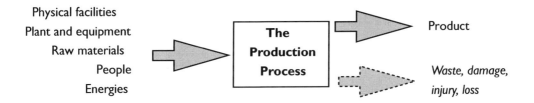

Figure 3.4   Loss in the context of the production process

The process of Loss can be modelled directly by identifying failures in the process flow of the organisation. A process flow diagram is a high-level image of how the process works and from which all single chain parts of the process can be quickly seen. Each link in a single chain is a critical point worthy of more detailed analysis.

Chains of Occurrences

It sometimes happens that the Outcome of one Occurrence becomes the Mechanism of another, as illustrated by the well-known case of the loss of the Titanic. The first Occurrence involved an Event which was a loss of control over the potentially damaging properties of the kinetic energy of the ship and an Outcome which damaged the ship's bow – emergency steering inputs were unable to avoid a Null Outcome. As a result of this damage, water flooded into the bow of the ship, eventually filling one compartment after another until the bow sank and dragged the rest of the vessel with it. Once largely filled with water, the steel hull was not able to remain floating near the surface and the ship started a journey to the bottom of the sea, eventually striking the seabed. This journey to the bottom was a distinct Occurrence, a gravity-energised fall, with gravitational potential energy being converted to speed (kinetic energy) and turbulence in the wake of the submerged ship. The Mechanism for the loss of control over the potentially damaging properties of the gravitational potential energy was the opening of gaps in the hull at the point of impact, followed by an uncontrollable ingress of water.

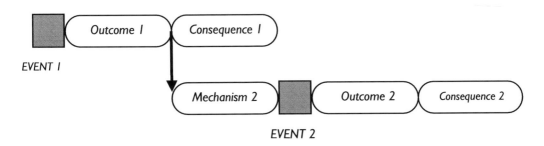

Figure 3.5   Chains of Occurrences

Practical Benefits from Use of the TSM

A small amount of effort to understand the essence of the TSM reaps rewards. It is no more complex than recognising that if something goes wrong there is a reason for it and then the effects of that unfold eventually leading to adverse consequences, or not as the case may be. The reality that this is an energy damage process if damage is involved or a threat loss process if not is all that complicates the idea, and that only to a slight degree.

For one person, a moment of understanding of the TSM came in a court case in which he was an expert witness when he suddenly realised this was the key to explaining his understanding in a simple manner that the judge, jury and lawyers could understand. He did so and with very positive effect. A number of years ago I was consulted by a government department because their workers' compensation system was being stressed by the large number and cost of injury claims in the government's own departments. They had made every effort to implement health and safety programmes and this was having no beneficial effect. Within an hour of talking to them it became very clear to me that their problem was probably little or nothing to do with Time Zone 2 but with Time Zone 3. In Time Zone 3 there was a well-entrenched system of legal process, insurance companies and doctors that had developed over many years but which was not particularly directed at the interests of the injured workers. It was not hard to identify this, given the statistics which they were able to provide and the knowledge they had of how the system worked. When I drew this to their attention, the light really did shine a little brighter in the room. Within three years, the Time Zone 3 system had been opened up, dismantled and given a fresh life in a manner that was of much greater benefit to the injured workers who were caught up in it. Reflecting on the meeting, it was evident that the very capable people around the table did not have any model of the process in their heads other than a belief that accidents can be prevented by looking for their causes. The simple TSM model released their minds from the bondage of accident theory.

Summary

Other fields of science point to the value of understanding the processes that give rise to the phenomenon of interest in facilitating objective understanding and research. A simple model of the process that leads to Damage can designed that shows the essential features of the way in which energy can create damage and from which a simple understanding of the time-based structure of this process can be made evident. Both of these features have been shown to be amenable to suitably simple description and result in the definition of concepts and terms that may be objectively defined and are of practical value.

Risk: Damage and Loss Processes are Uncertain to Occur

4

Introduction

The preceding chapter looked at the first two of three features of Damage and Loss, namely that they result from processes that take time to unfold – see Table 3.1. The third feature is that the process is uncertain. The well-known aphorism (usually attributed to Murphy) that if something can go wrong it will, is a simple expression of this. Another way of stating this is that if something is possible it is only a matter of time before it happens. The two questions, of course, are how long do we have to wait and how bad (we are talking about pure risk) will it be when it does happen? These are the unknowns and the essence of the uncertainty that makes us talk about risk.

For it to be possible for something bad to happen to me I must be exposed to the situation (Conditions and Circumstances) in which it is possible. If I am exposed, there is a finite probability that I will experience such things. For example:

1. It is possible for lightning to strike an aircraft in flight, so it is only a matter of time (exposure) before it happens.
2. If it is possible for a person intent on disrupting a flight to get into the cockpit, it is only a matter of time before it happens.
3. It is possible for a building to burn down if it consists of flammable materials, so it is only a matter of time before it happens.
4. It is possible for cars to run off the road in the country, so it is only a matter of time before they do.

In each of these examples, the resulting Damage could range from minor to serious. As we know from personal experience, if we have a car crash it is often pure chance whether the damage to the car is minor or major. Risk is essentially a statement of uncertainty. There is uncertainty that injury, damage or loss will occur and the magnitude of it if it does occur. While there are almost as many definitions of this term as there are drafters of legislation and national standards, there is one (Rowe, 1977) practically useful definition, which, with slight modification (in parentheses), is 'Risk is the uncertainty that an adverse consequence (of a given size) will occur'. Notice that this applies to pure risk only, not to speculative risk. In speculative risk, we would have to add that there was also a chance of something good happening.

It will be shown that a feature of this uncertainty is that the most severe Consequences generally, but not always, occur most infrequently. As a result the unwary may be lulled into a misplaced sense of security. It is almost certainly true that experience of past incidents is not a good indicator of the incidents that will result in the greatest Damage. As Captain Edward Smith of the Titanic is reputed to have said (Daino, 1998): 'I cannot imagine any condition which would cause a ship to founder. I cannot conceive of any vital disaster happening to this vessel. Modern shipbuilding has gone beyond that ...'.

Whoever wrote the Wikipedia article on risk (at the time of writing this text) used this: 'Risk is the potential that a chosen action or activity (including the choice of inaction) will lead to a loss (an undesirable outcome)'. Government regulations and various international standards also define the term in ways that suit their needs, not necessarily good or sufficient.

In what follows, Rowe's definition (as modified) will guide the discussion on what risk is and how to measure it. The reasons for this will become clear as the parameters that can be used to describe risk are identified. A functional definition of Risk is derived from this discussion. Rowe outlined a process of Risk Assessment that included:

1. Identifying that a risk existed, which he called Risk Determination.
2. Understanding how significant the risk is, which he called Risk Estimation.
3. Deciding what to do to reduce the risk, which he called Risk Aversion.
4. If nothing could be done to avert the risk, then the risk is accepted as it is.

Chapters 5 to 8 are based on a structure of Risk Assessment that follows a practical sequence which includes specific attention to what can be done to control a risk.

The Variables that Define Risk

If Risk is the uncertainty that an adverse Consequence of a given size will occur then the variables that determine Risk will be those that enable us to describe uncertainty and the adverse Consequence. Colloquial terms that describe uncertainty are likelihood and chance. They are often used with a qualifying adjective to describe the extent of likelihood. 'Highly likely' means close to certainty, for example. 'Most unlikely' suggests closer to impossible. Such word scales mean different things to different people or even to the same person at different times and so they are not of much value and certainly don't belong in a serious approach to the subject of risk.

In contrast, the mathematical understanding of uncertainty allows for a more explicit means of measurement. Uncertainty is described precisely in mathematics by the term probability. Probability is a number between 0 (impossible) and 1 (certainty). There is much benefit to be gained by using this real number scale of measurement for Probability, as there is for the other relevant variables about to be introduced. Uncertainty arises in all stages of the Occurrence. There is an uncertainty that an Event will occur, and of a particular Outcome if the Event does occur, and of the value of the Consequence as a result of that particular Outcome. The overall probability of the Consequence of a particular value is the end result of the process and so depends on all of the probabilities. Mathematically:

$$Prob_E \times Prob_O \times Prob_C \times Prob_{CV} = Prob_{Overall},$$

where:

- Prob$_E$ is the probability that an Event will occur (this depends on the different possible Mechanisms and their individual probabilities);
- Prob$_O$ is the probability that particular Outcomes will occur that have the potential to lead to Damage;
- Prob$_C$ is the probability that a particular Consequence Type will arise if those Outcomes do occur;
- Prob$_{CV}$ is the probability that this Consequence Type will have a particular value if it does occur;
- Prob$_{Overall}$ is the overall probability that this Consequence Value will be experienced.

The essence of this mathematics is not complex. It is easy to see that if the probability of someone falling on a flight of stairs is 1 in 1,000 times these stairs are used and the probability of a falling person experiencing a broken arm bone is 1 in 10 falls, then the overall probability of a broken arm from falling on these stairs is 1 in 1,000 multiplied by 1 in 10, or 1 in 10,000 broken bones per use of the stairs.

Probability has no dimensions as such, being just one dimensionless number divided by another. More generally in physics, all physical variables have 'dimensions' that are one or more of mass [M], length [L], time [T] and temperature [K]. For example, length divided by time [LT^{-1}] is the unit of speed (the SI units of which are metres per second, abbreviated to m/s), length divided by time squared [LT^{-2}] is the unit of acceleration (the SI units of which are m/s^2). Mass multiplied by acceleration is force, so force has the dimensions of [MLT^{-2}]. However, probability does have a meaning. For example, 0.5 is the probability of a head being uppermost when a coin is tossed. The probability is 0.5 [heads per toss]. In risk work, it is essential to ensure that the meaning of any probability is always explicitly stated. In any numerical work it is essential that the units are stated. The general meaning of probability is [cases per trial], where a trial is a single exposure to the situation in which something is possible. For example, [car crashes per trip or per km], [falls per use of a staircase], etc. To statisticians, probability is a theoretical variable that gives insight into the mathematical characteristics one would expect to see in empirical populations of data. In the coin tossing case, theory says that there is an equal chance (p = 0.5) on each toss that one or the other side of the coin will be uppermost on landing. If a coin is tossed many times an empirical population of results will be generated and the relative frequency (number of occurrences per total number of tosses) of heads or tails could be counted. If we had the chance to experiment with people on the stairs we would find that broken bones did not all occur exactly every 10,000 people. Rather, we would find empirically that they occurred at different times (that is, after different numbers of people had used the stairs). For a further discussion of this point, see Chapter 10.

The calculations above are of only theoretical interest if no one ever tosses coins or climbs stairs. But what if 10,000 people use the stairs each month? Perhaps the stairs are at a popular sports venue. What if they were emergency exit stairs and seldom if ever used, perhaps 100 times a year? Clearly the exposure to the situation is a relevant consideration in understanding the uncertainty attached to the Consequence Value of the broken arm. The number of occasions (per unit of time) the asset of interest (people who use stairs) is exposed to the situation in which the Occurrence (a fall onto the stairs) is possible is their Exposure to the situation in which the Risk exists. The unit of time of most use is the year, for reasons that will be made clear. However, any other suitable unit could be used, such as month, week, day, etc.

An estimate of Exposure makes it possible to estimate the time-based Frequency of any part of the Occurrence. Let us start with the Event. If the Probability of a person falling on the stairs is estimated at 0.001 [falls per use of the stairs] (this is one in 1,000) and the stairs are used (Exposure) 100 [times per year] then the Frequency with which falls are expected to occur on the stairs is:

0.001 [Falls per stair use] × 100 [stair uses per year] = 0.1 [falls per year].

That is, a time-based Frequency (per year) is obtained by multiplying the Probability by the Exposure. In general terms this is:

Frequency [Events per year] = Probability [Events/single exposure of the asset to the situation in which the Event can occur] × Exposure [number of times per year the asset is subject to the situation in which Events can occur].

For the Consequence Value of interest, the broken bone, we make use of the probability of a broken bone per use of the stairs in a similar way:

0.0001 [broken bones per stair use] × 100 [stair uses per year] = 0.01 [broken bones per year].

This is one broken bone per 100 years. Note the difference if the Exposure changes to 10,000 uses of the stairs per year:

0.0001 [broken bones per stair use] × 10,000 [stair uses per year] = 1 [broken bone per year].

The Risk in the first case seems quite small, whereas in the second it is clearly not as small. It is the Frequency that determines our perception of the Risk, not the Probability or the Exposure individually. Probability and Exposure are essential variables in understanding Risk, but only because they are the way in which Frequency is derived. Note that this Frequency is not to be confused with relative frequency which is a statistical measure associated with items in an empirical data set, for example, out of 100 broken bones, the proportion that occurred two months apart, three months apart and so on.

Frequency is a valuable parameter. In the first place, it is the form of our experience. It is often possible to look back at incident records and count the number of reported cases of whatever is of interest. You can't do that with Probability. In this field, Probability can only ever be calculated (or estimated by comparison with a previously calculated probability) via Frequency and Exposure. Frequency adds meaning to Risk. The Probability of something happening in a place which I never visit and to which I have no emotional ties is of no personal interest. The Probability of me having an allergic reaction to a medicine and dying is irrelevant if I refuse the medicine. If I don't refuse it, it is of the greatest possible interest to me.

Consequence Value is the third parameter used to describe Risk. Consequences for pure risks are always adverse, negative and unwanted. Consequences are also always very varied and can range from almost inconsequential to absolutely massive, such as the destruction of the earth. Consequences arise from the Outcome. Just as there is a probability that any one Outcome will occur after an Event, there is also a probability attached to the Consequence types and values that arise too. If we have a car crash the Consequence may range from minor panel damage to multiple fatalities, depending entirely on the situation in which the crash occurs. A fall when walking in an office could kill us if we happened to hit the edge of a desk with our head. That is possible and it has happened. It is far more likely, however, that we will simply bruise our ego, but probably the most serious injury is a broken arm.

Fortunately, the great majority of Risks normally give rise to minor Consequences, even though they do have the capacity to lead to Consequences of great severity. In fact, the Probability of a low Consequence Value is more often than not significantly higher than the Probability of a very high Consequence Value. Figures 2.1 and 2.2, from Heinrich and Bird, show what has been recognised for a long time: that higher Consequence Values occur less frequently than lower Consequence Values. It is not a law as such, but it is very common. Hence, it flies in the face of logic and experience to think that a Risk can be described by a single Consequence Value. We cannot ignore the range of possible values that is inherently a part of Risk. We can conclude that a good working definition is that Risk is the relationship between Frequency and Consequence Value.

The practical range of Consequence Values lies between the likely least and likely worst Consequence Values. The likely least Consequence (LLC) can be defined as the smallest Consequence that is likely to be of some concern. It is obviously a matter for some judgement. Some organisations are keen to report all 'near misses'. In other words, they are concerned even if there has been no actual damage or injury. In this case, the act of reporting carries a cost with it, no matter how minor. So, practically, some minimum level of value might be assigned to it. The likely worst consequence (LWC) can be defined as the largest Consequence that can reasonably be seen as feasible, rather than the possible worst case anyone could imagine. Again, this is a matter for judgement. The insurance industry is aware of these distinctions and uses the term Maximum Probable Loss (MPL).

Derivation of Risk from These Variables

In Figure 4.1, the curve shows an inverse relationship between Frequency and Consequence Value, because this is the general form that is known to exist in the great majority of risks. Mathematically, the simplest inverse relationship is of this form:

$$F \times CV = R \text{ or } F = R/CV,$$

where F is the Frequency, in cases per year, CV is the Consequence Value, say £ per case, and R is a constant.

More complex relationships are possible, for example:

$$F^a \times CV^b = R,$$

where a and b are powers to which the basic variables can be raised. Such forms of relationship are sometimes needed to produce a mathematical fit to observed data, but there are no such reasons in the development of this theory.

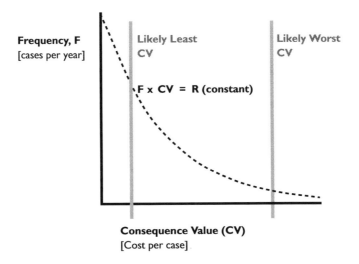

Figure 4.1   Risk as an inverse relationship between Frequency and Consequence Value

Taking this simple approach, the first observation is that the units of the constant R are very relevant:

Frequency [cases per year] × Consequence Value [value per case, e.g. £ per case] = R [£ per year].

Clearly, if the Frequency is greater than one it means that each year we experience Consequences (cases) of a given value. Most people would call the resulting constant (R) a rate of Loss, or Loss Rate (Browning, 1980). However, if Frequency is less than one it means that we do not experience Consequences of this value each year. In this case it is compelling to call the constant, R, Risk. Literally, the constant is either a real or a notional (meaning probabilistic) rate of Loss. Hence, with this simplest of all inverse relationships, the constant can be usefully renamed Risk and it has units of [£ per year].

With this simple relationship, mathematically the curve in Figure 4.1 can be thought of as a line of constant Risk, or an iso-Risk line. If the line is higher up and to the right on the graph, the constant is greater and hence the Risk is greater, and vice versa. In practice, a small change is needed to it, the reason for which is the possible size of the Frequency and of the Consequence Value scales. Both of these variables can have a value within a very large range. Frequency can range from, say tens (or hundreds, but this is uncommon) of cases per year down to as low as one case in several hundred years. Consequence Value can range from the start of our interest, let's say £100, to several hundred million pounds. It is not possible to show these huge ranges on a linear scale, say starting at £100 and proceeding, £200, £300, £400, etc. The line would simply be too long. It is a matter of convenience, therefore, to use a logarithmic scale. As the logarithm of a number is the power to which the base must be raised to give that number, 100 can be represented by 2 (being the power to which 10, the chosen base, must be raised in order to give 100, that is $10^2 = 100$), 3 represents 1,000, etc. Hence a line scale whose major gradations we might otherwise label as 1, 2, 3, 4, etc. can be labelled instead as 10, 100, 1,000, 10,000, etc. Each of these major gradations represents a range of one 'decade' (meaning a factor of ten) on the scale.

Mathematically, log (F × CV) = log R becomes

log F + log CV = log R, or log F = log R – log CV.

This means that the inverse line of constant R in Figure 4.1 becomes the straight line in Figure 4.2 in which log F decreases in proportion to the increase in log CV; in other words, if the log scales on each axis are of equal scales, the line has a 45° slope downwards to the right: a negative slope, as shown in Figure 4.2. Mathematically, the slope is –1.

Despite the mathematical clarity of this simple theory, the relationship between Frequency and Consequence Value is not actually the continuous function given by

F × CV = R.

The reason is to be found in the nature of the data. Consider, as an example, the sample data in Table 4.1. This lists all cases of a particular type of Occurrence (for example, corrosive chemical splashes requiring treatment of the affected workers) that have occurred in the period of one year (in this case). Like typical Occurrence data, the list contains a preponderance of low Consequence Value cases. Every now and again a larger Consequence Value case occurs, as you can see. Most of the cases lie in the Consequence Value range of £100 to £1,000. One of them lies in the range £10,000 to £100,000.

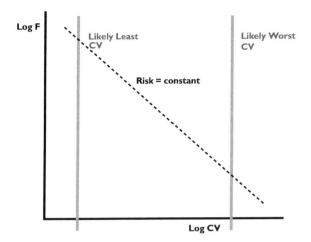

Figure 4.2   Risk with logarithmic scales: the Risk Diagram

Table 4.1   Sample occurrence data

Year 1 Occurrence No.	Consequence Value, £
1	650
2	925
3	375
4	250
5	875
6	23,490
7	635
8	175
9	475
10	990

It is not feasible to plot the frequency of each case against Consequence Value – as each Consequence Value in the sample data is unique, all we would get is a uniform Frequency of 1 [case per year] (e.g. 1 at £650, 1 at £925, etc.) and a scatter of points along the Consequence Value axis.

However, we can determine the average of the Consequence Value in the decade range of £100 to £1,000. It is £594 and there are 9 of them in the period of one year. Or we might have data for five years, or 6.3 years, etc., in which case a simple division gives us an estimate of the Frequency. In this case, though, the Frequency is 9 [cases per year] of a Consequence Value of £594 [per case]. It is possible to plot this discrete point on the Risk Diagram (see Figure 4.3) to represent all those cases.

If we had a lot of data collected over many years, we may well have cases whose Consequence Value was even higher. The line drawn in Figure 4.3 is really just a locus of possible points on the Risk Diagram. As explained, there can only be one point in each decade range of Consequence Value. The contribution of this individual Consequence Value decade to the total Risk could be called r, namely:

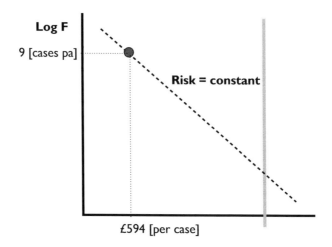

Figure 4.3   One data point on the Risk Diagram

$r = 9$ *[cases per year]* × *594 [£ per case] = 5,346 [£ per year]*.

If data points for the risk actually followed an iso-Risk line, the Risk contribution, r, for each would be the same. That is, at 0.9 cases per year (a factor of ten less), a Consequence Value of £5,940 (a factor of ten more) would be experienced, resulting in a contribution of £5,346 p.a. to the overall Risk, R.

If we were to plot data points representing a real risk on a Risk Diagram, it is unlikely that they will actually follow an iso-Risk line. There is no reason why they should. Figure 4.4 shows a series of hypothetical data points (one only in each decade range) representing the Frequencies with which higher Consequence Values occur. These points show that the Risk rises as Consequence Value increases: each of the data points is above an iso-Risk line through the first point that was plotted. There is no special meaning attached to this, they could also fall below the iso-Risk line. The total Risk (R) would nevertheless be the sum of the Risk values (r) at each of the individual data points.

Figure 4.4 includes real log–log scales over a realistic range of values. The Frequency values range from 10 (1E+01 in scientific format, meaning 1 times ten to the power of 1) down to 0.0001 (1E–04, meaning 1 times ten to the power of –4). The Consequence Value scales range from 100 (1E+02) to 100,000,000 (1E+08). Between each major scale line, the minor scale markers follow the progression of 2, 3, 4, etc., which is not a linear scale but a logarithmic one. Hence the first (upper left) point plotted in Figure 4.4 is (9, 594). The remaining points are chosen more or less at random simply to illustrate how an individual risk could be represented on the Risk Diagram.

Note that there is only one data point in each Consequence Value decade. The risk itself is represented by the string of points in the Risk Diagram: it is not one point only. The magnitude of the Risk in question, from this string of points, could be calculated as shown in Table 4.2 by reading off each point's coordinates from Figure 4.4. The first three points in this table, as the Frequency is greater than one, are actually Loss Rates, that is they are really experienced. The remaining points are notional losses. It is quite realistic to say that the first three points have a real Loss quality to them and amount to £37,486 p.a.

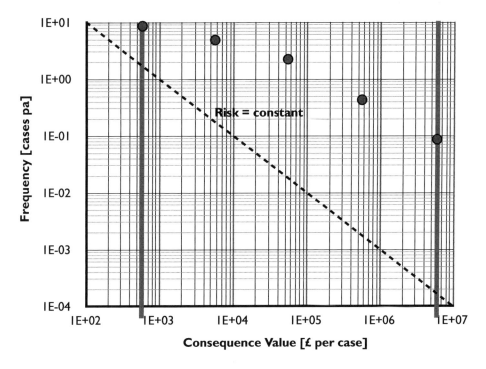

Figure 4.4   Hypothetical data points on a Risk Diagram

It is worth noting, though, that given a larger Exposure, all these notional points on the Risk Diagram could well become real Losses, not notional Risks. Similarly, given a smaller Exposure, all of them could become notional Risks. A range of data points such as shown in Figure 4.4 could apply to an industrial process in five factories. But what if these factories merged with a larger international group and now we are interested in 20 factories? Four times the exposure means four times the frequency, assuming the same, more or less, technology and management practices. Now, much less of this table is looking notional.

Table 4.2   Calculation of Risk from the points in Figure 4.4

Frequency, cases p.a.	Consequence Value, £ per case	Risk, £ p.a.
9	594	5,346
2.7	3,200	8,640
0.5	47,000	23,500
0.18	450,000	81,000
0.028	6,500,000	182,000
	TOTAL (Risk)	£300,486 p.a.

A special case of the Risk Diagram is the 'FN curve' or 'fN curve' used in portraying Risk associated with high-Hazard industrial plant such as nuclear power stations and oil refineries, where f is the frequency (and F the cumulative Frequency) and N the number of fatalities brought about by the risk in question. The purpose is to portray societal risks – how many members of the public might be killed and how often? Its appearance is identical to that of the Risk Diagrams shown above; see Figure 8.1.

The Domains of Risk

The very large ranges of the Frequency and Consequence Value scales on a Risk Diagram point to the enormous scope of Risk theory. On the high Frequency end are Losses of a relatively small scale and at the low Frequency end are possible Consequences of enormous implication. Figure 4.5 illustrates the four domains of interest distinguished by the different levels of data available to them as much as by the way in which they are managed.

Domain A is that of the maintenance and reliability engineer, whose concern is with reliable and productive functioning and handling day-to-day breakdown and preventive maintenance requirements. While most component breakdown data is not recorded in a manner that enables component reliability to be calculated, there are some critical situations in which it is, for example aerospace and nuclear power. Component reliability data and associated reliability theory

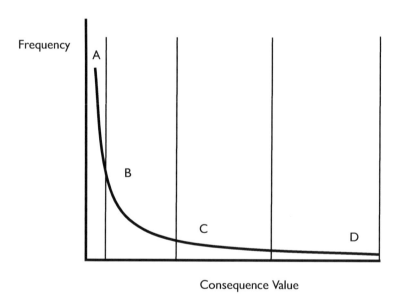

Consequence Value

A Component or Action failure. Potentially large quantities of failure data. Reliability principles.

B Personal injury. Some Occurrence data. Few risk analysis tools

C Plant and property damage (fire, explosions, collapses). Little Occurence data. Synthesis of risk scenarios. Good design guidelines.

D Catastrophes. High technology and high hazard system failures. Little or no Occurrence data. Synthesis of risk scenarios

Figure 4.5   Domains of Risk

underpins the theoretical basis of risk management work (not that it is seen as such) in this domain. Management understanding of this domain is forced upon them by the effect of poorly managed maintenance on production. This domain should not be thought of as one only attending to the failure of individual components in an industrial production process. Its wider context is that of the complete production process, whether it be an industrial or commercial process or a management process supporting these; see Figure 3.4.

Domain B is that of the occupational health and safety specialist, beginning with minor work injuries and extending through to multiple fatalities. Occurrence data collection capabilities (classification and analysis) are poorly developed, as is the theoretical underpinning of the domain. Management (and most other groups in society) understanding of this domain is poor and influenced by deep-seated human prejudices with respect to fault and blame.

Domain C is inhabited largely by insurance company engineers, building design standards bodies and land use planning bodies. Insurance companies have contributed greatly over the years to defining a body of knowledge arising out of fires and explosions and to encouraging good prevention standards amongst their insured.

Domain D is that of the risk engineer. The lack of Occurrence data is fundamental to this practice and methods are used (Chapter 9) to synthesise predicted values of Risk, based on component and action failure data, derived using the methods and data sources of Domain A.

Summary

When Risk is understood as an expression of the uncertainty surrounding the process leading to Damage and Loss it is possible to use logical argument to show how Probability and Exposure combine to produce an objective definition of Risk and Loss, which uses real numbers. This logical development shows clearly that Risk is a relationship between Frequency (of experience of Consequence Value) and Consequence Value, graphically represented by the Risk Diagram. Iso-Risk lines in the Risk Diagram provide both a means of defining Risk mathematically and a sense of meaning for points located on the Risk Diagram. It also becomes clear that Risk, as a probabilistic and hence notional rate of Loss, is distinguished from Loss only by the Exposure. The enormous scale of Risk becomes evident and it becomes possible to see the conceptual continuity between fields as diverse as maintenance and reliability, occupational health and safety and systems with catastrophic potential.

When the simple underlying variables on which a mathematical definition of Risk can be based are explicitly understood, a very simple understanding emerges that makes the continuity between Risk and Loss evident and shows how Risk may be estimated.

Identifying and Describing Risks: Prevention Depends on Knowing What Could Happen

5

Introduction

The idea that it is possible to comprehensively identify the nature of risks in any given situation (industry, organisation, activity and so on) is very difficult for many people to accept. A common perception is that accidents are mysterious, difficult to understand and especially difficult to predict. This view gives a perverse comfort to those who hold it, as it is easy for them to rely on the helpless position of 'who would have thought of that?' when something awful does happen.

This frame of mind is not conducive to accepting the essential premise of preventive activity, which is that (hopefully all) Occurrences are entirely predictable. As a consequence, relatively little actual preventive activity takes place, although it is often thought (erroneously) that learning from accidents is a preventive activity. Being busy with responding to cases as they arise has a certain self-satisfying urgency about it and those involved may well be seen as heroes. As is often the case, the presence of accident concepts in people's minds is an obstruction to understanding and effective action.

The truth of this view has been made evident to me on many occasions in my practice. In one organisation I was concerned by an overloaded and rusted coal conveyor gallery and made my concern clear in a conversation that took far longer than it needed to because those I was with strenuously denied it was a problem as such a thing had never previously happened at the very large site. That night the conveyor gallery in question did in fact fall down (without my help), with far-reaching adverse consequences to production. On another occasion I had been asked to speak at a company conference organised by the risk and safety department, on the subject of identifying risks. It was clear from body language that the audience were there because they had to be and were not paying any attention to my talk. Fortunately I knew something of this organisation and of a particular risk which had a high chance of killing more than one member of the public in circumstances that they could not possibly defend in the inevitable legal case. One of the managers was responsible for this department and I asked him if he could identify the risk after I had described the Consequence severity but not the details of the Occurrence. He could not. Nor could any of the other managers there. I had certainly got their attention and they did start to listen, but the rest of my talk was interrupted by requests to tell them what it was. At the time, I refused, mainly in an attempt to keep them interested.

On another occasion, I visited a large organisation that had for many years given a lot of attention to safety, employed safety officers, run safety committees and so on. It was a heavy engineering concern and I did a walk-around of the plant with the engineer manager. I asked about the energy isolation procedures in place and was told about the Danger Tag system and associated training. Much of the equipment was hydraulically powered, so I asked where the isolation valve was on the machine next to which we were standing, as it was not obvious to me. To his surprise and embarrassment, there wasn't one. Nor on the next machine, nor the next. This was a systemic problem. He hurried away and my tour came to an abrupt end. What were those safety officers and committee looking at for all those years?

Those who subscribe to the accident philosophy, see the subject matter of this chapter as being the hunt for hazards. With the common definition of hazard as 'anything that can cause harm' the hunt is one without end and encompasses anything and everything in the environment of interest, from frayed electrical cords to broken floorboards to light bulbs in need of replacement, rubbish on the floor and so on.

The risk approach to the subject views things differently and very simply: if something is possible, it is only a matter of time before it happens. A possibility can be objectively determined by the presence of an Asset and a vulnerability to a Threat (see Chapter 3). The probability of the Asset sustaining the possible Damage or Loss and the Exposure of the Asset to the situation in which it is possible determines the likely time interval before the Damage or Loss occurs. A later chapter is concerned with the estimation of these two parameters, but that estimation relies on understanding the Risk in some detail, particularly the factors that influence the probabilities (of Mechanisms, Outcomes and Consequences) and Exposure.

For that reason, this chapter is concerned both with determining these objective possibilities and describing the factors that influence the risk. It is hoped that the chapter provides a basis for combatting the prevalent view that this is a complex task, which it is not.

Determining Possibilities from Energies and Other Threats

Chapter 3 showed how risk arises from the presence of a Threat to which an Asset is vulnerable. These Threats were categorised as either energy-based (such as in Table 3.2) or non-energy-based (as in Table 3.7). These simple categories can be used to assist in the broad identification of such risks, by using our knowledge to describe where and possibly when (if they are not always present) these Threats exist. This will result in a high-level statement relevant not just to the specific situation for which it was produced but also to any similar situation and scope of interest. For example, all banks (or airlines, or insurance companies, or mines, or fish farmers) perform essentially the same function and all of them have the same types of risk. All tunnel-boring machines perform the same function and also have the same types of risk. The same can be said of all skyscraper window cleaners, and so on. So, whether the scope of our interest is a whole organisation, or a type of technology, or a specific task, it is possible to apply the generic Threat categories as a starting point for identifying relevant risks, as shown in Tables 5.1 and 5.2 below. Put another way, these categories give us an opportunity to consider each type of risk in the context of the situation. Each of the risks identified in this way can and should be described in greater detail with the aim of making its origin and presence clear.

Table 5.1   Energy-based preliminary identification of damage Risks in an open-cut mine

Energy form	Subform or description	Where found
'Potential energies'	Gravitational energy, including weight effects and waves in liquid–gas interfaces	Vehicles and people using pit access and haul roads People using haul truck steps People refuelling excavators etc. People replacing lights on poles and structures Tipping bodies of haul trucks Bulk storage bins Overhead conveyor runs
	Structural strain energy	Crusher shafts Drive trains of vehicles Drilling machines
	Stored energy in compressed fluids	Compressed gases in vehicle tyres Compressed gases in workshop
Kinetic energy	Energy stored in a body's mass due to its speed in a linear or rotational motion	Haul trucks and smaller vehicles Rocks thrown by blasting
Mechanical power	The rate of energy flow in machinery from the source of power to the point where the energy is absorbed in the action of the machine	Crusher drive mechanisms Powered workshop machinery Engine cooling fans Drilling machines Conveyor systems
Acoustic and mechanical vibrations	Noise (pressure waves in fluids)	Haul truck and excavator engine noise Crusher noise
	Acoustic shock waves	Blasting operations
	Mechanical vibration in solids	Haul trucks and smaller vehicles ride vibrations (affecting the driver). Vibration-induced stress peaks in chassis, suspension and associated equipment mountings
Electrical energy	Electrical potential energy (volts)	Power cables to excavators and lighting towers Power reticulation in workshops and offices Substations
	Electromagnetic fields	Substations
	Electrostatic charge	Lightning
Nuclear particle radiation	Radiation of a nuclear origin (e.g. X-rays)	Bin level detectors Ground radiation from pit
Thermal energy	Solids, liquids, gases (including flames)	Welding work Engine exhausts
	Ambient (atmospheric) condition	Pit and surface works ambient working conditions
Chemical energy	Molecular bonding energy released in oxidising reactions (e.g. fire and explosion, corrosion)	Fuel storage, distribution and use Corrosive dusts Explosive handling and storage

	Modification to the chemical processes of the body (e.g. acute toxic and non-respirable conditions)	Dust exposure Exposure to solvents, lubricants Exposure to diesel fumes
Microbiological 'energy'	Viruses, bacteria, fungi	Exposure of first aiders to blood-borne diseases Exposure to bacteria Food poisoning
Muscle energy	Attacks (purposeful) or inadvertent striking	Violence Manual workshop work
	Using muscles for work	Handling stores Handling components in the workshops

Table 5.2   Threat-based preliminary identification of non-damage Risks in an open-cut mine

Threat control failure types	Subtypes	Possible application
Influences of people	Actions with intended adverse effects (e.g. theft, fraud, sabotage)	Theft of stores or of the product of the mine, fraudulent transactions, e.g. contracts for work clothing or maintenance, sabotage of equipment
	Unintentional actions or actions with unintended effects (e.g. error in contribution to the business process)	Failure to order critical spares or consumables or mistake in ordering
	Loss of people (e.g. strike action, loss of knowledge and skill when people leave)	Industrial disputes
Failures of or in the system or process	Loss of permissions to operate (e.g. loss of licence)	Loss of environmental emissions licence Loss of mining licence Loss of transport licence
	Of something expected or hoped for to happen (e.g. a bank or investment vehicle fails, or a new product cannot be developed)	Loss of investments Failure to successfully install emission control equipment
	Loss of input supplies (e.g. raw materials, energy, labour)	Failure of diesel fuel supply Inability to attract suitable employees to the site
	Of function (e.g. computer system unable to function as intended, production equipment breakdown or unable to be brought into service)	Washout of haul road Crusher breakdown Critical conveyor failure Unreliable excavator or haul truck technology
	Of distribution of product or service and loss of market	Loss of road or rail way Loss of transport operator

Adverse external influences	Systematic adverse influences of the operating environment (e.g. corruption, competition, price reduction, inflexible business model, economic or fiscal conditions, political or social ill will)	High profile and prolonged protests by environmental groups Falling commodity prices Reduction in market for the output of the mine
	Random adverse influences of the operating environment (e.g. volcano eruptions affecting income of an airline)	Surface works damage by storm or earthquake or lightning strike
Liabilities	Derived from statutory or contractual requirements	Inability to supply product to fulfil a contract

Determining Possibilities Based on Equipment Types

An alternative to listing possible forms of energy and threats and then seeking where they are to be found is to list equipment types (or some other physical listing appropriate to the organisation) and seeking the energy or threat types that are related to the equipment, etc. It is helpful to consider, for each item of equipment, the energy that is contained in the item, the energy that is used by the item, the role the equipment might have in controlling risk from an energy source and the energy to which the item is exposed. This approach is illustrated in Table 5.3.

Table 5.3   Equipment-based preliminary identification of damage Risks in an open-cut mine

Equipment type	Attributes	Energy form
Haul truck	Contains energy	Kinetic Mechanical power (motor and transmission) Hydraulic power Noise Heat
	Uses energy of these forms	Chemical bonding energy in fuel and oils
	Controls risk from these energies	Gravitational potential energy of truck above the pit floor, of the tipper body and contents above the chassis and of the driver above the road surface
	Is exposed to these external energies in its operating environment	Ambient heat Solar radiation Other haul trucks Gravitational potential energy of overhead structures (conveyor galleries, bulk storage bins, etc.) Electrical power (lighting, excavator power)

Significance of Risk

The result of these efforts, however done, is a simple statement of the scope of the risk manager's interest. Clearly the various entries in the list will not be of equal significance. It is possible and useful to group risks by their significance to the organisation – see Table 5.4.

Operational risks can be defined as risks that arise in Circumstances and Conditions that are intimately associated with the operation of an organisation. Often, these risks involve unusually large intensities (energy per unit area of transfer) or inventories of energy (large voltages, large chemical stores, large masses, etc.) or energies in situations peculiar to the industry (e.g. transport vehicles, trains, microbes in hospitals) and they have the potential to result in major damage and loss. Because of this potential it is good management to explicitly recognise the special needs for the management of risk arising from them. Other examples of operational risks include high temperature and pressure steam in thermal power stations, gravity on construction sites, high voltage electricity in electrical distribution, explosives in mines, operation of aircraft in airlines, movement of trains on a railway and ships in a seaway, high water pressure in a hydroelectric power station, management of money in a bank, food poisoning in a restaurant, infections and iatrogenic illness in a hospital – see also Table 5.5. Often, the possible Consequences arising from these Risks are such that the existence of the organisation may be threatened either directly, because the equipment and facilities have been destroyed, or indirectly because of the customer or public backlash that results. Operational risks are often not the subject of specific risk management effort possibly because they are almost always under the control of specialists and the knowledge required to understand them properly is not accessible to a non-specialist risk adviser. This is not necessarily a good thing as these subject specialists may not have a good understanding of risk and risk management and their perceptions and judgements may seldom be subject to question.

General risks are all the remaining risks. While a petrochemical refinery will be subject to risks of an operational nature associated with the chemical bonding energy of the hydrocarbons it handles, probably every factory and transport company as users of the refinery's products has exactly the same energy source but in far less quantity and in far more simple and similar conditions. Risks arising in these situations can be managed by following regulations and good practice guidelines. Even in these less hazardous situations, it is beneficial to identify and draw attention to risks to which the greatest moral and ethical expectations are attached, hence the category of Critical. Below this level of criticality are to be found a multitude of general risk possibilities with lesser Consequence Values, which nevertheless require managing, as do the welfare and life quality matters listed next. Within the latter may well be found psychosocial stressors that can have a profound influence on the health of individuals experiencing the resulting physiological stress responses for many years.

Table 5.4   Groups of risks based on significance to the organisation

Group of risk	Description	Definition
1	Operational risk	Energy (or threat) exists in significant and unusual quantities and in circumstances closely associated with the function of the organisation, so there is a potential for a highly significant adverse effect on the organisation, possibly even threatening its existence. For example, petrochemicals in a refinery, electricity in a power station, flying or shipping or rail operations, haul trucks on mine sites.
2	Critical general risk	A general risk is one that arises from energy (or threat) exposures in circumstances that are common and that require control measures largely common in all industries with a similar risk type. For example, an oil store or electricity substation, use of small vehicles, noise, powered production machinery. A critical general risk is one for which the most likely worst Consequence Value is a fatality or multiple fatality or its equivalent (quadriplegia, comatose patient, etc.) or the equivalent in terms of damage to the environment, equipment, production processes or commercial processes.
3	Non-critical general risk	A non-critical general risk is one for which the likely worst Consequence Value is much less than that of a critical general risk and for which a lesser moral obligation exists.
4	Welfare and quality of life	Perhaps not thought of as risk as such, but these are matters that detract from the welfare of people or from the public image of the organisation or the morale of its employees and hence are in the category of adverse Consequences.

Table 5.5   Operational Risks in various industries

Industry	Example of Operational Risks
Mining industry	Fires and explosions underground Rock falls and rock bursts Roof collapse
Shipping industry	Running aground Collisions in seaways
Construction industry	Falls from height Collapse of structures
Petrochemical industry	Releases of contained fluids leading to fires, explosions, toxic effects
Financial industry	Institutional collapses
Road transport industry	Collisions Rollovers, running off the road
Electricity generating industry	Boiler explosion Steam release Turbine oil fire, turbine rotating kinetic energy Coal system fire

Steel industry	Gas release
	Structural collapse
	Loss of containment of molten metal
	Toxic fume release
Railways	Kinetic energy – derailing and collision
Financial industry	Fraud, embezzlement, trading losses
Commercial enterprise	Loss of licence to operate, loss of market, failure of supply

Describing the Damage Process

The simple statements in Tables 5.1 to 5.3 fall short of a full and satisfying description of the process that gives rise to each risk. To usefully describe the possible Damage or Loss processes, we need to know what could happen with each energy or non-energy Threat and to describe (by following the TSM) the possible Mechanisms, Outcomes and Damage forms and the environmental influences that are able to affect them. For example, in Table 5.6, one energy Threat is extracted from Table 5.1, the kinetic energy of haul trucks in an open-cut mine. Experience or consideration of everything in the haul truck's environment makes it possible to list what could happen involving this energy form. It is evident that this is actually a simple statement of Event, Mechanisms and Outcomes. As Outcomes end when Damage occurs, terms such as 'hits' and 'collides' are used. It is usually adequate for these purposes to identify Mechanisms using experience. Three such hypothetical possibilities have been shown to illustrate this.

Table 5.6   Describing a Risk

Risk arises from: Haul truck kinetic energy			
What could happen? (Event and Outcome)	Mechanisms	Conditions	Circumstances
Truck collides with small vehicle	Steering failure Brake failure Driver action	Haul truck mechanical design Maintenance regimes Haul and access route design Sight line from cabin Small vehicle visibility (flags, lights) Shared routes with small vehicles [250 haul truck movements per day, 50 small vehicle movements per day]	Night operations Dusty weather Glare from lights Increased traffic during excavator breakdown or service periods
Truck body sides hit structure supports	Steering failure Brake failure Driver action	Steel structure alongside truck discharge point into the crusher hopper Narrow access route to crusher loading bay [100 truck unloads per day]	Structure coated in dust and not distinct. New drivers unfamiliar with the site
Raised truck body collides with overhead conveyor gallery	Body descent hydraulics failure Driver action	Conveyor gallery over haul truck route No tipper body-up warning when forward drive engaged [100 truck unloads per day]	Night operations and associated poor visibility Driver fatigue New drivers unfamiliar with the site

The content of this table is succinct because excessive detail can be counterproductive. Becoming engrossed in too much detail too soon leads inevitably to a limited view of the overall scene, to the detriment of achieving a broad understanding. The content of this table should enable us to understand what the factors are that influence each aspect of the risk.

Risk Factors

A Risk Factor may be defined (see Figure 3.3) as anything that can affect the value of either Frequency or Consequence Value. In mathematics, a factor is something that is necessary to include in an equation in order to calculate the answer. For example, force and mass are necessary factors in the calculating the acceleration of a body. Risk Factors, therefore, include anything that influences the Probability of Mechanisms, of Outcomes and of Consequence types and Values and the Exposure. The factors can be expected to originate in the Prerequisites, Enabling or Concluding Conditions and/or Circumstances in which the risk exists. Any set of Risk Factors will be relevant only to the type of Risk being considered and the nature of the situation within which it exists; see, for example, the paper by Ferguson (2003), listing Risk Factors for young drivers as risky driving, alcohol use, seat belt use, driver distraction, fatigue and vehicle choice. To illustrate the essential differences, the Risk Factors for white shark attack in the waters off Western Australia (Western Australian Fisheries and Marine Research Laboratories, 2012) were determined by subjecting a collection of attack data to statistical correlation testing. They are listed as distance from shore, season of the year, water temperature, water depth and proximity to other sources of food.

A brief foray into the internet will show how useful Risk Factors are for health risks, for example cancer and heart attacks. Heart attack Risk Factors[1] are said to include obesity, lack of exercise and smoking habits. The Risk of heart attack (meaning the probability of it happening and the seriousness of it if it does happen) is higher for a person who is obese, who never exercises and who smokes. These factors are known to be relevant from scientific analysis of the data on heart attack victims – either by seeking correlations and testing them statistically or by understanding the aetiology of the disease.

Risk Factors based on Conditions can be used to understand a complex environment. For example, petrochemical plants all have a common risk, namely that arising from the flammability of the liquid or gaseous materials that are handled in tanks and pipes. The energy is normally under control because the pipes, valves and tanks do not leak. If a leak does occur, the amount of fluid discharged will depend on the size of the hole and the pressure of the fluid and for how long the leak exists. The duration of the leak will depend on the speed of response. Some systems detect leaks by the resulting pressure drop or flow increase and are designed to shut down the relevant pipe. Others will depend, perhaps, on gas detection in the area or on people noting the pressure drop and closing valves, etc. The factors that influence the Risk will be based on the likely quantity of fluid released and the likely Consequence of a release. The latter will depend on the nature of the fluid released, the presence of ignition sources and the presence of people. Risk Factors could be listed as follows:

- line pressure (more volume released for a given hole size)
- hole size (more volume released for a given pressure)
- response speed (more volume released the slower this is), depending on the response type (automatic, alarm response or manual response to pressure indications)
- volatility and flammability of the released fluid

---

1   An Internet search will reveal a number of heart attack risk calculators.

- presence of people and the number of them
- presence of sensitive equipment.

Risk Factors based on Circumstances can be used operationally to assist in making timely decisions about whether or how to conduct otherwise routine operations that are significantly influenced by Circumstance. For example:

- Given the unserviceability of the aircraft usually assigned to a particular route, or the unavailability of the normally experienced aircrew, and given the poor weather anticipated for the flight, would it be prudent to cancel the flight?
- Given the heart attack risk category of the patient, what treatment precautions and protocols are needed in the accident and emergency room?
- Given the nature of the process plant, the type of fluid being contained in the tanks and pipes and the proximity of sensitive personnel and plant, what precautions are needed for the proposed maintenance activity?

Given a set of relevant Risk Factors they can be used to distinguish between relatively high and relatively low Risk situations by the development of a suitable qualitative word scale for each of the Factors. This is illustrated for two of the factors from the petrochemical leak factor list:

1. Line pressure – a scale of line pressure from very low to very high would use typical line pressures and be divided in to a suitable ranges.
2. Line size – a scale based on pipe diameter from very small (instrument fittings) to very large.

Some Factors will have a detrimental effect on the Risk, for example both of those above, as the larger the pressure and the larger the line size the larger the volume released in a given period of time. Other Factors will have a beneficial effect on the risk, for example response speed: the higher this is, the lower the volume released. By associating the word scale used to describe the significance of the Factor with a number scale, it becomes possible to deduce an overall number, achieved by adding, multiplying or dividing as required, that can be used to rank the Conditions and Circumstances of a given situation against those of a different situation. A single representative number for the leak, limited to the three Factors mentioned, could be obtained by adding the line pressure scale number to the line size number and dividing by the speed of response number, as the latter has the opposite effect to the other two Factors.

Risk Factors are useful in qualitatively assessing any given risky situation, as this example shows. A heavy industry finished goods warehouse makes use of an overhead gantry crane to move the goods (which could be coils of steel, billets of metal, bundles of extruded steel, bags of granular material, castings, etc.) from the end of the production line to a warehouse from which they will be selected for export from the plant. This warehouse is a store of the finished product and an interface with the delivery to customers, which could be a railway or road vehicle loading bay. People work in the warehouse, finding locations into which finished product is to be stored or locating the required items for removal and directing the crane driver to them. A Risk that exists here is that of a person being struck by moving loads or being crushed between a load and a fixed object. What are the features of the environment (the Risk Factors) that influence this risk? Assuming the gantry crane driver is not intent on injuring someone (a criminal intent Mechanism) then the driver will do everything possible to avoid a person on the warehouse floor. The crane driver needs to be able to see these people, so they must not be out of sight behind the item being moved and preferably (for low risk) they must be highly visible against the background colours (they and their clothing must contrast with the background colours) and the crane driver must not be dazzled by any point sources of light or reflections of them. The control that the crane driver has over the movement of the product must be predictable, so the sensitivity of the controls and the stability of the load as it is moved are important. It would be helpful for the warehouse to not be a cramped space that is too small for the quantity of product stored there. It is easy to see here that a situation described in the following way is one which will give rise to relatively high levels of risk:

- The skin colour of the warehouse workers is dark (a Condition).
- The clothing of the warehouse workers is dull and blends in with the background (a Condition).
- The warehouse itself is a little small for the number of items stored in it (a Condition, possibly a Circumstance).
- The warehouse lighting is a few intense and high glare points because the shades have been lost over time (now a Condition).
- There are no reflective surfaces to spread the illumination (a Condition).
- The crane driver is not very skilled, having been recently employed (a Circumstance).
- The crane controls are coarse and their function is not well marked (a Condition).
- The production pressures are high (a Condition or a Circumstance).

I once saw just such a place and was virtually kidnapped to get me there (it was not part of my brief) by those responsible for it as they had experienced a fatality and were rather desperate to get someone to give them ideas about the prevention measures they could include in the accident investigation report that was expected of them. As they had worked in this environment for years, they were unable to see the Risk Factors in the situation and could not imagine anything different. It is not hard to see these factors if one has a good model in one's head and is not stuck in the accident mode of thinking.

Risk Inventory – The Risk Register

To complete a risk register in a thoughtful manner, it is necessary to use a definition of Risk that accords with some logical theory, such as that presented in Chapter 3, the application of which for these purposes is developed in some detail here. The alternative is to use the colloquial common meaning (of risk as a synonym for chance or probability) as the basis for identifying risks. Regrettably, this is a common basis for populating a risk register. The large number of entries from the resulting brainstorming make a register with this origin easy to spot as the large number itself is evidence that a structured approach has not been used. For example, in one organisation (responsible for the maintenance of a public utility) the register was so large (in excess of 1,500 entries) that a dedicated person was needed to run it. The register contained an odd collection of topics, but one that caught the eye was 'the design manual might be wrong'. Clearly, there is a chance (probability) of this happening but exactly what it had to do with actual risk was unstated. In this sense there is also the risk that the person in charge of the risk register might delete one by mistake. Without a structure based on a sensible understanding of what risk actually is (other than a synonym for chance), a register will absorb resources but eventually lead to the risk management process bogging down in unmanageable detail. This reality does not prevent the great majority of risk registers, in my experience, falling into this trap.

In any organisation, a structure such as those shown in Tables 5.1 to 5.3 can be used as the starting point. If we initially limit our efforts to the Group 1 (operational) risks (Table 5.4), the register will come straight to the point of the organisation's existence. For example, in an energy utility company a prime concern will be the risk arising from the generation, transportation or distribution of its energy. Hence, the risk originates in the energy source. The situations within which the energy exists can be used to provide some greater resolution of the risk, as typically this will include different amounts or intensities of energy (e.g. from very high voltage or very high gas pressure to lower levels of voltage or pressure). This distinction is sensible, as the technology (including that of risk control) associated with each will be somewhat different and the extent of its distribution (and hence the exposure of Assets to it) will be different. Typically the transmission lines or pipes at the very high voltage or pressure will be in different locations and of different overall lengths from those of the distribution into domestic or industrial outlets. A similar approach to providing more useful resolution of the risk would apply to railways (inter-city compared with suburban) or to vehicle highways (inter-city to urban to suburban) or to airways (international to domestic inter-city to terminal control zones). Within each such subdivision there may well be different types of technology and different conditions that apply. Table 5.7 illustrates this for an electricity transmitter and distributor.

Table 5.7   **Developing risk register content in a structured manner –**
electricity distribution

Risk from	Electrical energy		
	Event: Electricity flows through an unwanted and unexpected path		
Energy level	*Situation*	*Subclass*	*Conditions*
High voltage	Overhead	Urban, rural	Rural – forest, highway, farmland
	Underground	Urban	
	Substations	Urban, rural	
Low voltage	Overhead	Aerial bundled cables, single-wire earth return, etc.	
	Underground	Urban	
	Substations	Urban, rural	
	Transformers	Pole mounted, pad mounted	
Service voltage	Overhead	Urban, rural	
	Underground	Urban, rural	
	Street lighting	Urban	

There will be 17 risk register entries if you count each subclass as one item. The link between this list and the unstructured, colloquial-use form of risk register (the one that had a risk: 'the design manual might be wrong') is that the design manual is the way in which the organisation designs its transmission and substations, etc. The physical standards at the time of construction will be determined by this manual. These standards will determine the attributes of the systems, which will include functionality, reliability, longevity, aesthetics and risk control. As all risk controls have their limitations, it is quite possible that they may fail to prevent Damage at some point. This does not mean the manual was wrong as such, just that the control measure, like everything, has its failure modes. The word 'wrong' essentially arises from a value judgement made in hindsight. Accident theory seems to allow or even encourage the use of such judgemental terms. Risk theory does not and the inevitable result of using risk theory is that one achieves a greater and more objective understanding of the subject in question.

Supplementing the Insights from Theory

In my first day in one large and well-run heavy engineering factory I was able to identify over 60 situations in which:

1. I was either sure that the standard of risk control was not up to what would reasonably be expected of them in a court of law if subject to the scrutiny of barristers and experts, or
2. I was not sure what the common law standard was and wanted to go away and carry out some research.

This was despite the organisation employing several safety officers and the fact that it had been operating for many years. One of these safety officers was clearly astonished and said I had found more significant items in that single day than he had in several years of employment. It is definitely not how clever you are that makes the difference, it is what you think you should be looking for.

There are three ways to supplement the desk-bound tasks described above: peruse accident reports; walk around the plant; speak to people who do the work. The first two of these provide the plant insight that makes number three more fruitful. The largest possible collection of accident reports, going back as far in time as possible, is the Occurrence experience of the organisation. It is not what normally happens and what fills the minds of those who work there, it is what abnormally happens and which is often quickly forgotten by them. It may well be that you learn what the organisation has forgotten and certainly likely that you will learn what many of the people currently working there have forgotten or never knew. The best-quality information is found in the original narratives, not in a categorised and analysed report.

Observations of the working environment can be expected to provide clues about unexpected energy exposures and about Risk Factors that might not otherwise be identified. In complex industrial plants, people (operators or maintenance personnel) often do things that they forget to mention or don't wish to mention when involved in risk identification. They can get themselves into situations not envisaged by an office-bound person and the more of the plant that is seen in a walk-around the more likely it is that evidence will be seen. What follows in Table 5.8 is a short list of items that are examples of the types of observations that may be made when walking around a typical industrial process plant. Walk-around inspections have the limitation that one can only see what is visible at the time, but this may well include the traces of past activities on the equipment and facilities. A way of overcoming this limitation is to interview each type of worker or operator to understand the work they do. It is necessary to know not only what is normally done but also what is occasionally done. It is necessary to listen to them as well as getting them to show the place and describe the work, as it is only in this way that energy exposures will be made evident.

Table 5.8   Types of observations and their relation to Risks and control measures

Observation	What is observed?
Industrial plant is often dusty, and footprints in unusual places (e.g. on top of gantry cranes, on structures and outside walkways) or tools left behind in odd places are clues you don't want to miss. These tell a story about work for which precautions may not have been taken or which is uncommon and forgotten but which nevertheless happens and of exposure to various energies such as gravitational potential energy, heat, electricity and electromagnetic fields.	Exposures, from which energy types can be deduced Evidence of work being done without considered control measures in place
Broken wire ropes or fabric slings pushed behind something and in a dark corner. These tell a story about gravitational potential energy, not to mention training, preparation for work, maintenance practices and the efficacy of housekeeping inspections.	Evidence of damaging Outcomes Control measure failures
An old chair in a warm and quiet location is a common sight where round-the-clock shift work takes place. One story I heard, which I take to be true, was of a person who enjoyed a warming tea break in his chair, on night shift, in front of a microwave transmission antenna. Regrettably he was killed in his chair at Christmas time when the transmitter power was higher than normal.	Exposures, from which energy types can be deduced Control measures failures
Greasy hand prints or other evidence of repair work within the body of powered machinery gives insight into awkward maintenance work and the opportunity to question isolation practices and the extent to which breakdown maintenance dominates scheduled maintenance.	Exposures, from which energy types can be deduced
Missing fasteners on machine guards and loose fasteners on interlocked guards tell stories of poorly designed machine guards (very common) and the defeat of them (by removal or loosening) when essential maintenance work is done.	Control measure failures
Powered equipment that is provided with neither local isolation switches nor with clear identification placards points to possible problems with isolation practices.	Design standards Control measure requirements
Corroded and possibly overloaded structures are often not seen by site personnel as the process of change that has led to that state is so slow as to be practically imperceptible. Similarly, deterioration of electrical insulation.	Slowly developing Mechanism
The efficacy of access restriction signs (no entry, authorised people only) is easily assessed by observing the effect they have on people's movements. If they are routinely ignored, the evidence is easy to see as an informal pathway.	Slowly developing unintended exposures.
Impact damage (scrapes and dents) on structures alongside access routes.	The potential for a significant Consequence

Talking to those exposed to the risks is also important because of the incident experience they have which may well not have reached the incident/accident reports in the company files. Their experience of awkward or tense situations is invaluable, as Figure 2.1 shows.

Summary

In my experience, it is not helpful to use either accident theory or accidents alone to gain insight into what adverse events could happen. Risk registers, as the repository of the organisation's understanding of what could go wrong, need an efficient and objective means of filling them. Populating registers without a sensible understanding of Risk (i.e. seeing risk as a synonym for chance) is unfortunately very common as well as a certain way to ineffectually disperse the risk management efforts of the organisation. An efficient and justifiable approach can be derived from Damage and Loss process models. These can be used to develop a comprehensive understanding and form the basis of a structured approach to prevention efforts. These desk-based efforts need to be supplemented by insight from past Occurrences, from plant or process observations and by talking to those closest to the work. Once possibilities are identified, immediate insight can be gained by asking whether control measures are known to be adequate or whether what adequate means needs to be determined. Those responsible for populating risk registers or deciding on the approach to prevention need to be aware that their audience may find it very hard to believe that it is possible to list where 'accidents' are likely to happen.

6

Risk Estimation: How Significant is the Risk?

Introduction

If something is possible, it is only a matter of time before it happens. The next obvious questions are: How long will it be before we experience it? How bad is it likely to be when we do? The answers to these questions are not normally clear or precise. Nevertheless, we need to answer them: the massive energy sources that are now commonplace in our industrialised world and their artificial concentration and location adjacent to people create the need for answers. Is the risk imposed on us by these energies (or other threat) one that we are prepared to accept? How much money are we prepared to spend to control the risk before the benefit of the risk diminishes in our view? It is true that in some high profile cases the answer from the public is a resounding 'not in my backyard no matter how small the risk is', but in the great majority of cases these are valid questions. The questions cannot be answered without estimating the significance of the risk and the effect that the proposed control measures have on it.

If any attempt is to be made to estimate a Risk it is a task that needs to be taken seriously with due recognition of the capabilities of the method chosen, the uncertainty associated with categorical or numerical choices and of the assumptions that underlie them. There are three possible types of approach to the task, which range from the very simple to the most complex. The most simple is the so-called 'risk matrix', which is a two-dimensional tabulation of the parameters of likelihood and Consequence Value, making use of simple word scales to divide these parameters into a small number of categories from which choices may be made. This method does not make use of real number scales and for this reason what it gains in simplicity it loses in the ability to make any checks on the validity of the result. This very rough method is very popular, perhaps due to its simplicity. The most complex method is quantified risk analysis (QRA, see Chapter 9). This more formal method makes use of both real numbers and a complex representation of the structure and logic of the process leading to Damage or Loss. What it loses in complexity it makes up for in the use of real numbers to quantify the variables and the consequential ability to justify and validate the results. The use of QRA is largely limited in practice to the analysis of the technology of complex aerospace and petrochemical ventures, although this is not an inherent limitation of the method. Between these two lies the possibility of using real number scales to estimate the Risk directly using judgement. This method, called here quantified risk estimation (QRE), is uncommon but of much utility: it is less complex than QRA but the use of real numbers makes it possible to validate the result at least against experience or judgement. In QRE, estimating the risk means deciding where to draw a line on the Risk Diagram (Figure 4.4) that is a reasonable representation of the Risk in question, by estimating the Frequency associated with the Consequence (both LLC and LWC). If this can be done, then by estimating Exposure it becomes possible to also estimate the probability associated with the LLC and LWC. Possible control measure changes will affect any of the variables of Probability, Exposure and Consequence Value, so if we at least have an estimate of the starting point it may be possible to justify changes to these estimates resulting from the proposed control measure changes.

Each of these three approaches aims to make an absolute statement about the size of a Risk. The result can be used to compare Risks of very different types. For example:

1. Is the Risk associated with travel in cars higher or lower that the Risk of injury when rock climbing?
2. Is the Risk of falls in the factory higher or lower than that of eye injury?

There are times when it is convenient to have a method for comparing the same type of Risk but in different Conditions and Circumstances. This could be done by using estimated Risk values and sometimes is, but the task is made simpler by using Risk Factors for which word scales have been developed to distinguish between low, high and intermediate influences. Risk Factors are discussed in Chapter 5.

Uncertain Values

Many engineers and scientists are accustomed to dealing with deterministic calculations using numbers that are known with a high degree of accuracy. For example, the mass of a body may be accurately measured, as may its acceleration, and so it is possible to calculate the force that must have been imposed to produce the acceleration, to a degree of accuracy that is itself determined by the accuracy of the scale used to weigh the object and the accuracy of the instruments used to measure acceleration. Not all measurements are so certain. For example there is no single answer to the question: how tall is an adult female? The reason for this is that adult females vary considerably in size from one group of people to another as well as within a group. Consequently, the answer is given as a distribution of height measurements, showing what proportion of the population has a height greater (or less) than a particular height.

The presence of uncertainty in the numbers needed to estimate risk need not dissuade us from attempting the task, as there is really little point in identifying risks if we are quite incapable of understanding how significant the risk is. Any risk specialist must develop a good understanding and skill in the handling of uncertain numbers and all managers called on to make decisions regarding Risk need to understand the essential uncertainty and not use it to disparage the work done by others.

Rowe (1977) usefully pointed out that a Risk estimation can be regarded as objective only if all the variables are measured objectively. In the case of Risk, this means an objective determination of Probability, Exposure and Consequence.

Probability is only objective if it has been measured by repeated trials, which probably limits it to vehicle risks, public health (especially food-related damage processes) and to the history of industry as a whole. The common factor here is a very large Exposure. QRA makes use of component failure probabilities to estimate the probability of an Event by understanding the role that components play in the system under analysis, in other words by creating a model of the system for the purpose of risk estimation. Following the Event, a similar process is used to model all possible Outcomes and Consequences. In this way, it is in principle possible to synthesise the likely Risk associated with a system that has never before been constructed or associated with an Event that has never yet happened. The validity of the failure probability estimates used in such analyses is a constant practical concern. Failure probability values of typical mechanical, electrical and electronic components used in various critical industrial situations have been determined by major studies of statistically significant numbers of failures. However, variable influences include the operating environment and the quality of the original equipment. Psychologists have done their best in decades of research to develop means of predicting human failure probabilities. In the end, what can be used are at least representative values expressed usually as orders of magnitude. By definition, objective and modelled risks make use of real probability numbers. What these numbers are and the effect of using them has been discussed in Chapter 4.

Mechanism and Outcome to Consequence pathway probabilities are always best estimates that are most honestly treated as having a range of possible values, some of which are more likely than others. A simple variable like Exposure does not have a naturally occurring population as the base of its distribution of values. The simplest way to capture this information is as a single value estimate, based on the average value or the most likely value, for example. The more meaningful way to capture all the information given (during persistent questioning of those who know the answer to the Exposure variable) is as a distribution of likely Exposure values between limits of 'never less than' (a minimum) and 'never more than' (a maximum) and to attempt to fill in the likelihood of intermediate values in a graphical manner, similar to those shown in Figure 6.1. For simplicity, distributions B and C are shown as straight lines but they could equally be curved in some way. This would just be of academic benefit if it were not for the ease with which numerical estimates that are not expressed as algebraic relationships can be handled using spreadsheets. While the standard spreadsheet allows us to insert a single value into a cell, programs (known as plug-ins) that work alongside the standard spreadsheet enable us to insert a distribution of possible values in input data cells. This can be done using either mathematically defined distributions, such as the normal distribution, or freehand graphical distributions using shapes similar to those in Figure 6.1. In the case of probability, Figure 6.1 would be showing not distributions of possible Exposure values, but of possible probability values – the probability of a given failure probability number being the one to use.

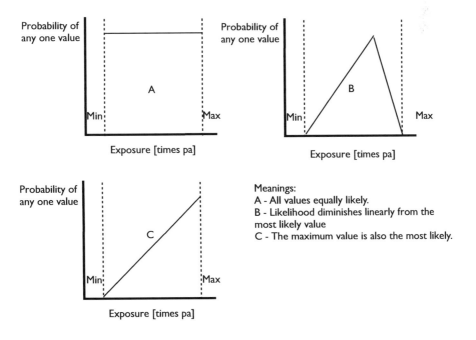

Figure 6.1   Describing uncertain values using Exposure as an example

Consequence values, as has been shown in Chapter 4, range from the LLC to the LWC and it is conceivable that there will be uncertainty in the estimation of these values. For example, if an industrial plant suffers a major fire that requires the demolition and reconstruction of part of the plant, there will be uncertainty in the likely cost of demolition and reconstruction as detailed quotes will not have been obtained at the time the risk is being estimated.

Consequence value is only objective for an individual case some time after the Event, often after many years and even decades. When estimating Consequences it may be necessary to think broadly beyond the most obvious and immediate effects of the damaging process, as illustrated by political responses to high-profile disasters. Following the Fukushima nuclear power station damage in Japan, after being hit by a massive tidal wave in 2011, many countries, including Japan, abandoned or reduced their nuclear power programmes, presumably because people en masse experienced heightened fear of nuclear power stations.

When real number estimates for each of the variables of Probability, Exposure and Consequence Value are made as a distribution of possible values it is simple, thanks to spreadsheets, to use Monte Carlo or similar statistical techniques to estimate the Risk not as a single value but as a distribution of possible values derived from the distributions of input variable values. Due to the essential measurement uncertainty of all the parameters that define Risk, this is in fact the most honest as well as useful way in which to convey the result.

Due to huge Exposure, the closest we may get to objectively determined Risk is to be found in the collected statistics of industry or transport operations as a whole or in the injury and health statistics of whole communities over long periods. It is, however, unreasonable to delay risk control action until specific objective statistical data is available, as this consigns people or the environment (as two sensitive and significant Assets) to the status of laboratory rats. Those exposing the community to new technology which is possibly injurious (for example microwaves, substances in foods, chemical pollutants) cannot logically or ethically justify inattention or inaction on the basis of a lack of statistical evidence. If the damage process is slow (possibly involving long lag times between Exposure and detectable injury), as was the case with asbestos, the Exposure needed to provide this statistical objectivity may be so great that the flaws in the argument only surface when it is too late to stop the illness of large numbers of people. Objectively determined risk is almost an anomaly, not a gold standard to be achieved before we respond to a risk.

The 'Risk Matrix' –
Subjective Estimates using Qualitative Word Scales

Qualitative word scales that allow a choice between a range of possibilities, also called ordinal scales, can easily be developed for each of the three parameters that define Risk. By way of illustration, the following is an approach suggested some years ago for health and safety practitioners (Steel, 1990):

Probability: impossible, unlikely, possible, even chance, probable, likely, certain.

Exposure: constantly, hourly, daily, weekly, monthly, annually, infrequently.

Consequence Value: scratch/bruise, laceration/mild ill-health effect, break (minor bone) or minor illness (permanent), loss of limb/eye or serious illness (temporary), loss of two limbs/eyes or serious illness (permanent), fatality.

Alternatively and conveniently, the first two parameters could be replaced by a single Frequency scale, for example:

Frequency: very infrequent, infrequent, frequent, very frequent, regular.

A more useful approach to such a scale would be based on actual frequency values, such as:

Frequency: less than once every 10 years, more than once every 10 years and less than once every 5 years, more than once every 5 years and less than once a year, between 1 and 9 times a year, more than 10 times year.

However structured, these scales are designed to elicit a response from the person doing the estimate. For example, if asked what you thought of the risks you face when travelling by car, you could check the provided scales and produce a result (from the first set of options above) that might look like this: unlikely, daily, laceration.

These word scales could be replaced by arbitrary number scales, or such numbers could be associated with the word scales. This makes it possible to perform addition or multiplication and calculate a single score to represent the result, instead of a collection of words as above. For example:

Frequency: very infrequent (1), infrequent (2), frequent (3), very frequent (4), regular (5).
Consequence Value: scratch/bruise (1), laceration/mild ill-health effect, break (minor bone) or minor illness (permanent) (2), loss of limb/eye or serious illness (temporary) (4), loss of two limbs/eyes or serious illness (permanent) (8), fatality (16).

The estimation 'infrequent, scratch/bruise' could then be written as (2) if multiplied or as (3) if added.

The apparent simplicity and convenience of these simple scales gave rise in the 1990s to a proliferation of different methods of estimation based on various variables similar to these even though the idea had first been published (in the form of a nomogram) some 15 years earlier (Kinney and Wiruth, 1976).

Those scales using more than two variables typically associated numbers with the word scales and used an algorithm to calculate an overall result, or presented the scales as a nomogram. The two-variable form (typically Likelihood and Consequence) has subsequently become very common and is widely known as 'the risk matrix'. It is not a matrix in the mathematical sense of the word but rather a simple tabulation of one variable against the other with no mathematical properties or use. A search of the internet will quickly show the idea applied in any field in which risk needs to be estimated. A common feature of these matrices is that the individual cells located by one combination of likelihood and consequence is given a meaning, typically not how big the risk is but whether it is acceptable or what needs to be done about it. This decision is the result of risk evaluation (if the risk is this big then we must do something about it, such as take immediate action, etc.), and as this is the subject of Chapter 8 it will not be pursued here.

Convenient though these simple scales appear to be, there are significant problems associated with their use. The problem of lack of repeatability arises from the descriptive and imprecise nature of the words used in the scale. This shows itself in three ways. First, for exactly the same risk, the same person at different times may not choose the same words and different people may choose different words. Very little research has been published on this repeatability problem.

I did some myself with a group of 40 students, each of whom was asked to make an individual (no consultation with others) estimation of the risk using five different applications of the basic idea, ranging from the nomogram of Kinney and Wiruth through to a by now superseded standard. The students were given a written description of a risk and a verbal explanation of it. The results were statistically analysed and the conclusion was: 'The study found substantial inconsistencies both within each method and between different methods' (Viner, Harvey and Borys, 2001). This result is little surprise to those who use such matrices but is not welcomed by those who are committed to their use, such as consultants and legislators.

Secondly, the true nature (that is, inverse) of the relationship between probability (or Frequency) and Consequence Value is not well represented by the typical matrix. Pickering and Cowley (2010) have drawn attention to this structural limitation, which arises from dividing the potentially large scales of each of the two variables into a small number of categories. Furthermore, the user may not be aware of this inverse relationship nor of the implications of attempting to characterise a Risk by one pair of values, when in reality the Risk is a relationship between the two variables. The Frequency word chosen may be for the 'most likely' Frequency but the Consequence Value word might be for the worst (or any other) case, which, as has been shown in Chapter 4, is usually also the lowest Frequency.

A third problem is that associated with the influence of the action statements with which regions of a matrix are endowed, which may be stated, for example, as 'manage by routine procedures' through to 'stop work and seek senior management attention'. Deciding what needs to be done when the Risk has been estimated as a particular combination of values of the two variables is Risk Evaluation, for a detailed discussion of which see Chapter 8. It is a matter of common knowledge that these action statements influence the estimation choices made by people, so that their use of the matrix does not force them into some action they do not believe is justified.

It would be helpful if these tools could be used for both short time scale (accident) as well as long time scale (chronic) Damage or Loss processes. The tools need to be provided with usage rules so that the likelihood/consequence value relationship is explicitly understood and used consistently by all users.

For short time scale damaging processes ('accidents', acute Damage and Loss):

1. the three fundamental variables (Probability, Exposure and Consequence Value) need to be present;
2. it needs to be made clear that the 'likelihood' scale is to be applied to either likely least consequence or likely worst consequence.

For long time scale damaging processes ('disease', chronic damage and loss):

1. The method must cope with cases where there is and is not a dose–response relationship. Dose is a measure of the intensity of energy or threat to which the recipient is exposed and the time over which it is experienced.
2. The method is able to cope with any latency period which may exist. A latency period is the time between the exposure and the onset of detectable consequences.

Word scales need to be appropriate to the scale in which they are used. It is incorrect, for example, to use a word such as 'infrequent' in a scale of likelihood as likelihood is a synonym of Probability, not Frequency. Similarly, a Frequency scale should not use Probability words such as 'unlikely'. It also makes little sense in a Probability scale to use a word such as 'probable', as the whole scale is about probability – every part of it is probable in that sense.

Despite these many basic problems associated with the matrix, it is very commonly used to decide on the risk before control measures are implemented and then determine the so-called residual risk afterwards. Apart from the impossibility of making any reasonable estimate of the risk, the idea that risk can be estimated in the absence of control measures is itself a fallacy, as made evident in Chapter 3.

Ranking by Significance and Opportunity

The significance of a Risk is only partly derived from its estimated size. The significance of Risks may be influenced by other matters, for example:

1. the effectiveness of possible control measure improvements;
2. the presence of significant moral obligations, such that it would be wise to draw particular attention to the LWC value of the Risk;
3. the existence of urgency due to threatened action by a Regulator if nothing is done.

If suitable qualitative numerical ranking scales are used for each of these, a final index number for each Risk can be developed using a suitable algorithm. All variables that contribute to increased motivation to do something could be multiplied and all that do not could be divided into the resulting ranking number, for example:

Risk × LWC ranking × Urgency × Control measure improvement potential / Cost of control measure

Alternatively, these contributors to the ranking index could be added if a positive motivator for action and subtracted if not. An alternative and very simple way to begin ranking a list of Risks is by their estimated LWC values. Subsequently, the availability and cost of control measure improvements can be assessed for each. Such rankings are a valuable way of discriminating between risks in a register and allow far greater resolution than does the simple risk matrix. There are no good reasons for using the risk matrix.

There follow in this chapter two further methods for estimating the size of a Risk, and these are both based on using real number scales, rather than these qualitative word scales. Each of these require more effort to complete than the matrix, but one could ask why use a simple method that is known to be virtually meaningless in practice? The methods that follow are of particular value in assisting with difficult capital investment or production cost implications.

What Does a Real Risk Diagram Look Like?

In Figures 2.1 to 2.3 data is presented that is suggestive of an inverse relationship between Frequency and Consequence Value. Figure 6.2 shows work injury history with a very large exposure as a Risk Diagram based on Probability of injury [cases per work hour]. This data distinguishes between self energy (energy within the body of the injured person) sources and external energy sources. Clearly the lines are not straight, but the evident tendency is to follow a straight line with a -45° slope.

Risk Diagrams of this form derived from past Occurrences have been seen in many different situations. However, this inverse relationship is not a universal law. Figure 6.3 presents data from 93 electrical transformer failures that tells a very different story (Bartley, 2003). If a transformer fails, it is far more likely to result in a very high Consequence Value than a low one.

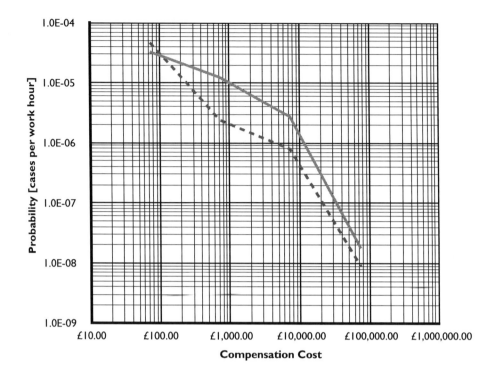

Exposure = 3.356 x 10^8 work hours pa, postal services company.
The solid line represents self-energy (see Table 3.1) and the dashed line external energy Occurrences.

Figure 6.2   Data from an organisation with a large Exposure base

Similar Risk Diagrams have been developed for eye injuries in manufacturing industry. This data tells a story about high-value assets that are very susceptible to damage. It emphasises the need to do any risk estimation thoughtfully and with real understanding of the nature of the Occurrence process.

Despite the possibility of non-inverse relationships between Frequency and Consequence Value, it is thought that these non-conforming situations are relatively rare. It is feasible to cautiously postulate an inverse relationship between the variables of the Risk Diagram. The mathematical simplicity of the iso-risk line provides an opportunity in risk estimation to venture into the realms of zero data and little experience.

QRE – Subjective Estimates Using Real Number Scales

The value of real number scales is that it is easy to establish the scales and the scales themselves are of universal application. Probability is naturally a number between 0 and 1 and Exposure is the number of times in a unit time period (conveniently a year) that the situation in which the Occurrence could occur is experienced. This number could be as high as thousands and as low as once in 10 years. Frequency, the number of times the Consequence is experienced each unit of time (conveniently the year), is measured naturally as number of times per year and a scale will range from perhaps once in 100 years to tens of times a year.

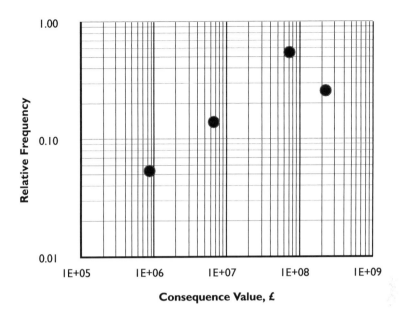

Figure 6.3   Electrical transformer failure Risk Diagram
Source: Bartley (2003).

Consequence Value is complicated by the presence of unquantifiable, or hard to quantify, components where human suffering and environmental damage exists. In practice it is sensible to recognise these difficult components but not allow this to deter us from measuring what is possible. A general principle is that Damage can be valued as the cost of the efforts needed to reinstate the Asset to its original condition: repair a car, remove the environmental contaminant, medical bills for treatment and medicines, rebuild the damaged structure, the value of lost production, the effect on share price of an embarrassing incident, the cost of fines imposed by courts and of lawyers' fees for our defence, etc.

What is not so easily quantifiable is the suffering of families and the long-term economic effects on them when a person is killed or maimed, or Damage to the environment when something incapable of replacement is lost (for example a species due to habitat destruction or toxic effects). Sometimes, damages are awarded by courts against parties considered under law to be responsible in an attempt to place a value on suffering and loss. One can think of these as ethical and moral constituents of Consequence and not readily amenable to simple quantification. However, it can be said that the larger the LWC, the greater the moral and ethical responsibility associated with the risk. The implication of this is that when estimating the size of a Risk with moral and ethical aspects it is not just the estimated Risk number that has meaning, but the LWC value as well.

Once we assign a real number scale to Consequence Value and understand it as the value of damaged or lost assets or the cost of reinstating them (a rule needs to be made here just as it does when taking out insurance – are you insuring for the cost of the item or the price you'll pay when getting another one?), it is relatively easy to determine the values of the LLC and LWC.

There are times when Exposure can be obtained directly from the production records of an organisation. For example, when analysing the risk associated with felling trees in a forest, the Exposure is simply the number of trees felled per year and it is no surprise that good records are kept and the number is known with accuracy. Similarly, if we are considering risks associated with the delivery of hazardous liquids from a road tanker into storage tanks we would expect to find the number of tanker deliveries per year in purchasing records. The answer to the Exposure question can alternatively be found in the experience of those doing the work. The response to the question may be: 'well it could be as infrequent as three times a year but could happen as much as 10 times a year'; 'It all depends' on – how many orders are received, how reliable a critical piece of plant is, how often this product is ordered, etc. When urged to do so, people will often be able to nominate a most likely value. As has been seen above, Exposure, too, is not that hard to estimate, despite the inevitable 'it all depends' response we get when asking about it.

Probability, however, is not so easy to estimate. If we understand the basis of probability theory or can ask a statistician, it may be feasible to calculate this from first principles. It is possible to calculate the probability of winning a lottery, for example, not that many of us feel competent to do so. It is highly uniquely in Risk work that probability can be calculated from first principles in any situation. While Probability is not a number that the brain is easily able to understand, the same cannot can't be said of Frequency. We are able to understand this as it is a matter of experience. Offhand, I have no idea what the probability of me damaging my car in traffic is, but I can tell you how often it has happened to me over the years – about five cases I can recall in 45 years of driving. Let's say about one case in 10 years, or 0.1 cases of damage per year. My Exposure to this risk can be measured either in terms of the number of miles (or kilometres) I drive each year or the number of trips I make each year. The latter is easier for me and I'd say it is about two trips a day, say 750 trips a year as a round figure. It is then a simple matter to estimate that the probability of me damaging my car is about $0.1/750 = 1.3 \times 10^{-4}$ [damage cases per trip]. This is a subjective estimate of the Probability.

As Risk is determined by the Frequency and the Consequence Value, I only really need to get an estimate of the Frequency. It is useful, however, to be able to work out the Probability, as often improved control measures will have an effect on this rather than on the Exposure. This underlying Probability will exist, even if I reduce my Exposure, so I can readily estimate the effect on Risk of so doing. If I undertake a defensive driver training programme or buy a car with a better braking system I can perhaps judge the extent to which this might reduce my Probability of having a panel damage accident. If I purchase a car with better ability to withstand minor collisions with less panel damage or which is cheaper to repair, I can estimate the effect of this on the LLC estimate.

I would say that the average cost of panel damage repair in my cases has been about £1,500 per damage case and I will assume this is my likely least Consequence Value (LLC). Hence the estimated Risk, or at least that component of Risk associated with this level of panel damage, is $0.1 \times £1,500 = £150$ per year.

This process is easy and repeatable. It is easy to do because I chose a level of damage with which I had experience. What this has done is provide me with one point on the risk diagram, similar to Figure 4.3. Table 6.2 is a suggestion of common ranges of values of real numbers for the variables involved in the estimation.

Table 6.1   Sample real number scales

Probability [cases per trial]	Exposure [trials p.a.]	Frequency [cases p.a.]	Consequence Value [£ per case]
10^{-7} to 1	0.01 to 100	10^{-2} to 10^{+2}	10^{+2} to 10^{+8}

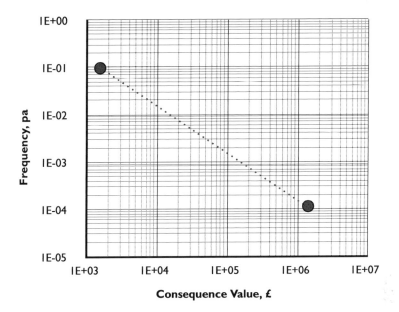

Figure 6.4   Estimating the Risk of car travel – Step One

The next part of the estimation task is to complete the Risk Diagram by estimating the position of the line that is the locus of (Consequence Value, Frequency) points in the range of Consequence Values of interest to me. The constant Risk line is drawn from the initial point estimate at the LLC until it intersects the LWC, just as illustrated in Figure 4.3. At this intersection the Frequency value for the LWC can be read off the scale. Continuing with the estimation of my risk with car travel, I'll assume that the LWC for me is a car write-off and my own death, and without justifying my estimate here, I'll assume this can be given a value of £1,500,000. This value is not far off the real cost to my family if I am a middle-aged person and it is conveniently similar to my assumption of £1,500 LLC damage. I am not very wealthy, so the LWC is not £15,000,000. An iso-risk line would associate this LWC value with a Frequency that is three orders of magnitude (factors of 10) smaller than my LLC Frequency because my LWC value is three orders of magnitude larger than my LLC value. With a spreadsheet set up to draw this for me, I get the result shown in Figure 6.4. The Frequency of the LWC is 0.0001 (or 10^{-4}) cases per year. When inverted, this gives me one such case in 10,000 years. The question is, do I believe this? My feeling is that I don't. A check of UK road accident statistics shows me there are 2,000 fatalities each year on the roads at the time of writing, and 44,380,782 drivers.

This is 4.5×10^{-5} deaths per driver year, or 22,200 driver years between deaths. My earlier estimate is not far off the large-scale reality and I can easily change the estimate to reflect this, as shown in Figure 6.5. The result remains close to a –45° line.

From this point, it is a simple matter to locate representative Consequence Value points in each decade of the Consequence Value scale, as shown in Figure 6.5 and Table 6.2. There is no specific justification for choosing points such as £1,500, £15,000, £150,000, but some point is needed to represent the contribution to risk made by the intermediate data between the LLC and the LWC.

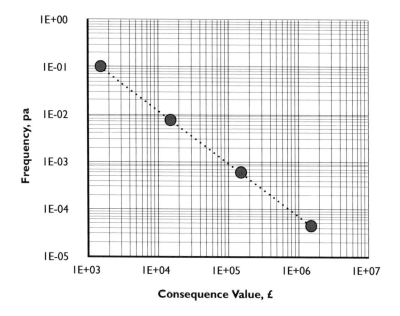

Figure 6.5   Estimating the Risk of car travel – Step Two

Table 6.2   Estimating my Risk in car travel

Frequency	Consequence Value	Risk, p.a.
1.00E−01	£1,500	£150
7.00E−03	£15,000	£105
5.00E 04	£150,000	£75
4.50E−05	£1,500,000	£67.50
	Total	£397.50

The resulting figure is uncannily close to my annual insurance premium of £414 at the time of writing, as I would expect.

What if I chose different representative points in each Consequence Value decade? Figure 6.6 and Table 6.3 show the effect of choosing differently. The estimated Risk has changed from £400 p.a. to £550 p.a. Perhaps this is a large percentage change, but the implications are negligible; I still know why my insurance premium is what it is. The relatively small size of this difference is due to the steep slope of the estimated Risk line: the flatter that slope the greater the effect of making different choices of intermediate Consequence Values.

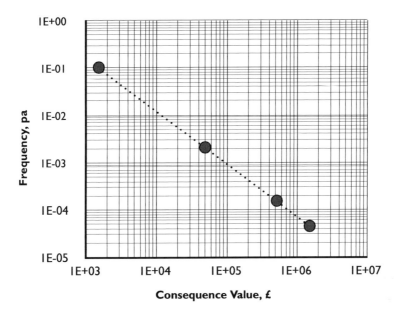

Figure 6.6   **Estimating the Risk of car travel using different representative Consequence Value points**

Table 6.3   **Estimating my Risk in car travel – changed Consequence Values**

Frequency	Consequence Value	Risk, p.a.
1.00E−01	£1,500	£150
2.00E−03	£50,000	£100
1.50E−04	£500,000	£75
4.50E−05	£5,000,000	£225
	Total	£550

To summarise the process illustrated by this example:

1. It is relatively easy to estimate the Exposure to the Risk in question.
2. The LLC and LWC are relatively easy to estimate.
3. Experience provides sufficient information to make a subjective estimate of the frequency of the LLC.
4. From this point, the probability of the LLC can be estimated. This is useful when efforts to reduce the risk are being assessed, see Chapter 7, but is of little relevance to the process of Risk estimation that follows from this point.
5. The LLC point on the Risk Diagram is used as the origin of a line of -45° slope to estimate the possible Frequency of the LWC. The inverse of the result is used to decide if the implied years between LWC experiences make any sense. In this case, I did not believe it. I was able to look at published statistics and determine that the result was actually not far from the community average. I changed the line to accord with this information.

6. Using this line (a locus of possible values of Frequency and Consequence Value) suitable values in the decade range of Consequence values between the LLC and the LWC are chosen and associated Frequency values read from the graph.
7. By multiplying the Frequency and Consequence Value pairs, a Risk contribution from each pair is obtained and then summed to produce a subjectively estimated total Risk value.

There are some variations on this process in practice, but the essential point is that the position and end points of the Risk line need to be estimated. One variation is when the LWC is something about which we have experience but there is no recorded information about the LLC. While unusual, this does happen. The process then is to work from the LWC point back towards the LLC, again using the iso-risk (–45°) line as a starting point. Examples of this in my experience are numerous and include the destruction of a cruise ship and loss of life following impact with a submerged rock, the loss of a space shuttle, the effects of a tsunami on a power station, large loss of life in a building collapse, a major oil spill in the ocean when a wellhead failed and the destruction of two aircraft with large loss of life in a runway collision.

When We Have No Experience of a Possible Consequence

A reasonable question is how such risks could have been estimated before the LWC cases mentioned above arose. Lack of experience of cases of damage need not be a complete hindrance to this. The first step is still to define the LLC and LWC. If we take a cruise ship hitting a rock as an example, it is not hard to think of the LWC as a hull loss with passenger deaths. Knowing the nature of the Occurrence, it is easy to see the LLC as a hull strike requiring berthing (and associated delay costs) to inspect the damage. If we assume the damage is assessed as a few scrapes that do not penetrate the hull it may be decided to continue operations but maintain a tighter watch over structural integrity. There will be costs associated with this, meeting with the maritime authorities, etc. It is not hard for someone working in the industry to decide what all this amounts to. For the sake of illustration, let us assume the LLC is £100,000 and that the LWC is £650 million (hull write-off, passenger deaths, lost business, etc.). We can now start to assemble a Risk Diagram with this information, as shown in Figure 6.7, which includes the LLC, LWC and some iso-risk lines.

In a curious way, the absence of experience of either the LLC or the LWC is a piece of information. If we assume that no one in this hypothetical cruise ship industry has ever heard of a grounding incident and that their collective memory goes back 25 years, we can feel reasonably justified (we could ask a statistician to give us a more formal indication of this) in assuming the likely Frequency of the LLC is neither 1 p.a. nor 0.1 p.a. This removes two iso-risk lines from the estimation. Do we then judge that the two possible LLC frequencies of 0.0001 p.a. (one in 10,000 years) or 0.001 p.a. (one in 1,000 years) are feasible? Probably not.

This leaves us with one iso-risk line, that which crosses the LLC line at 0.01 p.a. (one in 100 years). We could shift this up (or down) in accordance with judgement, because that is all we have in this case, to perhaps 0.02 p.a. (one in 50 years). If we leave it at 0.01 p.a., the iso-risk line indicates an LWC Frequency below 0.00001 p.a. (one in 100,000 years) and we can subject this to judgement: do we believe the LWC Frequency is likely to be of this order of magnitude, or does 0.0001 p.a. or 0.001 p.a. seem more plausible? In the absence of any data (and admitting to no inside knowledge of the cruise ship industry), I'd go for 0.001 p.a. – see Figure 6.8.

We now have a (very) subjective estimate of the Risk Diagram that may represent the potential for a cruise ship to strike an underwater object. An estimate of the Frequency of all possible Consequences and hence of the Risk can be derived from Figure 6.8, as shown in Table 6.4.

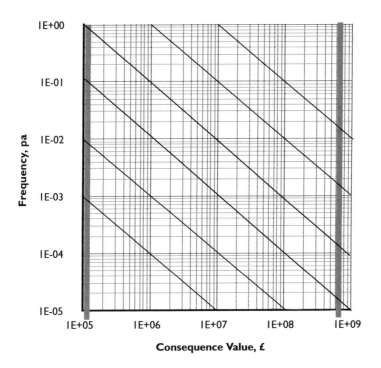

Figure 6.7   Cruise ship Risk estimation, zero data starting point

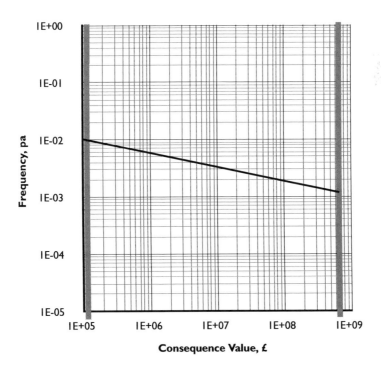

Figure 6.8   Cruise ship risk estimation, after application of judgement

Table 6.4   **Subjective total Frequency and Risk of cruise ship hull damage**

	Frequency, p.a.	Consequence Value	Risk, p.a.
	1.00E–02	£100,000	£1,000
	5.00E–03	£1,000,000	£5,000
	3.00E–03	£10,000,000	£30,000
	1.60E–03	£100,000,000	£160,000
	1.00E–03	£1,000,000,000	£1,000,000
Totals	2.06E–02		£1,196,000

A reasonable objection to this is that it is pure guesswork. With no knowledge of the shipping industry, it is. For someone with experience it is also guesswork, but to a much lesser extent. In any case, so is the choice of word scale options when faced with a risk matrix, but at least with real numbers, estimates can be checked against experience and judgement in a rational way.

A statistician would recognise that the lack of data over a period of time includes intrinsic information. If something has not happened over a period that includes 1,000 trials, for example, it seems unlikely that there is a one in five or ten chance of it happening, does it not? Quigley and Revie (2011) discuss the statistical implications of handling this problem, including the results of the efforts of others to solve this. They arrive at a simple conclusion, following an interesting and detailed theoretical derivation, that an estimate for the probability of the Consequence is given by the relationship

$p = 1/(2.5n)$,

where p is the probability of the Consequence occurring and n is the number of trials that have taken place to date without a Consequence. This assumes that each trial involves the same probability of a Consequence.

To illustrate the application of this, consider these assumptions about the cruise ship industry:

1. The industry has been operating in its present form for the last 30 years.
2. Between them, the cruise ship companies operate 100 cruises a year.
3. Each cruise has the same probability of striking an underwater obstacle, that is, the Exposures are alike.

The Exposure, n, is $30 \times 100 = 3,000$ [cruises].
The probability of a damage consequence occurring on a cruise is therefore estimated at

$p = 1/(2.5 \times 3,000) = 0.0001333 = 1.33 \times 10^{-4}$ [damage cases per cruise],

and the Frequency, f, at

$f = p \times n = 1.33 \times 10^{-4} \times 3,000 = 0.399$ [damage cases per year].

It is interesting to note that this is approximately ten times the result of my very subjective estimate in Table 6.4. My Risk Diagram could be modified to reflect this result. Now, if at the end of this period of 3,000 cruises, one such case arises of a grounding incident (for example the Costa Concordia incident of 2012), the estimate of the probability would become

$p = 1/3,001 = 3 \times 10^{-4}$ *[damage cases per cruise].*

Using Near Miss Experience

All of the estimates made above directly related the Frequency of Consequences and Consequence Values. A Consequence is simply the end of an Occurrence process that includes an Event and an Outcome pathway – see Chapter 3. The Event is often a point in time that is memorable (for example, a small fire starts in a workshop), because something has gone wrong and with serious implications. Many of these Events do not result in damaging Outcome pathways because control is regained quickly (an extinguisher is used) or the Outcome pathway is steered in a non-damaging direction (the fire is moved outside or away from other flammable materials). These experiences are commonly called near misses, but are more accurately termed Null Outcomes.

It is, fortunately, a matter of common experience that Events followed by Null Outcomes are more abundant than those followed by damaging Outcomes. The experience derived from these Events is more likely to be found in the memories of those close to the risk than in corporate data collections. Consequently, when Risk is being estimated there is no substitute for the time spent retrieving these recollections: for how long have you done this work and how many times have you experienced this Event in that period? I once needed this information when estimating the Risk associated with being hit by falling tree branches when felling trees in a forest. A questionnaire to all employed fellers asked them how long they had been employed in the industry and how often they had experienced tree branches falling when cutting a tree. The results were striking in their consistency and made it possible to make a good estimate of the Frequency of the experiences. Those with about 10 years of experience had been missed by falling branches once, with about 20 years twice and with about 30 years three times. By consulting industry production records, the exposure (numbers of trees felled per year) figure enabled the Frequency estimate to be turned into a probability figure. Having done this, the result was satisfyingly close to published fatality statistics collected over many decades.

QRA – Synthesising Risk Values

The process of QRA, which is this synthesising process, is the subject of Chapter 9. It suffices to say here that the Occurrence process can be mapped out in detail by understanding all the Mechanisms that could lead to the Event and understanding the various Outcome pathways that could then result. Risk analysis methods make use of logic diagrams suited to both of these stages in the Occurrence process. The logic diagrams provide a framework on which all the possibilities can be presented. The probability associated with each possibility can potentially be selected from failures in similar situations that have been subject to statistically significant methods of determining failure rates.

For example, it is possible to get lost (an Event) when using an electronic navigation system if the system fails. Such a system may never have been built before, but it will be made up of familiar components, including a power supply, an aerial, a gyroscope, signal processing and display electronics. As these components have been used in numerous other devices (for example and respectively: computers, radios, analogue inertial navigation systems, telephones, electronic displays of various sorts) it is likely that the components themselves have known failure modes and rates. Reliability mathematics is used to process failure data into failure probabilities with known statistical validity. Consequently, by knowing the logic of the processes used in the new navigation system it is possible to apply the failure probabilities of the components to predict the probability of the Event.

Our ability to do this successfully will depend on the adequacy of the model (the risk analysis) and the relevance of the probability values assigned to component failures. For example, we may have failure data for signal processing electronics, but not when these are used in the harsh environment of a fishing trawler in the North Sea.

Summary

The significance of a Risk is estimated to allow different Risks to be compared. The simplest way to compare the significance of different Risks is to estimate the LWC. Those Risks whose LWC is higher will attract attention because of higher legal and moral duty or other potentially serious implications such as major business interruption.

More completely, significance can be estimated qualitatively by applying judgement to word scales which describe the highs and lows of the relevant variables. The so-called "risk matrix" (actually a two-variable tabulation) is currently the most popular form of this. The apparent simplicity of this tool disguises underlying conceptual and design complexity which result in such significant structural and practical problems associated with its use, quite apart from the inherent subjectivity associated with any form of Risk estimation, that there is little justification for its use.

An alternative is to estimate the significance of a Risk by using real number scales, which exist for each of the relevant variables identified in Chapter 4. With real number scales, there exists the opportunity to check the result against experience and judgement through the estimation of Frequency and to use realistic estimates of Exposure and Consequence Values. Real number scales also make it possible to include in the estimation the reality of the range of Frequency and Consequence Values which are to be found in any Risk. This can be done even in the absence of any experience of the Risk.

The most rigorous method of estimation involves the development of a risk analysis model, which models all possible Mechanisms and Outcome pathways using logic diagrams to which component or action failure probability estimates can be applied.

7

Risk Control: Understanding Prevention and Cure

Introduction

Risk control is defined here, in a manner that follows naturally from the previous chapters, as anything that affects the Frequency or Consequence Value of a Risk. Risk mitigation is a popular and partly synonymous term, but the dictionary definition of mitigation is limited to the reduction of the severity of something adverse. The control of Risk involves much more than this and means anything that influences the value of the three basic variables of Probability (of a Mechanism, of an Outcome or of a Consequence Value), the possible Consequence Values themselves or the Exposure to the situation in which the Occurrence is possible. With this definition, any and all risks have existing controls, whether intentional or not. The risk controls associated with bare electrical conductors may be the lack of immediate exposure as well as common knowledge of the hazard and resulting high levels of caution when exposure is necessary. Something similar could be said about cliff-top walking paths. Removal of (for example fog envelops the cliff making its presence undetectable) or reduction in the effectiveness of a control (for example underage children approach the cliff without parental supervision) will result in an increase in the Risk, and vice versa.

The fact that we commonly seek improvements in controls (reducing Risk) does not deny the possibility of seeking to degrade existing controls. I have been involved in assisting an industry that historically was highly risk averse (due to political sensitivities around failing to deliver its services) to see what would be the likely effect of removing what had become seen as excessive (not cost-effective) risk control measures.

Some practitioners use the terms 'inherent risk' and 'residual risk'. The word inherent, meaning permanent and essential (OED), conveys the implication that nothing can be done to change the risk and so is an entirely inappropriate term to use for this purpose. Residual risk is simply the risk that remains after control measures have been put in place. As control measures are always in place, no matter how good or bad they are seen to be, all risk is residual at all times and there is no point in using the term. There is a current state of affairs, which is the current level of risk as we know it, and there is a changed level of risk after control measures have been changed. This may well change in the future as improved risk control measures are implemented.

Risk management practitioners are familiar with three types of risk control: insure, transfer and reduce. Buying insurance is an acceptance of the risk as it is and paying a relatively small annual premium to feel confident that if the LWC actually occurred it could be paid for. Transferring the responsibility for the risk is a control measure used when the risk has been evaluated (see Chapter 8) as too high under any Circumstances. Selling the process in which the risk exists, or subcontracting the process are ways of doing this. Reducing the risk is the possibility with which this chapter is mainly concerned – the systematic recognition of the possible types of control measures and their effects on an Occurrence and a Consequence.

Risk control measures are features of Enabling and Concluding Conditions and Circumstances (see Chapter 3). Imagination and experience can be used to identify risk control measures, but a specialist needs to use a structured method to ensure that all possibilities have been identified for consideration. Knowing what control types are possible in principle is helpful in understanding how suitable existing control measures are and what opportunities exist for improvement of them. Determining whether existing control measures are sufficient in themselves or whether proposed control measures are justifiable is the process of evaluation of a Risk, which is the subject of the next chapter.

A systematic approach can be based on a number of different ways of looking at types of risk controls. This chapter considers in detail two major classes of control measures:

- Class A control measures, being control measures over the Damage or Loss process. These are evident from detailed consideration of the EDM (or TVM), TSM and Risk theory.
- Class B control measures, being the organisational practices required to support Class A control measures.

There are two essential qualities required of control measures: they must be effective as control measures (effective Class A control measures have been used) and they must be reliable and so capable of doing their job predictably over time (as a result of organisational support, Class B control measures, for them).

Class A: Control Measures in the Energy Damage Model

The value of the energy damage concept in making it possible to develop a structured list of control measures was recognised by Haddon (1973). Table 7.1 is inspired by Haddon's approach but uses the EDM of Figure 3.1 to provide the structure: it is an expansion of the control measure tables in Chapter 3.

Table 7.1   Risk control measures derived from the Energy Damage Model

Control measure on:	Description and classification	Typical effect of control
Energy source	Eliminate the energy	
	EC1 Remove the energy completely, e.g. do not use a toxic substance	Damage or loss from this source is impossible – there is no risk
	Reduce the amount of energy	
	EC2 Reduce the amount of energy available for the Event, e.g. store smaller quantities of hazardous materials, limit the maximum pressure or torque in powered mechanisms, active reduction in power, speed, pressure, etc. if a Recipient approaches the damaging energy space	Consequence Value is reduced

Hazard control mechanism	Reduce the probability that the Event will occur (alter the Mechanism probability)	
	MC1 Reduce the rate of deterioration of the physical properties of the system that would enable an Event to occur, e.g. design improvements, preventive maintenance, enhanced control systems	Probability of failure is reduced (reliability improved)
	MC2 Reduce the rate of deterioration of compliance with required methods and practices of human interaction with the system through better-informed, -educated and -trained people, more suitable work methods more likely to foster compliance	Probability of failure is reduced (reliability improved)
	MC3 Reduce the occurrence of unusual situations or improve the likely success of people faced with responding to them using knowledge to analyse the situation and determine what to do, e.g. remove the need for non-routine types of operation of the system (for example testing and proving) or carefully predict and pre-plan activities associated with non-routine types of operation	Probability of failure is reduced (reliability improved)
	MC4 Reduce the probability of the system being subject to conditions that exceed its intended and designed for capabilities, e.g. restriction of vehicle loads on bridges, speed restrictions on railways and bridges	Overload Mechanism probability is reduced
Space transfer mechanism	Remove or redirect the vulnerability pathway (modify the Outcome) when energy is released	
	OC1 Divert the energy transfer pathway (allow the energy release to continue but direct it away from susceptible assets), e.g. blast barriers, flying particle screens, explosion containment, barriers around robotic machinery to prevent runaway arms encroaching on the operator's space, extraction ventilation, smoke control doors, water sprinklers	Probability of a damaging Outcome pathway is reduced or removed
	OC2 Interrupt the energy transfer mechanism (stop the energy release from occurring, including absorption of energy and prevention of changes of energy form in the Outcome pathway), e.g. noise transmission barrier, radiation barriers, vibration isolation, Faraday cage for electromagnetic field interruption, fire compartmentalisation in buildings, fire water sprinkler systems, fall arrest devices	Probability of a damaging Outcome pathway is reduced or removed or Consequence Value is reduced

Table 7.1   Risk control measures derived from the Energy Damage Model (*concluded*)

Control measure on:	Description and classification	Typical effect of control
	OC3 Increase the distance between the energy source and the Recipient in order to decrease the intensity of energy at the recipient's boundary, e.g. distance between electric transmission lines and houses, between motorways and houses, between people and noise sources and heat sources	Consequence Value is reduced
	OC4 Schedule movements of the energy source, e.g. traffic intersection sequencing controls, maintaining separation distances (arguably this could also be regarded as a Mechanism probability change)	Probability of a damaging Outcome pathway is reduced or removed
	Remove or redirect the vulnerability pathway when the Recipient moves towards the damaging energy space	Probability of a damaging Outcome pathway is reduced or removed
	OC5 Schedule movements of the Recipient, e.g. traffic intersection sequencing controls, maintaining separation distances (arguably this could also be regarded as a Mechanism probability change)	
	OC6 Block the movement of the Recipient, e.g. fixed fences and guards	
Recipient's boundary	Protect the asset	Consequence Value is reduced
	RC1 Strengthen the 'boundary' of the Recipient, e.g. personal protective equipment, tornado- and earthquake-proof buildings, corrosion-proofing	
Recipient	Remove the asset from the vulnerability pathway	Exposure is reduced or removed
	RC2 Remove the Recipient (asset) from the environment in which they could be affected, e.g. use robots to assemble car bodies, remotely controlled mining machines, explosion sniffer robots	
	Reduce the exposure of the asset to the threat	
	RC3 Limit the amount of time for which the asset is exposed or the number of instances of exposure to the environment in which they could be affected, e.g. time limits for unprotected ears, for exposure to a radiation environment, the number of deep water dives made per day	

For convenience of reference to Table 7.1 in the following discussion, each possibility is given an identifier. MC1, for example, refers to Mechanism Control Type 1, and so on. The underlying logic to Table 7.1 is very simple and the various situations described and examples used are for illustration rather than explicit definition.

If there is no energy (EC1 – Remove the energy completely) then the Occurrence process derived from it cannot exist and the probability of Damage is zero, meaning Damage is not possible. If the energy is reduced in magnitude (EC2 – Reduce the amount of energy available for the Event) then in principle the possible severity of the Consequence is reduced. For example, if the energy source of interest is speed, then reduction of kinetic energy can be brought about by reducing speed or reducing mass. Of course, there may not be a direct relationship between Consequence Value and the amount of energy: if you're travelling at 180 mph in a car, reducing speed to 150 mph does not necessarily reduce the amount of damage done if you hit a tree, as the energy quantity is probably well over the threshold for maximum damage anyway. Reducing speed in this case may actually improve the reliability of one of the control measures (for example the driver's capability) rather than reduce the damage potential.

In the majority of real-world cases, all the decisions about energy forms and energy quantities are decided by process designers long before any construction occurs and so these control measure strategies are mostly valuable for designers and those managing construction or implementation of the business process. Consider as an example the erection of a large steel-framed building. If the frame is erected before the steelwork had its final coat of paint a number of people will have to work at height painting it. This energy source could be removed, or at the very least the Exposure to it very much diminished (fewer people for less time touching up welds and bolts) by painting it at ground level before erection.

Reduction of the probability of Mechanisms is by changes made in Time Zone 1. Time Zone 1, it will be recalled from Chapter 3, is the here and now of our day-to-day experience of the Conditions and Circumstances in which the risk exists. The underlying categories of Mechanisms have been explained in Table 3.5. In Table 7.1 the MC1 (Reduce the rate of deterioration of the physical properties of the system that would enable an Event to occur) examples are limited to a typical industrial situation in which Mechanisms are failures in some quality of physical equipment or of the control system, which can include the role that people play in managing the equipment or the process for which the equipment is used. Equipment can suffer from deterioration of its relevant qualities over time (for example structural strength of steelwork deteriorates due to rust) or from exposure to 'stresses' beyond those for which it was designed (for example a structure is subject to loads beyond its design conditions). It is convenient to think of 'deterioration' and 'overload' when looking for these Mechanisms. Sometimes both can occur at the same time (see the example of a heavily loaded and corroded coal conveyor given in the introduction to Chapter 5). These control measures include equipment renewal, maintenance and inspection practices. In Accident Theory, Unsafe Conditions (Latent Failures) are cases found to be deficient when compared with an ideal standard, usually in hindsight.

Risk may also be affected by the way in which people behave. MC2 (Reduce the rate of deterioration of compliance with required methods and practices of human interaction with the system) is concerned with control measures intended to maintain or increase the conformity of people with a desired standard of behaviour. Examples of MC2 include training, education, skill, competency and experience requirements as well as the design of person–equipment/process interfaces. This is a huge subject and in order to not treat it lightly, the risk specialist needs to understand human capability, human variation and human performance deterioration (for example due to fatigue, distraction, lack of arousal). It is also necessary to recognise that each of the three different types of human activity (physical, perceptual or mental) involve different human capabilities and also that they are able to interact in possibly complex ways. A significant body of relevant science has been built up since the end of World War Two. In Accident Theory, Unsafe Acts (Active Failures) are things people have done or have not done that are found to be deficient when compared with an ideal standard, usually in hindsight.

One way to look at MC1 and MC2 is as separate features of process design: the equipment is like this and so people need to behave like that. A better way is to see these as interactive, so that process design features (MC1) reflect what people are more likely to do (MC2) and are also able to cope without disastrous Consequences when people (predictably) fail to do what is expected of them. As a generalisation, it can be said that people are far less reliable and predictable than machines. Human behaviour, however, is subject to complex influences. In some cases people are capable of extraordinary feats of perfect performance but in other cases error can be expected to be frequent and not easily predicted. Many texts have been and continue to be written on this subject and they range from the overview (Kletz, 2001) to the detailed and specialist text (Hollnagel, 1998).

MC3 (Reduce the occurrence of unusual situations or improve the likely success of people faced with responding to them) draws attention to another way in which people interact with complex environments. When:

- faced with a previously unseen requirement, one for which training has not been provided or for which experience has not been gained, or
- which requires a set of responses unique to the Circumstances being faced,

people need to decide what to do on the basis of their knowledge of the system or of the principles on which the system operates. People have difficulty solving problems from first principles when faced with competing demands for their attention, for example from control system error messages and unrelated communications. The success of their analysis and subsequent action can only be judged in retrospect. This has a lot in common with being faced with a new emergency, but here it is concerned only with Mechanisms of Events.

MC4 (Reduce the probability of the system being subject to conditions that exceed its intended and designed for capabilities) is concerned with avoiding situations in which a system is subject to an overload of its capabilities and avoiding the imposition of demands for which a system was not designed or intended.

Space transfer mechanism controls are to do with the prevention, diversion or sequencing of relative movements of either the energy or the Recipient or both. It is the space transfer process that is an aspect of the Outcome in the Time Sequence Model. This process sometimes includes changes of energy form, the most spectacular of which occurs in explosions when chemical bonding energy (the Energy associated with the Event) is released to be carried away from the source in heat and shock waves, light and sound, as well as the kinetic energy of flying particles, which themselves may carry heat or other energy sources, such as ionising radiation sources. Consequently, control measures of various types may be used in the Outcome pathway. Energy flows from the source to the Recipient or the movement of a Recipient towards an energy source can be influenced by diversion of the flow (OC1 – Divert the energy transfer pathway), by interruption (including absorption of energy, as in application of brakes on moving vehicles or the use of arrestor hooks on aircraft) of the flow (OC2 – Interrupt the energy transfer mechanism) or by increasing the distance between radiant sources and the Recipient (OC3 – Increase the distance between the energy source and the Recipient). In the latter case, as the distance increases the intensity of energy incident on the Recipient diminishes according to the inverse square (line sources of energy) or inverse cube (point sources of energy) of the distance.

Sequencing controls (OC4 – Schedule movements of the energy source and OC5 – Schedule movements of the Recipient) are appropriate to mobile energy sources and/or mobile Recipients and are familiar in vehicular movement (traffic controls at road and rail/road intersections and air traffic control) as well as in powered machinery where a person or part of them moves in and out of a damaging energy space (for example, no hand entry until de-energised, no re-energisation until the hand is out). OC6 (Block the movement of the Recipient) is simply the case of a fixed means of preventing incursion of a Recipient into the damaging energy space (for example crash barriers keep spectators from entering race tracks).

The boundary of the Recipient can be strengthened (RC1 – Strengthen the 'boundary' of the Recipient) so that it is able to withstand the intensity of energy to which it is subject without damage or with reduced damage – see Chapter 3 for a discussion of this. Examples include the use of skin, respiratory, eye and hearing protection, corrosion prevention coatings, vibration isolation of sensitive electronics, heat shields on equipment, impact damage protection on spacecraft. The precise logic of this classification for personal protective equipment can be questioned. Respiratory protection blocks the entry of the noxious substance en route to the susceptible organ (the lung, liver, etc.) rather than increasing the damage threshold of the organ as such. However, since it is worn by the Recipient, it appears to change their damage threshold. The Recipient could be removed (RC2) from the Outcome pathway altogether or the amount of time spent in the Outcome pathway can be reduced (RC3).

Class A: Control Measures in the Time Sequence Model

By providing a time-based structure to the Occurrence process, the TSM (Chapter 3) draws attention to time-based aspects of control measures that are not necessarily evident in the EDM. Tables 3.8, 3.9 and 3.10 list control measures in the three different time zones of the TSM. It is therefore convenient here to use the TSM to recognise possible active control measures, that is control measures that are able to respond to the Occurrence process as it is happening. As the Occurrence unfolds, there is an opportunity to detect and react to the imminently damaging Conditions and so avoid the damage by exerting some active control over the Mechanism, the energy or the Outcome and Consequence. These could be categorised as active control, avoidance or protection, respectively. Thinking of control measures in this way is particularly suited to situations that are amenable to the detection of Occurrences in progress and for which timely reaction is possible. Table 7.2 expands on the Time Zone 2 control measure possibilities in Table 3.9, in which each possibility is given an identifier. AMC1, for example, refers to Active Mechanism Control Type 1.

Table 7.2   Time Zones 2 and 3 active risk control measures (energy source external to Recipient)

Control measure on:	Description and classification	Effect of control
Mechanism (Active Control)	Where Mechanism types are predictable, efforts can be made to recognise when they are occurring and to actively intervene	Reduces the probability of an Event
	AMC1 Recognition of the presence and accumulation of Mechanism risk factors	
	AMC2 Automated Mechanism detection through sensing with associated information processing, either automated or by human review	

	AMC3 Manual Mechanism detection through testing and inspection protocols	
Event (Active avoidance)	Dynamically recover control before an Outcome has had the time to develop	Damaging Outcome pathway is avoided
	AEC1 Enable a dynamic recovery to a stable situation (permanent recovery)	
	AEC2 Enable a dynamic recovery to a metastable situation (temporary recovery)	
Outcome (Active avoidance)	Dynamically modify the Outcome pathway(s)	Reduces the damaging potential of the Outcome pathway
	AOC1 Actively interrupt energy type changes	
	AOC2 Actively interrupt energy flow	
	AOC3 Actively direct energy flow away from Recipients	
Consequence (Active protection)	Dynamically modify the Consequence Value	Reduces Consequence Value
	ACC1 Remove recipients from the Outcome pathway	
	ACC2 Protect recipients from the incident energies	
	ACC3 Restore recipients	

AMC1 (Recognition of the presence and accumulation of Mechanism risk factors) draws attention to the possibility of physically monitoring the Enabling Conditions and Circumstances in Time Zone 1 to provide a warning of the impending existence of or potential for an Event Mechanism or the increase in its probability. This control measure is particularly relevant to air transport operations as in a sense there is no such thing as a normal flight owing to the significance of Circumstance on each and every flight. Pilots adhere to strict procedures and checklists in order to ensure that routine compliance is an organising overlay on the disturbances of Circumstance. Flight crew capability, weather and visibility conditions, the serviceability of onboard and remote navigation equipment, the presence of other traffic, air traffic control clearance changes, etc. are all Time Zone 1 phenomena and all are subject to change with little or no notice. It is not hard to collate a set of these that clearly has the making of a Mechanism: imagine a tired crew, poor weather, unserviceable navigation equipment at the destination aerodrome, sudden changes of clearance by the controllers and the potential for a Mechanism associated with the primary energy source of this industry (kinetic energy) is not hard to imagine. An active control measure here is one that is able to recognise the collection of adverse Conditions and Circumstances and intervene in some way to ensure control is retained. In many cases, this is the role of the third pilot, who has the job of monitoring the work of the crew members flying the aircraft.

Consider this hypothetical case, which illustrates the way Circumstances may unfold in the flight and the nature of control measures. An aircraft approaches a holiday destination airport at a busy time. The approach to the duty runway requires a steep descent from high mountainous terrain. The air traffic controller directs the crew to fly an unusually lengthy entry into the traffic pattern, which consumes more fuel than is normally required. On this occasion also the Instrument Landing System (ILS) transmitter at the airport is unserviceable. The ILS provides pilots with an indication of their position both with respect to the centreline of the runway and their position relative to the glide slope down to the runway threshold. In the absence of the ILS signal, the crew are only able to use the VOR (VHF omnidirectional radio). The VOR is a radio signal that provides a readout in the cockpit of the position on the compass rose of the aircraft in relation to the airport's VOR transmitter. The task of flying a specific approach aligned with the centreline of the runway is made more difficult (the VOR transmitter is not at the end of any one runway) and there is no guidance given by instruments as to the position of the aircraft in relation to the glide slope. The steepness of the approach makes it more difficulty to attain a stable speed. Flying a stable approach (stable speed, lateral and vertical positioning) in this situation is not easy. On the first attempt and in accordance with established procedures the Captain calls for a go-around because of an unstable approach. The air traffic controller is now faced with a disturbance to the order of the incoming flights and directs the pilots to climb and fly away from the airfield but offers them no indication of his plan for the airliner to rejoin the traffic pattern. Attempts by the crew to be told what the plan is are unfruitful and it seems that the controller's English is perhaps not suited to trying to communicate in these Circumstances. The long entry into the traffic pattern, the subsequent go-around and climb to an unusually high altitude consumed a lot of fuel and the crew become concerned about fuel state and their distance from the airport. They are eventually able to assert their needs over the radio to the point where they are cleared to rejoin the traffic pattern and are able to land, but unusually close to having to make use of statutory reserve fuel content. Use of this reserve fuel is a trigger for the declaration of an emergency. This narrative is of a complete Occurrence, right through to a Null Outcome in that no actual damage was done. The Event, when routine ends and expectations start to not be met (perhaps most easily thought of as the 'Oh dear!' moment) is when the crew are required to fly a long and fuel-consuming initial circuit. It is at this point that the routine ends and two expectations become significant: that the controller will provide landing clearance quickly and that the aircraft can land on the first approach. Neither of these expectations are met and for the aircraft's fuel state not to become critical the next approach must be stable as there is insufficient fuel for a second go-around. The probability of the go-around became high due to the combination of high terrain on the approach and the lack of ILS assistance. The Mechanism of the Event is the act of the controller in not providing an expected fast inclusion into the traffic pattern and possibly seems innocuous enough not to be recognised as a Mechanism as such. For the airline and the pilots, AMC1 efforts are having skilful and experienced pilots and possibly rules about the acceptability of flights into such airfields in the presence of failed equipment on the ground. For the air traffic controllers, AMC1 efforts are to have acceptable pre-considered and specific air traffic control procedures to minimise fuel burn in the approach pattern at busy times and for handling missed approaches, possibly including rules to ensure an adequate number of controllers are on duty at busy times. An acceptable (to the airlines) standard routine for handling missed approaches on any of the possible runway directions is an Outcome control measure. For the operators of navigational aids, given the criticality of ILS in such a place, AMC1 is concerned with rapid response to ILS failures, possibly including the provision of backup equipment. The fact that nine out of ten or even 99 out of 100, or 999 out of 1000, etc. aircraft manage to land first time is irrelevant to any decision-making given the significant LWC. Rather, decisions need to be made using the imagination to predict what the accident enquiry would say in the event that the hypothetical Occurrence ended with loss of an aircraft and all on board. Not much imagination is required.

The management of public health is another example. The prerequisites of many diseases (that is, how they are linked to Time Zone 1 features such as age, lifestyle, nutrition) are well known and described as Risk Factors (see Chapter 5). It is feasible to recognise where those Risk Factors are collected together in an adverse way and assume that a relevant Mechanism is under way even if the Mechanism itself is not precisely understood.

In mechanical systems, measuring the ambient Conditions which support deterioration in materials comes into this category. For example, vibration measurement, air contamination measurement, heat, humidity, etc.

In AMC2 (Automated Mechanism detection through sensing) and AMC3 (Manual Mechanism detection through testing and inspection) there is the potential to recognise an actual Mechanism that is in progress and intervene to interrupt it. It is necessary to detect and respond sufficiently rapidly to prevent further development of the Mechanism, assuming that is possible. Examples are:

- crack and creep detection in metals; rates of crack length growth are able to be predicted and the time scale from inception to full fracture is often measured in months or even years (AMC2);
- detection of rot in timber, corrosion in metals and delamination in composite materials;
- contamination by solid particles or dissolved gas in oils;
- vibration monitoring in rotating or reciprocating machinery;
- acoustic monitoring of crack initiation in high pressure steam pipes;
- wall thickness measurement in structures (for example pipes) subject to corrosion or erosion;
- preventive health assessments by blood and other tests to see if there is any indication of the precursors of or presence of diseases.

Where faster Mechanisms exist, it is necessary to have faster detection and response measures, possibly including automation (AMC2).

AEC1 (Enable a dynamic recovery to a stable situation) and AEC2 (Enable a dynamic recovery to a metastable situation) are quite common where people are driving, flying and walking but it is not limited to this. There is an instantaneous recognition that an Event has occurred and if an instinctive reaction is possible and correct, then the instability can be rectified. The presence of an Event is an indication that control (over the potentially damaging properties of the energy source) has been lost (a Mechanism has occurred) albeit briefly. For example:

- A foot slips, a handrail is grasped and a fall (Outcome) is avoided.
- A car slides on the road, the driver corrects the slide and directs the car away from obstacles.
- An aeroplane wing stalls in a turn and the pilot instantly (quickly enough in the Circumstances) makes the correct control inputs to recover normal flight.
- Railway carriages have become unhitched but a secondary braking system automatically brings the carriages to a halt.

In these cases the instantaneous nature of the response ensures that an Outcome pathway has not had time to develop.

In all cases, the recovery may be to a permanent state of stability (AEC1) or into a fragile state of stability (AEC2 – metastable) in which a further disturbance can produce either an unstable or stable state: the slipping person may have arrested an incipient fall but still be on a very slippery surface in which a slip remains an imminent possibility.

In mechanical systems, examples of AEC1 or AEC2 include:

- Overpressure controllers (pressure relief valves). The pressure has risen above normal operating values but a relief valve opens to ensure that the pressure remains below the point at which a structural failure would occur. The reason for the rise in pressure (the Mechanism) has not been influenced in any way by this, it is just being responded to by ensuring that the energy level is brought back into control and so does not reach the point of a damaging Outcome.
- Rotational speed controllers. A steam turbine can overspeed rapidly with disastrous consequences if the main steam valve opens suddenly or the electrical load on the generator is suddenly lost (Mechanisms). The speed governor operates to stop this happening.

There is an opportunity once the Event has taken place to influence the way in which the Outcome unfolds. Depending on the source energy, energy type changes may occur in the Outcome pathway. A chemical explosion (chemical bonding energy) is the most prolific generator of different energy types – heat (possibly followed by further combustion), light and pressure waves and kinetic energy of flying particles. When gravitational potential energy is released the most common energy form transformation is to kinetic energy. The possibilities for all Event types have previously been analysed (Viner, 1991). AOC1 (Actively interrupt energy type changes) means that the production of other energy forms is minimised or removed by an active response to the release of energy in the explosion. Examples of AOC1 include:

- explosion overpressure relief doors in ducts handling dusts;
- blast-actuated water deluge;
- inert gas flooding of electronic equipment rooms;
- dumping of transformer oil on detection of initiation of an explosion and insertion of an inert atmosphere.

Active noise control is a good example of AOC2 (Actively interrupt energy flow), which is otherwise rare. In active noise control, a pressure wave (the unwanted noise) is sensed and (relatively) instantly countered by a pressure wave of opposite sign. Another example is the building of firebreaks in front of wild fires to interrupt progress towards valuable assets.

Examples of AOC3 (Actively direct energy flow away from Recipients) are easy to find and include:

- active opening of smoke control louvres in the roofs of turbine halls in power stations;
- active operation of extraction fans to remove fumes when these are generated by a fire or chemical process;
- active operation of smoke control doors and fire isolation doors in buildings.

Active Consequence modification is a familiar form of control measure. ACC1 (Remove recipients from the Outcome pathway) includes evacuation of people or removing assets from the path of a fire. ACC2 (Protect recipients from the incident energies) means the application of protective equipment when people are exposed to energies in the Outcome pathway. Examples include:

- self-rescuers in mines (personal air supply when air becomes unbreathable due to fire in the mine);
- smoke hoods used by flight attendants in the event of an aircraft cabin fire;
- the use of breathing apparatus by emergency response crews;
- the use of a water spray shield on fire trucks to protect them and the crew when trapped by fire.

ACC3 (Restore recipients) incorporates all the efforts made to treat and rehabilitate affected people and to restore other assets to their previous state, such as repair and replacement, clean-up of contaminants, etc.

Class A: Control Measures in the Risk Model

The one variable not explicitly mentioned in the EDM and TSM is that of Exposure, defined in Chapter 4 as the number of times per year that the situation arises within which an Occurrence could occur. Decreasing this number is a risk control measure. For example, if a person has to climb a ladder once per month in order to inspect something, extend the interval between inspections to once in three or four months.

EFFECTS OF CLASS A CONTROL MEASURES ON THE RISK DIAGRAM

Changes to control measures, whether in the EDM, the TSM or the Risk Model, have various different effects on Risk and consequently change the Risk Diagram in different ways, as shown in Figure 7.1. In Case A, the Event Frequency has been reduced, by Mechanism probability reduction or by Exposure reduction or both, or a change has been made to Outcome probabilities that equally affects all Outcome pathways. In Case B, the probability of an LWC has been reduced by reducing the probability of Outcome pathways that lead to the LWC. In Case C, only the value of the LWC has been reduced.

ORGANISATIONAL SUPPORT FOR CLASS A CONTROL MEASURES

The preceding detail is a useful aide to comprehensively identifying risk control possibilities, which, following the work, can be summarised. Reliability mathematics (see chapter 10) makes it clear that the functional reliability of any component depends on the interval between inspections of the component, the purpose of which is to check that the component is working and to repair it if not.

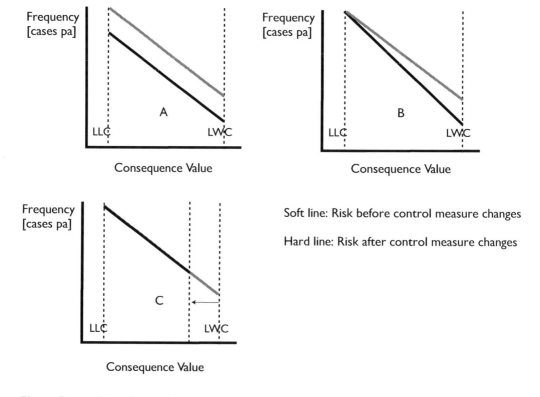

Figure 7.1 **The effects of different control measures on the Risk Diagram**

The same principles applies to behavioural control measures. We may conclude that any control measure is only as good as the inspection and maintenance activities which support it. Hence, an essential, though often neglected step, is to identify the organisational supports Class A control measures need if they are to be reliable rather than just effective when first implemented. Organisational supports, which can also be called administrative risk control measures, are identified specifically to support Class A control measures and include, by way of example:

deciding knowledge, skill, experience and information requirements;

defining and promoting work methods, restrictions and exclusions, performance standards etc. where relevant and appropriate;

evaluating the extent of conformance or achievement of the above;

determining the content and frequency of inspections of physical facilities and evaluating the outcome of them;

reviewing the above and using the results to modify expectations and optimise results to improve the effectiveness and reliability of the Class A control measures.

Organisational supports are indispensable. An example was given above for Class A control measure type AMC1, involving an aircraft landing with minimal fuel contents above the required reserve following an unusual experience approaching an airport with failed landing aids. The airline established rules for determining fuel requirements suited to individual destinations. The obvious Class A control measure this supports is that aircraft will always have enough fuel to complete the flight. The intent of all flights is to not need to use reserve fuel. By definition, the use of reserve fuel means things have gone wrong. Because the carriage of unnecessary fuel is a burden to a cost sensitive industry, operational efficiency is improved by minimising fuel carried above the required reserve in excess of that needed to complete a normal flight. This results in the rule given to pilots.

Any control system, even a risk control measure, requires the setting of a standard and the monitoring of system performance to that standard. If system performance is not what is required the system is changed to achieve a better result. In the context of this example, Class A support measures must include monitoring the actual fuel states of aircraft arriving at each destination to assess the extent to which they are approaching the limiting fuel state of required reserve fuel. Approaching the reserve fuel contents but not actually using them is an indication of success. However, the extent of this success needs to be monitored and evaluated carefully: the more arrivals close to the minimum fuel contents, the more likely it is that one will arrive having had to declare an emergency.

It is the nature of Risk that systems mostly perform as expected. If a performance standard is able to be defined that represents the limits of what is regarded as acceptable, the well managed organisation monitors Class A controls and their support measures to this standard. Then, when the standard is breached one can truly say there was a failure. This is proper management and is quite different from an investigation uncovering an 'unsafe' condition or action only after serious damage has been incurred in the operation of a system whose performance has not been monitored. Performance monitoring is aimed at noting the unacceptable tendency to approach the limit and determining the Class A control measure and support m improvements needed before the unwanted incident occurs. This can truly be said to be preventive activity.

Table 7.3 illustrates Class A control and support measures for chemical hazards.

Table 7.3   Organisational support for Class A control measures – illustrated for chemical hazards

Class A Controls	Support for Class A controls
Storage facilities –	Information on hazardous properties
1. separation of incompatibles and of empty and full containers	Training in the selection, use and care of personal protective equipment
2. maximum quantities	Training in transportation, storage, handling and
3. containment – bunds	disposal practices
4. containers	Work permit procedures
5. ventilation	Chemical register
Eye washes and showers	Chemical purchasing, transportation, storage,
Personal protective equipment	handling and disposal procedure
Change rooms	Emergency procedures
Defined work methods (transportation, storage,	Equipment and facility maintenance and inspection
handling and disposal)	practices

SUMMARY OF CLASS A CONTROL MEASURES

The numerous ways in which Class A control measures and their organisational supports are identified obscures an essential underlying simplicity. All such controls measures fall into one of three categories:

controls on physical and environmental risk factors;

controls over the way work is done;

administrative controls.

Administrative controls include all the necessary support influences to give effect to 1 and 2 above and the essential monitoring of performance.

Class B: Control Measures as Part of the Business Process

The influence of the organisation within which a Risk exists cannot be ignored. There are three significant points in the life of an organisation when Class A control measures and their supporting requirements need to be considered:

a) when planning future changes (importing Risks);
b) when changes actually happen (importing Risks);
c) when reviewing the adequacy of the status quo (managing present Risks).

Most of what organisations experience now are Risks that have been imported in years gone by with little explicit awareness of the intended Class A control measures or the requirements that existed for organisational support of them. That is, there has been endemic inactivity at points (a) and (b). Needless to say, this gives rise over time to a large backlog of problems, so that there is a large need at point (c). In an accident-oriented culture, this need may only be recognised or given any attention when an accident occurs. Risk controls may have been adequate at the time of commissioning, but over time regulations, codes of practice, technology and common industry practice change, not to mention the likely slow or fast deterioration of the Class A controls, management practices and organisational supports for the Class A control measures put in place in the early days.

Consider, for example, an organisation using powered conveyors for the transport of coal. Since commissioning, some 20 years previously, no efforts have been made to check the standards of design with modern conveyor safety standards. In the harsh environment, a fence around a take-up pulley has suffered from corrosion and impact with site vehicles. The gate provided in it swings a little insecurely on its hinges and is generally propped open by the cleaning contractors, as there is a regular need to clean up the fine material that falls off the belt as it runs around the pulley. This cleaning is done when it suits the cleaners, including when the conveyor is running. There was once a lock on the gate latch. If you know anything of machinery safety for conveyor systems it will be evident that this is a potential death risk (that is, the LWC is a fatality). The required control measure is a management system to ensure that cleaning is only done when the conveyor is stopped: an access permit system is needed in conjunction with an energy isolation practice. This requirement can only be communicated to the contract cleaners through the contract specification. The physical standard of the fence needs to be maintained, as does the ability to lock the gate. These remain responsibilities of the site owner/occupier and create an obligation that can only be satisfied through site maintenance practices. The gate must be locked when cleaning is not being done: this practice of the cleaners should periodically be checked to ensure that the practice is being followed. This simple case illustrates how control measures involve the procurement department (who determine the cleaning contract), production management (checking on the practices of the cleaners) and the maintenance department (ensuring the physical standards of the fence and gate are maintained). These requirements should have been recognised at the point that the site operators assumed control after the commissioning process. Management practices should have ensured all these requirements were being satisfied in the 20 years since commissioning. All this is highly improbable in a typical organisation and it had certainly not happened in the organisation in question. Since no accident had occurred here, the organisation was entirely unaware of it as a risk. In another organisation, an identical situation had resulted in the death of a cleaner. An accident-oriented organisation waits for accidents to alert it to problems. A risk-oriented organisation conducts reviews of the status quo.

Apart from fighting a rearguard action against the ravages of time, the risk advisers to this (and any other organisation) need to be alert to the changes being made to the organisation by the expansion of production facilities, upgrading to new technology (for example automated controls), decisions made in purchasing (for example new chemicals) and in reduction in manpower and the greater use of contractors (as in the example above), and so on. All these changes influence the nature of risk and the effects of control measures. Hence, organisational risk control measures need to be reassessed at an early point in the process of making change happen.

Organisational risk control points (a) and (b) need the inclusion of risk assessment at whatever stages the organisation makes use of in the development and implementation of change, whether that be the consideration of very large projects or relatively routine changes to equipment and consumables. Such risk assessment can be given whatever name is best suited to indicate at which stage in the process of considering new ideas they are used, for example preliminary risk assessment, project risk assessment, design risk assessment and so on. The earlier in the process, the less specific and detailed the assessment. The organisation will undoubtedly have processes to review financial, market, legal and environmental aspects of change, which will be increasingly detailed as the project moves on from preliminary to more detailed stages of assessment. Risk aspects need to be treated with just as much seriousness. The process of acceptance and approval which is needed to advance a project to the point of implementation needs to include a sign-off by the risk adviser at each stage. A further assessment at stage (b) above is required because stage (a) defines what is intended and at the point of delivery the organisation finds out what has actually been delivered. In one large organisation a plant extension went through major planning processes suited to the large investment, from which risk advisers were excluded, despite their clamour for involvement. After commissioning, the new plant was handed over to the operators and a major and very expensive refit was found to be needed immediately to suit the most basic of practical operational safety requirements. In another organisation, risk advisers were excluded from the largest public building project the organisation was likely to experience in a generation or more, in the belief that lawyers had completed adequate risk assessments at a preliminary stage in the project definition and that the constructors had done similar. The legal advisers had conducted adequate risk assessment of legal, commercial, cultural and heritage risks, as might be expected, but the project advanced to a significant degree before it was even recognised that the organisation was importing a public liability risk.

While examples have been given of major projects to illustrate the use of risk assessment at points (a) and (b) above, the same can be said of the need to consider even small changes in the same way. Changing from using employees to contractors for certain tasks can have significant implications, as has been made clear in the example above. Installing a new and larger printing machine in a dedicated room meant that in the event of a fire the power could not be turned off as the machine was so large as to block access to the power control. The purchase of new ride-on mowers by a grounds management organisation resulted in a rollover on a slope as the interaction of the new form of mower with the terrain had not been considered. It is generally very easy to predict and understand an accident in the imagination and far better than waiting for it to occur in the real world, but time needs to be provided to allow the imagination to work, rather than rushing in and hoping for the best.

Organisational risk control point (c) above is the routine of everyday plant operation; the activity that should be evident in Time Zone 1. Improved ways of doing things can be identified at any time and do not only arise from surveys commissioned for the purpose or because of incidents. The most significant aspect of risk control point (c) is that, over time, legal expectations, technology and the practices of industry change, so that what was an acceptable degree of risk control at the time of commissioning is no longer one that would withstand scrutiny in a court of law. There is a need to periodically subject existing Class A risk control measures to review.

An organisation that welcomes new insights into improved ways of controlling risk needs to have a process in place for managing the ideas that arise. In the absence of such a process, there is a very real chance that good ideas are suppressed by the manager faced with a request to make change happen, especially when that means expenditure. On the one hand managers know they need to show that they take safety seriously and on the other hand they are rewarded for managing their budget – a classic conflict occurs here. If the budget does not contain the necessary slack to pay for the proposed changes, the temptation to delay a decision or ignore the suggestion is strong.

An example will illustrate the point. A local government authority had crews installing water supplies in new suburbs in an area very prone to bush-fires. These crews used angle grinders for pipe cutting, but were not provided with any firefighting equipment. After a few (unrecorded but vivid in their recollection) scares in which they had started grass fires and only as a result of frantic stamping managed to suppress them, they asked their manager for a fire extinguisher for each truck. The manager, intent on the importance of managing his budget in the face of cuts, refused. The workers had no effective avenue through which they could raise their concerns (the safety committee was dominated by the same manager), but did talk to a visitor about the problem. The visitor had an opportunity to ask the Chief Executive Officer what would happen if one of their crews started a major bush fire and quickly got his full attention. He had hardly finished explaining the problem before the Chief Executive telephoned the stores and ordered them to supply extinguishers to the outside crew trucks.

The lesson to be learned is simple: the decision about whether a proposal for improved risk control measures is worth spending money on is one that naturally belongs to the manager at the level at which responsibility would rest in the event that the foreseeable LWC happened, not the manager at whose level the expenditure is to be accounted for.

These management attributes could be provided by the:

1. creation of a register of all proposed risk control improvement ideas, accessible to all levels in the organisation;
2. creation of a process for the assessment of all entries in the register that ensures decisions are made at the appropriate level of responsibility.

Much could be written about the desirable qualities of such a register and process, but it is at least clear that it would benefit from:

- all involved having a sensible idea about what the register is supposed to contain;
- entries being reviewed and developed by a specialist to ensure retained entries are well researched and contain intrinsically worthwhile ideas;
- managers understanding the dynamics of evaluating the proposals and approving funds or not as appropriate.

These control points are closely related to the practical evaluation of risk control possibilities, a subject discussed in Chapter 8.

The Necessary Qualities of Control Measures

As has been seen above, control measures can be on physical features of equipment, the way work is done or administrative features of work. In every case, it is a suitable combination of all three that is needed. In all cases, control measures need to be suited to the Risk in question and reliable. Suitable control measures result from a proper evaluation of the Risk; see Chapter 8. Reliable control measures mean they can be expected to be effective over significant periods of time. To a degree, reliability is an inherent quality of a control measure, but it is in all cases dependent on the frequency with which the control measure is inspected or checked on; see Chapter 10. Control measures that are ignored quickly fall into disuse.

Summary

As the primary purpose of any risk management activity is to ensure that control measures are effective, there is no activity more worth attending to than that of ensuring that risk control possibilities are understood and that control measures remain in place over time. When the risk in an organisation is largely determined by invariable Conditions it is these to which most attention is needed. When the risk in the organisation is significantly affected by Circumstance, the need for dynamic and responsive controls, perhaps largely working in Time Zone 2, is of more importance.

A distinction is made between Class A and Class B control measures. Class A control measures are derived from a detailed understanding of possibilities made evident by the EDM (or TVM), the TSM and the Risk model. Effective control measures are those that are explicitly understood and technically suited to the risk in question. Class A control measures are only as good as the organisational support they are given and the extent to which their effectiveness is monitored by actively seeking evidence of partial Occurrences and using these for insight and for improving risk control measure effectiveness. Class A control measures may be categorised as being either controls on physical and environmental Risk Factors, on the way work is done or the administrative practices of the organisation. Class B control measures are those which ensure the organisation actively assesses risk control measures at appropriate times, including the planning of change, implementation of change and also the periodic reassessment of control measures on existing risks to ensure the standards of control remain appropriate.

8

Risk Evaluation:
How Safe is
Safe Enough?

Introduction

This chapter concludes a logical sequence of topics from the identification and description of Risk (Chapter 5), through to understanding how to estimate its significance (Chapter 6) and understand possible control measures (Chapter 7). Risk Evaluation is the process of deciding if the Risk is acceptable and, if not, what will be done about it. The total process (Chapters 5 to 8) is one of Risk Assessment.

The evaluation of Risk requires the establishment of criteria on which this decision can be made. There are two ways in which evaluation can be understood, based on the existence or not of moral and ethical obligations. Where such obligations exist, called, for convenience, Type I, acceptability is determined by comparing existing control measures to the required standard of care. The existence of obligations is expressed in legal terms as a duty of care and the required standard of care can be determined by understanding how courts are likely to view control measures in the event the Risk gives rise to a case in court.

In the second way (Type II), where no moral or ethical obligations exist (or are being ignored), the purpose is to determine whether the degree of Risk is acceptable to the person or organisation. A popular way to understand this is that above some threshold value the level of Risk becomes something the evaluator finds increasingly uncomfortable or intolerable. This tolerable Risk approach (Type IIa) makes sense, for example, when faced with a purely financial Consequence. Is the evaluator willing to afford the LWC in the event that it occurs? If not, they should not become involved or should take out insurance. An example is the decision about whether to take out travel insurance in case luggage goes missing. It is typically mainly the LWC that is the focus of attention in these cases, with the likely Frequency of it being of somewhat less interest. For me, the value of clothing in my luggage is not great and I feel able to buy replacements without financial concern, so I decide not to take out insurance. In this example, there is little I can do to avert the Risk so I decide to reduce it slightly by putting my computer in my hand luggage but not to insure my baggage. There is another way of dealing with Risk in this situation (Type IIb) and that is to consider the cost-effectiveness of improvements to Risk controls. There is no tolerability as such, just the law of decreasing returns making more and more Risk controls unattractive as the cost of improvement is greater than the perceived value of reducing the Risk.

Table 8.1   A classification of Risk evaluation situations

Type	Basis of evaluation of an individual Risk
0	Nothing about the Risk can be changed, including Exposure, so there is no point in attempting an evaluation. There are no possible criteria of acceptability.
I	Moral and ethical obligations exist, expressed legally as a duty of care. Evaluation involves understanding the required standard of care in the situation.
IIa	No moral or ethical obligations. Evaluation involves deciding if the risk is tolerable.
IIb	No moral or ethical obligations. Evaluation is based on considering the cost–benefit of risk reduction proposals and is affected by the law of diminishing returns.

If we think of a Risk over which we have no control, including the ability to escape from it (remove ourselves from Exposure), it will be evident that there is really no purpose in Risk evaluation. An example that attracts a lot of interest is radiation from a supernova explosion hitting the earth with an intensity that will kill everyone on the exposed hemisphere, or even all life on earth. Naturally, efforts have been made to see just what the Probability of this is. There is, however, no reason to ask if this is acceptable as there is nothing, we may reasonably assume, that any one of us could do about it. It is a Risk we can describe and make efforts to estimate the value of but there is no point in evaluating the Risk. This can perhaps be thought of as a Type 0 situation. See Table 8.1 for a summary of this classification of Risk evaluation scenarios.

It is often possible to develop a long list of Risks for which control improvements are justified (in Type I or II). In one organisation I was able to develop a list with some 40 entries over a two-day period. I also recall a government regulator generating a list of a similar size when it sent its inspectors into three chemical storage facilities following a major fire in one of them. Their list consisted only of failures to comply with regulations whereas my list resulted from a slightly broader scope. As is easy to imagine, the cost of acting on every item in these lists is likely to be significant, certainly more than any organisation is likely to be able to afford in its current year, as a budget allocation is yet to be made. Budgets will be needed and the work may take more than one year to complete. The evaluation process now involves a decision about how rapidly the changes can be funded: over how many years is it reasonable to implement the justifiable changes? Another aspect to this question is how much money can the organisation afford?

In either Type I or II, the process of evaluation inherently involves judgement. Consequently, in this chapter, a natural process of evaluation is described and what is known of the way people and organisations apply judgement when faced with Risks is reviewed. Obviously, Risk evaluation is essentially a decision-making process and it is possible to critically assess every aspect of it according to decision-making theory. I am not, however, versed in decision-making theory and will confine this chapter to the Risk aspects of the process.

Acceptability Criteria in Type I

In Type I, acceptability criteria are based on or significantly influenced by moral and ethical considerations. Almost always, this arises because the possible Consequences affect people (their health or their wealth) or the environment. In the industrial world, the way in which moral and ethical requirements are expressed depends on the relationship between the body responsible for the Risk and the people or environment potentially suffering the Consequences of it; see Table 8.2.

The criteria listed in Table 8.2 can be expressed in a general or a specific form. General statements of responsibility in much of the English-speaking world are to be found in the common law expression of the duty of care.

Table 8.2 Relationships and risk acceptability criteria in Type I evaluations

Relationship of responsible and affected entities	Risk arises from	Origin of criteria
a) Employer–Employee	Exposure to industrial processes and social/organisational environment	Detailed expectations developed since the origin of the industrial modern world and expressed in a legal framework out of which general and specific expectations are formed
b) Company–Client	Provision of services and advice	A statutory framework for the profession or service, including self-regulation
c) Government–Public	Decisions made affecting public health (health services and land use planning) and transport planning	A tendency of governments to form acceptability (tolerability) criteria for the associated risks with reference to the decisions and practices of other governments
d) Company–Public	Provision of products and services; exposure to industrial processes	A statutory framework for the service or profession, including self-regulation Environmental legislation
e) Company–Environment	Exposure to industrial processes	Environmental legislation

An aspect of the duty of care that is of particular relevance is that owed by an organisation to:

- those who are employed by it, including contractors;
- members of the public or the natural environment affected by its operations, for example as a result of noise, vibration, fumes, chemicals escaping the boundary of the operation and exposing the public;
- members of the public who seek advice or services from the organisation.

These common law obligations are often repeated in statutory law and even in the regulations made under this. It is also common for codes of practice to be framed by legislators (or industry bodies) or given some authority by them through such statements as 'one way of satisfying the Regulation is to comply with the Code of Practice'. Regulations and codes of practice may be written for management practices or for hazard-specific purposes. National standards bodies are also prolific writers of both management practices and hazard-specific standards.

In many parts of the world, the tendency over the last several decades has been to write performance-based standards rather than prescriptive ones. A prescriptive standard could, for example, provide precise guidance on how best to store dangerous goods or guard a specific machine. A performance-based standard would, by contrast, say that it is necessary to store dangerous goods in such a way that adverse interactions between chemicals are prevented, or even, more generally, 'safely'. The user then has to do the research for themselves to determine how to achieve that – in other words, go out and do the Risk assessment and make their own decisions that suit their circumstances. With a performance-based legislative background, there is the opportunity for industry-based codes of practice to be more prescriptive: an industry-based group does the research for all members. This discussion is relevant to cases (a), (b) and (d) in Table 8.2.

In case (c), reference to common and statutory law is unsuitable as the government cannot prosecute itself in the event of a failure to comply. The government, through its departments of health, transport and land use planning (at least), makes decisions that affect public health and safety. Examples include:

i.   providing medicines and health screening services;
ii. deciding on standards of road design, such as the provision (or not) of separation barriers between opposing lanes on motorways;
iii. deciding whether to accept a development proposal for a new petrochemical installation.

One approach to decision-making is the cost-effectiveness of the proposed expenditure: how many lives will be saved per £? This approach is practical for (i) and (ii) above. Clearly a decision needs to be made as to the value of a life saved and much has been and can be written on this subject and guidelines are needed for estimating cost-effectiveness.

Another approach, suited to (iii) above, is to establish the level of Risk that is acceptable. This is typically used for planning decisions where significant fires and explosions are possible, ranging from hydrocarbon refineries and large storage facilities to compressed gas installations. Risk engineers are able to model heat flux from fires, explosion over-pressures and toxic fume plume geometry and in that way estimate the possible numbers of people (beyond the boundary of the installation) adversely affected. Modelling estimates the number of the public killed (the Consequence Value) by the Occurrence as well as the likely Frequency of this Consequence. The result is shown in a specialised Risk diagram in which the Consequence Value is measured in number of deaths (N) and the Frequency either as the estimated frequency with which a specific Consequence Value is estimated to occur (f) or as the cumulative Frequency (F) with which N or more deaths are expected to occur. These give rise to what are commonly known as fN and FN curves. The United Kingdom Health and Safety Executive (n.d.) has published acceptable and unacceptable Risk profiles in the FN curve; see Figure 8.1. The position of these iso-risk lines is specified at the 50 fatalities point and said to extend beyond this in either direction with slope of –1, but the limits of this are not specified, particularly at the high Frequency end. Predicted Risk levels from a new hazardous industry installation should lie beneath the lower line for the increased Risk to the public to be tolerable. If the predicted levels are above the upper line they will add significantly to the sum total of all Risks currently existing and hence be regarded as unacceptable. Needless to say, when such criteria are made use of by a government instrumentality, much protocol surrounds their use and the decision-making process.

Case (e) in Table 8.2 is worth a separate explanation. Environmental damage, one may presume or perhaps hope, is something that imposes a moral and ethical obligation on polluters. However, in practice little use is made of the general duties of care arising from common and statutory law. Instead, government agencies (for example environmental protection agency and similar) license polluting processes by specifying pollution limits for defined pollutants, such as chemicals in water, noise and dust in the environment, noxious gases released to the atmosphere, etc. A problem arises for the polluting organisation if the limit is crossed and if this is discovered by the agency.

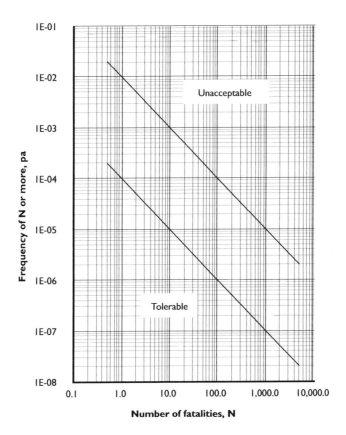

Figure 8.1   Societal risk criteria
Source: United Kingdom Health and Safety Executive.

Type I in Practice – 'Must Do', 'Should Do' and 'Could Do'

Type I gives rise to situations in which improvements to Risk controls either must, should or could be made. Arguably, if there is a regulation that is specific in its expectations or which gives authority to a code of practice, any responsible organisation would feel that it must comply with the rules. National standards and industrially developed codes of practice may not quite have the authority (or potential for prosecution) of a regulation or approved code of practice, unless given that authority in the regulation or code. However, the fact that these documents originate from respected bodies creates a powerful urge to comply: compliance should be achieved for Risk controls suggested in this way. Where an improvement to a Risk control is either a 'must do' or 'should do' it becomes hard to argue in a court of law, perhaps when facing a prosecution, that it was acceptable to ignore it or that it was not done because there was no money in the budget.

The great majority of Risk control improvement options do not fall into the must or should category and so are 'could do' items. The effort could be made to improve the Risk control, but is it really worth it?

Type I – Financial Justification of 'Could Do' Proposals

There is every reason to subject a 'could do' proposal to a financial justification, as long as this is done in full recognition of how to include the essential moral obligations in the decision-making process. Cost–benefit analysis is simple in principle: if the benefits outweigh the costs, the proposal is justifiable. The analysis can be made more complicated (and more real) by using net present values in establishing the value today of costs and benefits delayed in the future. In a simple financial investment decision, the question is usually a matter of how much profit will be made per year if we invest a lump sum now in some productive process. At the very least, the same lump sum could be put into the bank and earn interest, so we would wish to see a return greater than that baseline.

Most proposals for capital expenditure in industry and commerce are for investments in the production process that give rise to improvements in profitability, or for new profitable ventures. A proposed improved Risk control measure may not be seen to be doing either of these. Rather, it is likely to be seen most immediately as an avoidable increased cost. Most budgets contain allowances for unforeseen costs but also most managers are loath to spend the whole budget as their performance is judged by their ability to come in under budget, not over it.

A manager's view of a request for funds to improve Risk controls is affected by the fact that the benefits of reduced Risk are notional (probabilistic and hard to prove) and in the future. Those who have to be convinced to release the funds are very seldom those whose life or health is at risk – the negative Consequences of the Risk are not experienced directly by them and they probably do not have a personal relationship with those who are at risk. The requirement for funds to implement the improved control measure is real and immediate, however, so the disadvantage of agreeing to the proposal is a direct experience.

If the proposal is for a safety improvement, a dilemma arises: on one hand the organisation probably makes public statements about how important safety is (possibly even 'safety is our number one priority') and on the other hand managing the budget is most important. As with all dilemmas, either position is uncomfortable. The manager may turn to various strategies to avoid a decision, such as asking for more information, setting up a committee to investigate the options and similar. The heat can be taken out of the Risk dilemma by subjecting the management of all Risk reduction proposals to a suitable process in which the inherent value of a proposal is the first stage of assessment and the question of funds a second stage, responsibility for which is removed from the dilemma level of management and placed on the organisation's agenda at the appropriate level of responsibility. Table 8.3 is an outline of such a process. There is much to be gained by assisting the risk adviser to put forward well-researched proposals and the manager to understand when and how it is acceptable to decline a proposal.

Table 8.3   A decision-making process for Risk control improvement proposals

Stage	Description
1	Is the proposal inherently justifiable?
	a) It is a 'must do' or a 'should do' proposal, i.e. to comply with legislation, standards and codes of practice.
	b) It is a 'could do' proposal: is the expected reduction in risk commensurate with the amount of money needed to achieve it? To what extent does the moral argument influence the cost–benefit argument?
2	To what extent can we afford to implement all of these inherently justifiable improvements?
	a) What annual budget is affordable, given the legal and moral obligations?
	b) With this annual budget, how long would it take to complete all inherently justifiable proposals? Is this reasonable or should the annual budget be increased?
3	In what priority order should these proposals be completed?

If, however, the proposed control measure is aimed at reducing a Loss the suggested benefits will be seen as real and immediate and amenable to normal cost–benefit analysis. The dilemma disappears because most organisations are familiar with making such decisions. As has been seen in Chapter 4, the difference between a Risk and a Loss is simply Exposure. The bigger the organisation the more likely it is to be able to see adverse Consequences appearing as Losses and to find it easier to make decisions about control measure proposals as they more readily fit into the normal capital investment or operating cost decision-making process. However, if the decisions are made in small units within the larger organisation, those making the decisions will see them as Risks and find the decision harder to make. This reinforces the need for decisions to be made at the correct level in the organisation. The process outlined in Table 8.3 has the ability to achieve this.

It is an oversimplification to see proposed control measures simply as demanding an initial injection of funds. The cost of implementing a control measure may include annual costs for training, inspection and maintenance. Also, the benefits of a control measure may include an improvement in productivity, a direct benefit also measured as a £ p.a. value. Proposals which combine real improvements with the notional benefits of Risk reduction are more likely to be successful. The overall benefit of a Risk control measure improvement proposal is:

Benefit of control measure [£ p.a.] = Reduction in Risk or Loss [£ p.a.] + Improvement in productivity [£ p.a.]

The basis of a cost–benefit decision where a one-off provision of funds is required is the payback period. The payback period is calculated by dividing the one-off cost by the annual expected benefit of the control measure:

Payback period = Capital Cost [£] / Benefit of control measure [£ p.a.]

The units of this are obviously [years]. The result is notional in the case of Risk and real in the case of Loss.

The basis of a cost-benefit decision where no capital is required but the risk control measure requires an increase in annual operating costs, for example providing a second person to accomplish a task, is not the payback period. All that can be done is to compare the increase in operating costs directly with the notional reduction in Risk.

Type I and the Moral Argument

Law is a vehicle for conveying community expectations for the harmonious conduct of all social interactions whether in the community, industry, commerce, health care or transport. In many English-speaking jurisdictions it is the common law that provides the guidance on the responsibilities that people in general have towards one another. In its simplest form this responsibility is expressed as a duty of care: each of us has a duty to care for others where we are in a position to do so. It is the nature of the relationship between people that determines the standard of care expected, for a discussion of which see below. When a Type I Risk evaluation is being made it is necessary to make the decision in full recognition of the moral implications. One aspect of this is the need mentioned above for the decision to be made at the appropriate level of responsibility. Both the level of responsibility and the practical meaning of the moral implications are determined by the magnitude of the LWC: the greater the LWC the more heavily the moral obligation weighs on the decision-making process.

In some jurisdictions, notably many of those in the English-speaking world, the standard against which Risk control measures are judged is expressed as the need to provide a safe place and safe system of work with adequately trained personnel. The emphasis (see Table 8.4) is on the importance of a safe place of work supported by a safe system of work with little reliance being placed on requiring safe behaviour of those at Risk. Indeed, leading cases over the years have pointed out the need to expect workers to exhibit all the normal vagaries of the human condition, such as lack of attention, inadvertence, tiredness, emotional upset and psychological disturbances: the need to take people as they are and not assume some ideal type of person who does not in the main exist. This concept is closely related to that expressed in Chapter 7, where it is suggested that behaviour should not be judged against a hypothetical perfect standard.

Table 8.4   A hierarchy of controls based on common law judgements

Name	Meaning
Elimination	Eliminate the hazard
Substitution	Replace the hazard by something less hazardous
Engineering controls	Build something to make the hazard less accessible or less able to produce damage
Administrative controls	Establish processes for the way work is done – rules, methods of work, training, etc.
Personal protective equipment	Protect the exposed person from the hazard

This expectation is popularly promoted as a hierarchy of controls. The first in the hierarchy is the provision of a safe place and so on down to the lowest order in the hierarchy which is to expect certain behaviour of the affected worker, such as wearing personal protective equipment. Table 8.4 is a hierarchy of controls suited to an industrial hygienist's view and it is best understood using examples from that field: eliminate the chemical, substitute for a less hazardous chemical, provide extraction ventilation or covers to prevent exposure to the chemical fumes (engineering controls), make rules about when the process can be used or who uses it and in what way, and finally provide the exposed people with protective equipment. The industrial hygiene model is not very amenable to application in many other areas of Risk, such as electricity, transport, chemical process plants and automated machinery, to name a few. For example, how could one apply elimination or substitution to a petrochemical refinery? Nevertheless, the principle of preferring safe place controls to safe people controls can be applied to any area of Risk, just not necessarily using the names given in Table 8.4.

There is a significant disparity between the expression of the moral obligation and the conclusions of accident theory (see Chapter 2). Accident theory emphasises the fact that 80 percent or more of accidents are caused by unsafe acts of people and 10 percent or so by unsafe conditions. With the concomitant notion that it is necessary to remove the cause to prevent the accident, it is easy to see an emphasis being placed on safe person control measures, as indeed it has been over the years, in direct conflict with the legal obligations that have existed over the same period. Interestingly, the philosophy of Risk deduces that the best control measures are those that are reliable, see Chapter 7, as these maintain low failure rates over time. The most reliable control measures are those that are designed in to the technology, not those that rely on human behaviour. This coincides with the moral argument of the law.

Type I and the Standard of Care

The risk adviser needs a detailed working knowledge of the standard of care in their jurisdiction. A specialist could write a whole book on this subject, so it is hoped that the succinct summary offered here does not contain so many inaccuracies arising from its brevity that it is misguiding.

When expressed as common law, the duty is to take all reasonable care to prevent injury, ill health, damage or loss. The duty is stronger (the standard of care is higher) when those to whom it is owed are less skilled or capable than the average person, for example, under-age, low-skilled and handicapped people or people to whom a service or advice is being given who are unable to understand the complexities of it. This consideration of the standard of care is to be determined in each individual case, not to a group as a whole. It is necessary to take into account known special weaknesses or peculiarities, physical and mental attributes, degree of experience and prior education or training. Also, people may be expected to be distracted at times, possibly emotionally upset and so on: such natural states should not be enough to lead to a severe Consequence.

Where the potential for injury or damage is concerned, the duty is satisfied by providing:

a) A safe place of work with safe equipment/materials and facilities. This implies proper initial design and appropriate inspection and maintenance programs.
b) A safe system of work, including adequate levels of supervision; for example, how many people, of what skills, how supervised, using what methods, proper procedures to reinforce these expectations.
c) Adequate numbers of competent personnel.
d) An overall system that is monitored and modified as experience shows this to be necessary.

Failing to provide the required standard of care is called negligence, which is assessed after an adverse Consequence has occurred. Those claiming that there has been negligence (the plaintiff) need to show the following, called the tests of negligence:

- a direct causal link between the breach (what they claim failed to be done) and the injury or damage sustained by the injured party;
- the potential for injury/ill health was reasonably foreseeable to the person or legal entity that owed the duty of care;
- that reasonably practicable control measures were available.

The argument relies on the interpretation in the specific situation of the meaning of safe, reasonable, foreseeable and practicable – each of which is sufficiently subjective to support lengthy legal arguments. A practical definition of the term safe (as an acceptable level of Risk) has been proposed earlier and will be discussed further below. The reasonable person is a legal concept rather than an identifiable type of individual. One can imagine that such a person must be aware of their duty and the technicalities of it and be intent on behaving responsibly.

For something to be foreseeable to a reasonable person, logic demands that the knowledge of the possibility must be available to them, either through their own experience or the experience of others whose advice they could reasonably obtain (a subject specialist or an industry specialist). If knowledge costs money, for example to engage a specialist environmental scientist, then the more affordable the fees (presumably, the larger the organisation) the more foreseeable the knowledge reasonably is. If the knowledge is freely available and only needs to be looked for, then it should have been found, as a reasonable person would be diligent in seeking it.

'Practicable' has a legal definition, which is that due regard must be given to:

1. The severity of the Risk. The larger the Risk, or specifically the larger the LWC, the more justifiable a proposed control measure becomes. See further discussion of this point below.
2. The state of knowledge about the hazard and ways of removing or reducing the Risk. Knowledge mainly available to people who consult to similar organisations or to others in the same industry would reasonably be considered accessible knowledge. Inaccessible knowledge would be that only recently known to narrow specialist researchers or not known at all to anyone.
3. The availability and suitability of control measures. It is common, after an accident, for improved control measures to be rapidly implemented, thus demonstrating the practicability of better controls. Some legal advisers argue against implementing improved control measures in order to not expose their practicability. This is perverse and immoral logic where personal injury is concerned.
4. The cost of implementing the control measures. The affordability of control measures is discussed in greater detail below.

Items 1 and 3 are interactive and subject to the preference for safe place over safe system control measures. The best available control measure technology is expected where the LWC is very high (for example fatality upwards), with the best practical technology being acceptable when the LWC is less than this. This is also discussed in more detail below.

It follows that control measures that are commonly found in the industry in question are considered reasonably practicable. The converse of this is that if suggested control measures are uncommon or not present within the industry this is possibly an argument for them not to be impracticable. This, however, could be evidence that the whole industry is lacking in this regard, rather than a defence against negligence for one member of it.

A common but unsupportable view is that the perceived misjudgement, inattention and inadvertence of the injured person is a significant defence against a charge of negligence. While the defence of contributory negligence may be considered in court, it is not common for it to be given anything like the weight given to the tests of negligence.

'Safe' and the Law of Diminishing Returns

The question of how much needs to be done to be able to say something is safe is a common one in industry and commerce and is conveniently illustrated by the law of diminishing returns.

A poorly controlled Risk may be reduced significantly (project 1 in Figure 8.2) by the most obvious control measure improvement project. The benefit is the reduction in Risk. This project has a high benefit:cost ratio due to the large reduction in Risk possible for a relatively modest outlay. Project 2 has a benefit:cost ratio of about one and Project 3 a very low benefit:cost ratio, showing how increasingly costly control measures may only provide minor reductions in Risk. Project 1 would be easy to justify. Project 2, while being less cost-effective than Project 1, still gives an even return. Project 3 is really not attractive from a financial investment point of view.

The term practical in 'best practical technology' carries the connotation that it is relatively easy to make the change technically and the cost of it is affordable. Where it is acceptable to look for this, it is by implication acceptable to use a cost–benefit assessment (appropriately weighted to reflect moral obligations) to determine whether the control measure changes are inherently justifiable.

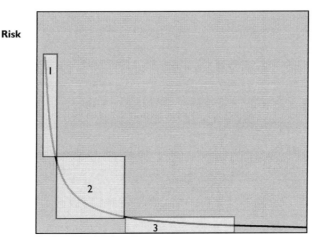

Cost of risk control measure

1. A high value for money project
2. A even value for money project
3. A low value for money project

Figure 8.2   The law of diminishing returns in risk control

The term available in 'best available technology' means the technology only needs to be available as an option for its use to be justified. The best available technology requirement applies to situations of the most significant moral obligation, practically meaning those where the LWC is single or multiple deaths and severe disability or major property damage, major loss and similar. Project 2 is indicative of what might be thought of as the best practical point on the diminishing returns curve. Project 3 may represent the best available technology and so still be justifiable from a moral perspective. Those assessing proposals for improved Risk controls need to be informed of the standard of care requirements expected of the organisation. The 'as low as reasonably practical' (ALARP) criterion is very commonly promoted as the Risk control goal but the 'as low as possible' criterion is generally not accorded the same degree of recognition. It should be noted that even ALARP is only relevant in appropriate Type II evaluation situations.

These standard of care criteria mean that as technology changes and new ways of controlling Risk become available so situations that had been thought of as safe become unsafe. An organisation needs to keep its standards of Risk control under surveillance as the years pass, as noted in the discussion on Class B control measures in Chapter 7. Examples of changes to available relevant technology occurring in recent decades are:

- earth leakage circuit breakers (core balance relays): these sense an unbalanced flow of current and shut it off very rapidly, thus preventing electrocution;
- 'Man-down' alarms: when a person wearing the alarm is not upright, an alarm is sent;
- Intelligent building access: this both allows access into a building and enables use of doors, etc. to be traced. The technology can be used to alert security after hours that a person is in a building; a check can be made if the person does not leave the building in a reasonable period.

Is it Affordable?

It is also true to say that as time passes, what was not affordable may become affordable and so fall within the bounds of a reasonably practical change. This question relates both to an individual proposal to improve Risk control measures and to the whole collection of proposals. So long as an organisation is only prompted to consider suggested improvements after an accident has happened, it is unlikely to be faced with the cost of a collection of proposals. This makes the acceptance of accident theory attractive to many. The (rare) proactive approach to looking for inadequate Risk control measures produces a collection of proposals. The earlier discussion will have made it clear that this is the approach to which an organisation should aspire.

A proposed control measure may be justifiable in itself but not affordable either immediately or in the long term. When a proposal is first conceived and presented to the organisation, unless it is very cheap and can be paid for in the present year's budget for contingencies, it will not, by definition, have been budgeted for and it becomes a candidate for inclusion in some future budget. A manager may well be faced with saying that it simply cannot be afforded at all. To an organisation with an annual budget for developments and improvements of £100,000, a single Risk control improvement item of £100,000 may not be considered affordable if it ever became a topic of discussion in a court case, depending on the significance of the LWC. In a Type I evaluation, the responsible manager making the decision needs to understand the expression of moral obligation in the jurisdiction within which the organisation operates. However, the same amount has a very different meaning if the organisation has an annual budget for developments and improvements of £1,000,000. It would be hard to argue that it was not affordable.

When a group of proposals exist, the combined cost of implementing them may be such that long-term planning is required. As an example, if a list of inherently justifiable improvements has a total capital value of £500,000 but the organisation is not able to invest more than £50,000 p.a. in them, all of the improvements could be completed in 10 years. Is this a reasonable period? The question can only be answered by senior managers or even by the board of directors. If the idea of tolerable Risk has any practical meaning it is in this decision.

Once decisions have been made to fund a collection of proposals, the second decision is in what order of priority should the works be done on these improvements? A sensible answer is to sort the list according to the benefit:cost ratio and, if this includes Type I evaluations, also check to ensure that this has not reduced the items attracting the greatest moral obligation (based on LWC) to an unreasonably low position on the list.

The Meaning of Safe

In Figure 8.1, the area below the lower line is labelled 'tolerable', which is a somewhat grudging judgement that Risks in that area are regarded as perhaps acceptable. Above the upper line (where the area is labelled 'unacceptable') there is no such equivocation, as it is easier for a government body to be more clear about what is unacceptable than what is acceptable, owing to their propensity to be highly Risk averse. It is evident that the top right-hand corner of the Risk diagram is the highest level of Risk in this diagram and the lower left-hand corner is the lowest level of Risk.

In Figure 8.3, a Risk Scale (broken line) has been superimposed on Figure 8.1. On the Unacceptable line, the product (the numerical value of Risk) of Frequency and Number of Fatalities is everywhere 0.01 (1.0E–02). The Risk Scale shows this product (the Risk) at each point on the scale. The iso-risk lines have a slope of –1 and the Risk Scale a slope of +1.

If ever there was a region in the Risk diagram that deserves the label 'safe' it is clearly towards the lower left corner. Even in the lower left corner there remains a possibility that a fatality could occur.

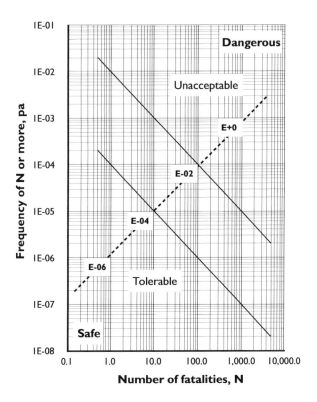

Figure 8.3   Defining the terms 'safe' and 'dangerous'

The reason for the possibility is that the energy source that gives rise to the Risk still exists, as does the exposure to it. Zero Risk only occurs where something is impossible: no Threat (energy or otherwise) or no Exposure. It is evident that somewhere towards the upper right corner is the opposite, where 'dangerous' is.

These insights virtually compel the rational being (including the Risk specialist) to define 'safe' as an acceptable degree of Risk and 'dangerous' as an unacceptable degree of Risk. Neither safe nor dangerous are definable points on the scale, but they are terms more likely to be applied at the extreme ends of the Risk Scale. The question that naturally arises is: acceptable to whom? The inherently judgemental nature of these terms is evident. The answer to this question must include those at Risk, those with a duty of care towards those at Risk as well as the larger community. Precisely who is interested depends on whether the Risk is occupational, environmental, recreational, public, financial, organisational and so on. One can be confident that the law has something to say about it in each case. As will be seen later in this chapter, each affected entity (person or other legal entity) may well bring different points of view to bear on the answer so that what is objectively the same Risk can be regarded as either safe or dangerous. The answer given by any interested party will arise from their perceptions, which are influenced by a number of different factors. It can generally be said, however, that an acceptable Risk is one in which the Risk control standards are acceptable to the individual and the interested community at large.

Surprisingly few attempts are made in the literature or in safety legislation to define these terms. A review of health and safety legislation in various English-speaking jurisdictions found phrases such as 'safe and without risks to health', 'without risks to health and safety' and 'protect health and safety', but in each case without an accompanying definition of 'safe' or 'safety'. In contrast, risk is often defined in a manner that is quite consistent with that presented in this text. Unfortunately, the general impossibility of the risk-free goal implied in the phrase 'without risk' appears not to be evident to legislators.

The Social Context in which the Risk is Experienced

The social context in which the law of diminishing returns is experienced is very significant because of the influence of the benefits of accepting the Risk. This is most apparent in the huge variation in choices of acceptable means of transport between wealthy and poor countries. In poor countries people are delighted to have an opportunity to travel in a car that would be condemned and scrapped in a wealthy country. Even small improvements in roadworthiness are unaffordable.

We may be exposed to the Risk at work, as a result of a neighbour's activities, at home for our own benefit, as a result of recreational or sporting activities, or have Risk imposed on us as members of the community through the way in which food, health services, energy, transport, policing and defence services and so on are provided. We may respond to what is objectively the same Risk in different ways as a result. We accept Risks in recreation and sport that we probably would not in employment. We expect the government will be working towards a safe community, health services and transport system, yet accept food products grown and processed in unknown ways and medicines largely without question. We may privately evaluate Risk we take for recreational purposes, unless these expose others to Risk, in which case we need to be conscious of acceptable standards of care. Where Risks arise from occupational origins, we must be aware of the required (legally acceptable) standard of care.

Our perception of these situations is so different that it is not possible to infer from our acceptance of a Risk in one situation that we will respond similarly to the same Risk in another situation. Climbing into a high place for our employment as an industrial painter may not make us feel the same way as it would if we were abseiling for pleasure in the mountains and this would be especially so if we did not have faith in the level of planning done by our employer. It is also the case that employment Risks may be different in kind from those found in private life: a steel worker is not going to be exposed to the heavy industry hazards of a steel plant when at home.

It is not uncommon for managers in industry to complain about health and safety laws on the grounds that the workers take far more Risks when at home and in recreation. The comparison is pointless, not least because of the duty of care owed by an employer to an employee. Domestic and recreational Risks, by contrast, are self-imposed and voluntary. The manner of imposition of the Risk and the awareness the affected person has of the Risk are two essential considerations in determining how someone will respond to a Risk. I will rely here, again, on the pioneering work of Rowe (1977) in risk philosophy.

Table 8.5   The context in which a Risk is experienced, after Rowe

Context	Category	Explanation
Imposition of the risk	Endogenous	Self-imposed by the risk agent.* Typically recreational and domestic – e.g. sports, cleaning gutters, using cleaning chemicals.
	Exogenous	Imposed upon the risk agent by others, by nature, e.g. being drafted into the military, having to take avoiding action in traffic, escaping from a violent person, finding the building you are in on fire, being exposed to an extreme weather event like a tornado or flood, etc.
Exposure to the risk	Voluntary	Choosing an exposure in which free will can be exercised, with options and without coercion, e.g. seeking employment as a fireman, recreational parachuting, voluntarily becoming a racing driver or jockey.
	Involuntary	The exposure does not involve choice, e.g. feeling morally obliged to enter a burning building to help occupants, caught in a violent storm, forced into a hazardous occupation to support family as no other employment choices exist.
The receipt of benefits from being exposed to the risk	Equitable	The risk agent has the opportunity to weigh the benefits against the risk, e.g. wages are the benefit of employment, pleasure and success are the benefits of recreational activities.
	Inequitable	The risk agent is not able to weigh the benefits against the risk, e.g. forced labour, being unaware of the risk (see below).
The state of knowledge of the risk	Aware	The risk agent is aware the risk exists and understands it, e.g. the level of noise is known and information about its effects on hearing has been given.
	Unaware	The risk agent is not aware of the risk (they have not made the effort to find out when the chance has been offered, knowledge has been withheld from them or no one knows about the risk) or they don't understand the nature of the risk.

Note: *Rowe calls the person evaluating the risk the Risk Agent.

Table 8.5 explores the nature of imposition of a Risk and the type of exposure that occurs. What is objectively the same Risk can be perceived in very different ways. Deciding to go parachuting for fun is an endogenous voluntary Risk, but being in an aeroplane whose engines have failed and deciding to parachute out instead of chancing the landing would be an exogenous voluntary Risk. I know of two pilots who had to use their parachutes to escape their glider when a wing broke off during a display. Immediately on landing in front of the crowd, they were offered free membership of the local parachuting club. They declined the offer, evidently with some passion.

An equitable exposure means that the individual exposed to the Risk is aware of the Risk and receives some direct benefits from being exposed to it so that the opportunity exists to decide if the benefit is adequate recompense for being exposed. A person employed as a painter might expect to work at height and be exposed to the possibility of a fall. The pay they receive gives them the chance to decide if they are happy to accept this Risk. This does not mean that they must be able to identify a component of 'danger money' and decide if that extra pay makes it worthwhile. Outside of employment, the benefits a person receives from being at height may be personal satisfaction at overcoming fears when rock climbing, to hoping to be a winner and receive congratulations. An acceptable Risk is essentially one for which possible adverse consequences are accepted because of the immediate benefits derived from it. Pay is only one form of benefit and only applicable where employment is offered.

A notorious example of knowledge of a Risk being withheld is that of asbestos. Despite expert knowledge that exposure leads to cancer being available to companies mining the substance, it was many decades before the knowledge became public and much has been made in the media of the efforts of boards of management to suppress the knowledge, apparently to the benefit of their business and the detriment of the whole community. When knowledge of a Risk is withheld, it is not possible for anyone to make a reasonable decision about their exposure and an otherwise voluntary and equitable situation becomes the opposite. This, no doubt, is the reason financial regulators require investment promoters to explicitly mention the Risks inherent in the opportunity they promote.

The Personal Context in which Risk is Experienced

It is hard not to be aware of the sometimes extreme sensitivity of the public to some classes of Risks but not others. This can appear quite illogical. Members of the public appear unconcerned by the annual death toll from car use (presently about 2,000 p.a. in the UK) but individual aircraft crashes (15 reported fatalities in the UK in 2010) may evoke a far more emotive response. Television programmes appear to exploit this fascination (or is it horror?) with aircraft accidents far more than they do car crashes.

A Risk can be described objectively but the response of an individual or group of individuals to it ('do I accept it?') is essentially subjective. This subjective perception may be based on highly relevant and specialised information, on missing or incomplete information, on simple prejudice or on a desire to conform to the norms of or express the views of a significant group. It may even be a surrogate for a completely different concern (Clark, 1980).

The need to understand something of this subjective response arose particularly in the 1970s and 1980s as public concern about various relatively new Risks (chemicals, nuclear power and weapons) became apparent. The work of Rowe, mentioned many times in this book, arose out of this need. In 1987, Slovic (1987) published the results of a substantial study to describe how people as individuals and groups perceived Risks and responded to them. The reasons for these perceptions may be a subject of speculation but the facts of them are amenable to description and of practical interest to the practitioner. A very brief summary of Slovic's conclusions is that people's perceptions of community Risks is determined by three factors: the 'dread' factor (a state of dread, influenced by the perceived worst consequence and the perception that it could not be controlled), the state of knowledge factor (familiar through to unknown and new) and the number of people affected. Slovic studied the response of four groups of people: the League of Women Voters, college students, active club members and experts in the Risk being considered. Interestingly, in cases where expert groups existed (for example guns, nuclear power, aviation), the experts often had a very different perception of the Risk from that of the other groups. Nevertheless, the responses tended to cluster in predictable areas of the graph. For example, nuclear power was considered high on the 'dread' and 'unknown' scales. Domestic matters were rated low on both scales, and so on.

If we experience first-hand the Consequences of a Risk, or could readily imagine that the Consequences could be experienced close at hand, we are more concerned by the Risk – see Table 8.6. People who have actually had a family member affected, or who have seen someone else affected, are very concerned about a Risk. This personal proximity factor weighs more heavily the closer the experience is. One's family, friends, acquaintances, local community, society, culture and so on are of importance but in decreasing order. For example, a flood affecting a remote culture weighs less heavily than one in which one's own family members are involved. Surgeons whose lives are spent mending bodies broken by car crashes are more concerned about them than the community in general. A government regulator whose work involves handling the complaints made by people affected by unprofessional providers of services is more concerned about the need for reform than the public in general. This experience also suggests that a manager being asked to approve expenditure for an improved Risk control measure will value the proposal less than the people whose well-being is at Risk. Proponents of the proposal would be advised to draw attention to the implications for the manager of not approving the funds, for example how a negative decision would look in a court of law after the anticipated Consequence had occurred.

Perception of Risk is also affected by the period that has elapsed since the consequences of the Risk were last experienced or known about. The same applies to the potential for a Consequence in the future; the further into the future the Consequence is likely to occur, the less concerned we tend to be. Our community has heightened awareness of terrorist activity, but this will diminish if terrorist activities do not occur for some time. There is a (seemingly small) reduction in the numbers of people flying after a highly publicised aeroplane crash. We feel anxious about driving for a period after we have seen a serious crash. Workers modify their behaviour, probably only for a short period of time, if one of their colleagues is involved in an accident. Psychologists see this as a positive mental attribute, as we would be a very anxious person if the fear of adverse experiences stayed with us forever. We need to discount the seriousness quickly and move on.

Table 8.6   Influences on people's perception of Risk

Influence on the risk agent	Meaning
Personal proximity of the Consequence	The closer the actual or possible Occurrence or Consequence the more highly it is valued. This ranges from me (or my loved ones), wider family and friends (including workmates), my community, my country, my culture, other countries and other cultures.
The time since the Consequence was last experienced	The more recent the experience of the actual Occurrence or Consequence, the more highly it is valued.
The possible worst Consequence	The extreme value of possible Consequence is emphasised to the exclusion of any other considerations.
The frequency of the least Consequence	The most frequent Consequence results in a high degree of sensitivity towards the occurrence, even if it is trivial.
Feelings of horror	An experience of fear or revulsion when understanding the nature of the Occurrence or Consequence. Outrage occurs if this is accompanied by the perception that the responsible organisation was unconcerned about the risk.

Experience in industry suggests that people discount the importance of serious incidents typically within a six to eight week period. Within that period, people's priorities and behaviours will be affected, although to a decreasing extent, by the Consequences they have experienced. After that period, life returns to normal. Pre-existing values, concerns and perceptions of what is important will again be dominant in determining their behaviour. For example:

- A month after a colleague was killed by heavy powered equipment, those remaining in his team were observed repeating the (unapproved but possible) short-cut behaviour which had led directly to his death.
- Workers in a steel plant would habitually walk across the frozen crust on a ground-level pot of molten metal. Periodically one of them would break through the crust and suffer serious burns to the lower leg, following which people would walk around the pot, not across it. Behaviour returned to normal after about six weeks, until eventually another person suffered injury and the cycle would repeat. Three cycles of this behaviour were observed.
- Following a very serious fire in a large petrochemical storage facility, managers' attention was entirely on complying with the (lengthy) list of requirements of the government's inspectors. By two months later, the urgency had diminished and the implementation of these requirements became harder and harder to achieve. Life had returned to normal.

There is evidence that people and groups of people will, at times, focus their concerns on either the multitude of minor Consequences of a Risk or on the potential for a major catastrophic Consequence. Very frequent minor Consequences can so engage people that any other Risk is ignored. In one company, people's entire safety concern was about dust nuisance in the car park. The safety committee could address nothing else, even though other very serious Risks existed.

Similarly, communities become so concerned about very high Consequence possibilities that arguments about their low probability are ignored. An example of this is the possibility of major nuclear plant catastrophe. The community clearly indicates that the Consequence is not acceptable no matter how low is the calculated probability. For us as individuals, the probability of a Consequence is not relevant if the Consequence to us personally is seen to be very high. I was once told by a doctor that the probability of me experiencing a fatal reaction to a penicillin injection was 'only about one in one hundred thousand'. The notion of this was so unacceptable to me (I had a friend who had died this way) that the probability was irrelevant.

Hence, when discussing Risks that have a personal meaning to the particular audience, Probability or Frequency of Consequence has little meaning to the audience. Morally this is true also. The focus of discussion should rather be on what can be done to control the Risk. If the cost of any proposed control measure is seen by the group as being unreasonable in relation to the Risk, the group may change its perception of the significance of their concerns.

Table 8.7 summarises the context of Risk evaluation.

Table 8.7   Risk evaluation in context

Context	Application
Occupational: Employer–employee or employer–public relationship	The purpose of evaluation is to understand and satisfy the standard of care. In the absence of specific guidelines this means doing everything that is practical or possible. The emphasis is on providing a safe place, not on encouraging safe behaviour. The estimation of probability or frequency is only relevant when establishing priorities for jobs to be done or the economic efficiency of proposals for 'could do' work. There is no practical meaning of the phrase 'acceptable level of risk'.
Business–customer relationship	The purpose of evaluation is to understand and satisfy the standard of care, often expressed as a 'must do' or 'should do' depending on government- or industry-based regulation.
Government–individual relationship (transport, health care, etc.)	Government agency decisions based on lives saved per unit of expenditure. Government agency approvals (land use planning) based on anticipated increase in the frequency of fatalities if approval is granted.
Individual to other members of the public	The purpose of evaluation is to understand and satisfy the standard of care.

The Abuse of Risk Evaluation

Slovic reports research that suggests that: 'Risk concerns may provide a rationale for actions taken on other grounds or they may be a surrogate for other social or ideological concerns'. He concludes that in these cases 'communication about Risk is simply irrelevant to the discussion'.

I have on three occasions been asked to contribute to workplace disputes based on the assertion by one party that either work method changes cannot be made because it would be unsafe, or work should be allowed to continue in the way it was because it was not unsafe or physical changes needed to be made because it was unsafe. On the first occasion it was the affected workers making this assertion. On the other two, it was the government inspectorate. On the first occasion, my rational contribution may have made the assertion disappear but not the underlying concern about workplace changes. On the second and third occasions, the assertion was withdrawn in the face of evidence to the contrary, but there were suggestions the assertions were made in the first place because the inspectors involved were trying to demonstrate their power to people who were disrespectful of it.

There was another occasion when I provided assistance with Risk theory to someone who had been commissioned by a government forestry department to assess the Risks to forestry officers from falling branches when walking in the forest. As the theory developed it came into conflict with the scope of the exercise as framed by the government department. The scope had been skilfully written to ensure that no matter what the outcome of the exercise, the result would be declared 'safe'! On yet another occasion, I was assisting a group of engineers with understanding the theory and practice of Risk analysis for their work on the design of new suburban rail cars. The highly Risk-averse government department to whom they were contracted had set a (very low) target Risk level (fatalities per year) to be achieved. The organisation for whom the engineers worked had set up a process that ensured that the target Risk level was an input to guide the subjective selection of equipment failure rates. The process was the inverse of what a logical process would have been.

The risk matrix (mentioned in Chapter 6) is used in an enormous variety of situations, despite evidence of its unreliability. As a Risk estimation device, it needs some discipline and knowledge to use with a modicum of meaning, but is still unreliable in the sense of producing unrepeatable results. As a Risk evaluation device, it is seriously conceptually flawed, as it offers a coarse distinction between acceptable and unacceptable based purely on unreliable choices from subjective likelihood and Consequence scales and an arbitrarily selected boundary between the two states. It is no surprise, then, that, in the hands of a person intent on using this blunt instrument to promote their viewpoint, innocent members of committees find themselves faced with an assertion that 'it's not safe'. It seems that community groups are especially vulnerable to this misuse of Risk evaluation when considering plans for the annual fete, an outing into the woods or whatever.

Summary

Risk evaluation is the process of deciding whether the existing standard of control measures is acceptable. It is necessary to recognise three different situations in which risk evaluation tales place, as these affect the criteria on which evaluation may be based. Only in very particular situations is this achieved via an estimation of the size of Risk and only in particular situations can a decision be made about what needs to be done be based on this. Consequently, and respectively, the popularity of estimating tolerable risk, seeking the ALARP standard and the popularity of the risk matrix is largely misplaced. The task is not to decide how much Risk is tolerable, nor is it to select a cell in the matrix, rather it is to determine the acceptable standard of Risk control measure (see Figure 8.4).

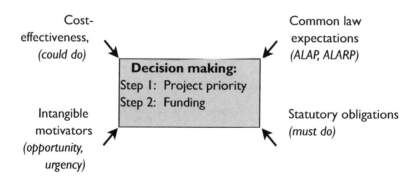

Figure 8.4   Summarising Risk evaluation

An understanding of how people perceive risk is useful as a means of explaining their responses, whether in the occupational, recreational or private environment. An understanding of how to determine the likely requirements of the standard of care in any one situation is needed to evaluate the acceptability of the current or proposed control measures. This understanding can be used to both investigate an individual risk and to see how management practices in organisations can be designed to facilitate effective risk-related decision-making.

Understanding how to evaluate risk makes it possible to understand how to define the meaning of both 'safe' and 'unsafe'.

9

Classifying and Analysing Risk: Damage Aetiology through Logical Analysis

Introduction

The primary purpose of Risk analysis is to:

- accurately describe how something adverse can happen and the results of it, if it does;
- provide a means of synthesising estimates of the Frequency and value of the associated adverse Consequences.

Risk analysis uses logic diagrams, which reflect the logic of the failures and processes needed to produce adverse Consequences. Their origin (Ericson, 1999) is to be found in the Cold War need to determine methods to test intercontinental ballistic missile launch systems up to the point of launch but being sure not to actually launch. Application to the design of aircraft quickly followed, then the nuclear power industry, rail, road and the petrochemical industry. These methods provide the most structured means available to us to gain insight into the detailed minutiae of Occurrence processes and potentially provide us with the insight with which to direct control measures at specific predictable processes.

Despite this long history, it is not clear that the methods of risk analysis are well developed or well used, or perhaps adequately used where needed. Significant disasters are the best evidence that can be advanced in support of this assertion. A minimal list of these, amongst many that are easy to retrieve from the internet record and all documented well in numerous places, is the Bhopal disaster of 1984, the Deepwater Horizon oil spill in 2010 and the Fukushima nuclear power plant in 2011. Post hoc judgement finds it easy to identify equipment and management failings and much along these lines has been written about each case. What is of concern to anyone interested in the management of risk is the lack of prior awareness of the failings and their implications. Unfortunately, relatively little is written in this vein. These disasters occurred in the industries most involved in the application of risk analysis since its inception. One possible conclusion, probably out of many, is that it is hard for day-to-day managers to keep in view the assumptions and implications made in risk analysis at the plant design stage. A more productive response to such cases, rather than censuring and fining the individuals or organisation on whose watch these disasters took place, would be to improve the technical management of risk in high-energy industries. For this reason, an emphasis in this chapter is on the organisational implications of the assumptions made when risk is being analysed. A later chapter is concerned with the technical management of risk and the structures and processes required in the engineering management of high-hazard industries. The reader should recognise, however, that these techniques are as applicable to non-energy threats (business processes) as they are to energy-based ones.

Risk analysis makes use of two types of logic diagram, one to understand the logic of system faults, known as fault tree analysis (FTA), that lead to a significant Event (called a Top Event in FTA), and the other to show what can follow the Event by describing the logical pathways (here called Outcomes) that lead from it to Consequences. This latter is known, somewhat confusingly, in the petrochemical industry as event analysis (EA) and so this is the term that will be used here to refer to the analysis of possible Outcomes following an Event. A search through the literature will make it evident that these terms can be used in a conflicting and hence confusing variety of ways by different authors. These tools are used by engineers to understand the Occurrence scenarios that are possible in typical industrial electromechanical systems. All that is said in FTA is what needs to happen to create the Event. For example, that for a leak to happen in a pressurised system either a valve is opened unintentionally, or at the wrong time, or a failure of the vessel to contain the pressure occurs, perhaps due to a structural failure or to the operation of the pressure relief valve. These are Mechanisms of failure. It could also be that for something to occur two simultaneous requirements exist, for example the tank must be pressurised and the valve must be opened. FTA is based on the construction of a logic diagram (shaped like a tree root) that places all these OR (either this or that will produce the result) and AND (it requires this and that to produce the result) logical operators in their appropriate place. The endpoint of an FTA is the discovery of the individual component failures or human action failures needed to produce the Top Event. Once the leak has occurred the EA looks at how it is identified and responded to, which may involve automatic functions or manual reaction, themselves capable of failure.

Industrial safety practitioners have discovered these forms of analysis in relatively recent times, adopted them for their own purposes and given names such as 'cause analysis' to them. A simplified version of risk analysis, given the name 'bow-tie' because of its appearance, has become increasingly popular from the 1990s onwards. While their appearance as logic diagrams may be similar, their content may be and is often very different from that of FTA or EA, either because they contain causes (which are not the same as Mechanisms of Failure) or because their purpose is more to demonstrate the variety of possible reasons for Events and to summarise their effects, rather than include the logic of these options. Hence, it is necessary to emphasise that the terms 'accident' and 'cause' have no place in FTA and EA, which are solely concerned with physical possibilities (i.e. following the universal laws of physics) capable of objective description. Any term that is clearly judgemental has no place in an FTA or EA, for example 'insufficient', 'ignorant' and so on. This chapter is concerned with FTA and EA, and not with bow-tie (although this is mentioned briefly) or with cause analysis.

One aspect of what can be taught about these tools is the simple structural conventions associated with them and the mathematics of deducing from component failure probabilities the Frequency of possible Consequence Values. Specialist texts devoted to the former, for example that of Sutton (2007), are readily available. Boolean algebra is the form of mathematics that handles probabilities through AND and OR points (known as 'gates') in the logic diagram. To these are added VOTING gates, to represent the way in which replicated multiple inputs are handled by automated control systems. Where three devices provide the same input (for reliability purposes), the control system may, for example, take any two inputs that agree with each other as the correct input and ignore the dissenting input. Similarly, explanations of this simple branch of mathematics are easily found on the internet. Consequently, in this chapter the very simplest of explanations will be given. The intention is to not obscure the underlying logic and purpose of the analysis with matters whose complexity is best understood at another time and through dedicated sources.

It is particularly important to realise that the choice of failure probability at the component or human action failure level is what determines the Risk. Representative values of failure probability are fortunately available to the risk engineer, but actual failure probabilities depend on everyday management decisions about operating, maintenance, inspection, equipment renewal and training practices. I have never met, in high-energy industrial plant, operating managers who have taken the time to understand the assumptions of the design engineers. This is akin to pilots jumping into the cockpit without bothering to enquire too deeply about the designed performance of the aircraft they are about to fly: unheard of! Of interest in this context is the revelation that in the operation of NASA's space shuttle, the failure probability estimates made in risk analysis at the outset were shown to be incorrect in practice by a significant amount (NPR, 2011).

What I have found, in decades of teaching this topic, is that risk analyses are surprisingly susceptible to the interpretation of the individual. This problem can be partly overcome by following a formal process and some practical guidelines, both of which I attempt to explain succinctly here. Not all systems that can fail are made up of tanks, pipes, pumps and controllers connected together in a simple and defined way that is relatively amenable to being analysed in the same way by different people. An extensive search of the literature reveals a dearth of papers providing either a theory for or critical appraisal of FTA. The paper of Russo and Kolzow (1994) is an exception. These authors are concerned with the structure and content of fault trees and assert that most fault trees are inaccurate, suggesting that this is due to exclusions from the analysis not being explicitly stated and to ambiguity in the details of what is analysed. Much of their argument depends on the presence of a standard branch in fault trees, called 'all other events'. Not being further analysed, this branch is a convenient but obscure location for anything of which the analyser has not thought. It is the intention of this chapter to address these failings.

The TSM (Chapter 3) conveys the underlying architecture of the way in which FTA and EA are connected through the defined Event. It follows therefore that, in principle, any Event that is capable of being identified and described is amenable to the analysis of Mechanisms and Outcomes. For example, I have used this to construct successful risk analysis diagrams of such diverse matters as:

- a biped (human, robot) falling;
- being struck by a tree branch when felling trees in a forest;
- a car hitting a fallen tree branch on country roads;
- a car and train reaching a level crossing at the same time;
- the loss of an air operator's certificate by an airline;
- the failure of an aircraft to achieve take-off safety speed;
- a person unable to leave a walk-in freezer;
- the complete operations of an open-cut mine up to the point of loading coal at the railhead;
- numerous Events at thermal power stations;
- errors while carrying out switching instructions on an electricity distribution system.

The form of the energy-damage theory that is presented in this book specifically defines an Event in terms of an energy source, as well as extending this to accommodate non-energy threats. For any type of industry or commercial organisation, it is therefore feasible to determine all the Event types of concern. It follows that all possible Mechanisms and Outcome pathways are also able to be modelled. This is neither a gigantic nor an improbable job. It is arguably the most useful contribution a risk engineer or adviser can make.

The skeleton of a risk analysis is determined by physical possibilities and there is a natural limit to these. For example, a risk analysis of the Event 'a person starts to fall' (on a surface) uncovers six basic Mechanisms that can be expanded to 17 subcategories, an application used in this chapter to illustrate a theory for determining Event Mechanisms. One could expand this almost without limit if one started to add banana skins, oil leaks, rainy weather and so on to the slip category. All this circumstantial material detracts from a proper understanding of the basic principles and reinforces the perception that everything is very complex. With very few exceptions, it is not. First let us obtain a thorough understanding of the structure of possible Occurrences and only then add relevant circumstantial detail.

To illustrate this important point, all airlines are equal when it comes to what they do: fill aircraft with fuel, food, baggage and passengers, taxi, take off, climb, cruise, descend, land, taxi and disembark passengers. However, not all airlines experience the same Circumstantial influences of environmental, culture, economics and people. An untimely emphasis on Circumstances is distracting and unproductive. It is inefficient to start our understanding of risk by studying these Circumstantial differences, even though research at into this may uncover some valuable insights, it is highly likely to be reactive insight (studying crashes) and not at all proactive.

There are two possibly unexpected benefits to be gained from the intellectual capital that a risk analysis represents: the work can be used to assist with the analysis of Occurrences (investigation of accidents) as well as to classify them by type. It is very useful to have a guide to investigation that has preconsidered all the options. The benefit works both ways as an investigation may expose omissions and other weaknesses in the risk analysis and be a very useful partner in the development of quality risk analysis models. The classification of cases that have occurred is useful in the development of historical data, which can be used to measure performance in risk control over time.

Classifying Risks and Mechanisms

In Chapter 5 it was argued that risks could arise from one of two sources, either from exposure to energies or to non-energy threats. There are 10 or so different forms of energy, depending on how they are classified, each of which we could therefore say gives rise to a unique type of risk. Gravitational risks are quite different from those arising from ionising radiation, for example. Chapter 5 identified four different types of non-energy-based threat. Each of these risk types can give rise to an Event, being the point in time when control is lost over the potentially damaging or loss-making properties of the Threat. Figure 9.1 shows this with the convention that items to the left are subsets of items to their right. That is, energy-based threats are subdivided into the various

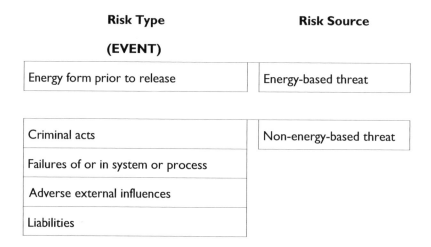

Figure 9.1   Classification diagram of risks by source and type

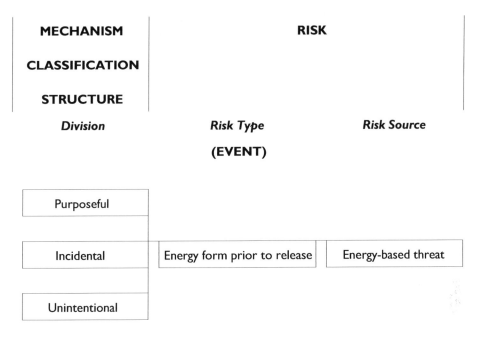

MECHANISM CLASSIFICATION STRUCTURE	RISK	
Division	*Risk Type* **(EVENT)**	*Risk Source*
Purposeful		
Incidental	Energy form prior to release	Energy-based threat
Unintentional		

Figure 9.2   Classification diagram of Mechanisms for energy-based threats

forms of energy, not listed here due to their number. Non-energy-based threats are subdivided into the four categories introduced in Chapter 5.

In our role as risk engineers or managers, we are most commonly concerned to understand and manage unwanted Mechanisms of Occurrences. It is useful to understand the types of possible Mechanisms before delving in great detail into those associated with specific Conditions and Circumstances. In Figure 9.2, use is made of Divisions proposed by Rowe (1977) and which were described in Table 3.4 as types of Hazard Control failure Mechanism. Each of these is potentially the Mechanism for an Event based on the energy form of interest.

A Theory for Analysing Unintentional Mechanisms

The objective is to understand all possible Mechanisms that could give rise to an unintentional Event. On some few occasions, these Mechanisms may appear self-evident from the context. Chapter 5 describes a structured approach to identifying risk, based on energy sources and Threats, and by way of illustration shows how these can be associated with Mechanisms and Outcomes without resorting to the use of special techniques. Such simple methods (using experience and judgement) are a valuable way of filling in details. However, a greater sense of certainty results from using a structured approach based on a set of rules or conventions. If we expect risk analysis, as suggested in the introduction to this chapter, to be the basis of a predictive approach to risk engineering and management, we need a theoretical basis, however simple it might be. It is a long way from saying we are interested in an unintentional Mechanism for the release of the potentially damaging properties of a chemical bonding energy source to the point of being able to decide on the Top Event that is suited to an FTA of a part of an automated petrochemical plant.

If a small and self-sufficient item of plant is to be analysed, the Top Event is probably self-evident from the context, as it simply describes whatever it is that is to be analysed.

As examples: the fire alarm fails to operate, the standby generator fails to start on demand, the tank is overfilled. All that is needed to complete the FTA is an understanding of the logic and how to make the logic diagrams reflect that adequately. None of this is especially complex in itself, although even simple electromechanical systems can lead to a surprising and undesirable variety in the FTA produced by different people. If, however, we are concerned with the potential for an Occurrence involving a large energy source in a far larger and more complex piece of plant, we can see that each of these examples may be a small part of something bigger – but what?

The contention here is that if an analyst follows a process, they are more likely to create a reproducible result. This process benefits greatly from first describing the intended positive functioning of the system, as the analysis of failure to do so is then more understandable to others. The process is a simple one and involves:

1. Rules for determining the Top Event.
2. Selection of the Mechanism Division (Figure 9.2).
3. Question 1: What abilities does the system have that normally prevent it from falling? An explicit statement is made of what enables the system to control its hazardous properties under normal operating Conditions and Circumstances: the abilities or capabilities of the system in this regard. The basic ability may be subdivided into functional abilities, for example the ability to control temperature in a domestic hot water service will depend on the functional ability to measure water temperature and then influence energy input to the service.
4. Question 2: What mechanisms does the system have that give it the abilities determined by Question 1? An explicit statement is made of the Mechanisms (called Hazard Control failure Mechanisms in Chapter 3) which enable the system to have these functional capabilities. For example a thermocouple and an electric heating element (alternatively a person using a finger to sense temperature and a wood fire under the hot water tank).

The process is conveniently illustrated by analysing something everyone has experienced, namely a person falling. The Event, being defined in Chapter 4 as the point in time when control is lost over the potentially damaging properties of the Threat in which we are interested (which is the gravitational potential energy of the person in this case), can be stated as 'a fall begins'. The Risk Type from Figure 9.2 is 'Gravitational Potential Energy – fall begins.' In the purposeful Division, a fall is a voluntary jump. No incidental Mechanisms are envisaged. In the unintentional Division, which will be analysed here, falls do not normally begin, because of the abilities that we have to hold our body upright, to know what upright means and to so arrange ourselves that forces and moments are balanced in the vertical direction and the horizontal plane. Forces and moments arise from gravity, inertia, the wind and other forces (such as pushes) acting on us at the feet, hands or other parts of the body. We need to be able to balance forces and moments whether stationary or walking. These system abilities are:

*   the ability to hold our skeleton in shape;
*   the ability to balance forces and moments by moving our body as needed to provide support when and where required – our movements must not be constrained;
*   the ability to balance forces and moments by developing the necessary support forces at points of interaction of our body with its surrounds.

If any one of these system abilities is taken from us, then an Event will exist – a fall will begin. A negative statement of abilities is the way to describe the nature of the Mechanism, for example the inability to hold our skeleton in shape. For brevity, in Table 9.3, the failures of these abilities are called Collapse, Constraint and Release respectively. The word failure, depending on context, could mean one of the following:

- a literal failure of a component, for example a bone breaks or a ligament snaps;
- a missed visual cue or other sensory input, for example not seeing a banana skin on the floor;
- a missing or inappropriate output of a processing function, for example the brain makes the wrong decision or no decision.

Further analysis could and arguably should be completed using terms uninfluenced by the technology of the bipod being considered – which could be either a mammal or a robot. However, at this point a person is referred to in order to avoid obscure generalised terms. Collapse means the person is no longer able to hold their body upright. This ability is derived from the functional abilities of the neuromuscular system:

- the ability of the brain to know what is needed and to tell the muscles what to do;
- the ability of the muscles and tendons to hold the skeleton in the necessary configuration.

Each of these abilities exists because of the ways in which the system works. The way in which the neuromuscular ability is provided is that:

- The brain receives inputs from the eyes, ears and the rest of the body – the 'seat of the pants' senses that pilots make use of (called \sensory input problem').
- The brain processes that information and decides what needs to be done to stay upright (called 'brain processing failure'). For practical reasons, the functioning of the proprioceptors in the body, which provide feedback to the brain about the position of joints, is included in this.
- The brain sends action signals to the muscles (called 'signal failure').

Knowing what the system has to do (system ability) and how it functions (system functional capability), it is possible to know how these functions can be disrupted. In Figure 9.3 the terms Class, Order, Family and Genus are used to name these levels in the analysis as, apart from being readily recognised as part of the biological classification systems, they have inherently relevant meanings and it is useful to have names for the various parts of the Mechanism. In the biological classifications, Kingdom and Phylum precede Class. Here, Kingdom is analogous to Risk Type and Phylum to Mechanism Division.

Question I is asked as many times as necessary. The ability to keep the body in a controlled posture relies on the ability to decide what is needed and give effect to that decision. From then on, we can't answer this question meaningfully, as we have to ask in what ways (Mechanisms) are these abilities made possible? Generally it is a physical mechanism that does this or a procedure that encourages people to behave in a defined way. Notice that the abilities (Class and Order) are of general applicability and do not depend on the technology employed for the Mechanisms – either a mammal or a robot. The technology of the bipod could be brains, blood, nerves and muscles, or electronic processor, power supply, signal cables and electric actuators. The generality of the analysis is derived from the need of the system being investigated to comply with physical laws. In this case, our bipod exists on earth with gravity and to remain stable all forces and moments must be in either static or dynamic balance. This applies to the body itself, since it is made up of joints and linkages, as well as to the body as a whole as it interacts with its environment by standing or walking or being pushed or pulled and so on.

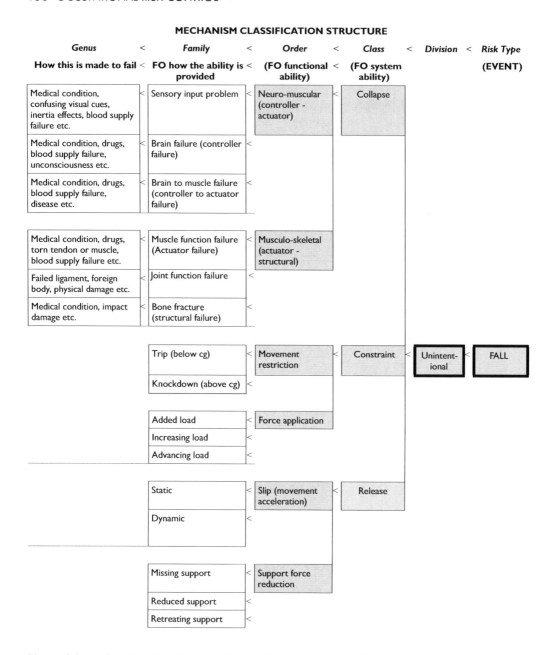

Figure 9.3   Classification diagram illustrating the theory of Mechanism structure

Note: < denotes hierarchical connection. Used in place of lines for a compact figure.

Successful FTA Requires a Suitable Top Event

The example of the fall shows how the use of Question 1 above leads to an understanding of the Class and Order of the Mechanism. These are capable of being expressed in a generic form that should not depend on the actual technology of the system, even though it may be useful to use technology-specific terms for brevity. Further analysis below the Order, which is what FTA does, necessarily depends on the technology in use (people or robots?) and the specific design of the system. As argued previously, the ability to conduct a high-level Mechanism analysis is valuable as it enables Top Events for FTA to be derived from logical analysis rather than intuition or guesswork.

As an example, consider the ejector seat used in high-performance military aircraft, the functions of which can be succinctly described as follows. Once triggered by the pilot, the cockpit canopy is jettisoned, the legs of the pilot are pulled back and restrained, the seat together with the pilot is propelled up its launching rails, its motion stabilised by drogue parachutes before the pilot is released from the seat and the pilot's parachute is deployed. Mostly, the logic is of the type: if this happens then that happens. This is akin to a chain, as the failure of any one link in the chain will lead to a complete failure of function. What is the Top Event on which a failure analysis could be based? A pilot abandons an aircraft if its use as a support against gravity is compromised – it is going to crash. In Table 9.3 this is the release/missing support route to a fall. In this case, however, the support of the aircraft is replaced by the support of a parachute, as both a parachute and an aeroplane can be landed. The successful function of the device is to provide the pilot with the support of a parachute when needed. The failure of this function is well described as failure to do this, so the Top Event would be stated as 'Failure to provide the support of a parachute when needed'. The phrase 'Missing support' is highly relevant with the qualification 'when needed'.

The need for careful consideration of the logic when identifying Top Events can be illustrated by another aeronautical example. Aeronautical engineers are familiar with a design condition for multiple engine aircraft known as 'engine failure on take-off' or EFTO. At take-off, weights are high and speeds are low. Low speeds reduce the power of aerodynamic control surfaces, but high weights require larger forces. If an engine fails, the aeroplane must be able to maintain a controlled climb (the design condition for roll and yaw control) and maintain a minimum climb gradient (the engine power and maximum take-off weight design condition). Hence EFTO is intuitively also a Top Event. EFTO essentially means that the thrust from the engine in question (an outboard engine in the case of a four-engine aircraft) is no longer being delivered to the airframe. Obviously, this can occur in one of two ways: either the engine stops working or the engine separates from the airframe. Because the former is far more likely and because the phrase EFTO is in common use, it is easy to regard this as being the Top Event for the case. One day, the much less common 'engine separates' case did occur and the Outcome was that the engine accelerated past the wing, destroying all the triplicated hydraulic control lines that lay in its path, hence disabling all roll control devices on that wing. The aircraft rolled on its back and crashed near the airport boundary, killing all on board. As will be explained later, different Mechanisms can lead to different Outcomes. It is clear that an inaccurately stated Top Event can result in significant omissions from a risk analysis.

The Structure and Content of a Fault Tree

The earlier figures in this chapter illustrate the relationship between different levels of classification. The style used has been chosen because it is similar to the form of logic diagrams used to construct an FTA. By convention, an FTA is constructed either downwards from the Top Event, or from the Top Event towards the left. Because the horizontal form replicates the style of the TSM, this is the form that will be used here. By convention, in engineering and science time is shown on a horizontal axis moving from earlier times on the left to later times on the right. Mechanisms give rise to Events and, as Mechanisms always take time to unfold, the Event usually occurs some time after the Mechanism begins. Certainly, the Event logically follows the Mechanism and, of course, Outcomes follow the Event.

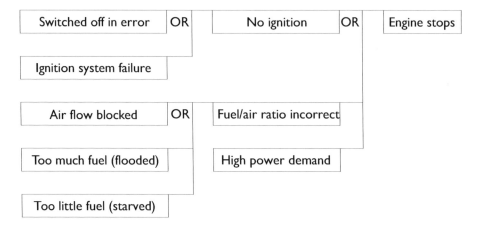

Figure 9.4   A fault tree with OR logic

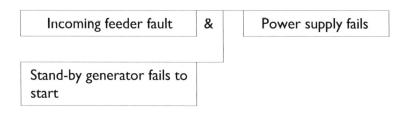

Figure 9.5   A fault tree with AND logic

In an FTA, the logic shows what needs to happen to produce the fault of interest. For example, if a petrol engine stops (the fault) it is due either to there being no ignition spark, or to the fuel/air ratio being incorrect due to too little or too much of either or because the power demand exceeds the capability of the engine. Each of these OR logic possibilities is shown diagrammatically to the left of (or below) the fault. Other faults may require two or more things to happen simultaneously, for example for the power supply to an industrial process to fail it may be necessary for the primary (the normal electricity supply) AND the backup (the standby generator) power supply to fail. Figures 9.4 and 9.5 illustrate these examples in the form of logic diagrams in which 'OR' and '&' show the logic appropriate to the node. In either example, the analysis could be continued further to the left to uncover the ways in which any of the faults could be produced. For example, air flow to an engine could be blocked by ice in the carburettor or (unlikely but possible) by a blockage in the exhaust pipe. Carburettor icing will only occur if the dew point is close enough to the current temperature. The increasing level of detail is taken to the point where there is no intention to analyse the Mechanisms further. Usually, this is the point at which the expected function of a component has failed (for example ignition failure, standby generator failure), a person acts inappropriately (for example switched off in error) or a sufficient or relevant environmental condition exists (for example air flow blocked by ice).

A functional failure means that the normal and intended purpose or function of a component or condition is not satisfied. The inappropriate interaction of people with the system being analysed refers to their choice of working method or procedure, receiving and acting on information, direct personal interaction with the environment and so on. This is inappropriate in the sense that it would lead to the unintended Mechanism.

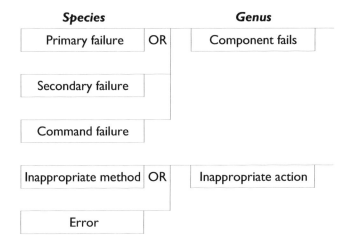

Species   *Genus*

| Primary failure | OR | Component fails |

| Secondary failure |

| Command failure |

| Inappropriate method | OR | Inappropriate action |

| Error |

Figure 9.6   **The endpoints of an FTA**

Very commonly, the analysis of the ways in which a Mechanism develops ends at the Genus with either a component failure or an inappropriate action by a person – see Figure 9.6. For example, either a tank structure fails and releases hazardous liquid or a person opens a valve and releases the liquid. Proponents of accident theory would be comfortable calling these Genera 'unsafe conditions' and 'unsafe acts'. The scientist's objection to these terms is simply the use of the essentially judgemental qualifier 'unsafe'. An unsafe act is better seen as an inappropriate interaction of people with their environment (being more objective and capable of further analysis). Wigglesworth (1972) saw the benefit of replacing the term 'unsafe act' with 'human error' and in defining 'error' as 'a missing or inappropriate response to a stimulus'.

There are two aspects, for which the (biological) term Species would apply, to this Genus of inappropriate action: an inappropriate method properly (or even incorrectly) followed or an appropriate method incorrectly followed, called error for brevity. In the former, the person is doing what is intended (or makes a mistake doing this) but this intended method is inappropriate. A detailed understanding of these two Species is essential for the risk engineer, but this would require a substantial digression from the subject of this chapter. It is the subject matter of the study of what is known as human factors or ergonomics.

Functional failures of components are the subject matter of reliability and maintenance engineering. For the purposes of FTA it is sufficient to note the three commonly accepted Species of component failure:

1. A primary failure is one due to the malfunction of an item under conditions for which it was designed. Typically these failures occur due to a deterioration in the component arising from corrosion, fatigue, erosion, embrittlement and similar ageing processes. Examples include:
    * an electric motor fails while subject to load within its design capacity;
    * a tank or pipe develops a leak due to corrosion;
    * a valve leaks due to damage to the valve seat or ageing of gaskets and packings.
2. A secondary failure of an item occurs when it is subject to conditions which are not part of its designed operating condition. Typically, these failures are due to the imposition of excessive loads on an otherwise healthy component. Examples include:
    * a pump fails when solid objects are sucked into it;
    * pipework fails when hit by a vehicle;

- a conductor is destroyed by excessive current arising from a lightning strike;
- a conveyor bridge collapses under the weight of spilled materials.

3. A command failure occurs if the item is made to operate or to stop operating at a time or in a manner that is not appropriate. The command can either come from an automated control system or from a person in the case of a manually controlled process. Examples include:
   - a person or automatic controller switches a pump on (or off) at the wrong time;
   - a pilot inappropriately switches off a hydraulic system.

More could be said about the classification of ways a component can fail to perform as intended, but a digression into the details of reliability and maintenance engineering is not appropriate. As with error and work methods, knowledge of this detail is essential for a risk engineer.

The term component is intended to be interpreted loosely here. In an industrial plant, the term is used for electrical, electronic, pneumatic, hydraulic and mechanical components of the plant. The structure of the plant itself, the structure of tanks and their bunds, of conveyor galleries, pipe racks and so on are also components of the plant. Outside the industrial environment, the term can be applied to all physical components that contribute to the function of any system, as the examples in Table 9.1 illustrate.

Table 9.1   Examples of physical components

Field	Components include
Railways	Trackbeds and tracks, electricity supply hardware, bridges, tunnels, cuttings, drains, platforms, signalling apparatus
Airports and airways	Terminal buildings, service tunnels, aerobridges, taxiways and runways, drainage works, lighting, radar, radio communication equipment, navigation aids
Forestry	Trees and tree branches, winches, mobile equipment, portable equipment
Civil works	Drains, trenches, mobile powered equipment
Commerce	Computer systems, communication pathways, records facilities

Defined methods of work exist in many situations, for example electrical switching work, electrical live-line work, piloting/driving work, operating machinery, energy isolation work, maintenance activities, tapping a furnace and so on. Commercial examples are also numerous: how loans are approved, the way advice is given, the way investment or planning decisions are made and so on. It is entirely possible to subject a defined method of work to FTA. An inappropriate method can be said to exist if:

1. The method is formal (probably in writing) but is incorrect or impractical. Examples include:
   - an electrical switching instruction that is intended to apply to the job in which it is used but there is an error (for example wrong action or missing action) in it;
   - an energy isolation procedure that is complex and time consuming to the point of being impractical;
   - a required work method that is not up to the required standard of control measure, given the nature of the risk intended to be controlled by it.
2. A method that is adopted to do a job lacks the qualities necessary to avoid damage. An example is a method of isolating plant that has developed over time but which ignores relevant energy sources.

Error, in the simplest sense, means that a person acts in a way that was not intended or that is subsequently shown to be inappropriate in the circumstances. Many errors of judgement or action occur without ever resulting in a complete Occurrence. Table 9.2 shows the context in which this needs to be understood. While in most cases people are aware of what is required, this is not always the case. It is not uncommon for people to have no intention of complying with an approved or expected method of work. It is common to hear of people deciding to 'work to rule' as a form of industrial action as this means delays can be expected as the work takes far longer to do when done to rule. In this case, compliance is nonproductive (and hence not feasible in this sense) and noncompliance has been accepted as the norm, with managers turning a blind eye to the expected method of work. Ordinary errors do not normally constitute negligence and even intended noncompliance with rules may not be negligent if the rules are known to be seldom followed or impractical. Negligence requires careful definition having consideration of relevant laws.

Table 9.2   The context of error

Knowledge of what is expected	Intention	Compliance feasible?	Result	Interpretation
Aware	To comply	Yes	Correct	What we hope for
		Yes	In error	Error type 1
	To not comply	Yes	In error	Negligent action
		No	Irrelevant	Unsuitable method
	Unintentional action	Yes or No	In error	'Accident' type 1
Unaware	—	—	Correct	Luck
	—	—	In error	Error type 2
	Unintentional action	—	In error	'Accident' type 2

Error type 1 is in the normal context of understanding the term. The correct action is known and appropriate and the person has every intention of complying, but does not do so. Pilots are familiar with this as the piloting task involves numerous required actions, including following checklists, making radio calls, making navigational decisions and flying the aircraft. Pilots are retrospectively aware of the number of incorrect or missing actions or decisions they have made during a flight. Error type 2 applies to a situation in which the person has no awareness of the need to behave in a particular way and by chance acts in an inappropriate way. For example, a person on a farm enters a slurry tank with no awareness of the need to check the atmosphere is breathable. Whether of type 1 or 2, error is a Species of great variety and theoretical development and requires detailed study in its own right.

Table 9.3 is an analysis of the structure of a controlling function. Automated systems are (typically) electromechanical devices that replace the human as the system controller. A controlling function, whether human or automatic, always involves the three sequential steps of detection of the system state, understanding whether that state is different from a desired state (cognition) and taking action to correct any discrepancy. An automated system does not suffer from the problem of intention with regard to compliance to which human beings are subject. It may nevertheless make errors at either step due to functional failures or limitations in the provided capability.

Table 9.3 **The structure of the controller function**

Step	Human responder	Automated system responder
1. Detection (perception)	Attention is directed towards relevant indications. Able to see the indications because these can be seen, heard or felt (e.g. smoke, leaks, overflow, noise, flames) and the presence of them is not masked.	Serviceable and calibrated sensors detect abnormal conditions. Sensor transmitters function as intended and the signal is received by the controller.
2. Cognition	Correctly understands the meaning of what is perceived (e.g. that is an alarm siren). Correctly deduces the implications of what is perceived. Correctly decides on the action required.	The controller function is designed to process the received signals.
3. Action	Correctly takes the action. The action is timely and effective.	The controller sends commands to actuators, which function as intended, or alerts to human operators.

Developing Understandable Fault Trees

It is easy to develop an FTA that has no evident incorrect features but which nevertheless is obscure in that it fails to capture or make evident the essence of possible Mechanisms. For example, in a typical industrial environment, almost every FTA will include equipment failure, operating method failure, power failure and control system failure. One can list all the equipment and provide detail of the logical connection of all the components, but without making the nature or implication of the possible failures evident to the user.

On the other hand, if the analyst has an understanding of what normally happens routinely and successfully (e.g. when tank temperature reaches a set point then a valve is opened after a time delay to transfer the contents to the next stage in the process) then it is easy to express the opposite of this in failure statements, for example: the tank temperature exceeds the set point; the valve does not open; the contents are not transferred. That is, the failure modes of the subassembly of the tank and its associated components are being described. Different failure modes may make different contributions to the Top Event.

Alternatively, the analyst can first understand what set of conditions could bring about the Top Event and then use a plain language statement of this to guide the development of the FTA. For example, for an explosive gas/air mixture to exist in an oven the rate of gas flow into the oven must be high in relation to the rate of air flow. This may result from gas flowing (leaking valve or valve opened) when the blower is off or from low blower flow (blocked inlet, blower failure, etc.) when the gas is on. It is generally not the fact that doggedly constructing an FTA in the absence of this understanding will make the reason for the Top Event clear to the analyst. An FTA will be created in this way, but its meaning may be very unclear. Not only will the analyst be no wiser but the result may bear little resemblance to someone else's analysis.

Of equal importance is the fact that the resulting FTA will not provide insight into what conditions need to be guarded against in the operation of the plant. This is of great importance in determining realistic failure probabilities, as discussed below. Consequently, plant operating and maintenance practices will not be sensitive to these conditions.

Estimating the Probability of the Top Event

As shown in Figure 9.6, FTA ends at the Species level of component or action failure. If the probability of these failures can be estimated, then it is possible to follow the AND/OR logic of the diagram to deduce the probability of the Top Event happening. The ability to do this relies on an understanding of the mathematical meaning of the logical operators AND and OR when associated with failure probabilities. For this discussion, it will be assumed that component or action failure probability can be estimated and that it can be represented by a single value.

The point has been made in Chapter 6 that although probability is a dimensionless number, it nevertheless has the meaning of the number of failures per unit of Exposure and it is of great importance for this meaning to be explicit. The exposure denominator can be of three types:

1. On demand – the demand for the service being provided by the component occurs occasionally. Examples include components on standby (such as fire water pumps, emergency generators), alarms, smoke or flame detectors, fire suppression devices, security systems, switching devices, batch delivery (for example tanker supply from or to a fuel tank) and transport arrivals (for example trains at a station). The Exposure is the unit of demand and the failure probability has the meaning of [failures to work per demand].
2. Process time – the demand for the service is continuous when the system of which it is a part is in use and this may be measured by natural time or production cycles. Examples include duty pumps, power supplies and engines, sensors and gauges. The Exposure is the running hours of the component and the failure probability has the meaning of [failures per running hour]. Failure may alternatively be measured per operating cycle, related obviously by the number of operating cycles in an hour, day, week or year.
3. Permanent – the demand for the service is continuous during the lifetime of the component. Examples include structures of all kinds (gravity never rests) such as bridges, buildings, and towers, and continuous services such as electrical or gas power supply and radio communications. The Exposure is the same in principle as that of routine Exposures but the unit typically taken is that of the year, so that the meaning is [failures per year]. This is indistinguishable from Frequency, of course.

Using Figure 9.4 as an example of OR logic, ignition failure can be brought about either by an action failure (switched off in error) or by a component failure (ignition system failure). As this is only of interest when the engine is running, the running hour is chosen as the unit of Exposure. For the purpose of illustrating the logic only, probability values are chosen as below:

$p_A = 0.001$ [action failures per running hour],

$p_C = 0.0001$ [component failures per running hour].

The overall probability of an ignition failure arising from p_A OR p_C is properly given by Boolean algebra as:

$$p_A \text{ OR } p_C = p_A + p_C - p_A \times p_C = 0.001 + 0.0001 - 0.001 \times 0.0001 \text{ [ignition failures per running hour]}.$$

It is common practice in risk engineering to ignore the second-order product term (in this case $p_A \times p_C$) as this has a value orders of magnitude less than the other terms and probability estimates are not precise. The equation is simplified to:

$$p_A \text{ OR } p_C = p_A + p_C = 0.001 + 0.0001 = 0.0011 \text{ [ignition failures per running hour].}$$

In words, the more failure types that individually could bring this state of ignition failure about, the greater the probability that it will happen.

Using Figure 9.5 as an example of AND logic, as power supply failures are only of interest when the power is being used, the hour is again selected as the unit of Exposure for the feeder. As the standby generator is not normally running, its exposure is best expressed as the number of start demands, which is the same as the number of incoming feeder faults. For illustration, probability values are chosen as below:

$$p_{C\,Feeder} = 10^{-5} \text{ [incoming feeder faults per running hour],}$$

$$p_{C\,Generator} = 10^{-2} \text{ [start failures per incoming feeder fault].}$$

Boolean algebra gives the overall probability of a power supply failure as the product of these:

$$p_{C\,Feeder} \text{AND } p_{C\,Generator} = p_{C\,Feeder} \times p_{C\,Generator} = 10^{-5} \times 10^{-2} = 10^{-7} \text{ [power supply failures per running hour].}$$

In words, the more failure types that must happen to bring this failure about, the lower the probability that it will happen. This is true only if the two failures are independent of one another. Because of this it is very important when constructing fault trees to ensure that this independence condition really is satisfied when using AND logic. When two failures are not independent, they are said to have a common mode of failure. For example, if a gas turbine control system makes use of two air pressure sensors for reliability purposes, the analyst would need to be satisfied that these two sensors really had no common modes of failure in order to use AND logic. Common modes of failure for such components could include dust build-up and insect nests. Situations can also arise in the testing of plant when AND logic protection devices are intentionally overridden in order to test a final level of protection. Many cases have occurred of failures in such circumstances. AND logic in an FTA results in low Top Event probabilities and potentially to a perception that the Risk is very low. Common mode failure possibilities increase the Top Event probability and result in an increase in the estimated Risk.

The simplicity of the mathematical treatment of the logic diagram is countered by the complexity of finding appropriate failure probability values. To properly understand the nature of failure probability, it is necessary to understand something of reliability mathematics as well as have access to a source of data. Reliability mathematics is introduced in Chapter 10, where it is explained that components in general may exhibit early failures (so-called infant mortality or burn-in failures) as well as late failures (commonly called wear-out). Between the end of the early failures and the start of the late failures there is often a lengthy period in which the failure probability is reasonably constant and assumed to be due to random processes. It is possible to find sources of random failure probability data and extract a value that seems to be relevant. However, actual failure probability depends on many factors. Some components may have more than one failure mode and the probability of failure may be different for each. For example, the failure modes of a pump will include fail to start, fail while running and fail to deliver the required flow. It will be no surprise that failure probability also depends on the manufacturing quality of the component (usually reflected in the price), the physical environment in which it operates as well as the inspection, maintenance and equipment renewal practices in the organisation.

With regard to component failure probability, one can generally (there are few exceptions) take it for granted that the user organisation will not have had sufficient failures to properly determine failure probability. While the fact of component failure is often stored in a maintenance management system, it is unlikely that the time in service (which is often the relevant measure of exposure) of the failed component will have been determined or recorded. It is also unlikely that the component manufacturer will be able to supply data. There are exceptions to this observation, such as the aircraft industry, where manufacturers carefully monitor engine and other critical equipment failure rates and modes, and the nuclear power generation industry.

Action failure probability depends not only on the task to be done but also on a number of factors that influence the performance of the individual. These factors are both external (that is, derived from the organisation or the physical and social environment) and internal (that is, state of knowledge, fatigue, stress imposed by an emergency condition). As has previously been noted, human error is a complex subject on which much has been written over many decades and of which a risk engineer needs a detailed understanding. Due to their significance, action failures have been studied (Gertman and Blackman, 1994), particularly in catastrophe-sensitive industries. Efforts have been made to estimate human error probabilities in commerce and the medical industry – for example, Edmondson (1996).

As a search of the internet with search terms such as 'failure probability data' and 'human error probability' will show, this is a field that has attracted much attention over many years, particularly in the nuclear power industry (US Nuclear Regulatory Commission, 1984; International Atomic Energy Agency, 1988). There are many sources of component and action failure probability data of which the risk engineer should be aware.

To avoid the general difficulty of obtaining plant-specific failure probability data, it is common practice amongst risk engineers to use representative standard values (see, for example, Table 9.4) for different classes of components. A benefit of this approach is that the Top Event probability can be estimated consistently and with relative ease, at least to within a reasonable order of magnitude. At the very least, representative probability values make clear the relative significance of different branches of the fault tree as contributors to the Top Event. In Chapter 10 the mathematical origin of these values is explained, particularly that they assume random failures and not age-related failures. If the plant being analysed is reaching old age, if maintenance practices are reactive and equipment renewal investment minimal, the estimates of failure probability used in FTA must reflect this reality.

Human error probability possibilities cover a wide range from one error in less than five chances to one in millions of chances. This is influenced by the context. Many formal data collections arise from studies of people doing skilled tasks, with the implication that they intend to succeed. Examples include opening a valve or replacing a circuit board. The resulting probabilities cluster around one error in 1,000. However, people often do not intend to comply. In my own experience, unskilled people working in a loosely managed environment may fail to do what is expected of them as many as once or more in three opportunities. I have seen this even where a fatality has happened in very recent memory. I have even seen zero compliance (error probability of one) when a rule is seen as impractical even when associated with severe or fatal likely Consequence Values. On the other hand, I have also seen people performing production tasks which could readily be automated with an apparent error probability of less than one in a million actions: the body is doing a learned physical task with extraordinary reliability. When using error probability estimates it is important to break the task or activity down into its component parts. For example, the act of reading a gauge consists of identifying the gauge to be read, reading it and recording the result. Any of these parts of the task could be done incorrectly and each has its own probability of error.

Table 9.4   Representative failure probability estimates (various sources)

Failure type	Exposure base (prob. denominator)	Failure probability
Human error (occasional tasks, unskilled process operator)	per task action or decision	10^{-1}–10^{-2}
Skilled human error (maintenance tasks)	per task action or decision	10^{-2}–10^{-5}
Small component failures:		10^{-3}–10^{-4}
Sensors and logic controllers fail	per operating hour	
Small pipe and gasket leaks	per operating hour	
Alarms fail to sound	per demand	
Relief valve fails to open	per demand	
Engineered large component failures:		10^{-5}–10^{-6}
Inspected major mechanical controls fail	per operating hour	
Storage vessels spontaneous rupture	per operating hour	
Valve rupture, major leaks	per operating hour	
Human error in rapid routine tasks (manual production work)	per task	10^{-5}–10^{-6}
Pipe spontaneous rupture, containment weld failure	per operating hour	10^{-7}–10^{-8}
In-built design failures (e.g. unsuitable material selection)	per operating hour	$< 10^{-8}$

Outside the industrial field, 'component' failure probabilities are unlikely to be so readily available. Estimates can nevertheless be made by asking people how often they have experienced the failures in question; see Chapter 6.

When modelling Mechanisms using FTA it is common for component and action failures to have Exposure denominators of different types. The example given above of electrical supply failure (see Figure 9.5 and the associated discussion) is pertinent. In the case of AND logic, the resulting probability has a natural meaning that is derived from the individual meanings. In the case of OR logic, as probability figures are being added it is necessary that each has the same meaning, that is the same Exposure denominator. It is nonsensical to add a failure probability based on an occasional demand to one based on a routine running hour. It is feasible, however, to convert the demand-based figure to a per-running-hour-based figure by multiplying by the estimated number of demands per running hour. When quantifying a complete FTA this process needs to be followed right through the logic structure to ensure a meaningful figure for the Top Event probability. The logic of this result should become evident as the work proceeds. The Top Event probability will have an Exposure denominator that is a characteristic of the system under consideration. For example, if the risk of a production system failing to provide raw materials for delivery to market via a supply train is being analysed, a natural unit of exposure for the whole plant is a 'per train' figure. Likewise, if the risk of a person being trapped in a freezer is being analysed, the natural unit of exposure is 'per freezer entry'.

An essential conclusion to the quantification of an FTA is a reality check on the estimated Top Event probability. This can be achieved by converting the probability into a Frequency, the number of estimated Top Events per year, and comparing this with experience, or at least with judgement. For example, if the FTA estimates the Frequency of a person being trapped in a freezer as one in 100 years, but this is known to have happened once in the first five years of the freezer's operation, one may conclude the probability estimates do not accord with reality and adjust them accordingly. Reality does not fit the assumed failure probabilities, they have to fit reality – see also the discussion in Chapter 6 on estimating probabilities in the absence of data. Naturally, the more sensitive the result and the less evident the discrepancy with reality, the more useful it will be to involve a statistician in interpreting the confidence that may be placed on the estimated Top Event probability.

It is their common interest in component failure probabilities that unites the risk engineer and the reliability engineer. For this reason the risk engineer needs to be familiar with reliability mathematics and to have access to a source of failure probability data. The risk engineer also needs a good working understanding of error (action failures) and the situations that promote them.

Modelling Outcomes

The second part of risk analysis is the modelling of the Outcome process possibilities associated with the Event, Event Analysis. The purpose of the model is to show all physically possible ways in which the Outcome and associated Consequences could unfold. It is the end of the Outcome pathway that results in the Consequences: it is not the fall that hurts, but the impact at the end of it.

It is generally, but not always, true that the great majority of Outcomes do not result in any, or any significant, noticeable Consequences. In some cases, the energy or non-energy Threat is brought back under control so that the Event is short-lived. In Figure 9.7, this is the short pathway shown as the Null Outcome. Examples are numerous, but include by way of illustration:

- A roof tile begins to slide on a sloping roof but is soon brought to a halt by the presence of an obstruction on the roof.
- The primary system that controls pressure, temperature and/or level in a chemical plant reactor vessel fails to keep these within normal control boundaries when vessel outlet flow is stopped by a failed pump. Within a short time, the standby pump starts and outflow resumes, leading to conditions becoming stabilised.
- A driver realises their vehicle is about to enter a slide on loose gravel as a bend is rounded at high speed but is able to reduce speed and change steering inputs so that a slide is averted.
- A person is trapped inside a freezer room in a pharmaceutical company when the powered door fails to open, but is able to use the backup manually operated door to leave the room.
- In a petrochemical plant, a gas leak develops from a failed control valve, but the automatic control system recognises the leak from increased flow and reduced pressure indications and shuts a nearby stop valve, thereby ending the leak.

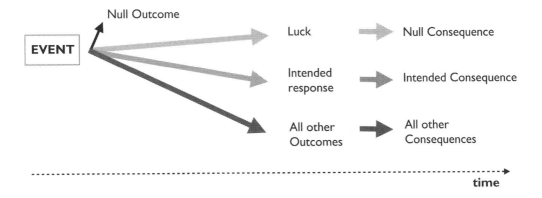

Figure 9.7 Outcome possibilities

On the other hand, an Outcome may result in a Null Consequence because of the pathway that develops. In this case, after the Event, the energy or non-energy Threat is not brought back under control but the process unfolds in a way that leads to no significant (Null) Consequence. Examples include:

- A roof tile begins to slide on a sloping roof and gathers speed as it drops over the edge of the roof and onto the ground beneath, fortuitously missing the builders standing there.
- The primary system that controls pressure, temperature and/or level in a chemical plant reactor vessel fails to keep these within normal control boundaries when vessel outlet flow is stopped by a failed pump. Conditions inside the vessel continue to develop until a pressure relief valve operates, which prevents a pressure explosion from rupturing the vessel. Operators trigger a water deluge system which contains the temperature and further reduces the pressure rise. This gives the operators a chance to implement an emergency shutdown of the process, which proceeds successfully and leads to no damage to equipment or to injury.
- A driver finds their vehicle sliding on loose gravel as a bend is rounded at high speed and successfully responds so that the car stays on the road.
- A person is trapped inside a freezer room in a pharmaceutical company when the powered door fails to open and the backup manual door opener does not work, but the alarm is sounded and others are able to respond successfully to open the door before the trapped person is adversely affected by the cold.
- In a petrochemical plant, a gas leak develops from a failed control valve. It is some time before the operators of the plant detect and respond to the problem as it is night time and the leak is not visible. A large vapour cloud forms, which drifts over the nearby plant boundary and then disperses over nearby fields without igniting or creating any known adverse effects due to its toxicity.

Null Outcomes and Null Consequences are both colloquially known as near misses.

Table 9.5 Physical possibilities and situational effects in Outcome pathways

Outcome/Consequence process affected by:	Explanation and examples
Energy form changes	Explosions result in heat and sound waves and in flying objects. Fires result in fumes and heat flux. Fumes and spilled liquids may result in chemical changes in water. A fall results in the conversion of gravitational potential energy into kinetic energy. The way in which Recipient exposure occurs may be different for each energy form.
Component operation	Devices such as pressure relief valves, alarms, fire suppression, smoke extraction, emergency shutdowns, backup power supplies, emergency lighting and similar may fail to operate.
Environmental Circumstances and Conditions, including weather effects	Wind or water may affect the process once the Event has occurred. If a flammable gas leak occurs, wind may blow the gas towards people or towards an ignition source. If it is raining heavily when the leak occurs the gas may dissolve in the rain water and the run-off may contaminate adjacent farm land. A flammable gas leak at a remote desert wellhead has very different Outcomes from one within a petrochemical plant surrounded by critical equipment and in close proximity to people. Contaminated dust may settle on crops and flowers and the contamination may affect mammals and insects some distance from the source of the release.

Geometrical uncertainty	The direction in which a tower or tree falls may be uncertain. The location along a train line where a derailing might occur is uncertain. The location of a hazardous goods vehicle accident along a route is uncertain. The location and direction of a landslide, rock or tree fall may be uncertain. An electricity transmission line fuse capable of dropping hot materials may operate over flammable ground cover or not depending on its location.
Uncertainty in the way in which Consequences could arise, including random chance	A gas leak or fire occurring in normal working hours will expose more people to the chance of injury than if it occurs outside those hours. If train doors fail open during rush hours, the chance of passengers falling out is increased, as is the chance of them being hit by passing trains. Random chance that a sensitive Recipient is in a location affected by an Outcome pathway at the same time as the Outcome occurs can be called a space/time coincidence. A landslide/tree fall/rock fall hits that point on a road or path that is occupied by a car or person. A car arrives at a road/rail crossing at the same time as a train.
Human behaviour	Response by control room operators to plant fault indications. Response by drivers, pilots, etc. to incipient unstable vehicle movements or to possible collision scenarios, to warnings and instructions.

The general purpose of Event Analysis is to identify all other Outcomes and their associated Consequences. The first need in Event Analysis is to understand all the physical possibilities and situational effects, up to and including the way in which Consequences arise. In Chapter 3 the point was made that Outcome processes are influenced by the situation and the Conditions and Circumstances within which the Event takes place. See Table 9.5 for a summary of these.

The second need in Outcome Analysis is to understand how the unfolding process can or should be responded to. Much of this will be sequential: if this happens then that should happen and after that something else, as in: leak detected, pipe flow shut down, alarm sounds, suppression operates, people evacuate the area, emergency response team gathers and does its job, and so on. Some of the Outcome may be in parallel, as in the activation of the alarm being at the same time as the operation of stop valves.

Modelling of the Outcome pathway is based on the expected sequential (or parallel) response process, while recognising that what is intended does not always occur: the excess flow sensor may not work, the stop valves may not operate, the alarm may not sound, a person under a breaking tree branch may not hear the sound made by the branch and so on. If all these things happen as intended the pathway proceeds down the preferred, intended, expected or hoped-for route, if not then different and adverse Outcome scenarios get played out. Intended and preferred Outcome pathways will exist where Events have been predicted and the equipment or process has been designed to accommodate a predicted Outcome process. There are many examples of this:

- the provision of fire-hardened structures, fire detection and suppression mechanisms, smoke control doors, evacuation alarms and evacuation plans;
- the provision of gas detection apparatus where toxic or non-respirable gases may leak;
- the provision of core balance relay circuit breakers in electrical reticulation;
- the provision of automated emergency shutdown ('soft landing') capability in complex plant;
- the provision of an uninterruptible electrical power supply;
- the protection of power transformers by gas detection (Buchholz relay) devices, venting and inert gas flooding;
- the provision of emergency communication devices in building lifts for use in the event of breakdown;
- the provision of explosion overpressure vent doors in dust handling plant;

- business interruption plans;
- the provision of emergency and first aid personnel on standby during events attracting large numbers of people;
- plans for managing large numbers of passengers at short notice when an airliner becomes unserviceable or environmental conditions make it impossible to fly.

When an Event has occurred, it may be responded to only if it has been detected. The earliest and most desirable detection is of the Event itself, but detection may only occur at later stages in the unfolding Outcome pathway. If neither the Event nor the pathway are evident, detection may only arise when the Consequence becomes evident. This is obviously undesirable, but the path of history is paved with such cases, particularly in the exposure of people to toxic substances (artists to lead paint, asbestos workers) whose presence is unknown due to general ignorance of the processes involved.

Outcome Logic Diagrams – 'Event Analysis'

Analysis of the 'All other Outcomes' pathways in Figure 9.7 relies on a structured understanding of the process possibilities (Table 9.5) and possible responses. This understanding is conveyed in a logic diagram in which the intended or hoped-for route through the Outcome is defined by a series of individual stages that interpret the general ideas conveyed in Table 9.5 in a manner that describes the sequence of the Outcome pathway for the system under analysis. Each of these stages is conventionally written as a question, such as 'Fire alarm operates?', as this enables a binary choice logic diagram to be drawn for both the affirmative answer (yes, it does operate) and the negative (no, it does not operate). The sequence of affirmative answers describes what we intend to happen in the Outcome (because it has been preconsidered and planned for), or at the least the best we could hope to happen. Negative answers at any or all points in the sequence define the various possible pathways through the 'All other Outcomes' of Figure 9.7. As the answer 'Yes' or 'No' can be given to each of the questions, at each question the logic diagram branches in two ways. This concept is illustrated in Figure 9.8. For the purpose of illustration, this is a very simple three-stage Outcome based on a response process only.

In Figure 9.8 each of the questions that define the Outcome sequence is expressed positively and the 'Yes' response pathway proceeds upwards, as indicated by the 'Yes'/'No' convention shown at the first question. This convention results in the best possible Outcome pathway being the uppermost one and the worst possible pathway being the lowest one. Whatever convention is adopted, it is good practice to ensure that all questions are stated in the positive sense or all in the negative, as a mixture is certain to lead to confusion in the construction or interpretation of the analysis. Notice that not all questions have to be relevant to all the pathways. If the alarm does not operate then the second question in Figure 9.8 is irrelevant.

The theory is disarmingly simple, but the practice is not always so. A good logic diagram is one that contains sufficient detail to be a useful model but not so much that the analysis becomes hard to understand and use. To achieve suitable simplicity, the analyst must define the stages in the Outcome with care, such that there are just sufficient of these to adequately describe how Consequences arise and no more. It will be evident that Figure 9.8 could rapidly become very complex (many more pathways) if the number of questions was doubled, for example. One means of achieving this practical simplicity is to collapse a series of complex possibilities into a single result, which is what has been done in Figure 9.8. The question 'Alarm responded to as planned?' could be subdivided into such detail as: 'Can the alarm be heard?'; 'Is the meaning of the alarm understood?'; 'Is the correct action taken as a result of it?'

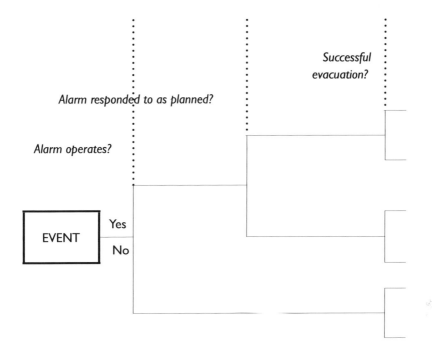

Figure 9.8   Outcome logic diagram concept

Doing so, in this case, would add significantly to the complexity of the analysis diagram without adding value to the result. The substructure of this 'top' question can be considered when determining the probability to be associated with the Yes/No responses.

It is common, when working with complex industrial plant, to find that different Event Mechanisms can lead to different Outcomes. In such cases, a separate Outcome Analysis should be created for each Mechanism.

As with FTA, there is no substitute for learning from experience or for looking at examples based on real situations.

Estimating Outcome and Consequence Probabilities and Values

The probability associated with any given Outcome and Consequence pathway can be estimated from the probabilities of YES or NO answers to each of the questions used to describe the pathways. In Figure 9.8, the alarm is a component the failure probability of which can be estimated as discussed above for FTA component failures. With an estimate of the probability of the alarm not working (NO), the probability of it working (YES) can readily be determined as $(1 - p_{NO})$. Put another way:

$$p_{NO} + p_{YES} = 1.$$

Table 9.6 (derived from Table 9.5) illustrates the many different ways in which Outcome probabilities can be estimated.

Table 9.6   Outcome pathway probability estimation methods

Outcome process affected by:	Outcome pathway probability estimation
Energy form changes	In most cases, an Event gives rise to one form of energy. Where multiple forms can occur it is likely that they will occur (YES probability = 1) and the Outcome pathway will be unique to the energy form.
Component operation	Component failures estimated as discussed for FTA. Each component-related functional failure in the Outcome Analysis can be analysed using its own FTA if necessary.
Environmental Circumstances and Conditions, including weather effects	Meteorological data provides the probabilities of wind strengths and directions (relevant to geometrical uncertainty) and of rainfall. Lightning strike data is used to estimate probabilities of a strike happening on a given sensitive area. Likewise with earthquake, storm and sea surge data.
Geometrical uncertainty	Analysis of the geometry, for example: the damage-sensitive area within the possible impact area divided by the possible impact area; the length of train line with damage-sensitive assets within the derailment zone divided by the total length of train line; the length of road with damage-sensitive areas in the event of a hazardous goods vehicle accident divided by the total length of road; the length of road typically affected by a landslide divided by the total length of road; the number of transmission line fuses over flammable ground cover divided by the total number of similar fuses.
Uncertainty in the way in which Consequences could arise, including random chance	Analysis of presence, for example: the number of working hours or rush hours in a week divided by the total number of hours in a week; the number of times a day trains pass others that are stationary at railways stations. Analysis of random chance is an application of AND logic, for example: A landslide occurs AND a car is on the road below the land slide site. A car must be on the level crossing AND a train must arrive too. The presence of a vehicle on any particular stretch of road or rail is dependent on the number of vehicles using the route per year, their speed and their length.
Human behaviour	Analysis of human error possibilities and probabilities. This is a specialist task, but generic figures can be used, as discussed for FTA.

With probabilities estimated for each of the Outcome and Consequence logic diagram branches, it is possible to multiply them through from the Event probability onwards to estimate the probability of any one pathway occurring. As before, care must be taken with the meaning of these probabilities to ensure that the Exposure denominator has been handled in a sensible manner.

The end of each Outcome pathway is a point at which an adverse Consequence does or does not (Null Consequence) occur. Knowing the way in which the Occurrence has unfolded assists the analyst to make a statement of the nature of the Consequence and to use this to estimate the likely Consequence Value, as shown in Figure 9.9.

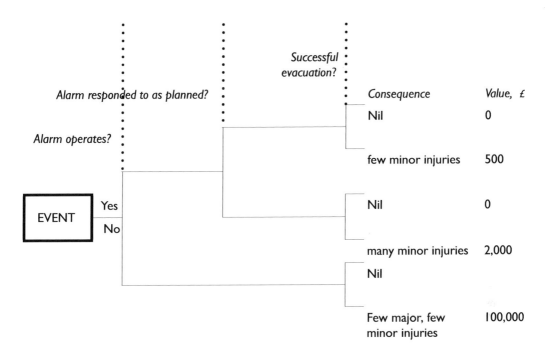

Figure 9.9   Adding Consequences and their Values to the Outcome analysis

A complete quantified risk analysis consists of the FTA joined to the Event Analysis by their common feature, the Event itself, and with probability estimates included – see Figure 9.10.

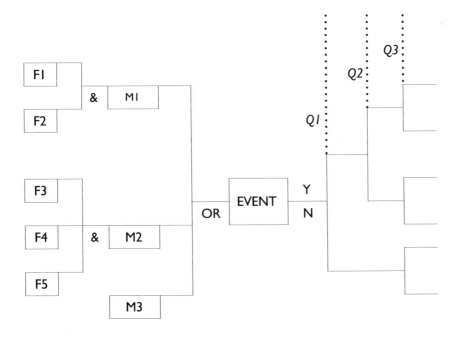

Figure 9.10   Completed analysis of Mechanisms and Outcomes (generic form)

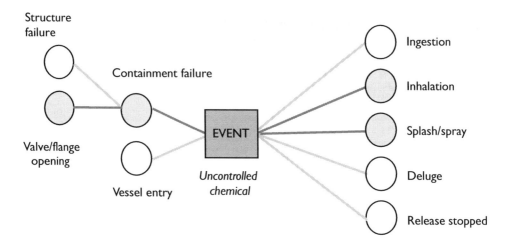

Figure 9.11 'Bow-tie' representation of a simplified risk analysis

Bow-tie Diagrams

The origin of these is to be found in the general shape evident in Figure 9.10, which at its simplest conveys the idea that there are many possible reasons for Events and many possible results of them. Figure 9.11 is a style of diagram I used in teaching in the late 1970s and early 1980s to illustrate the essential points being made by the risk analysis methods of FTA and EA. Figure 9.11 is a simplified version of a complete analysis in order to illustrate the point rather than be a comprehensive analysis of chemical exposures.

This type of analysis can be quickly completed for a number of different Event types and has the advantage that a person investigating an incident involving chemicals (in this case) has a ready reference of the possibilities to be investigated. The figure shows in bold the route taken by a particular Occurrence, in which a flange of a pipe under pressure was opened, resulting in an escape of carbon dioxide and an acidic liquid. The similarity of the shape to that of a bow-tie is obvious. The concept is at its most useful if Events are defined as suggested in this text. Bow-tie analysis methods are now widespread and of increased complexity, including control measures for each line in the diagram, as well as including causes, as a brief exploration of the internet on this subject will make clear.

The Effect of Management Practices on Risk Analysis

The obvious results of a risk analysis are first a structured understanding of the different ways an Event can occur and how these can lead to adverse Consequences, and secondly an estimate of the size of the Risk. The first of these is of value for one main reason – it enables the most likely pathways to be known. The second is of value because it enables the Risk to be compared with others, possibly also with respect to acceptability criteria (see Chapter 8) and it enables the cost-effectiveness of any proposed risk reduction measures to be calculated.

A less obvious result is that the analysis draws attention to the assumptions that have to be made in order to quantify the analysis: to estimate the various probabilities. As previously noted, component failure probabilities depend on the quality of the original components, on the inspection and maintenance practices adopted for them and the equipment renewal practices of the organisation, as well as the physical environment in which the components do their work. Component failure probabilities most often used in risk analyses are the single figure that represents a random failure, preferably including a range of values around this figure to account for uncertainty in its value. A real component will often have early-in-life and late-in-life failure probabilities that are quite different and much higher than this. The following chapter provides a more detailed discussion of this point.

The literature on human error shows that the probability of action failures depends greatly on performance-shaping factors. These factors reflect the organisational, social and physical nature of the environment in which work is done. Experience shows that the cautious behaviour and working to rule that occurs in the aftermath of an accident has a life of only some six weeks. Social researchers (see Chapter 8) call this phenomenon 'discounting in time': the value or meaning of the event is discounted over the time since it happened or could happen in the future.

It is an inevitable conclusion that the result of a quantified risk analysis is only as good as the technical knowledge and organisational contextual assumptions made at the time it was done. If this knowledge changes or if this context changes over the life of the plant, the estimated Risk will necessarily also change. Some industrial examples help to illustrate this point:

- Flammable material storage tanks are required to be earthed and there is a requirement for the earth resistance to be less than a certain value. Over time, the contract to annually measure earth resistance lapses. Because the contracts department is unaware of it as a requirement, its absence is not noted. The effect of this is that the natural steady rise in earth resistance resulting from deterioration of the earth rod bond with the earth is not noticed.
- Bulk chemical storage tanks are provided with bunds to contain spills from them. There is a technical requirement that incompatible chemicals cannot be stored in different tanks that share the same bund. The sales department of the storage company is rewarded for increasing the occupancy of the tank facility and over time their knowledge of this requirement diminishes so that it becomes common practice to have incompatible chemicals sharing the same bund.
- A standby pump is used as the duty pump after the duty pump fails. The company is going through a hard time financially and the order for a new duty pump is delayed for many months.
- A critical conveyor gallery carrying coal in a steel plant is subject to an increasing dead load over time as coal spillage is not cleaned up. The gallery structure has not been painted for a long time as there is no preventive maintenance programme on site. Over time, the structure corrodes. The gallery structure fails due to both overload and weakening, leading to a critical loss of production capability.
- A critical temperature sensor in a power plant is not calibrated to its required schedule as it is very difficult and uncomfortable to access. For thermal efficiency reasons, the boiler is controlled to the highest steam delivery temperature that the delivery pipework metal is able to withstand. Potentially, an unintended high temperature could lead to an early delivery pipe failure with catastrophic results.

The EDM (Chapter 3) shows how Mechanisms arise from Prerequisites. FTA shows how the probability of the Mechanism is affected by these Prerequisites (enabling Conditions and Circumstances). The analysis of Outcomes shows how Outcomes are similarly affected by the situation (concluding Conditions and Circumstances) in which they arise.

Summary

A theory is developed for the classification of possible Events and their Mechanisms. The value of these in both predicting and analysing Occurrences, including accident investigation, is noted. The theory contributes to the identification of Top Events for FTA and in developing the analysis in an understandable and repeatable manner. The chapter discusses component, action and controller function failures and the choice of failure probability, drawing attention to their sensitivity to operational management decisions during the life of the process.

A detailed understanding of the development and possible content of the logical analysis of Outcomes (Event Analysis) is given.

10

Risk Numeracy: Numerical Insights into Failures and Incidents

Introduction

An understanding of risk is necessarily founded on an understanding of probability as the mathematical expression of uncertainty. Most of us are not statisticians but do need a practical understanding of the subject, sufficient to understand the limits of our knowledge and sufficient to talk with a statistician. The risk analyst needs to understand the theoretical origins of probability estimates (of component failure and of action failures by people or automated controllers) in order to have an understanding of their meaning and limitations. Of interest also is if and how probability theory can be used to understand bulk Occurrence ('accident') data.

Reliability theory assists engineers working in industries sensitive to component failures, particularly the aerospace, power and petrochemical industries. In most cases, equipment failure leads to production or functional losses of some sort. Sometimes, it can lead to much more significant adverse Consequences and attract attention as a loss or a significant risk. The only reason that one is of interest to the maintenance department and the other to the risk engineer is the value and frequency of the Consequence. Maintenance theory and practice is based on the assumption that failures occur frequently and that failure data will be available in large quantities. Risk theory and practice is based on the assumption that adverse Consequences occur infrequently and that there will be little usable data. Efforts to increase the quantity of data lead to the promotion of incident (near miss) reporting. It should also promote the collection of failure data (the inverse of success data) associated with known possible Mechanisms. Despite the distinction between the two departments managing the problem and the amount of data they have, there is no conceptual difference between the two organisational functions. Reliability theory explains the origin of component failure probabilities, which (as has been seen in Chapter 9) determine the probability of Events as well as Outcome pathways. Maintenance theory helps us to understand the nature and effect on failure probability of the different possible maintenance practices.

In an engineer's ideal world, actual maintenance practices would be deduced rationally from reliability requirements. In practice, maintenance departments are often overwhelmed by the sheer volume of components in a complex industrial plant and this ideal is not approached. The risk analyst is concerned with the real way in which components are being managed as this affects the likelihood of component failures which in turn affects the likelihood of Events.

Any discussion of component failure has its counterpart in a discussion on human action failure or in automated systems failure. Human behaviour is dependent on so many factors: emotional state, education, experience, training and skill development, equipment design, expected work methods, organisational culture, management systems, etc. While human reliability can approach that of machines, see Chapter 9, in many significant situations it does not do so and the part of the risk analysis that is dependent on human behaviour is usually that with the highest failure probability. Human behaviour in production departments is influenced mostly by that department in the cultural and supportive (or otherwise) context of the larger organisation. It is in this area that risk theories can be applied to commercial organisations as these rely on large numbers of people following guideline methods of work.

The mathematics of reliability are explained in detail in dedicated texts so no attempt will be made to replicate it here. The purpose of this chapter is to provide a succinct summary of the theory sufficient to support an explanation of its implications for the risk analyst.

The other reason for the risk adviser to understand something of statistics is to properly understand the meaning of collections of incident data and so to interpret and use them in sensible ways.

Component Failure Probability is a Function of Time

Conventionally, the possible way that component failure rate changes with time is shown in the so-called 'bathtub' curve, a stylised representation of which is the solid line in Figure 10.1. Unrecognised manufacturing problems and failures arising from the installation of the component are considered to give rise to failures early in life, otherwise known as infant mortality (as this also occurs with human beings) or burn-in failures. After this initial period, the diagram shows a constant failure rate until the component begins to suffer increasingly from age-related failures and the failure rate rises over time. This latter period is known wear-out. Human fatality statistics show a similar function of time, with a (regrettably) relatively brief central portion and a lengthy period of increasing failure rate with age. Conceivably, when wear-out mechanisms exist, the failure rate asymptotically approaches the age beyond which it is hard to imagine that any component will have survived. Wear-out failures arise from an age-related reduction in the capability of the component, for example wear of rubbing or sliding parts, corrosion, embrittlement, perishing of rubber parts, fatigue and so on. Age may be either due to cycles of use or to calendar time.

By exclusion, it is possible to define the constant failure rate portion of the diagram as arising from mechanisms of failure that are none of those previously mentioned: not due to manufacturing problems or installation error and not due to time- or operating-cycle-related changes to the capability of the component. Typically these mechanisms are random happenings, with examples that could include:

1. lightning strike affecting electronics;
2. earthquake and storm effects, tidal waves;
3. a valve being struck by a falling toolbox;
4. an air pressure sensor being blocked by insects or dust;
5. a vehicle being damaged in a collision.

With people, these random happenings could include murder, suicide, vehicle accident, falls, electrocution, industrial accidents and so on.

There is no particular reason why any given component has to display the bathtub failure rate vs time characteristic. Possibly, a component has neither burn-in nor wear-out mechanisms, as shown by the dotted line in Figure 10.1. Also possibly, a component may have a slowly rising probability of failure with time, as shown by the broken line in Figure 10.1. It is even possible to postulate an upside-down bathtub relevant to certain circumstances (Glaser, 1978).

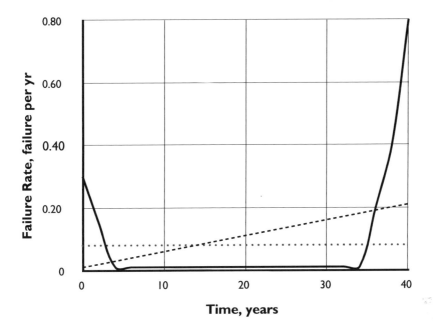

Figure 10.1   Illustrating three different failure rate time functions

These various possibilities make it evident that it may not be a simple matter to determine component failure probabilities to use in the FTA and EA of Chapter 9. It is, however, often the case that sources of component failure data are derived from what are believed to be random failure processes so that the quoted values are assumed to be constant over time. The nature of the random influences that gave rise to the failure data is not specified in these collections, other than to say the data was obtained from certain industry types. The implication is that these random failure modes are common to the industry, rather than to a location. This assumption may not be correct in any one case. For example, in hot and dusty environments, exposed equipment may behave differently from the same item in an icy environment.

Note that a failure rate can be a high number: in a plant with many similar pumps, the failure rate for all the pumps may be many times per year, if that is the time unit chosen. It is even possible to have a single unit fail more than once per year. Failure rate, represented by the Greek letter lambda (λ), is equivalent to the Frequency of adverse Consequences, with all cases being simply described by the Consequence of 'failure to function as required'. In Chapter 4 we saw that Frequency [cases per year] and Probability [cases per statistical trial] are related by Exposure [trials per year]:

$p = Frequency/Exposure.$

In component failure notation, the relationship is as follows for the probability of failure:

$p_f = \lambda/Exposure.$

As described in Chapter 9, component Exposure may be based on demand, process time or continuous function. The meaning of failure probability for the first two is therefore one of these:

p_f [failures per demand] $= \lambda$ [failures per year] / Exposure [demands per year],

p_f [failures per hour] $= \lambda$ [failures per year] / Exposure [operating hours per year],

p_f [failures per cycle] $= \lambda$ [failures per year] / Exposure [cycles per year].

When Exposure is a continuous functioning of the item, probability is indistinguishable from Frequency [failures per year].

Failure rate λ is obtained by counting the number of cases in a year. In this context, a constant failure rate in any situation also means there is a constant probability of failure: it is assumed that Exposure remains constant as a characteristic of the situation. A constant failure probability (or rate) means that over time more and more of a batch of components will have failed or it is more and more likely that a single component will have failed.

To illustrate this, assume that a component in a Fault Tree is a liquid level sensor in a tank containing flammable liquid. The tank is filled twice weekly on average for 50 plant operating weeks a year and the signal from the sensor is the trigger that stops the tank being overfilled. Assume that the Exposure unit relevant to the sensor is of the 'per demand' type. The Exposure, assuming only one tank is in operation, is

Exposure = 50 × 2 = 100 [sensor operating demands per year].

If the sensor has an assumed constant failure probability of 1 in 10,000 demands (10^{-4} [failures per demand]) then the failure rate (Frequency) will be:

$\lambda = 10^{-4}$ [failures per demand] × 100 [demands per year] = 0.01 [failures per year].

At the beginning of the first year of operation (at time zero) the probability of failure of the sensor will be 0 as we will prove its operation during commissioning. With a failure rate of 0.01 [failures per year], on average 1 percent of a batch of such sensors will have failed after one year. This is equivalent to saying that the probability that our one sensor has survived will have reduced to 0.99 after one year in operation. After two years in operation, 1 percent of this hypothetical remaining 0.99 sensors (in our 'batch' of one sensor) will have failed, meaning that the probability our sensor is working after two years (that is, has survived up to this point) is now 0.99 − 0.0099 = 0.9801, and so on. This result is described mathematically by the negative exponential function $e^{-\lambda t}$ and called the survival function by statisticians and reliability by engineers. Figure 10.2 shows the cumulative survival chance (reliability) of the component at each point in time as the solid line and the cumulative probability of failure as the dashed line. As the component has either survived or failed at any point in time the sum of these probabilities must be one:

$p_f + e^{-\lambda t} = 1$, or $p_f = 1 - e^{-\lambda t}$.

Reliability, r, is defined as one minus the probability of failure: $r = 1 - p_f = e^{-\lambda t}$.

In fact, of course, a batch of ostensibly identical components operating in a given situation will be exposed to a variety of random failure mechanisms and the individual failures arising from these will occur at different times in the life of the components in the batch. The discussion above implies that this has happened so that a batch of failure data is available to us. All of the failures that constitute the batch of data are represented by an average value, λ [failures per year]. The inverse of λ evidently has the meaning [years per failure]. It can be shown mathematically (and is

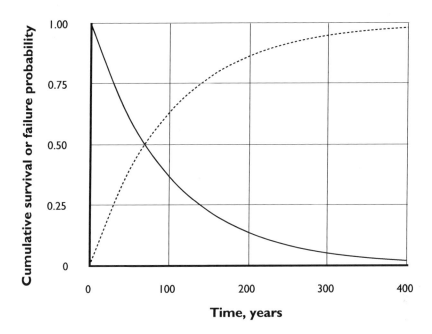

Figure 10.2 Cumulative failure and survival for λ = 0.01 failures per year

perhaps evident to the reader intuitively) that this is also the mean time between failures (MTBF) when the average failure rate is constant over time and the failure mechanisms are suited to this random process. MTBF is a term much used by reliability engineers.

Figure 10.2 applies if a component is never inspected and we simply allow it to run to failure. However, if we institute an inspection programme in which we verify that the sensor operates properly and perhaps carry out any repair or cleaning found necessary, then at each inspection we return the probability of correct functioning to one and the probability of failure to zero. Figure 10.3 shows the effect of this. The changed time scale expands the view of the first five years of operation and it is noteworthy that the $e^{-\lambda t}$ function is approximated by a straight line, as is also evident in Figure 10.1. In Figure 10.3, an inspection interval (T) of two years is assumed, after which the reliability time line restarts at one. The reliability time function now has a saw-tooth shape, with the dotted line indicating the mean reliability over time. In fact, the reliability at this two-year point, before the inspection, is 0.9801, so that the mean reliability over the two-year period is (0.9801 + 1)/2 = 0.9901 [survivals per year]. Consequently, with this inspection regime, the probability of sensor failure is (1 − 0.9901) = 0.0099 [failures per year]. It is this figure that should be inserted in any quantified risk analysis of the system using the level sensor, illustrating the point made at the end of the previous chapter that in a FTA or EA all component and action failure probabilities depend on the management practices of the system in question. Figures of component reliability obtained from tabulations such as Table 9.4 are the starting point, not the end point.

As seen in the previous chapter, a human being can be regarded as a component in an FTA or an EA. The simple theory just explained could apply to action failures as much as to component failures, if we assume that action failure (an action that produces an unwanted result) occurs at random. This is not necessarily a good assumption, as there is evidence to suggest that in some circumstances the motivation of people to behave in a preferred manner deteriorates rapidly with time – an age-related failure). Nevertheless, the point that inspection (in this case reinforcement of the desired behaviour) determines failure rate is applicable.

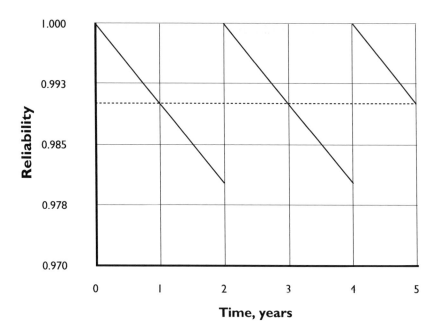

Figure 10.3   Mean reliability (dashed line) with an inspection interval of two years and $\lambda = 0.01$ failures per year

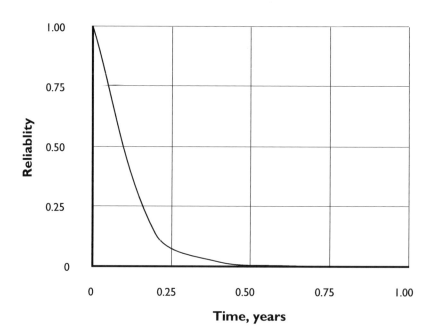

Figure 10.4   Human action reliability with $\lambda = 10$ failures per year

Typically, but not always, action failures occur with a higher probability than component failures. This is certainly true where the action expected or hoped for is optional as far as the person is concerned, as then the expectation requires regular reinforcement. This interval between times of reinforcement is conceptually no different from the time between inspections for a component: is the person still doing the task the expected way? Personal experience suggests an MTBF for a person in these circumstances as being generally of the order of six weeks ($\lambda = 8.7$ [failures per year]) and as low as three weeks. Figure 10.4 illustrates how unreliable people can be in this situation and the need for very frequent reinforcement of the requirement.

Reporting on Incident Data

Incident data can be used to show absolute numbers or cost of incidents or relative measures based on Exposure. As an example, for vehicle incidents the data could show the absolute number (or cost) of incidents, the number (or cost) of incidents per 100,000 vehicles (the incident incidence) or the number (or cost) per 1,000,000 miles travelled. It will be evident that counts with denominators based on the unit of Exposure give an indication of the underlying Probability (as defined in Chapter 4). Absolute numbers, not based on an Exposure denominator, do not make it clear whether the changes are a result of changed Exposure or not. These measures may have different uses: an aeronautical engineer is interested in the probability of mission failure of the aircraft (crashes or fatalities per flight or per flying hour); the travelling public may be sensitive to the actual number of crashes or fatalities being reported. In the workplace, relative measures are:

1. LTIFR: the number of cases with at least a defined number of days off work (commonly more than one shift) divided by the number of millions of work hours in the time interval over which the number of cases is counted. Also calculated in this way are the Medical Treatment Frequency Rate or the All Injury Frequency Rate.
2. Injury Incidence: the number of cases in the counting time period satisfying a suitable definition of injury severity per 1,000 people exposed, or other stated denominator.

Any change in overall Consequence Value will be a result either of change in the number of cases or in the Consequence Value per case. Calculating and graphing the Consequence Value per case will make it possible to identify any underlying influences – see Table 10.1.

Table 10.1   Measures of Occurrence experience

Measure	Definition	Meaning
Number of cases, N	The sum of all cases that satisfy the collection requirements in the reporting time interval	Changes may be a result of underlying changes in Occurrence probability or in Exposure
Number of cases per unit of Exposure, e.g. crashes per million passenger miles, etc.	As above but divided by the Exposure measure in the reporting time interval	Changes are a result of underlying changes in Occurrence probability, not Exposure
Incidence, being N per number of exposed assets (such as people, vehicles)	The sum of all cases divided by the number of asset units	As above
Consequence Value	The total cost associated with the damage and due to replacement or repair or reinstatement, fines, legal expenses, etc.	Changes in the Consequence Value suggest either improved control over Consequences or risk factors or that the response to Consequences has improved
Consequence Value per case	Total Consequence Value divided by the number of cases in the reporting time interval	Changes are a result of changes in the management of damage or in the magnitude of asset damage value
Consequence Value per unit of Exposure	Total Consequence Value divided by the exposure measure in the reporting time interval	As above

The time interval used for the purpose of counting cases may be either the day, week, month, quarter or year. The number of individual cases within the selected time interval is counted or the Consequence Values summed. These numbers may then be plotted as a time series; the shorter the time window, the more apparent the fluctuations in the data. Short time windows draw attention to the fluctuation and encourage the observer to see the problem as random and unpredictable and possibly forming the conclusion that the underlying reasons are uncontrollable. Very long time windows relative to the number of years for which data is available make it impossible to see if any trends in the data can be observed. It is generally practical to make use of an interval of a quarter of a year for relatively short data collections, as in Figure 10.5, and an interval of a year for long period collections, as in Figure 10.7.

An alternative form of data presentation is to make use of a cumulative sum – see Figure 10.6. In a cumulative series, the data in each time interval is the sum of all data in the period up to and including the current time. It is feasible to accumulate the numbers of cases or the cost of cases, but obviously not any of the measures relative to exposure. The result is a steadily increasing number showing how the measure is accumulating. The immediate effect of this is to remove much of the appearance of fluctuation. Further, if the rate of accumulation is changing (increasing or decreasing) this is often very evident on the graph. Statistical theory (CUSUM) can be used to decide whether the change in slope is significant. The thin line in Figure 10.6 is a straight line of best fit, a trend line. A trend line is one in which there is as much difference between data point values and the line above the line (positive difference) as there is below it (negative difference). Spreadsheets make it very easy to draw a line of best fit.

The absence of a wealth of Occurrence data is either an indication of a safe operation or that operations are characterised by essentially low Frequency but high Consequence Value

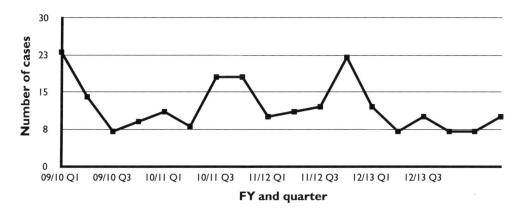

Figure 10.5   Time series of the number of reported incidents

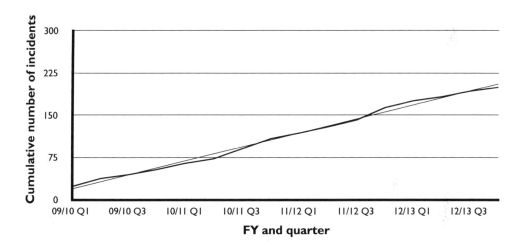

Figure 10.6   Quarterly cumulative plot of the same incidents as Figure 10.5

Occurrences and the risk adviser should not allow the organisation to be lulled into a false sense of security by this. In the absence of completed Occurrence data (that is, based on Damage), there is much to be gained by monitoring incomplete Occurrences. Given the often significant influence of human actions on the probability of these, failure to achieve intended standards of behaviour can be monitored as an indication of potential failure. Where performance standards are clearly defined, the extent to which these are achieved can also be monitored, see for example the airliner example given in Chapter 7. Here, it is better to monitor the actual fuel state of arriving aircraft than to wait for the collection of data about declared fuel emergencies. This is the same principle as adopted for condition-monitoring of fire extinguishers.

Interpreting Incident History

Figures 10.5 and 10.6, from a real collection of data, are typical of many collections and are useful in demonstrating some simple observations:

1. There is a high level of variation, with the numbers per quarter varying from 8 to 23 about a calculated average of 12.5 incidents per quarter. Another way of looking at this is that the variation occurs in a band which is 16 incidents per quarter wide – the variation is bigger than the average value.

2. There is no evident trend when the data is seen over the whole collection period of 16 quarters. If we looked at shorter overall periods we may have been led to the conclusion that the number of incidents was either increasing or decreasing, depending on when we looked. A simple conclusion is that the greater the overall collection period (and number of data points) the greater the confidence we have in drawing conclusions such as 'things are getting better (or worse)'. When there is pressure (generally political) to use such time series to show how successful a prevention programme has been, the wise risk adviser will engage a statistician to properly evaluate the confidence in making such an assertion and refuse to sanction any reference to the data without the qualifications written by the statistician.

3. The cumulative graph supports the idea that the rate of accumulation of incident numbers is static for all practical purposes. In the figure, the fit of the trend line is very good. In other words, the average value appears to be a good statement of the overall experience.

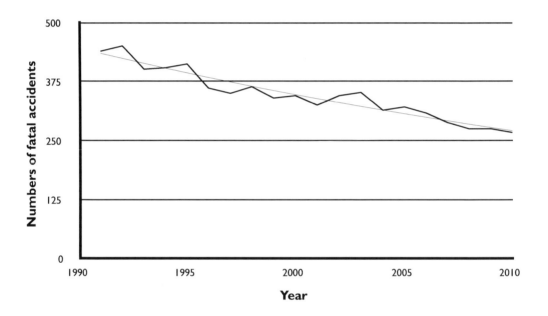

Figure 10.7   US general aviation numbers of fatal accidents

Figure 10.7 shows data from the US National Transportation Safety Board.[1] The existence of a downward trend in absolute numbers of fatal accidents is evident and there is a possible reduction in the variation about the trend line. Both of these features are characteristics of a risk under control, as the process of risk control is one in which we intend to reduce the overall number of cases by increasing the certainty of wanted outcomes and reducing the number of surprises. Figure 10.8 shows how this appears when plotted as a cumulative graph.

---

1   http://www.ntsb.gov/data/table10.html, accessed in January 2014.

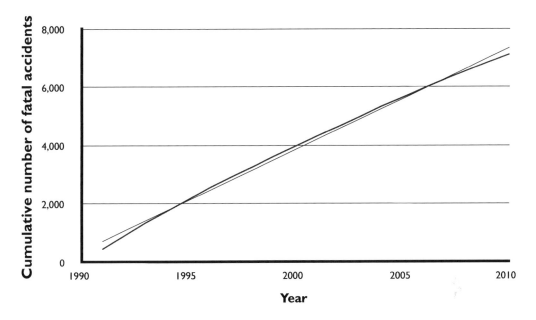

Figure 10.8   US general aviation cumulative numbers of fatal accidents

A straight trend line is shown to make the steady curvature of the cumulative graph evident. A steadily decreasing rate of accumulation of cases (Figure 10.8) shows itself as a steady decrease in the slope of the cumulative curve. The amount of data in this collection (20 years) increases our confidence that the appearance of Figure 10.8 is not deceptive. The extent of the slope change of the cumulative graph from the beginning of the collection to the end of it is an indication of the extent of change over the total period. As previously mentioned, a statistical test (which should be done by a statistician) is possible on this change of slope to assess the confidence that it is indicative of a real change.

Testing for Evidence of Randomness

Do Occurrences occur at a constant average rate over time and hence are they a result of random processes? Reliability theory could be employed to check, considering an incident to be a failure and survival to be no incident. For any collection of incidents there will be a date at which the collection began and a date at which the collection ends for the purpose of the analysis. From this the number of days represented by the collection can easily be calculated. The total number of incidents divided by this number of days is the mean failure rate, λ.

A collection of 228 actual work injury incidents over a period of a little over three years was analysed by sorting them into date order and calculating the interval (in days) between each incident and the preceding one. This is the same data that is shown in Figures 10.5 and 10.6, and is presented in Table 10.2.

Table 10.2   Partial data set of work injury incidents

t	0	1	2	3	4	5	6	7	8	9
n_i	45	27	10	9	15	12	7	12	10	6
tn_i	0	27	20	27	60	60	42	84	80	54
n_i/N	0.21	0.12	0.05	0.04	0.07	0.06	0.03	0.06	0.05	0.03
$\lambda e^{-\lambda t}$	0.134	0.12	0.11	0.09	0.08	0.07	0.06	0.05	0.05	0.04

The interval (t in Table 10.2) varied from 0 days to 44 days between incidents. The data was then counted to show the numbers of cases (n_i) which occurred the same number of days after the previous claim. Table 10.2 shows only the first 10 such sets. The weighted number of incidents in each interval t is the product tn_i. In the complete data set, the total of all tn_i, $\Sigma_i tn_i$ (t being the total number of columns), is 1,617 days. This, divided by the total number of incidents, N, gives the MTBF for the data set:

$$MTBF = \Sigma_i tn_i \,/\, N \; [days].$$

For the complete data set, MTBF = 7.08 days and λ = 1/MTBF = 0.141 [incidents per day]. This result is more simply obtained by dividing the overall number of incidents by the total number of days represented by the collection of incidents.

It is tempting to see what the actual data looks like in comparison to the theoretical negative exponential distribution, $e^{-\lambda t}$. To do this we need to derive from the real data an indication of the incident probability figure as a function of the 'time between' intervals. This is simply n_i/N in each column, the proportion of the total number of incidents that is in this 'time-between' column. The theoretical value of this probability is based on the mathematical expression of the negative exponential distribution. As has been shown (Figure 10.1), $e^{-\lambda t}$ gives a probability of no incident arising in each time-between interval.

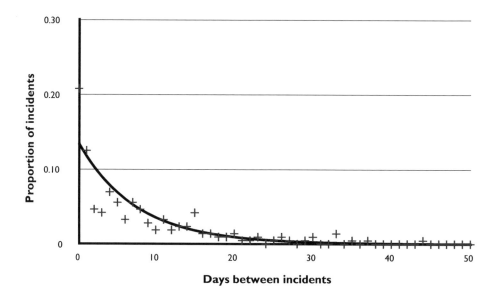

Figure 10.9   Work incident data compared with the negative exponential distribution

Multiplying this by the actual incident average frequency puts this probability into proportion, so to speak, so that the product $\lambda e^{-\lambda t}$ provides the rate at which we would expect to accumulate incidents in each time-between interval. Statisticians call $\lambda e^{-\lambda t}$ the probability density function. Figure 10.9 shows the result of completing these calculations for the set of data: both the actual data points and the theoretical line.

Inspection of the result suggests that the data is approximately distributed in a random manner, as suspected from the appearance of the time series in Figure 10.5.

Summary

Component failure probability is a function of time. There is one special case of this function, namely constant failure rate, that is amenable to mathematical analysis, which shows how the probability of failure is related to the mean time between failures through a negative exponential relationship. It is this special case that is generally represented in the component failure probability databases used to quantify FTA and EA. In practice, the actual failure probability of an installed component is dependant on the interval between inspections. The same can be said of action failure probability, which is dependant on the interval between efforts made to encourage needed standards of behaviour.

The various types of incident data and their potential to provide insight into the effectiveness of risk control efforts, when analysed as a time series, is explained. A means of testing for evidence of randomness in real accident data is given as a back-up to the simple visual assessment of this quality in accident data presented as a time series.

11

The Management of Risk: Strategy and Tactics

Introduction

The term 'managed risk' connotes a systematic preventive approach as distinct from one that is ad hoc and reactive. The process of managing a risk is simple and is in fact the subject of Chapters 5 to 8, although it is more commonly stated in the order: identify, evaluate and control. The order of the chapters in this book is because evaluation cannot take place in the absence of understanding control options. The actual practice of managing risks in any situation is complicated by many factors, including the preconceptions of those involved (often, that it is not possible to predict what can go wrong), the complexity of organisations (political posturing, protection of empires, problems of communicating between divisions) and the fact that the practices required to manage risk are easily glossed over under day-to-day pressures as they do not appear to add any immediate value. Risk management practices need to be maintained year after year and require a continuity of attention and effort that is hard to achieve in the dynamic and restless human environment of typical organisations, with people entering and leaving and little recognition of the need for a corporate memory. Fortunately, the use of management system standards subject to annual audits has become widespread in industry and commerce. Actual management practices have become subject to audits conducted by people not constrained by the politics and problems of the organisation. Audit results communicate directly to the top of the organisation and bypass internal barriers. These so-called quality and risk (also environment and health and safety) management systems standards share common management practices beneficial to the management of anything. The implementation of any one of them helps in the development of management capability of great value to the management of Risk. The organisational risk manager, however, needs a deeper understanding than is to be found in these standards if Risk management activities are not to be reduced to the paper evidence expectations of auditors.

The generic features of a standardised Risk management programme cannot be expected to draw attention to the specific technical and managerial details of the organisation using it. While the risk management process will be the same in principle, the details will differ significantly between mines, banks, shipping companies, share brokers, power generators and so on. It may be less obvious, but the details will depend also on the organisational structure and the culture of each organisation. Risk management belongs to the whole organisation, not only to the risk manager's department. It is rare to find a department or a management decision with no influence on risk management.

An organisational tendency towards a reactive approach (and therefore not Risk management) is often based on a deep lack of understanding of risk at the highest levels of management. Possible problems, by which is meant feasible potential Consequences, generally carry less weight in the manager's mind than actual problems, meaning experienced Consequences. Risk management practices may also be in conflict, in the manager's mind, with the route to success, however that is perceived. Risk management is clearly a line management activity, as responsibility resides within the line management structure. The role of the risk adviser is akin to that of a coach in providing leadership, encouragement and truthful observation.

The economic, political, commercial, legal and social environment within which the organisation exists also has a profound effect on the management of risk. Economic conditions determine employment levels and the availability of maintenance, equipment renewal and training expenditure. A common short-term strategy to improve profits is to stop much of the expenditure on these items, often with adverse effects on risks in the following years. If cost-centre managers see anticipated expenditure on risk controls as a cost, not an investment, they may avoid the expenditure and be rewarded for ending the financial year under budget.

Internal political pressures to get the job done no matter what may result in the conservative advice of engineers, operating managers and other technical or commercial specialists being disregarded or devalued. A high profile example of this was NASA's space shuttle Challenger disaster. Political or commercial expediency may have a greater influence on senior management values and decision-making than any technically correct advice. Examples of this in the airline industry are often publicised. Ideally, engineers approve the operation of an aircraft and ignore inappropriate commercial and managerial pressure to release an aircraft for service. Conflict of interest can be pervasive and unseen. Some years ago, an explosion killed many people and destroyed a factory. The investigation implicated a chemical unrelated to the work of the factory but which had been the basis of a lucrative trading activity. Risk management proposals regarding the development of much-needed chemical management practices had been resisted for many months, possibly to avoid uncovering this somewhat under-the-table activity.

Laws define liabilities and responsibilities often with scant regard for how practical this is in the management of Risk. It is, for example, easy to legislate that factory managers are responsible for work injuries, despite the fact that it may be (and often is) the underlying design of equipment that has the greatest influence on their occurrence and that this is outside the control of the manager. Perversely, those same laws may define a 'hierarchy of controls' that places design at the top of the hierarchy. Much of health and safety legislation in the jurisdictions with which I am familiar does little more than to define the rules for prosecution rather than establish an effective country-wide approach to Risk management.

The claims handling practices of insurance companies can be a powerful disincentive for management if liability is accepted by a clerk with no knowledge of industry. Also, the lack of understanding of Risk amongst barristers and judges may reduce years of good preventive effort within the organisation to nothing of value.

It is for these diverse reasons that the purpose of this chapter is to offer the risk specialist a perspective based on first principles and objective measures.

Reactive and Ad Hoc: The Common Approach

In the too-common reactive approach to risk, attention is paid primarily to Consequences that have already happened by responding to the specifics of individual cases as they occur. As the majority of Consequences are of relatively low value they typically elicit relatively minor and localised responses. In only responding to actual Consequences and the specific Outcome pathways associated with them, the opportunity to promote a deeper exploration of the Occurrence and Consequences is lost. An extreme example of this approach is to be found on the highways of a country in which I have worked. At random points along the road there are makeshift speed humps that have been placed there by the locals at the precise point at which pedestrians have been injured or car crashes have occurred. In another country and industry, after someone was injured by a piece of wood flying off a docking saw, the response was a small metal shield placed in the exact flight path of that particular piece of wood.

With the reactive approach, over time a larger and larger number of Consequences are known about and a sense of comfort may well be derived from this. However, in the absence of a comprehensive model of what the Risks are, nagging doubts arise that 'we don't know what we don't know'. It is also true that a number of problems from the past (and their hard-won control measures) may well be forgotten over time.

The reactive and ad hoc approach can best be exposed by considering what the opposite might look like. A systematic and prevention-oriented approach to managing Risks requires there to be someone, somewhere, monitoring risk and that this monitoring is used to facilitate a detailed understanding of it from the small symptoms that have yet to shock it into action. One of the Consequences (not Occurrence, note) that defines our period historically is the tragic 11 September 2001 Twin Towers disaster in the USA. What was new about these attacks was chiefly the precise nature of the Outcome and Consequences. Aircraft hijacks motivated by politics have a long history, as a search of the internet will quickly make evident. One pertinent example, of many that can be cited, is that of an airliner over Africa (British Airways Flight 2069 on 4 December 2000) which was subject to an attack by a person who had no difficulty entering the cockpit. During the struggle with the flight crew the aircraft entered a vertical dive from which it was recovered by one pilot moments before that pilot judged recovery would have been impossible. According to the report, the single attacker was clutching a prayer book and seemed delirious before the attack. The role of monitoring organisation naturally falls on an industry body, in this case perhaps the International Civil Aviation Organisation (ICAO), rather than on any individual member of the industry. The purpose of the monitoring function would be to monitor symptoms (Mechanisms, Events and Null or minor Outcomes), understand through conscious analysis the potential implications and promote preventive action before any significant Consequence had been experienced, certainly before the Likely Worst Consequence.

The premise would be that if something is possible it is only a matter of time before it happens (otherwise the probability is zero and the Risk does not exist). The process of analysis by the monitoring body might proceed as follows. As the likely interval between cases (Events) is determined by both Probability and Exposure, it is relevant to understand the motivations of hijackers (Probability) and the implications of growth in passenger numbers (Exposure). Hijackers will include people who suffer from psychological conditions, so mental health statistics will assist in understanding how probable this is – what the incidence of this is in the world community. Hijackers may be people with criminal intent who wish, for example, to use the aircraft and passengers for ransom demands. Other hijackers will have political aims, perhaps particularly because they are politically disenfranchised; previous hijacks suggest this may be true. As large numbers of people travel, it becomes increasingly certain that some flights will carry passengers who wish to use the flight to further their criminal or political aims or that their psychological problems will emerge on the flight. Regardless of motivation, attacks in the aircraft cabin have the potential to endanger the whole aircraft if they involve weapons such as bombs or guns. If an attack reaches the cockpit there is the potential to endanger the whole aircraft either by disabling the pilots or by forcing them to fly to unsuitable or unwanted destinations. In any circumstance, the LWC value is very large as passenger aircraft have much kinetic energy, a large amount of chemical bonding energy in fuel and many passengers.

Control measure options (obviously derived in this case from the TSM, for which see Chapter 3) might include:

1. screening passengers for psychological condition, criminal intent or for possible adverse political motivations;
2. screening passengers for weapons;
3. having the ability to respond to attacks when they become evident (trained cabin crew, immobilising gases or devices, etc.);
4. having the ability to prevent, or make very difficult, entry into the cockpit;
5. providing the flight crew with means of defence in the event of an attack on the cockpit.

It is easy to reflect on the implications of these control measure options on passengers, airports and on aircraft design. Any changes will involve the whole industry, which includes equipment suppliers, airports, baggage handling, the management of air transport routes and legislators. The limitations of an individual airline in managing this Risk are evident. The monitoring body or function would therefore need to have the ability to promote its analysis to the point of gathering industry-wide recognition of the Risk and agreement on control measures.

Purposeful Control

Certain capabilities and communication pathways are needed for any system to be controlled in an organised way – see Figure 11.1. It must be possible to influence the behaviour of the system as well as to know what the desired behaviour is. It must be possible to observe the actual behaviour of the system and to compare this with the desired behaviour. The comparison between observed and desired behaviour gives rise to a need to exert an influence, the control input, on the system. The operation of such a system is known to us all when we drive a car. The driver is the comparator and the desired behaviour of the system is to arrive at the destination without having hit any obstacles en route. To do this, our eyes provide feedback to our brain and our brain decides what control inputs (steering, brakes and acceleration) are needed.

It is necessary for influences on the system to be timely. If control inputs are too late or in the wrong direction (out of phase) the system will perform in a manner which is inappropriate. The timing and phase aspect of this is known to drivers who have experienced a rear-wheel skid: the skid can be made much worse by the wrong phase of steering input, meaning the steering wheel is moved in the wrong direction. Many systems with which we are familiar respond rapidly to control influences but a number are very slow in their response. For example, a ship's pilot is in command of a system with a long lag time between control input and system response: it takes the ship a long time to begin a turn after a rudder movement and a long time to slow down when power is reduced.

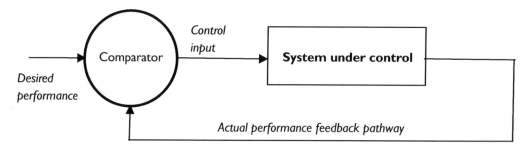

Figure 11.1   Schematic of a control system

When a system is under control, the actual performance of it approaches the desired state and then maintains that state. Effective control inputs achieve this quickly and show evidence the comparator has learned to be effective in the nature and timing of control inputs so that the system responds as and when needed. Practical experience of this may be had by giving a small child the steering wheel of a car and asking them to steer through a gate. To begin with, control inputs are often large and held for too long, resulting in emergency swings in the opposite direction. After a while, however, the child's brain learns how to do it efficiently with minimal steering inputs and the owner of the car experiences less anxiety.

The relevance of this to risk management is to be seen first in the idea of what a system is and what desirable performance is. The system is the organisation or industry of interest together with all its influential connections to the world beyond its immediate borders. Its desired performance is that the experience of unwanted incidents is reduced over time and that the fluctuations in the number of incidents in a year reduce over time. This is equivalent to saying we want our child to go through the gate and to use minimal steering wheel input to do so. From stressful early efforts they will quickly achieve this. Evidence of these learning features is shown in Figure 10.7. There must be ways of measuring the performance of the system, the possibilities of which have been discussed in Chapter 10. There must also be some entity that is actually concerned with all of this, as without anybody looking at the performance of the system no control is possible. This entity must not only have access to performance data, it must also be in a position to influence the system in an effective manner. The 'system' of relevance in risk is any and every item that represents a component of the system – the individual communities that experience the adverse Consequences, the providers of raw materials, energy, equipment and systems and processes to those communities, the providers of people to them, the legislative framework within which they exist and the bodies and professions which support them or chastise them in the aftermath of an adverse Consequence. All of these exist in the modern world, but to be labelled a 'system' it is necessary for them to be connected in a meaningful manner, for links between them to exist and for at least one common purpose to be shared; that a reason for their connection is to provide synergy towards the common goal of risk reduction.

Systemic Risk Control

Rowe (1977) introduced the term systemic risk control for the whole-of-industry approach, described above and in the earlier Twin Towers example. He reserved the term risk management system to describe the more limited potential of a programme within an individual organisation. Systemic risk control requires an intentional coordinated effort by every relevant body able to influence risk and risk control in some way: employee and industry associations, equipment suppliers, education and training bodies, the legal system, insurance companies and government regulators. The national environment potentially influenced by government regulators includes the way in which industries and individuals are licensed to operate, the legislative framework of permissions and responsibilities, the availability of educated and skilled people, the role of regulatory inspectors, the role and relationship with employee unions and industry associations, insurance companies and so on. These may work together towards risk control as a systemic feature of their relationships, or they may not: it depends on whether there is a defined relationship and whether risk control is a part of it.

An example of an approach that has many of these desired characteristics is to be found in the constitution of industry associations (Berufsgenossenschaften) in Germany. In that country, it is necessary for any business to belong to a relevant industry association. It is to this association that work injury insurance premiums are paid. A proportion of the premium is kept by the association to fund, for example, a research and development and training facility. This facility has as its goal the development of improved equipment and processes to increase efficiency and safety/health and to provide good training for industry people. The association is in a good position to solve problems and to influence the designers of equipment used by the industry and potentially the educators of trades and others employed by the industry. In short, the association is an industry memory and quality improvement body giving the industry combined knowledge, purchasing power and a continuous improvement process.

A country can influence much more than an individual company. Government can set up self-regulating processes to influence the education, knowledge and training of the people employed by anyone in their jurisdiction. They can also set up industry-specific processes to ensure that industry learns from its own experiences.

Within a country, for example, it is possible to:

a) License company operations and exert control on company behaviour by imposing licence conditions. In Germany, apart from government inspectors, the industry association sends out inspectors to educate, inform, encourage, coerce, etc.

b) Ensure that trade trainers include relevant risk-related knowledge and skills in the training provided. Conceivably, individual trade training institutions could become centres of specialisation in relevant industries and as of right obtain bulk industry incident experience from insurers. In Germany that is a definite role of the industry association. Who better, as they learn from the injury claims they process?

c) Ensure that industry professionals, e.g. engineers, scientists and managers, are appropriately educated in relation to risk by their educational institutions.

d) Gather and evaluate national injury/damage statistics and use these to influence industries, educators and trainers. In Germany this is made possible by the claims agent role of the industry association.

Each of these not only needs to exist but to operate in a coordinated fashion with the others to achieve the effects shown in Figure 10.7. It is this coordinated cooperation that gives the individual items their power. Figure 10.5 shows none of the signs of a controlled risk and we may reasonably presume that there is no shared objective and cooperative effort at risk control within the system that gave rise to the results, or that the system itself was unable to identify effective control inputs.

Table 11.1   Systemic management of risk in regulated (after Rowe) and deregulated environments

Regulated environment	Deregulated environment
A philosophy of controlling and minimising risks as a major emphasis in the design and operation of the system	The 'system' itself is probably nonexistent, but an industry association may have a loose form based on common interests. Consistency of philosophy around risk is possibly hard to achieve, depending on the purpose of the association.
A means for regulation of the total system to ensure maximum safety	If there is an industry association, it needs to have an ability to input controls to the system through the power to encourage (preferably) or to coerce.
Inclusion in the system of:	
Quality assurance	This may be possible within individual organisations due to the presence of an audited quality management system.
Redundancy of critical systems	Assuming a critical system to be either the feedback pathway from or control inputs to the 'system', the presence of a loose or nonexistent system makes it unlikely that either will exist in a robust manner or at all.
Training, licensing and certification of personnel	It is unlikely that there is a nationally or internationally coordinated scheme and this will be left to the efforts of the individual organisation and training provider.
Inspection of equipment and operations	Often this right is retained by government. An industry association could be so constituted that this is possible. Alternatively, individual sites in the same organisation could be open to inspections from other sites. Head office inspections by qualified people can also achieve useful results.
Licensing and registration of operation	If this is retained by government, it may become a clerical exercise rather than one with the purpose of making control possible.
Ongoing review of system performance to meet goals	The absence of a system means that the control system comparator is nonexistent or weak.
Enforcement and auditing system	Fines for visible failures, fear of major loss. External management system auditing on individual organisations will have some effect.

Rowe identified the qualities required of a system whose purpose is systemic risk control and these are listed in the first column of Table 11.1. Clearly, these are more likely to exist in an environment regulated to a degree by government, but could also exist in the cooperative environment of an industry association which has consciously taken on this role. Increasingly, in the modern world, governments are loosening the reigns of regulation in many, but not all, industries. Table 11.1 shows the potential for weakening arising from the loss of all forms of either regulation (government) or cooperation (industry association).

Systemic Failures

There is no shortage of documented examples of systemic failure to manage risks, or of books written about them. In April 1989 many people died as a result of crushing at Hillsborough Stadium in the UK during a football match and the legal aftermath of this is still in progress 25 years later. The final report of the inquiry by The Right Honourable Lord Justice Taylor had this to say:

> It is a depressing and chastening fact that mine is the ninth official report covering crowd safety and control at football grounds. After eight previous reports … it seems astounding that 95 people could die from overcrowding before the very eyes of those controlling the event.
>
> … in 1986 … Mr Justice Popplewell said: 'almost all the matters into which I have been asked to inquire and almost all the solutions I have proposed, have been previously considered in detail by many distinguished Inquiries over a period of 60 years'.
>
> In my Interim Report I set out what happened at Hillsborough and why. That it was allowed to happen, despite all the accumulated wisdom of so many previous reports and guidelines must indicate that the lessons of past disasters and the recommendations following them had not been taken sufficiently to heart. (Taylor, 1990, p. 4)

The report becomes an end unto itself. The job is done, the report accepted and shelved. The task of implementing systemic change is probably underestimated and perhaps ignored or perhaps the task of maintaining the changes over a period of more than half a century is too hard for people whose time horizon is limited to five years or less. Possibly, the underlying problem is that there is no 'heart' to which to take the recommendations and also no corporate memory. That is, there is no entity in government with 'a philosophy of controlling and minimising risks as a major emphasis in the design and operation of the system'.

Risk Management Systems

A risk management system (RMS) exists when an individual organisation has a means of directing and managing its approach to the management of risks – those things entirely in its own control. The approach is organisation-wide and no wider.

By definition, an RMS is limited in its scope and power to that which the site can do by itself. In my experience, even in large multinational companies, risk is managed at a site level, even if there is a need to report to the global head office on corporate performance indicators. On one occasion, I was called into a multinational's site by the site manager to see if they had the same set of circumstances that had recently killed a worker on another continent. After travelling for most of a day to get there, within half an hour of being on site it was very obvious that they did have the same situation. The situation that killed the worker existed for these reasons:

1. The as-built plant did not comply with the relevant equipment design standard. This is commonly because commissioning engineers don't know what the standard says and the tendering process is so competitive that the supplier can't afford to add the compliant features, despite the motherhood statements in contracts about complying with all applicable legislation, etc. A deficiency in the education of those designing the product and a conflict with commercial pressures makes this possible. These features of systemic risk control are lacking.

2. Once in operation, this deficiency is not noted by people. There is no government expectation or means of ensuring that their education or training includes such knowledge. These features of systemic risk control are lacking. Once constructed, operational staff may not be able to identify this problem and any RMS may not specifically encourage them to do so.

3. Compliance with the relevant equipment design standard may have prevented the fatality, but probably the design would have been circumvented because of the contractual conditions of the worker and the need to work quickly under a lean payment system. The presence of the contract created an arm's length relationship between the site and the small contracting company. In effect, the risk management programme, such as it was, belonged to a small and unsophisticated small country town contractor.

This work method problem is not recognised by the site's procurement office, who think they have done a good job by getting a cheap contractor and ticking all the boxes of the company's procurement system. The nature of this problem is not evident to the safety officers as the scope of their work does not direct their attention to such matters and their education does not make the nature of the risk evident to them.

Despite the use of similar technology and management systems all around the world, at a practical level, each site was managed as though it was a small company. One positive feature, albeit reactive, of corporate risk management was that bad experience and the lessons learned were promulgated to all sites and led to the enquiry at the site visited.

There are six essential features of proactive and systematic (not systemic) management of risk in an organisation:

1. There must be an explicit overall purpose to manage risk, including the maintenance of risk controls over long periods of time. This purpose must be understood by the individuals presently occupying the highest level of management and must be promulgated to those who succeed them. The purpose can be conveyed in a Risk Management Plan. This is a high-level statement of the arrangements an organisation makes to manage risk. It will include a policy statement, objectives and strategies and nominate who is responsible for implementing the strategies. The components of the risk management process will normally be evident in these elements, as will be the features of a management system (including incident investigation, documentation standards and so on), such as is defined by international quality management standards.

2. The development and maintenance of an inventory or register of risks, see Chapter 4. It is necessary to know what the risks are and to be specific about the control measures required by each. Generic risk management practices are no substitute for directed effort, especially where operational risks (Table 5.4) are concerned. Effective risk management practices are those directed at the origin of risks. A risk register should identify the specific control measures for each risk, see Chapter 7. Control measures will generally be in the form of plant strategy, maintenance, inspection, contractual requirements (outsourced activities), work process flows, work method statements and training documents. There is in the majority of cases absolutely no need to make an estimate of the size of risk, for example by selecting a category from a risk matrix – see Chapter 8. In the majority of cases it is sufficient to identify the LWC value associated with the risk, as this is what mostly determines the standard of control measure and the efforts needed to maintain them over time. Likelihood, in any event, is virtually impossible to guess meaningfully from the word scales provided in a typical risk matrix.

3. Periodic review of the adequacy of control measures in the risks listed in the inventory. The risk register can be designed to prompt this at suitable intervals, such as five years. Not only do the details of risks change over time, but the standards against which the adequacy of risk controls is judged changes over time as regulations, standards, codes of practice, community expectations and technology change. The review also looks for missed opportunities to properly or better control risk. To borrow a term from quality management standards, these are rightly and positively called opportunities for improvement (OFI). Some use the term Latent Failure for these. The risk register should be designed to trigger such reviews.

4. Conscious recognition of the organisational requirements for the maintenance of the tangible risk control measures noted in 2 above. Each cited control measure document should be formal and subject to document control. The risk register should link these to an audit plan, the purpose of which is to determine the interval between checks on the implementation of the control measures. This is the inspection interval discussed in Chapters 7 and 10, which is so important for the reliability of control measures. Implementation checks need not be complex or time-consuming. They are a demonstration that the organisation is making an effort to actually implement what it says is the management system and purposeful supervisory activity. They are an opportunity to discover action failures in the implementation of the defined risk control measures and by understanding them discover ways of improving the reliability of those measures. Some use the term Active Failures for these. Inadequacies of the coverage of risk control measures (see above) may also be discovered at the same time.

5. The ability to revise all the above through learning lessons from partial and completed Occurrences as they are experienced. Quality management systems include a system for learning from things that go wrong (variously known as 'issue-action', 'opportunity for improvement' or 'corrective action' practices). Each time an Action Failure is noted, there is a documented response to it.

6. A means of ensuring the continuity of this comprehensive approach as staffing and the organisation changes over an extended period of time. If the risk management purpose and the mechanisms of giving effect to it are not communicated to new arrivals it will dissipate rapidly. The time between significant risk Events is lengthy. Risk engineers are accustomed to thinking in terms of 10s to 100s of years between catastrophic events, but within a 10-year period there may have been two changes of management. Each 'change of watch' often comes about with a loss of knowledge and one of the first things to be lost is the intention of the previous management team. The Risk Management Plan needs to be incorporated as closely as possible into the management practices of the organisation. It is this that provides the essential continuity of effort and intent without which it is not possible to manage risk. Formality in the management of the documents which define risk control measures is what provides the corporate memory which is so essential in risk management.

With this context, the widespread adoption by industry of so-called quality management systems is encouraging. These management systems (based on ISO9001) essentially encourage an organisation to commit its policies and processes to writing, ensure knowledge (by training programmes) and compliance (by internal audits) with them and set up a system for learning from things that go wrong, thus satisfying requirements 3 to 5 in the list above. By filling in the gaps (particularly items 2 and 3) an RMS can be created that is part of a quality management system. Because of this, related standards such as ISO14001 (Environment Management Systems) and ISO31000 (Risk Management) are all based on the quality management system structure.

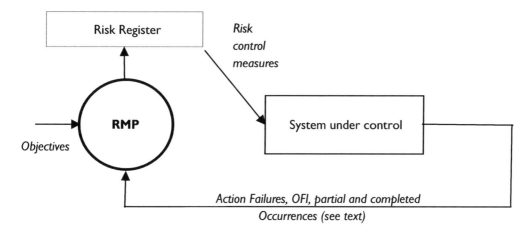

Figure 11.2   A Risk management system

Risk Management System Failures

The Concorde disaster of 25 July 2000 is a high profile case that has received much attention and which has been revisited by lawyers in recent times (Samuel, 2012):

> Claude Frantzen, 75, the former head of France's civil aviation authority, had also faced prosecution for negligence. He was accused of ignoring warning signs from a string of tyre incidents on Concorde over a 15-year period, but was acquitted of any offence.

While details are not provided in the press reports seen, the judge is reported as saying that:

> 25 years of operation ... were littered with numerous cases of tyre damage following more or less serious incidents. Mr Frantzen ... should have proposed 'suspending Concorde's flight permit' ... his scrutiny of the jet's flight fitness had 'not been up to the mark'.

The point of knowing about Events with minimal Consequences is that it provides an insight into possible major Consequences. A large number, as in this case, of minimal Consequence Value cases is invaluable in estimating the Risk itself, as shown in Chapter 6. A system needs to understand this basic characteristic of risk. If true, this is an example of a very fundamental failure of an RMS – if there is no feedback or if the comparator is not paying attention, then there is no risk control.

The Qualities of a Controlled System

A system that is under control, in the sense of Figure 11.1, has certain attributes and desirable qualities that are relevant, by analogy, to the control of risk. An understanding of these assists us to see how an operational system can direct its attention towards meaningful specific measures in support of risk control. It is otherwise easy for an operational system to be distracted by activities with apparent general relevance but little specific purpose. The RMS needs to explicitly attend to the provision and maintenance of these characteristics.

Table 11.2   Control system functional capabilities and desirable qualities

Control system attributes	Operational system attributes
Functional capabilities	
F1: Predictable response to perturbation	All Occurrences or part Occurrences (e.g. partial
Normal disturbances produce a predictable response.	Mechanisms, Null Outcomes, completed Outcomes)
	are perturbations which receive attention.
F2: Conforming behaviour	The nature of the response to all perturbations is the
No matter what the nature of the disturbance, the	same. They are analysed and decisions made about
response is the same.	the need to change features of the operating system
	that influences them.
F3: Reliability	The organisational processes that are involved in these
The components of the system seldom fail.	responses are of high reliability and maintained over time.
Desirable qualities	
Q1: Robust design	Physical risk control features of equipment and
The system is able to operate even when faced with	processes are able to withstand the extremes of
the extremes of the environment in which it works.	environmental stressors. The management system is
	strong enough to cope with organisational hard times.
Q2: Responsive to failures	risk control features of equipment and people-oriented
When functional failures occur, the system is designed	processes default into a safe mode when failures
to fail into a safe mode of operation.	occur. The management system explicitly determines
	the features of day-to-day operations that constitute
	early indications of Occurrence processes and
	devises practical means of ensuring safe Outcomes.

A physical control system has three main functional capabilities (F1 to F3 in Table 11.2), which ensure it functions in a satisfactory manner to return the system to its desired state when a perturbation occurs, for example the control of liquid level in a tank when the level begins to rise. To be satisfactory the system must have predictable appropriate responses (to bring the level back to the desired point) and be reliable. It must also have two main qualities (Q1 and Q2 in Table 11.2) that make it practical in the environment in which it is intended to operate. One is its ability to withstand the stresses of the environment (which may be high temperatures, vibration, acidity, etc.) and the other its ability to work satisfactorily in the face of component or operating method failure (what happens to the system when the controller itself fails). Given these, the control system will not provide any surprises in the operation of the system and if it fails it will do so safely. The exact way in which these capabilities and qualities are provided depends greatly on the system itself. A liquid level controller will require a powered control system with sensors, logic and powered valve actuators and these will operate continuously. A simple pipe containing hazardous fluids will need an excess flow or low pressure sensor and a powered valve actuator that will operate only when the fail conditions of a leak are experienced. Process plant engineers routinely design plant to have a 'soft landing' capability when failures occur, meaning that the failure is detected and the plant shuts down in a manner designed to minimise damage and maximise the speed with which it can be brought back on line. Foreseeable Occurrence processes are predicted and automated responses provided to create a preferred Occurrence path.

However, not all high-energy systems have these characteristics. For example, modern airliners rely on pilot judgement ('seat of the pants') to identify inadequate take-off performance due to any one of a number of possible and predictable Mechanisms other than engine failure and to react appropriately. The first task of a risk management system is to pay attention to the technology surrounding high Consequence risks and attend to the quality of its design and operation.

In many control systems automation has not replaced people, who do not behave in the predictable manner of machinery. The nature of F1 to F3 and Q1 and Q2 in Table 11.2 will be very different where the role of people is significant. In the control room cabin of a process plant or vehicle, perturbations of the system (F1) may be signalled to the controller by error messages or abnormal operating conditions. The conformity of the person (F2) to the preferred (intended, hoped for, possibly post hoc judgement) response to the perturbation will be less certain than that of an automatic controller and affected by how routine the perturbation is and therefore how learned the response is. Conformity can be expected to be high if the perturbation is routine and the operator is experienced, but less so for a new operator. The reliability of an operator in making the preferred response (F3) will depend on the detail of the operator–system interface. A detailed understanding of how human beings respond to control room displays is needed to understand this properly. Obviously, and for example, indicators of highly significant operating conditions (for example the engines on an aeroplane) need to be clear and unambiguous, not small and hard to discern amongst the clutter of other indications. The system needs to be designed so that it is possible for people to make appropriate decisions as to the significance of display indications in the face of background clutter and competing demands for attention whether system driven (masses of error alerts) or arising from other people (Q1). For example, error alerts can be filtered by significance and interruptions from others not allowed or ignored, an example of which is the 'sterile cockpit' in aircraft. When faced with an escalating situation (the Occurrence process is advancing) few people are equipped to think clearly and solve novel problems at the same time when under time pressure. If, after all, incorrect actions result, the system needs to be designed in some way to allow the system to come to rest, so to speak, without major energy release (Q2). As an example, the crew of a large airliner inbound to a major city were faced with a last minute offer (a perturbation) of an alternative runway which would reduce flight time and fuel use. Are they able to accept? The crew referred to performance charts, made complex (influenced by weight, temperature, airfield altitude and wind strength) end-of-flight weight and approach speed calculations (the runway was short and they were required to 'land and hold short' to avoid crossing the main duty runway). These stressors make demands on Q1. They accepted the offer and did manage the landing, but in the hotel and in the calm of the following day reconsidered the charts and discovered errors that meant the decision should have been to reject the offer as the landing could not be completed with the required performance safety margins. Q2 could have been enacted here by providing a rule that no late changes to clearances or expectations requiring such decisions would be accepted, as a matter of policy.

The second task of an RMS is to develop organisational capabilities, and this task needs the same attention to detail. Continuing the analogy, perturbations (F1) come in the form of evidence the system is not performing as desired, in other words noticeable features of possible Occurrences are detected. Only those aspects of performance that are relevant to feasible Occurrence processes are of interest. To be aware of these as perturbations, it is necessary to understand the possible processes in the system – see Chapters 5 and 9. This is Item 5 in the earlier explanation of an RMS (the six essential features of proactive and systematic management of risk, above), in which it is also easy to locate F2 and F3 in Item 6. All such performance perturbations can be captured either as a matter of routine or by periodic sampling of performance.

For example, a tank level control system may be triggered by a high level indicator to reduce the level, but failure to do so may lead to the second level of alarm being triggered, requiring manual intervention. This is a perturbation depending on a potentially low reliability component (the operator) to avoid an escalation of the process. The risk management system should monitor how often the operator is required to act on this and how close the operator comes to failing to achieve level control in time. As another example, airliners are expected to land with at least a legislated minimum level of reserve fuel. Monitoring how close fuel reserves come to this minimum will give an indication of the likely Frequency of transgression of the rules. Monitoring flight situations in which unexpected amounts of fuel were used due to non-routine operating conditions, such as unanticipated and adverse clearances, missed approaches, etc. gives insight into perturbations upstream in the Occurrence process. It is an organisational concern that such matters are recognised and performance monitoring requirements set.

A robust organisation (Q1) is one that does not sacrifice its risk management activities in order to save money in hard times and certainly one in which the influence of the RMS does not wax and wane with changing people in the management structure. Of far greater complexity, in the sense that there is a larger amount of detail to be managed, is the need for the identification of significant functional failures (Q2) and the methods of responding to them to produce the desired 'soft landing'. Over the last decade, efforts to promote Q2 qualities have been promoted under the name of 'resilience engineering' (Linh et al., 2012). Resilience means the capacity to recover from adverse situations (OED). The promotion of these attributes of a controlled system is perhaps most evident in aviation. All aspects of a flight are predicted in the flight planning process and the flight itself conforms to rules used throughout the organisation. Efforts are made to ensure that operational reliability is suited to the responsibilities of the flight: as larger numbers of people are transported in one aircraft, the number of flight crew increases and one role of the additional pilots is to check the actions and decisions of the flying crew members. Pilots are trained to respond to equipment failures, difficult weather conditions and complex navigational practices in flight simulators. Aircraft are designed to cope with in-flight equipment failures, with major systems being triplicated, for example.

It is easy to see why proponents of accident theory correctly define accidents as unpredicted, unexpected and unwanted; these are the opposite of the positive attributes of a controlled system. If accident prevention is seen to mean the strengthening of the positive attributes of the controlled system, it is identical to the purpose of a risk management system.

The positive attributes discussed here are also of general value to the organisation, as they can lead to predictable etc. outcomes in all facets of the business. Contributing to these attributes does more than assist to manage risk, it helps to manage the organisation. What needs to be done to operate an airline safely is the same as what is needed to operate efficiently.

Risk Management in Real Organisations

Some organisations are more able to develop the required capabilities than others. As a subset of management, risk management can only be as good as the organisation itself. The Risk manager needs to understand the character of the organisation and promote management capabilities that are of general value (assisting the development of management capability generally) and risk management strategies that are both relevant to the needs of the organisation and feasible in the sense of achievable by the organisation. Any RMS is an artificial introduction to a situation in which some forms of risk management already exist. A common view is that risk management is a normal part of managing anything and this may well lead to the criticism that an RMS is unnecessary. People at the most senior levels of management of industry will almost certainly have a career that imbued them in their formative years with a very simple understanding of industrial safety, which, when extrapolated into risk management and expressed in the boardroom, can result in the promotion of ineffective and outdated beliefs and management strategies typically based on a less than thorough understanding of even accident theory. In attempting to impose structure and order, an RMS unavoidably disturbs the status quo as well as the individuals with power and influence in the organisation.

It is the nature of the interaction of the RMS with the culture, beliefs and politics of the organisation that leads to a good or poor result. It is no surprise therefore that some promoters of risk management are primarily concerned with promoting group beliefs and shared values rather than challenging the conceptual understanding of senior managers. There is a danger that a general approach to risk management may be seen as valuable in its own right. If efforts are not actually directed towards real risk control measures we live in a fool's paradise and are at the mercy of statistics. Risk identification and analysis not only gets to the heart of the matter (of what can go wrong), it also has the ability to predict what could happen. Twenty–twenty hindsight can be supplemented by something close to that in foresight.

All types of industry and commerce do the same things over and over again, often for decades at a time before significant technology changes occur. For example, airlines book passengers on flights, gather them in the terminal, load aircraft with baggage, fuel and food, fly the aircraft to the destination, unload the passengers and give them back their baggage. This happens thousands of times a week. From an operational risk point of view, there are a limited number of operational scenarios that require analysis:

1. operations on the apron, near the aero-bridge including cleaning, refuelling, baggage and food handling;
2. ground manoeuvring, including taxiing;
3. take-off and initial climb;
4. en-route climb;
5. cruise;
6. descent;
7. terminal area manoeuvring including holding;
8. landing;
9. hostile acts (hijack, war).

Passengers don't really care if an airline has a risk management programme in place or what the beliefs of managers are, but there are some qualities of the operation that passengers care about very much. With some relevant knowledge, this is my list:

- that aircraft are reasonably new;
- that engine and airframe maintenance is done on time by well-trained and content people;
- that airworthiness decisions on individual aircraft are made as of right (no interference by managers with commercial or internal political interests) by the engineers and, as necessary, by the responsible captain;
- that pilots are well-trained, experienced and content in their employment. If I know more about this subject, I find myself very interested in how the flight crew relate to each other in the cockpit, whether they are a cooperative team (good) or have a tense hierarchical structure (bad);
- that I am flying in well-equipped and managed airspace.

If an RMS contributes directly to the really important qualities of risk control it is useful. The RMS will do so if it defines standards of control of each predictable risk and monitors the extent to which these standards are achieved day-after-day and year-after-year, risk control standards are an essential feature of any RMS and a suggested simple way of categorising them (see Table 7.4) is as controls on physical and environmental risk factors, controls over the way work is done and administrative practices. These categories are used to group all the control measures a comprehensive risk assessment of the specific operational scenarios has found to be necessary.

Organisational culture is important if it is able to adversely influence risk assessment or the attainment over time of the standards determined by the risk assessment. The relevant facets of organisational culture that may have an adverse effect are:

1. Shared unhelpful beliefs. A common belief is that by far the greatest number of problems are caused by people not doing what they should and hence risk control efforts promote personal responsibility rather than look more deeply into the design of work methods and equipment. This belief arises from a misunderstanding of accident theory that equates risk control measures with the removal of perceived causes (Chapter 2, the Fourth Axiom). Another common but dangerously erroneous belief, in industry at least, is that the measure of numbers of injuries, such as lost-time injury frequency rate, is also a measure of operational safety capability (Chapter 2, the Fifth Axiom). The chemical industry, for example is known for both low lost-time injury frequency rates and for periodic catastrophic fires or explosions.
2. Misunderstanding Risk. This commonly exhibits itself as the inability of people to believe that 'accidents' can be predicted and being unaware of the implications of LWCs. When unaware of the distinction between likely least and likely worst Consequences, people will not understand why control measures need to be designed with the latter in mind and feel that risk control measures are unnecessarily complex.
3. Misunderstanding the significance of the law and insurance. When legislation is prescriptive about control measures, managers can sometimes be motivated to conform with these if the penalty of not doing so is made to seem plausible and awful. Performance-based legislation, for example specifying risk assessment processes to be followed, probably has less immediate influence on the behaviour of managers although may be used to justify risk management processes. Common law (where it exists) effectively defines the practical meaning of moral obligation and a detailed explanation of it can have the effect of making managers understand both their role and the need for a systematic organisational approach to risk management. Managers of operational activities (e.g. operating the ships, running the hotel, investing the funds) may be insulated from the costs of failure by separate insurance and maintenance budgets: 'I don't pay for it, it is not part of my performance measures'. They are often also insulated from the decisions of courts as insurance companies manage claims and typically do not mount vigorous defences. The implications of judgements made against them are often not considered within the organisation, perhaps as a result.
4. Unsuitable accountability structures. In promoting qualities and activities that may not be easily connected to the immediate needs of the business, an RMS asks people to do things the purpose of which may not be immediately evident. A significant aspect of the design of any RMS is the ease with which the people who occupy relevant positions can be held accountable for continuing to perform their RMS tasks. If accountability practices in the organisation are poorly developed or adversely influenced by other cultural factors, the ability to implement the RMS will be compromised. People are held accountable for action rather than beliefs or commitment. Statements of action requirements can be developed, to suit the individual organisation, from the international quality (or risk, environment or occupational health and safety) management standards. These standards define what is needed and from each listed item strategies can be developed that include what needs to be done, how and by whom, to meet the requirement. It perhaps is not necessary to say that while the risk adviser may suggest the content of this, it is essential that the most

senior management executive group knowingly approve it. Risk management is necessarily a line management activity. A significant omission from these standards, however, is the need for risk control standards specific to the nature of the risks faced by the organisation.

5. Conflict of interest. The pressure to reduce costs or achieve politically desirable goals overrides technical judgement, for example when a manager is given what may be conflicting values to maintain a safe operation and cut the operating cost budget by 25 percent. If the coupling of these two values is not understood risk control standards may well be compromised. Alternatively, a manager may wish to achieve a goal that promises great rewards but can only do so if risk control standards are ignored. At a workforce level there are often conflicts between expected productivity and required work methods. The latter are normally the casualty in this conflict, as is made evident when a dispute with management results in the workforce working to rule. See also the discussion on safety and productivity below. A particularly dangerous version of this is when a high-level manager subject to pressure to achieve a goal imposes pressure on someone lower in the organisation to allow something to happen against that person's better judgement. In the airline industry, this might take the form of an operations manager putting pressure on a maintenance technician to release an aircraft for service or on a pilot to operate with unserviceable equipment or in poor weather.

6. Corruption. An opportunity for personal gain overrides technical judgement. This is a hidden and (possibly) illegal aspect of conflict of interest. In corrupt societies the presence of laws and rules and of positions of authority create an opportunity for a payment to be made to remove the obstacle by issuing licences, approving works done and similar when the required conditions have not been met.

7. Authoritarian communication styles. In vertical (within a department from one level to the level below or vice versa) interactions between people, any culture that interferes with open communication in either direction is potentially problematic in an RMS. If management requirements are expressed as orders or if displeasure is evident when the wrong response is forthcoming from the level below it is likely that the only response that is given is that which is wanted, whether it is true or false. Information that should be passed up the line may be repressed entirely if it will bring an angry response. In one case in my experience, the CEO of a very large organisation personally inspected storm drains at each production location prior to the monsoon season as he knew he could not rely on drain cleaning progress reports to ensure cleaning actually occurred and knew of the loss of production that flooding caused. In such organisations, there is little point in trying to implement any system. A variation of this is when high-level managers express strong needs for specific outcomes, for example a desire for the LTIFR to be below a particular value. A common consequence of this is dishonest accounting for injuries: one set of records that please the general manager and another that reflect reality. In horizontal (between departments) communication, the presence of impenetrable organisational barriers makes it difficult for cooperation to achieve common goals. As an example, a radar operator is said to have watched an aircraft fly into a mountain but felt unable to intervene because this was happening in a flight region managed by another part pif the organisation and on a different radio frequency.

The way in which these seven cultural determinants express themselves in any one organisation creates the character of the organisation, which in time becomes evident to an outsider — see Table 11.3. In Chapter 3 (Time Zone 1 discussion), the point was made that, despite its complexity, the only features of culture with significance to prevention work are whether the organisation is supportive of it and capable of doing it.

Table 11.3   A view of the character and culture of organisations

Character	Description
Welcoming	Belief in openness and respect for the views of all leads to advice or suggestions regarding anything (including risk) being welcomed and considered seriously. The organisation values improvement and change. Vertical and lateral communication pathways are open.
Resisting	People doubt their and their organisation's capability and feel that their position is fragile, possibly because of authoritarian management style. They will not wish to provide useful information to the risk adviser. Alternatively, performance in risk management is clearly unrelated to accountability in all areas of the organisation and hence is seen to be an irrelevant concern. Change will be resisted.
Passive	People feel the organisation can be neither threatened nor changed in any way and so advice or suggestions are seen as largely irrelevant. Bureaucracies often have this character.
Secretive	There are strong undercurrents and hidden agendas, possibly arising from conflicting interests and/or corruption. Information of any value is hard to obtain and change is almost impossible to conceive. There are possibly one or two people in the organisation whose influence is felt everywhere but it may be very hard to discover who they are.
Arrogant	There are strongly held beliefs in the existing qualities of the organisation, particularly of its culture. Advice or suggestions threaten this perception and are unwelcome. In the extreme, the beliefs of the organisation are sacrosanct and absolute acceptance of them is necessary for a person to work in the organisation. Alternative view points are not welcomed. The organisation has the potential to become totalitarian.

Despite the number and complexity of adverse influences on an RMS, annual audits of performance against the requirements of a Risk management standard are potentially valuable in communicating the facts simply and without implied judgement or criticism. All that is required to begin the process is agreement to begin and agreement about the content of the standard used. Annual repetition of the audits keeps the facts fresh and the pressure on the organisation to improve its Risk management capability. This apparently simple process can be frustratingly difficult to make a reality and success depends on very careful consideration of how the actions are framed in words. How does the auditor know when the action requirement really has been completed? Some actions will be to develop a capability, for example a Risk register, which may have several stages of development with different responsible people to decide on its structure, select or design suitable software and commission it. All departments will have a responsibility to populate the register, but how are poor quality entries or inappropriate scope to be treated by the auditor? Relying on the dictum that what gets measured gets done, the Risk adviser needs to be sure that what is being measured is of real value in improving the management of Risk.

One of the first attempts to establish a useful standard was the International Safety Rating System, derived from an earlier document (c.1975) of the National Occupational Safety Association of South Africa. Based on performance against a number of criteria, subscribing companies were rated up to five stars, similar to the hotel rating scheme. The more stars supposedly the better safety was managed. After some time, an independent study (Eisner and Leger, 1988) assessed the value of the ratings: did high ratings mean safer organisations? The conclusion was that despite the enthusiastic comments of the supporters of the system, there was little objective evidence that increased star grading was a reflection of improvement in safety. The process is only as good as the content of the standard.

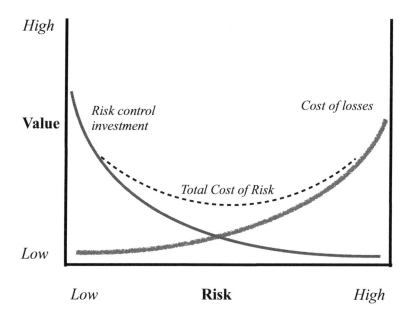

Figure 11.3   **Representation of the total cost of Risk**

Risk Control Effort and its Cost – The Total Cost of Risk

Figure 8.2 illustrates a possible application of the law of diminishing returns when adding risk controls – the more one tries to reduce Risk the greater the cost for smaller increments in risk reduction. This relationship assumes that the early risk control measures will be simple to implement and have comparatively large effects on Risk reduction, but then it becomes increasingly harder to achieve reduction. Another way of looking at this relationship is in Figure 11.3. If it is possible to imagine an organisation with nothing other than unconsidered risk controls, one might expect the cost of the losses it faces to be as high as they can be in the context of the industry. Assuming always that subsequent risk control activities are well directed, as more is invested in risk control the losses will keep reducing. Ultimately we would expect the law of diminishing returns to be demonstrated – the amount you have to invest to achieve a small reduction in loss becomes increasingly larger.

Here, the total cost of risk (TCOR) is defined as the sum of the cost of loss and the investment in risk control, alternatively thought of as the cost of reacting to losses as they arise and the investment in preventive activities. It is the sum of the two curves in the figure and naturally has a minimum value, if the assumptions are correct. Figure 11.3 makes it clear that an organisation can experience the same TCOR either through a large cost of loss or through a large investment in risk control activities. If an effort is made to define the components of the two parameters and estimate their values, many organisations appear to operate with a high cost of reaction and low investment in prevention. As emergency preparedness (first aid, fire precautions, business continuity plans) and insurance are all components of the cost of reaction it is not hard to see how this is so. Where a moral obligation exists, it is also not hard to see that the obligation is more likely to be satisfied by operating with an investment in prevention that is higher than the cost of reaction. Both the concept and the measurement of TCOR has the potential to provide senior levels of management with a strategic view on the adequacy of their efforts.

An organisation uses its input resources to pay for the people and equipment needed to provide its services or products. Some inefficiency of use is expected in the conversion to services or products: in other words, some losses occur. In a for-profit organisation, one of the possible outputs of this conversion is profit, despite this being susceptible to accounting manipulation and influenced by taxation regimes.

The relationship between these variables is:

profit = value of services or product value – cost of input resources (cost of operation) – cost of losses.

Where profit = 0 (a not-for-profit organisation), the equation still applies and

minimum value of services or product value = cost of input resources (cost of operation) + cost of losses.

Occurrences result in a number of possible disturbances to the desired state. For the purpose of this discussion there are two ways of looking at Occurrences:

1. as an unwanted outcome of a process that normally produces desirable outcomes; for example, a conveyor system malfunctions and spills its contents outside a delivery chute.
2. as an unwanted process that is not normally experienced and which produces only unwanted outcomes; for example, an unexpected exchange or loss of control of energy, as when a vehicle accident occurs or chemicals being transferred spill.

There are three possible ways in which Consequences produce loss which would be added to the cost of reaction:

1. The need to repair or replace/rehabilitate/pay damages and fines and legal bills, etc. produces an increase in the cost of loss.
2. There may be an increase in the cost of input to compensate for the unproductive consequences of the loss (consequential loss in insurance terms); for example, a casual is employed to do the work of the injured person, or a service has to be purchased to cover for the damaged machine.
3. There may be a decrease in the rate of production or quality of services or in the profit output of the operation; for example, an employee is injured but not replaced, so the work is done by those who remain over a longer period of time. Over a year the total amount of work done by the organisation will be less than it would otherwise have been.

Other components of the cost of reaction would include, for example, the cost of an emergency response and first aid facility including training, the cost of treatment and rehabilitation specialists, hospital, medicine, special equipment needs, the cost of fines and legal costs.

Prevention 'investments' may include the use of capital or a change in the amount of recurrent (operating) expenditure. These can be incurred in various ways:

- physical items (assets are capital expenditure and consumables are recurrent expenditure);
- administrative practices – that is, work methods that have a risk control reason; for example, checking certificates, working two in a team where one could physically do the job (recurrent expenditure);
- supervision (a higher level of supervision for risk control purposes may result in increased recurrent expenditure);

- information, education, training given to at-risk or other people (recurrent expenditure);
- personal protective equipment (consumables – a recurrent expenditure).

Other components of prevention investment would include, for example, the direct employment costs of internal advisers and external consultants, library, equipment, the cost of defined items of formal training, information provision and education (relating to safety, operation and maintenance, not to organisation development or professional development training) and the cost of personal protective equipment.

Safety and Productivity

If one goal of risk management is to reduce the number and Consequence value of Occurrences, it follows that the burden of Consequence costs will reduce, thereby possibly improving profitability (more production per unit of cost) and possibly also productivity (more production per unit of time). However, these efforts themselves may come at a cost that reduces gross profitability and productivity. In the extreme, risk management efforts could cost more than the benefits, resulting in productivity and profitability reductions. The benefits of risk management may well be probabilistic but the costs of it will always be immediate and real. As discussed in Chapter 8, real and immediate concerns weigh more heavily on people than possible future benefits. Because of these variables and realities, it is not possible to make any definitive statement that better risk management always improves profitability and productivity. This does not stop proponents claiming that it does, but the thoughtful risk adviser will consider the situation before making such claims.

When an organisation experiences routine losses from easily identifiable types of Risk that are readily able to be reduced by investment in improved production process design, the benefit:cost ratio can be used to justify the investment and reduced Risk (actually Loss) results directly in improved productivity and profitability. Post hoc studies in such industries will show a direct relationship between such improvements and reductions in Risk. For example, the use of greater automation in mining will, by removing susceptible human bodies from a hazardous environment, improve personal safety as well as possibly improving rates of production (machines don't get weary). It is questionable, however, whether the safety programme can claim the accolades. In Chapter 1, it was pointed out that nearly a century ago it was recognised that good management practices were apparently indistinguishable from safety management practices. The previously mentioned study by Cohen (1977) many decades ago showed how apparent improvements in safety (as measured by time off work from claimed injury) could be attributed to a humane and supporting work environment in which due allowance was made for the fact that adults need time off to attend to family matters (sick children, etc.) and not to any actual improvement in safety.

A review of the recent literature discussing this matter uncovered a preponderance of studies showing a direct correlation between productivity and safety and a slightly lesser number that either uncovered an inverse relationship or drew attention to the difficulty of determining what was influencing what. Correlation, after all, does not equate to causation, although many papers appear to imply this is the case. Even if it does, is it safety that causes productivity improvements or vice versa (Hopkins, 1994)? Automation is a steady route to productivity improvements and by removing the Exposure of people, it will also reduce the experience of injury, but it is unreasonable to say that the driving reason for this is a safety programme. In (unpublished) work of my own in the 1990s, a number of manufacturing companies were visited who had distinguished themselves by performing much better on injury compensation cost metrics than others in their industry. Detailed insights were gained during site visits, two of which illustrate the possible variety of reasons for a connection underlying the correlation:

- A small company with a family atmosphere and in which birthdays, marriages and newborns were celebrated in a working hours (production stopped) party. The Chief Executive Officer saw his main task as keeping the employees happy 'as their work is very tedious and repetitive'. The equipment and methods in use had not changed for many decades.
- A medium-sized company with an icy atmosphere of stand-off between management and unions pervading all personal interactions. There were only two significant Risks in the process, arising from muscle effort and from noise. The factory had been designed from the ground up with professional advice on both matters and control measures in place were excellent.

In some organisations, however, losses are from predictable sources but there is no or little opportunity to reduce Exposure or Probability. In such situations, there may be a very weak or even negative relationship between spending on safety and the benefit of Risk reduction. A transport company is a good example of this. Until automated vehicle technology becomes available the most that can be done is to retain maintenance practices, provide defensive driver training and implement strict vehicle loading and driver fatigue regulations. These will increase direct costs with only a diffuse and probabilistic improvement in losses. As safety increases (more driver training, shorter work periods before rests, more maintenance) productivity and profitability reduce. Add this to a competitive tendering environment and the systemic scene is set for inevitable periodic disasters that are of value mostly to lawyers. In such industries it is essential for regulation to make it necessary for all competing companies to achieve the same standards of safety practices. Before statistical reality delivers its benefits, the conscientious organisation working on its own will probably have gone bankrupt.

In other organisations, of which the chemical industry is a good example, very few minor injuries arise due to limited exposure of people with plant for operational and maintenance reasons and major Consequences make surprise appearances that are so infrequent as to be seen to be unrelated to safety activities. Reducing spending on safety and on maintenance will improve productivity and profitability in the short term to the benefit of the short-sighted manager's reputation.

While productivity may be relatively easy to measure, 'spending on safety' is not easy to separate from spending generally. Attempts to measure this in different organisations have met resistance and many practical problems. Also, the relationship between these two variables is diffuse and probabilistic, not deterministic. Individual safety projects requiring money may not improve productivity and they may be ignored without immediate effect on safety. Sometimes safety considerations require more people to do a job and hence reduce productivity. Sometimes automating a task improves productivity and improves safety, as people are no longer involved; for example, using radio-controlled aircraft tugs.

If there is any relationship between these two variables, is it so dependent on specific circumstances that it is pointless generalising? The immediate financial benefits of reducing such spending, combined with the lack of immediate effect on 'accidents', means that this is a route for easy gains in profitability. The motivation to seek such gains and the lack of knowledge of the implications leads to behaviour that erodes the continuity of risk control measures, the reason for which has been forgotten.

By reducing expenditure on risk control measures (for example inspections, training, maintenance, equipment renewal) organisations can gain the immediate benefit of improved financial performance. If these reductions are made in ways that actually reduce the effectiveness of risk control measures the uncertain nature of risk makes it highly unlikely that something adverse will happen quickly. The reward of improved financial performance will appear to have been gained without paying for it.

If the organisation has been operating in a highly risk-averse way, as many government organisations do (production 'without risk' at any cost), it may well be that significant cost reductions can occur before any adverse effects become apparent. Examples of such risk-averse organisations in some countries are electricity generators, transmitters and suppliers. For many years these were owned and operated by governments that were very averse to power failures because of the negative effect on the public (voters). Operating and maintenance practices developed over years reflected the risk-averse policy: supply must be maintained at all costs. For example, lightning protection is expensive to install and maintain and analysis may show that it contributes little (less than its cost) to supply continuity in areas of low lightning activity. As these organisations have become more commercially oriented, the extremely low levels of Risk have become more apparent and there is a desire to move towards a higher Risk but lower cost method of operating. Practically, this might mean that less money is spent on equipment, inspection and maintenance (remove or don't maintain the lightning protectors) or on training, for example. In this case, it might indeed be true that less spending on safety means more profitability and perhaps productivity. The financial rewards can be significant and encourage the new commercial managers to seek further improvements at the expense of risk control. The problem with this is that in the absence of a specific understanding of the risk effects of the cuts there is nothing to dissuade the organisation from continuing in this direction, until a significant loss event occurs, which, statistically is quite possible, though the time interval may be long and those who began the process no longer on watch. After some time, it is fortunate that the problems caused by this cost reduction strategy are likely to first become evident in breakdowns, operating errors and similar as the probabilities of these is much higher than that of a completed Occurrence with a severe adverse Consequence. To set out on this path with some sense of caution, it is very desirable that the organisation makes every effort to monitor these early indicators of the health of the production process.

Contingency Planning and Crisis Management

Any organisation is sensitive to Threats of political, social or physical origins. A disgruntled customer may enter the building and shoot a person, a strike may bring production to a halt, a fire may burn down the electricity supply on which the company relies, what are considered safe investments may suddenly be without value, an extortionist may threaten an attack unless money is paid, the building may burn, the computer system may be hacked into and records destroyed.

There is often little or no warning period. It is never good to be forced to decide how to manage a crisis while the crisis is happening. It is always better to have a preconsidered plan that suits foreseeable needs and which is practised. Every major company should consider itself to be a potential target for extortion or terrorist attack and should have contingency plans to deal with such circumstances. The objective of a contingency plan is to manage the unfolding crisis as best as possible, minimise the adverse influence and recover to normal operations as quickly as possible.

Summary

A useful way to understand the desired qualities of risk management is by analogy with the block diagram representation of a control system. A systemic approach to risk is possible if a large view is taken of the ways in which all inputs to the whole industry to which an operating organisation belongs can beneficially influence risk within the industry. This is the role of government and legislation, but it is seldom enacted where occupational risks are concerned. By contrast, a risk management system is limited to that which the operating organisation itself is able to influence.

The control system model also makes it possible to identify the functional attributes and operational qualities of a system attempting to control risk. The way in which these apply to both the technical origins of risk and the management system are described. Particular note is made of the need for any risk management activities to be purposefully directed at specific risk-related matters derived from an understanding of Occurrence types, Mechanisms and Outcomes, rather than becoming busy with generic activities the purpose of which is hard to relate to individual risks. Risk control standards are suggested as a means of keeping the attention of the organisation on real needs. Despite this, the beneficial influence of quality management standards is noted, as these promote management activities and attributes that are of much value in the management of risk.

Efforts at risk management within individual organisations are often of limited effectiveness because of a lack of understanding of what the task involves or an unsupportive or incapable culture. A way of understanding how the culture of an organisation influences its ability to support risk management activities and understand its capability to make good use of them is given. If a Risk adviser is able to recognise these limitations, they may perform a great service to the organisation by encouraging the development of general management capability while at the same time beginning to incorporate elements of what will contribute to a complete risk management structure as the organisation achieves the needed qualities.

Attention is drawn to the fact that the management of operational risks particularly demands attention to specific risk control measures and the monitoring of their performance at all stages of development of Occurrences to proactively understand how achieved performance approaches critical states and improve those controls that prevent the critical state being reached.

The Total Cost of Risk is defined and described as a means of understanding the adequacy of the efforts of an organisation through the proportion of effort put into both prevention and reaction. From this, it is possible to make informed strategic decisions about the adequacy of the risk management efforts of the organisation.

In a discussion on the relationship between productivity and safety it is concluded that there is little logical support for the contention that increased risk control necessarily improves productivity.

12

Engineering and the Management of Technical Risks: Prevention by Technical Management and Design

Introduction

Of the three basic types of control measures (design features of equipment and facilities, administrative practices of the organisation and the behaviour of people) it is generally true that the most reliable are those designed in to processes and the least reliable are those that depend on prescribed or hoped-for behaviour of individuals. Somewhere between these two is the hoped-for behaviour of the organisation. The common support for these three is the management system, which can be thought of as an organising principle. In an industrial environment, engineering is influential in both the design of the process, equipment and facility and its support during operation. Unfortunately, process design does not always foresee operational requirements and operational methods do not always conform to the assumptions of the designer. The situation is complicated by the fact that equipment and facilities are commonly modified during the life of a process, for example to install modern control systems or to increase productivity. Some years after the initial commissioning, the actual state of the plant will show evidence of these changes as well as the maintenance and equipment renewal practices of the organisation. Because equipment designers are usually remote from operational experience, the problems originating in their designs may not be known to them. This restriction does not apply in those few industries and countries in which a systemic approach to risk control exists (as described in Chapter 11). Consequently, various influences combine to produce a less than desirable quality of risk control with new plant (possibly) and increasingly so with the age of the plant.

The application of good engineering principles can do much to create safe plant throughout its life. These can be derived from the control measure strategies outlined in Table 3.3, particularly control measure types 1 to 4, which are concerned with the energy source, the containment mechanism and the space transfer mechanism. Behavioural controls are relevant when people interact in any way with the process. Where Recipients include equipment and buildings, engineering design has a role there too. Consequently, it is possible to categorise engineering risk control measures, the specifics of which may depend on the energy source and the nature of the process.

Risk control measures in design may directly affect the process or equipment or may be subsidiary to it. For example, in the design of a thermal power station detailed design decisions about steam handling cannot be separated from risk considerations. Decisions about the design of access, routing of controls, fire suppression and the provision of fugitive gas sensors may be seen to be subsidiary to the basic design but are of great significance to operational risk. As in all things, one can have an expensive high quality design and low operating and risk costs or a cheap and poor quality design and high operating and risk costs. However, a well-thought-out design may not have an initial cost any different from a poorly considered one. What is the difference in cost between an elevated walkway obstructed by a large duct and one not so hampered?

Designers of industrial plant and of buildings are contractually required to ensure that their design complies with standards and legislation and possibly codes of practice. Those specifying these requirements may well be (and often are) lulled into a sense of confidence in the risk control features of the design that may in fact be misplaced. For example, all access in an industrial plant can be expected to conform to routine design standards, but their location may be inappropriate and their number insufficient. Designers may leave the routine detail to the contractors building the equipment (by passing on the requirement to 'comply with standards and legislation') who are constrained by competitive tendering to try to squeeze meagre profits by cutting corners. If these details are unknown to commissioning engineers, the as-built plant will have ticked boxes on a checklist but not in fact comply with the specified standards, or it may comply but be less than useful in practice. A very common example of this is industrial bulk conveyor systems, which are often commissioned with what appear to be guards (they may even be painted yellow to proclaim their presence) but which do not satisfy the standards, or common law expectations. Other more subtle practical problems may exist in the provision of start alarms (for example multiple conveyors in the same location all with the same-sounding start alarm) and emergency stop (E-Stop) functioning. These are often not minor matters and significant expenditure can be required to modify the plant to a sensible standard.

The same problem may arise from building designs. The offices and laboratories of a power station may comply with applicable codes and standards but be located alongside large energy sources in a situation never imagined by those who wrote the codes. Access stairs may be assumed to comply with requirements but always be the steepest allowable, as this minimises floor space, without regard to their likely use in an emergency. In public buildings stairs built to this minimum standard may be used by the elderly or by a pregnant woman with a toddler on her hip and in the rain and darkness.

Also within the Risk domain (see Figure 4.5) is the management of plant reliability. From a Risk perspective, this is directly concerned with the potential for significant production failure with its associated large Loss values. While not normally thought of as part of risk management, it is not conceptually distinct from it.

The purpose of this chapter is to provide a structure for the elucidation of engineering and design risk control principles such that their application in situations not envisaged by the illustrative examples will be apparent to the reader.

The Importance of Design Quality in Risk Control

In the English-speaking world the importance of design in risk control first became evident during the industrial revolution (see Chapter 1), with people being exposed to powered machinery en masse in factories and in the fields. As injuries from interactions with unguarded powered devices multiplied to the point of amputees being a common sight in towns, the law changed from the protection of employers (workers were thought to have accepted such risks by accepting employment) to the protection of workers (employers required to provide 'safe' equipment). This revolutionary change in the attitude of society eventually led to a set of principles based on common law judgements, which may be summarised as follows:

1. A danger cannot be made safe by relying on the good behaviour of an attentive worker.
2. Both the likely and the unlikely actions of workers have to be taken into account when devising barriers against dangers.
3. The provision of hardware barriers is required whether or not such barriers are commercially practicable or mechanically feasible. While the legal meaning of 'reasonable precautions' is strict, in practice the level of risk which remains after the provision of barriers of various sorts is subject to commercial and mechanical feasibility and may be made respectable by publication of acceptable designs by government departments, standards bodies, professional bodies or even trade groups.
4. With regard to operator behaviour, dangers are disregarded only if they are the result of deliberate action or action that could not be reasonably anticipated. Responsibility with regard to 'reasonable' is satisfied when the only danger remaining is due to the unlikely and unforeseeable actions of the incalculable individual. In essence this means that when reliance is placed on a worker for the safe operation of the system then the demands on the worker should be realistically assessed in terms of the worker's response to all the stressors of life (for example hangovers, lack of sleep) and work (for example piecework rates, peer group pressures).
5. Ignorance of the existence of a danger is not condoned and in particular it is irrelevant whether previous accidents and reports had alerted the responsible party to the presence of a problem.

It is clearly irrelevant to ask why a person would place themselves in such a position of danger or to argue that precautions are not necessary because this has never happened before. Consider the possibilities in Table 12.1.

Table 12.1   Mechanisms for access into damaging energy spaces

Mechanism type	Example
1. Inadvertent movement (e.g. slip)	• While working with the DES
	• In proximity to the DES (e.g. walking near)
2. Purposeful action into the DES	• Aware (e.g. for blockage clearance or adjustment)
	• Unaware of DES
3. DES energised by other or by functional interlock while the DES is occupied	• Intentional
	• Unintentional
4. Entangled with and possibly pulled into the DES	• By material moving into the DES
	• By a machine part such as a chain
	• By tool being used for cleaning or setting
5. Caught by an unanticipated movement of a machine part outside its apparent boundary	• Robot arm position control fails

While these principles were developed in the context of powered machinery in the industrial revolution, they are a good set of engineering design guidelines for equipment using any energy source, be it powered machinery, tanks or channels of hot liquid, pools of aerated water, enclosed spaces with toxic or non-respirable atmosphere, locations containing ionising radiation and so on. They require the designer to go out and look for the ways in which equipment is able to injure people and develop designs to prevent injury while ensuring that decision-making about complexity and cost is undertaken with a sober understanding of moral obligations. There are good rational reasons for this emphasis as it is generally true that well-designed equipment removes the potential for injury or its probability far more reliably than careful human behaviour. It is generally accepted that the designer has the responsibility to explicitly consider all stages in the life cycle of the equipment: construction; installation and commissioning; routine operation; maintenance; disposal. The designer must also consider all modes of operation of the equipment, for example under normal power supply, with backup power, when there is a power failure and possibly when there is an emergency, such as a fire.

Intrinsic Safety and Reducing Mechanism Probability

The first task of the designer is to create equipment that is intrinsically safe, which may be thought of as control measure types 1 and 2 in Table 3.3. Intrinsically safe equipment is either designed around minimal energy sources (a desirable but generally impractical goal) or around limiting the energy potential to the minimal amount needed to accomplish the task of the equipment. For example:

- Movement of a compressed-air-powered machine may require only a fraction of the pressure available from the supply of compressed air, so supply is provided through a pressure limiting valve. Alternatively, pneumatically or hydraulically powered closing movements can be pressure limited until the closing movement is complete, when full pressure may be applied.
- Where movement has the potential to injure, for example entangling, trapping and shearing points on powered equipment, the design removes these points. Abrasive moving surfaces and sharp edges are removed at the point of design.
- Storage of hazardous fluids in a number of small vessels rather than one large one.
- Applying surface treatment to steel structures when the steelwork is lying on the ground rather than when it is erected.

Control measure types 3 and 4 (Table 3.3) are concerned with reducing the probability of injury from the available energy sources. It is perhaps not necessary to say that many of the strategies listed below are subject to detailed national regulations, codes of practice and standards There is much variety possible in this, but examples include:

- Provision of torque or force limiting devices such as slipping clutches, limited drive belt tension to limit the maximum transmitted torque and drive train shear pins or weak links. Current limiting devices may be provided in the supply of electrically powered equipment.
- Provision of core balance relays in electrical circuits to shut off supply in the event of an unwanted current flow path.
- Designing clutches to open, brakes to be applied and pneumatic or hydraulic powered closing movements to stop or reverse when power fails. Upon restoration of power, the machine will remain in a passive state until commanded to operate.

- The provision of barriers to prevent access to damaging energy spaces or to de-energise those spaces before access is possible. This is achieved on powered machinery by the provision of fixed and interlocked guards. The same strategy may be applied, for example, to hot water channels and hot wire runs as well as to access to incomplete structures. A discussion on guards and other forms of access control follows.
- Providing controls designed appropriately for both normal operation and for maintenance use in isolating equipment and for providing power required for maintenance purposes.
- The provision of excess flow or low pressure sensors connected to automatic shut-off valves in pipes containing hazardous fluids, the intent being to limit the amount of energy released. This so-called 'soft-landing' capability can be designed into a number of different types of processes. This is also called 'resilience engineering'.
- The provision of intrinsically safe electrical equipment in hazardous gas locations.
- Providing fire hardened containment structures, smoke control and smoke venting, automated fire suppression systems.

Guards and Access Restrictions in Industrial Process Plant

The objective is to positively prevent access to places within which injury could occur, in other words into a DES. Either the energy is removed before access is possible or access is made impossible. These simple statements hide a complex reality: what does it mean to 'remove' energy from a space into which it may be introduced and what has to be done to make access 'impossible'. In both cases, the answer is to do what is generally regarded as sufficient and the reader will not be surprised to know that both points are the subject of many and detailed codes of practice and standards that are applicable in common industrial manufacturing and process situations. Different approaches are relevant for small powered machines in a manufacturing or materials handling environment and for large and complex industrial processes such as a coil rolling mill in a steel plant. As always, the engineer may expect to find situations not envisaged by legislators so an understanding of principles is valuable.

The term 'guard' is used to describe ways of preventing access into the DES of relatively small manufacturing or materials handling equipment. Access prevention applies to small body parts, such as fingers, up to the whole body. Where mesh is used for guarding, the allowed hole size depends on the distance from the guard to the DES. The longer the body part that could gain access, the larger the distance must be to the DES. Consequently, guarding standards provide specific guidance on the size of openings with respect to distance from the DES, based on anthropometric data. Collections of anthropometric data are based on racial body types and care needs to be exercised to ensure the guidance material used is relevant to the body types of the envisaged workers. In particular, guards suited to the large body types of Western Europeans may not at all suit people from Far Eastern nations.

All types of guards may be categorised in one of two ways: fixed in place or interlocked. A fixed guard is suited to preventing access to a DES for which there are no routine access requirements, for example drive shafts and belts, various pulleys in belt conveyor systems and similar. These guards are bolted or screwed on and will only be removed when major maintenance is being done with the whole system de-energised under an isolation procedure. An interlocked guard can practically be regarded as any device that de-energises the equipment when access into it is required, for example to remove a blockage, setting tools and cleaning. The act of opening a panel for access or the act of approaching the DES with a part of the body will influence the control state of the machine and de-energise it.

It is entirely possible to produce a 'guard' the detailed design of which satisfies relevant standards but that is nevertheless inappropriate for the application. An appropriate type of guard is determined by understanding which user (for example machine setter, production operator, maintenance technician, engineer, cleaner and any others) has which acceptable access needs (for example setting, normal production, blockage clearance, breakdown, tool change, cleaning, planned maintenance) into the DES and how frequently. In the detailed design of a guard it is necessary to consider the realities of time pressure when access is needed and also the likely ways in which the function of the guard could be circumvented by a person in a hurry. Setters and operators commonly feel this time pressure and will often go to extraordinary lengths to defeat guards in the interests of productivity. Maintenance technicians may do the same if breakdowns and blockages are commonplace.

Having identified the access requirements of the various users, the first guard design strategy is to remove or reduce the needs for access to the DES, for example by bringing adjustment points, lubrication points and electronic control cards to the outside of the machine and making it possible to inspect operation without the body entering the DES, perhaps by the use of mirrors. Having minimised access requirements, the second strategy is to provide guards to make access impossible or limit it in some way while the DES is energised. The most effective approach to this is to design a fixed guard around the precise DES (point where injury will occur). This potentially results in small fixed guards, which only require removal during major maintenance. Very often this is not feasible and an access control perimeter is required some distance from the actual DES. The feasible location of this perimeter will determine who has what access requirements past the perimeter. When operators and setters require access an interlocked guard will be needed. When they do not require access, a fixed guard is a possibility on the assumption that the requirement for maintenance access behind the guard is occasional and will always occur under the protection of an isolation system (for a discussion on which see below).

The task of detailed design is made far simpler by choosing to put a fixed guard around the whole machine in the form of a fence. However, this necessarily means that people will require access behind the guard and an interlocked gate will be required. Once behind the guard it is almost certain that some reasons for access, such as setting tasks, will require the power to be made available and so this apparently simple possibility has only deferred a proper solution or is only a part of a proper solution.

Table 12.2   Strategies for the protection of people from damaging energy spaces

Safeguarding strategy	
1. Reduce the need for access into the DES	
(a) Remove the need for or frequency of access into the DES	Access needs may be reduced by locating lubrication, adjustments and electronic circuit cards, etc. outside the DES, by providing line of sight to critical points from outside the DES, e.g. by using mirrors.
(b) Reduce the frequency of or time pressures of access into the DES	Reduce the rate of or time criticality of access for blockage clearance, troubleshooting and breakdown by design improvements.
2. Provide a fixed guard to prevent access into the DES	
3. Remove the damaging energy before access	

(a) Provide a guard interlocked with the controls of the machine	This is applicable to routine operational and running maintenance access requirements. The effect of the interlock may be to stop all damaging movements in the DES or to make energy available in a restricted manner (movement or pressure limitation) to allow tasks to be completed. There are three types in this category:
	
	  i. A physical device such as a gate or door the movement or removal of which is interlocked to the controls or power supply of the machine.
	  ii. A sensing device that detects the presence of a body part and affects the controls or power supply of the machine. Various sensors can be used to detect whole body access behind fences.
	  iii. A device that requires the operator to place the controls or power supply of the machine in an acceptable state in order for it to be possible to remove the guard, e.g. a captive key system.
	
	When machines have long spin-down times, controls or power supply are placed in the off state and access is given when a latch opens the guard either after a time delay or when a movement sensor detects the machine has stopped.

(b) Isolate all energy sources	This is primarily applicable to major overhaul. It may also be used for breakdown maintenance access where the size or complexity of the machine makes the provision of an interlocked guard impractical or proper guarding has not been fitted. It is similar in intent to 3 (a) (iii), but it relies more on behavioural practices. The intent is to remove incoming energy supplies and any stored energy from the system, not just to influence the control state of the machine.

The guard design decision process is summarised in Table 12.2. While this set of strategies has a compact machine or DES in mind, it acts also as a starting point in the design of safeguards for larger machines and DES. The larger a DES the more likely it is that safeguarding efforts favour a fence for reasons of simplicity. A fence can be designed to satisfy the needs of safeguards to positively prevent access, but a fence is only one of a small number of strategies to control access into hazardous areas. It is necessary to draw attention to the fact that Table 12.2 does not include a form of interlocking that relies on human behaviour to throw a switch or put the controls in a particular mode prior to entry into the DES. Owing to the unreliability of people, this does not satisfy any common standard of care test unless perhaps the worst possible injury is of almost complete insignificance.

Table 12.3   A hierarchy of DES access restriction

1. Prohibited	No access for anyone while the DES is energised (e.g. the machinery is operating). This restriction is used, for example, if machinery in the area is unguarded (e.g. because of age or size) or if other hazards (heat, radiation, chemicals) are or could be present and an acceptable standard of protection cannot be achieved by compliance with defined work methods or use of personal protective equipment.
	Access to the area would be allowed only under formal conditions (e.g. defined by a Permit to Work) for the de-energisation of the DES by a competent person and compliance with any permit conditions by all who enter the area.
2. Authorised access only	Access is allowed at any time to authorised people only. Written work procedures are required to define the way in which the person is protected when in the area. This restriction can be used when the nature of the hazard is such that an acceptable standard of protection can be provided by work methods or personal protective equipment use. The definition of these areas is needed to prevent inadvertent entry by others (for example contractors, visitors, cleaners, etc.) who either
	• have not been trained in the required procedures, or
	• cannot reasonably (in a legal sense) be relied on to behave responsibly if they were so trained.
	When such people need access it must be provided under the direct control of an authorised person.
3. Maintenance access only	Similar to 2 above but the only people who can be legally regarded as adequately responsible are maintenance tradespeople. This can be expected to require the use of a formal isolation procedure defining control and communication requirements.

The perimeters of and access points into restricted areas can be defined in various ways that range from positive exclusion to polite requests for compliance:

1. A positive exclusion barrier. This is a substantial fence which complies with published design standards for robustness and height which define what is practically sufficient for the intended purpose. Swimming pool fences designed to prevent access by children are of this type.
2. A physical barrier which is not of positive exclusion standards. Examples of this common form are fences along pathways, wheel stops in car parks, balustrades on the edge of ramps, tapes to define access routes. Less formal but nonetheless effective barriers include hedges and borders planted with robust shrubs.
3. Visual barriers, evident only to the eye, which offer no physical restriction to movement. These are typically indicated by signs, line marking on floors or by the use of colour on floor surfaces.

The standard of barrier suited to a given application will depend on the degree of risk associated with noncompliance and the standard of care expected in the circumstances. Balustrades will not stop an adult from jumping over them but they are designed to prevent a child doing so. Lines on the floor are unlikely to satisfy the standard of care required in most jurisdictions when there is a significant DES behind the line although common practice may make them acceptable, for example to keep passengers back from railway station platform edges.

Once a safeguard concept has been established, the remaining task is to design the guard in detail. Both fixed and interlocked guard design standards are specified in detail by various national standards bodies. The design standard for fixed guards specifies methods of fixing (a tool is required to remove them), reach-over or -around distances and the hole sizes of mesh used as infill. When a fixed guard is a fence, the climb-over height is specified.

The design standards for interlocked guards specify the quality of the interlock devices, whatever they might be (see Table 12.2(3)(a)). Interlocked guards are often used to protect skilled maintenance tradespeople when they need rapid access to fix a running production problem, as they are unlikely to resort to isolation (see below) in such circumstances. Higher quality interlocks are likely, through their detailed design, to fail less frequently than lower quality ones. For example, a simple form of interlocking, using one switching device putting the controls into pause or stop mode, may be suited to situations where there is an opportunity to escape upon failure of the interlock or if only a relatively minor injury would be experienced or if Exposure is infrequent. On the other hand, where escape is unlikely and a severe injury or death would result from interlock failure, a higher standard of interlocking is required, possibly including multiple switches of different types, monitoring of their condition for failure and an interlock action on the power supply, not just the control circuitry. As many machines make use of programmable logic controllers (PLC) for their control functions, the interlock may either be an input to the PLC, perhaps with special authority, or a separate hard-wired function that interrupts any output signal from the PLC. The latter, being of higher reliability, is more suited to higher risk situations. The required integrity of the interlock depends on the standard of care appropriate to the situation and methods of risk assessment are included in standards to achieve a uniform and acceptable approach to this decision-making. The standard of interlocking needs to be based on the most critical user group, determined by time pressures on access, frequency of access and injury potential.

The design standards for functional interlocks, which make the machine perform its functions, are different from those of safety interlocks, a fact that is often not appreciated by tradesmen doing the detailed design and installation of interlocked guards. Safety interlocks should always be of the normally closed type, with normally open types only being used in conjunction with a normally closed type. The reason for this is that the installation of a normally closed type is harder to defeat, and these types have safer failure modes. Similarly, the design standards for electrical, electronic and programmable electronic systems that provide safety functions are different from those that do not, again because of integrity concerns. Safety-related equipment is designed to satisfy safety integrity levels (SIL) published by authoritative bodies (International Electrochemical Commission, 2012).

Whatever interlock technology is used, it is inadequate if acceptable precautions have not been taken to avoid it being defeated by removing fasteners, adjusting distances, providing custom keys and tools and similar.

Design of Power and Functional Controls

Safeguard design in general cannot be separated from consideration of the design of the power and function controls of the energy space, and not just because controls may be influenced by interlocks. Powered machinery is of such variety of function and size that it is not a simple matter to generalise about the design of power supplies and function controls. Possible control modes include inching, stepping, nudging, creeping, manual operation, single cycle, automatic and maintenance. The effect of the control is indicated by its name. For example:

- inching means the machine position is moved a short distance for each operation of the control;
- stepping means the machine advances a defined amount before stopping;
- nudging means the machine is given a very brief movement;
- creeping means the machine moves continuously but very slowly;
- manual operation means the machine is controlled entirely manually in its cycle of operation;
- single cycle means the machine completes one cycle before stopping;
- automatic means the machine continues cyclic operation;
- maintenance means that power is provided in a manner suited to the maintenance needs while the maintenance person is not protected by the guard, eg. nudging. This is intended to allow a skilled maintenance person to operate the machine under restricted conditions in order to rapidly respond to running problems, using a special key or code. An obvious and common way for this to be defeated is for the key or code to be given to the machine operators. As the ease of defeat is a prime consideration in all aspects of safeguard design, administrative control measures are needed to retain the integrity of the intention.

Design details are significant in promoting or reducing control operation error by operators. Some details for designers to consider include:

1. Physical features of controls
   a) size (suited to fingers in gloves if necessary, for example, or to a moving hand in vehicles);
   b) nature of operation (push/pull, turn left or right, slide up or down) suited to the effect of the control and consistently applied both to the individual machine and the whole factory;
   c) ability to lock in position if needed as part of an isolation system;
   d) shrouded if necessary to avoid inadvertent operation of critical controls (including protection around fluid power control levers to make inadvertent operation less likely).
2. Location
   a) suitable relative positioning and grouping of common functions;
   b) separation distance between controls to minimise unwanted actuation;
   c) so that the user can see them in a direct line of sight, not just feel them;
   d) so that they are not at arm's length from the preferred operator's position;
   e) emergency stops need to be located at places from which they may be operated in a foreseeable emergency, not only at the control panel.
3. Identification
   a) tactile discrimination (shape, texture, size);
   b) visual discrimination (consistent and standard colour – red for stop, green for go, etc.);
   c) labelled as to function to avoid confusion of the purpose (including use of diagrams which mimic machine function) and especially to make the function clear to someone responding to an emergency and who may not be familiar with the machine;
   d) location of labels with respect to their control is consistent (above, below, etc.);
   e) complex alphanumeric strings derived from control diagrams should be avoided as a sole means of identification; names of controls should relate to local usage (an out-feed conveyor for one part of a plant may be the in-feed conveyor for another);
   f) permanently disconnected controls should be clearly marked as such and removed as quickly as possible; temporary disconnections should be clearly marked;
   g) on complex control panels, indicator lights should be used to indicate the status of a control, and the function of the lights must be checked routinely.

4. Function
   a) stop controls self-latch and bring the machine to a halt in a preferred manner and subsequent operation after unlatching requires a positive start control actuation;
   b) inch, step and nudge controls operate once per press;
   c) creep controls operate continuously while the control is actuated;
   d) emergency stop controls lock in place and bring the machine to a halt in the shortest possible time without consideration of consequential production loss;
   e) start controls include a delay and an audible warning (for example in conveyor systems).
5. Hierarchy of their operation
   a) safety interlocks override functional interlocks;
   b) when a machine has been stopped manually, controls should revert to the manual mode of operation, i.e. the action of stopping also deselects an automatic control function;
   c) safety interlocks should be hard-wired into control systems that use PLCs or microprocessors rather than being wired into the electronic unit.

It will be evident that many of these features are familiar and we associate attributes based on expectation. For example, stop buttons are red, moving a lever up or a knob to the right implies an increase in movement or power. These stereotypical associations may be carried through to the relative position of different types of controls, if for example a group of machines from one manufacturer all conform with that manufacturer's normal designs. A similar machine but from another manufacturer may not conform to this and result in inadvertent operation. Control stereotypes are the subject of detailed study, the results of which may be found in human factors and ergonomics texts.

Isolation of Equipment

Equipment needs to be isolated when major repair or recovery work (for example clearing major blockages) is being carried out or when it is not in a serviceable condition. Isolation is not a substitute for guarding. It is either primarily done for the protection of tradespeople undertaking maintenance, or is under their control if others are also working on the equipment, for example cleaning or greasing. Isolation means positive disconnection of the equipment from its sources of energy and the removal or blocking of all forms of stored energy. These principles apply whether the equipment is a powered machine, a process plant vessel or a confined space.

The removal of supply sources of energy may be brought about by interrupting electricity supply or preventing flow in incoming pipes. In pneumatic (or some hydraulic) power systems the equipment is disconnected from the air receiver (or accumulator). In hydraulic systems without an accumulator, isolation is by removing the power supply from the pump.

Stored energy can take many forms and the overall goal of removing or neutralising it is achieved in various ways depending on the situation. Examples of stored energy include:

- stored pressure in air and hydraulic lines and cylinders;
- gravitational energy in raised parts, for example the raised back of a haul truck;
- heat arising from operation, for example in ovens, boilers;
- vapours, fumes and non-respirable atmosphere retained in vessels, for example process vessels;
- structural strain energy in transmission systems, for example the drive shaft of a blocked crusher;
- stored electrical energy in capacitors.

A simple piece of equipment which is very small, such as a machine driven by a single electric motor located at the machine itself, can be isolated without fuss if the motor is equipped with a local isolation switch. The more complex and large the equipment and the further away from the machine the power controls are, the more complex the isolation process needs to be. Very complex plant exists in many industries, in which numerous energy sources and control points may exist for a single machine. Exactly what has to be done to isolate such plant is something best understood in a methodical way when not under time pressure. It is clearly not reasonable to rely on local knowledge of isolation requirements when the likely Consequence of an isolation failure is death or severe disablement. Predetermined methods of isolation can be committed to paper in the form of a standard isolation sheet, which then means that when the job has to be done no time is spent deciding how. Such preparation is especially valuable when maintenance work is outsourced and the plant knowledge built up by employees over many years is lost.

Precisely what is meant by interrupting the incoming energy supplies depends on the desired standard of isolation, which depends on the standard of care required in the situation. For example, when a process vessel is to be isolated from incoming supplies, is it sufficient to close a valve or is it necessary to dismantle the pipe and physically separate the vessel from the supply? Is it sufficient to turn a hand-operated valve and place a tag on it, or it is necessary to chain and lock the valve in place? Is it sufficient to turn off a local electrical isolation switch at a motor or should the supply be de-energised by removing fuses? Methods of risk assessment in given situations are sometimes found in standards and codes of practice to ensure uniform and reasonable decision-making. These decisions are best made before checking that the required hardware exists in the plant. Any deficiencies can be rectified, for example by providing lockable isolation switches or valves as necessary.

The specific isolation requirements (as recorded in a standard isolation sheet) of a given piece of equipment exist in the context of an isolation procedure, which defines the rules and practices of isolation. This procedure is itself a part of a wider procedure for controlling the work done on a plant – the work permit system. Those needing to perform work request a permit from a permit-issuing officer. This officer's role is to assess the request with respect to other work being done that may interfere with the requested work either functionally (can that system be shut down?) or spatially (will the requested work affect work being done on other systems but in the same location in the plant?). Depending on the situation, either the permit issuer arranges for isolation to happen or the permit receivers do this. The isolation procedure is designed to provide positive control over access to the plant in each of the three stages of isolation shown in Table 12.4 and particularly recognising the possible isolation failure modes. The procedure also has to control the access of each individual in a group of people working under the protection of the isolation. This is commonly done by using a group isolation board which stands in a prominent position and to which each person attaches a personal lock, as evidence of their presence. It may also be done by having a sign in/out sheet. No change to the isolation state can be made while any person's lock remains in place or any person has not signed out. Similarly, no work can be done unless the isolation board indicates isolation is in place and the process of removing isolation has not begun.

Because of the ease with which failure can occur in the establishment mode, three practices are common:

1. The isolation is made by one person and independently verified by a second person who follows the first, but not too closely.
2. Only when isolation is complete is this fact publicised, for example on the group isolation board.
3. Before any work is done, the fact of isolation is verified again by a cautious initial approach: for example electrical equipment is tested to verify it is dead, flanges or valves are opened assuming the pipe or vessel is not isolated, by the worker standing away from any possible discharge and being provided with suitable personal protective equipment.

Table 12.4   The stages of isolation and their failure modes

Stage	Failure mode
1. Establishing isolation	1.1 Incomplete/incorrect isolation made
	1.2 Access achieved before isolation established
2. Isolated	2.1 Failure of the isolation mode of an energy control device
3. Removing isolation, temporary or permanent	3.1 Too soon, work still being done

In complex plant, failure mode 1.1 is common because of confusion over the identification and purpose of switches, valves, etc. The error of switching off or closing the incorrect component is common and made more so by indistinct or confusing component identification placards. The likelihood of this may be reduced by simplifying identification placards, using colour coding and similar strategies as well as by providing photographs on the standard isolation sheet. These errors may also be promoted by isolation being undertaken with a sense of haste or urgency. Where the same type of plant is side by side, for example a row of transformers, it is important to ensure that numbering is sequential (there are many reasons why it may not be so), of large size and visible from all four sides.

Maintenance Strategies for Components

In the industrial world, maintenance strategy possibilities are commonly listed as:

1. Run to failure, then replace. This breakdown strategy is applicable to components whose function is not critical.
2. Fixed life. This strategy is based on a predetermined expectation of the point at which age-related failures begin and the rate at which the probability of failure increases. It has been applied to components whose function is critical to system operation, for example aircraft engines. When taken out of service, the component is stripped and repaired as necessary to bring it back to an as-new condition. The strategy is less used than it was as inspection often showed that there was nothing seriously wrong with the part and the work done was found to promote failures that otherwise would not have happened.
3. Preventive maintenance. The component is inspected, cleaned, adjusted, greased, has its oil and filters changed, etc. This is applicable to components such as conveyor systems, compressors, some types of rotating machinery. Aspects of it are similar to the fixed life strategy and to condition monitoring.
4. Monitor the condition. Condition monitoring is relevant for components which have known wear-out possibilities and for which methods of monitoring exist. It is typically applied where the function of the component is critical to system operation. Criteria are required for the limit of the acceptable state of the monitored property, so that when this is approached, the component is considered to have reached its useful life and is replaced prior to failure. Monitoring methods include:
    a) functional testing (for example pump outlet pressure, power consumption, alarm operation, calibration of sensors, testing of earth resistance, operation of pressure and vacuum valves, operation of standby components including emergency generators);
    b) vibration monitoring (suggestive of bearing wear, damage to rotating assemblies);
    c) oil debris monitoring (suggestive of bearing wear);
    d) monitoring cycles of operation (for example cold, warm and hot starts in power stations, flight cycles of aircraft);

e) crack detection and monitoring.

Maintenance strategies need to be determined in conjunction with spares holdings. Running to failure may be a sensible option for an item of equipment but only if suitable spares holdings can be ensured. Software to assist in the choice of maintenance strategy for an individual item uses estimated random and wear-out failure rates and the estimated costs of the different possible maintenance strategies to point towards financially optimum strategies for maintenance and spares holdings.

Of interest to the risk engineer in a complex industrial plant is the reality of the maintenance activity. In an ideal world, maintenance engineers would be able to demonstrate that the plant had been analysed in detail to determine classes of equipment for which a particular maintenance strategy was appropriate and that this analysis was based on both productivity (to minimise unwanted downtime) and risk (to avoid adverse other Consequences, such as fire, structural collapse). The results of this analysis would be evident in the population of the maintenance database with appropriate maintenance strategies. Many maintenance databases contain aspects of strategies 3 and 4 almost as a default, with little evidence that intervals between planned actions have been determined based on the needs of the plant or the component. A rough assessment of the adequacy of maintenance practices and strategy in a plant can be made by seeing what proportion of work is breakdown and what scheduled and how much work is actually being completed to schedule. A high proportion of breakdown maintenance and a low proportion of work being done to schedule is potentially of concern with regards to risk.

Maintenance personnel in industrial plant commonly focus their attention exclusively on the function of equipment. A conveyor may be operating well but, with missing, broken or slack emergency lanyards and silent start sirens, it can not be said to be doing so safely. The risk adviser may need to work hard to bring about the needed change so that safety-related features are given the same priority as functional attributes.

Critical Plant and Production Failure

A maintenance focus on individual items of equipment, necessary though it is, may distract from an understanding of total failure of production capability. Such failures are the infrequent high Consequence Value end of the plant failure Risk Diagram. Significant production downtime results from failure of plant which is critical in the sense that without it production is either much reduced in capacity or cannot continue and reinstatement of its function takes a long time. The reinstatement of the plant may require the purchase of a major component, for which it is not feasible to hold spares, or reconstruction of parts of the plant. For example:

• a large transformer, pump or motor;
• a new conveyor gallery, new bulk materials silo.

An overall understanding of plant criticality assists first with determining design requirements for critical constructed plant, for example to protect them from predictable vulnerabilities, and secondly with establishing beneficial maintenance strategies and associated spares holdings policies. A plant criticality analysis at the design stage will illuminate ways in which an adequate functional design can be made more robust in the face of critical plant failure, for example:

• replacing one large tank with a number of smaller ones;
• providing standby pumps;

- providing higher levels of protection on large power transformers;
- protecting structures from mobile equipment.

The relationship of equipment (such as pumps) to the business process can be obtained by expanding a map of the production (or business) process into increasing levels of detail, from plant (collections of equipment and facilities) to the individual items of equipment or facility. At each level of detail both parallel and series connections are looked for. Series connections, like the links of a chain, imply a single failure can interrupt the whole process. In this way, critical items of equipment can be identified and an assessment made of existing design, maintenance practices and spares holdings.

Maintenance Strategies for People's Behaviour

Action failures are not different in principle from component failures: the person is a component in the system. In commercial organisations there is much reliance on people following process and little on plant and equipment as people are the major component. In organisations that rely on equipment, be it manufacturing, mining or transport, at some level people are involved in every aspect of operation, not least in interacting with the equipment.

In Chapters 7 and 10 the point was made that while the reliability of control measures is an inherent quality of whatever risk control measures are chosen, it is in all cases dependent on the frequency with which the control measure is inspected or checked. The properties of equipment deteriorate over time and the behaviour of people can do the same if the behaviour has not become habitual or cultural and especially if there is no apparent benefit received from it. When the behaviour of people deteriorates away from a desired standard, Table 9.2 sees this not as an error as such, but rather as an aware intention not to comply or, if what compliance means has long been forgotten, unaware. In practice, therefore, we should design systems to reduce action failures by paying attention to design details of equipment and paying attention to management and supervisory systems to reduce problems associated with awareness and intention. Therefore, one maintenance monitoring practice is to record and analyse action failures. If these change over time, there may be an underlying reason. By way of illustration of the possibility, Table 12.5 contains real data from a study of electrical switching errors. It is entirely feasible to conduct such a study where errors have significant operational implications.

Table 12.5   Action failures (errors) in electrical switching tasks, after Table 9.2

Type of case	Error modes (after Hollnagel)	Operator No. of cases	Controller No. of cases	Installer No. of cases
Error type 1 – erroneous action	Wrong time – too early		1	
	Wrong type – direction	2		
	Wrong object – similar object	9		1
	Wrong place – sequence omission	13	4	1
	Wrong place – sequence reversal	2		
Negligent Action				
Error Type 2 – unaware		2		
Accidental type 1		1		

The other people-monitoring practice is to identify where the deterioration of desired behaviour is of concern or the existence of individual action failures cannot be allowed to remain undetected. Table 12.6 indicates the types of situations for which this practice is relevant. There is much experiential evidence (and probably psychological evidence too) to support the view that when it is possible to do work in a variety of ways, people will tend towards the most time-efficient ways of doing it even in the presence of a visible and tangible serious hazard.

Table 12.6   Action failure (error) situations and management strategies

Situation	Example	Maintenance strategies
1. The risk control task is an additional task that is unrelated to carrying out any function.	The compound of an electricity substation needs to be kept clear of weeds and plant growth. This task can be ignored for a long time without evident problem as plants grow slowly.	Include as a maintenance task. Monitor compliance through routine plant inspections.
2. The risk control requirement is an aspect of a task that does not have an immediate effect on the productive outcome of the task.	Adding a blank to the flange of a valve after closing the valve and removing the attached pipe. The blank is a backup to the valve, which may leak despite being closed, but the chance of that is small as valve seats deteriorate very slowly.	Modify equipment to make it impossible to complete the task in any other way. Modify equipment to simplify the task. Observe and supervise.
3. Avoidance of risk requires an effort but offers no immediate reward.	Taking short cuts through hazardous areas (railway lines, underneath metal pouring operations, etc.). Getting a piece of equipment to assist with a handling task. Getting a permit to undertake some quick inspection or cleaning task. Following a detailed work procedure with many embedded risk controls but with much urgency or time pressure.	Make physical changes so that avoidance is more difficult than compliance. Make physical changes so that compliance with a procedure is unnecessary. Remove time pressure. Remove urgency by automating response to malfunction.
4. Failure has a critical effect and cannot be allowed to happen.	After cleaning an aircraft, tape is left covering the static pressure sensor holes. Pressure relief valves left gagged after testing.	Independent inspection on completion of the task. Duplicate inspections.

While equipment generally deteriorates relatively slowly over time, the behaviour of people can deteriorate very quickly. Various examples of this have been given in Chapters 8 and 10.

Managing Operational and Technical Risk

The ability for operational decisions to be made by those close to the operating reality of technical plant is not just important, but in some cases critical. Probably all design is based on engineering assumptions and compromises and all has limitations. All equipment ages and many types of equipment deteriorate with calendar time or process time. Some equipment is susceptible to temperature, vibration and other environmental influences. It is seldom possible to precisely and objectively understand the implications of all these variables. A serious problem arises when managers of high energy plant or activities have little technical knowledge but their position of power allows politics and expediency to override engineering judgement on day to day decisions.

It is for this reason that pilots and airline line maintenance staff are given the power to make decisions about whether the conditions are suitable for flying or the aircraft is airworthy. It is not uncommon for technical judgement to frustrate the desires of a manager and to be seen as inconvenient, expensive and unreasonable. When relative power and influence in the organisation is introduced into the dispute (as it will be) the technical argument may find it hard to succeed in the face of political expediency. When the technical argument fails but the feared Consequence does not arise (aided only by the vagaries of probability or skill of the operator and with reduced safety margins), the manager feels justified and the value of the technical judgement is diminished. This is not an argument that can be won or lost on the basis of past experience, but rather one that should be decided as a matter of principle – what is right? This point is so important that it should be explicitly recognised in risk management policies so that no one is in doubt about who has the final authority to make a decision. As a reflection of this logic, it is appropriate for risk advisers to have the right to report directly to the chief executive.

Over most of the life of equipment it is the productive reliability which is the subject of most attention. As a plant ages, the ability to perform its productive or risk control function is compromised by ageing processes, for example corrosion, erosion, fatigue, metallurgical change, waste product contamination, electronic component deterioration, etc. The effect of ageing on the reliability (the probability of it performing both productive and risk control functions) of the equipment will depend on the original quality of the equipment, the deterioration mechanisms, equipment renewal practices and maintenance strategies.

Also over time a lot of change occurs as plant is modified and added to, has its operating life extended and new control or other technologies introduced. The origin of technical risk management lies in knowing what the plant is and what it does and having a strategy for managing it that recognises both function, maintenance and risk. A formal change management process is needed that establishes a change approval and authorisation process, publicises cautions prior to implementation and ensures that plant drawings are changed as the change is completed. Plant change management and plant strategy documents become the basis of the technical management of operational risks. Change management is concerned with the formal approval of changes based on the criticality of the plant rather than on the size of the change, the cautious management of the plant until the change is completed and the timely completion of plant documentation. The purpose of plant strategy documents is to record functional and safety significance of the plant and decisions made about the maintenance and renewal policy for the plant. In this way, the technical management of risks can be made explicit and integrated with day-to-day activities.

Engineers responsible for managing the technical risk associated with plant use their detailed knowledge to develop an informed judgement about what needs to be done. This judgement is not easily expressed in the simple rational terms commonly used to evaluate operating cost or investment decisions. It involves weighing up competing values and uncertain outcomes, as no one knows with any certainty what the probability of adverse Consequences is. In practice, those deciding whether to accept these judgements may not properly understand the reasons for them but may find it easy to criticise them for lack of objective support. Even when proposals are subject to an operational cost or investment evaluation process, it is very likely that this process is not amenable to handling the essential uncertainty (risk) of the argument or the moral values associated with possible adverse Consequences. As the adverse Consequence feared by the technical proponent of the idea is not certain to happen, it seems to decision-makers that the decision can be delayed with impunity. This lack of certainty is comforting for the manager delaying the decision and it can also lead to the proposal being lost in the more immediate demands of running the plant. The unfortunately common simple and inadequate understanding of risk and its management at board level can have an important negative influence on the productive discussion of engineering judgement and consequently on the effective management of technical risks.

One way of avoiding these adverse influences is to bring technical risk management ideas into the realm of day-to-day technical management by instituting a process that:

1. Maintains a register of risk control improvement suggestions of those closest to the technical management of the plant as well as suggestions arising from periodic reviews. Such reviews can be done to populate a register at any stage of the plant from preliminary design onwards, are usually needed following commissioning and should be conducted periodically (say every five years) to assess the implications of any changes to legislation and standards, community expectations and technology change. See Chapter 8.
2. Involves a method of reviewing the efficacy and value of the ideas captured in the register in the competition for attention time, operating expenditure and capital investment and which is able to give appropriate weight to any moral aspects of the argument.
3. Retains register entries and reviews them on a regular basis.

The attributes of effective risk registers are discussed in Chapter 5.

Summary

Good standards of technical design of plant and processes are necessary not just for good process function but are also essential for good process risk control. Where injury is possible, the expectations of common law for design standards needs to be known by the designer. Intrinsic safety is a desirable design quality that needs to be considered before lesser options are considered.

The principles and desirable features of both design and procedural methods to prevent people from entering DES and the desirable features of power and functional control design are outlined.

The maintenance strategies which are possible (for both plant that is critical for operational safety reasons and for the maintenance of safety-related aspects of plant), are explained in the context of their value as risk control measures, in which case maintenance activities need to be based on safety as well as functional requirements. The importance of understanding the extent to which maintenance activities are preventive rather than reactive is explained. Technical management strategies whose purpose is to avoid action failures include both the monitoring of performance with respect to expectations and analysis of the potential for failure to occur. These are significant proactive risk control measures.

Technical judgement about risk controls needs to be given high standing in an organisation and immune from being overridden by commercial, political or operating expediency influences.

The good management of operational and technical risks requires an understanding of the management of operations and maintenance that is integrated with that of specific rather than general risk control measures. Included in this is the formal management of change and the development of plant operating, maintenance and renewal strategies which recognise contributions to risk as much as contributions to operations.

Appendix 1:
A Note on Accident Investigation:
Why Did the Horse Bolt?

Late one morning the telephone rang in my office and I recognised the voice of a client. His quiet and sombre intonation was unusual: an explosion in the scrap smelter had killed more than one person and burned a number of others. Could I come over as quickly as possible?

When I arrived, the plant was deserted except for the security guard on the gate. The silence that descends on the scene of a tragedy following the departure of ambulances is a heavy one. I walked towards the smelter building. Blown-out wall cladding, a pool of blood, spattered aluminium, a fork-lift truck in frozen movement, its driver fled. Nearby, my client was waiting for me with two others. With little introduction, I was told they thought they understood what had happened and they wanted me to look around for myself and see if my deductions agreed with theirs. I well remember walking around the empty shell of the smelter building, which was pervaded by an uncomfortable and unfamiliar silence. The air held the shock. Fresh pools of blood stained a concrete plant road. The windscreen of the fork-lift truck had received violent impact damage. Cladding had been ripped from the building and flung across the yard. The busyness of police and regulators had yet to be imposed on this scene of raw and frozen brutality.

This smelter took scrap aluminium and melted it down to form ingots for resale. A salt (ordinary sodium chloride) flux was used to assist in the removal of impurities from the molten metal. The salt loading platform was intact, as was the empty crucible in which the metal was melted. There was no cladding left on the building, exposing the steel skeleton of the structure. There was a lot of aluminium splatter on the structure, all over the concrete floor and over the fork-lift truck – mostly small globules of metal the size of a pea.

The most common problem in any scrap smelter, whatever the metal, is an expanding water vapour explosion. Scrap is loaded which contains moisture, perhaps in an unseen void, and this rapidly becomes superheated steam reaching great pressure until escaping in a violent outrush which flings molten metal everywhere. I knew the possibility of this but had never seen the total metal load in a smelter scattered by such a Mechanism. Wet scrap is avoided and scrap which contains cavities is broken up to ensure an enclosed wet cavity is not loaded into the melt. Where did the pressure wave come from that had blown off all the wall cladding? How had the now dead smelter attendant come to land on the roadway outside the smelter? Was he blown off the platform by an explosion or did he simply fall from it in shock? If the latter, how was it that the pool of blood from his body was halfway across the roadway?

I walked back to the waiting group and said that I thought this explosion was not due to expanding water vapour but to a violent chemical reaction. I admitted that I didn't understand the chemistry and would need to research that. They nodded in agreement. They also told me that many men had had the clothes burnt off them by a wave of radiant heat. The newspapers the next day printed a respectful picture of some of these men, clothed only in safety boots, wandering dazed on the plant roadway. Some men had all the sweat glands burned off their body. This confirmed the chemical explosion theory, as a vapour explosion does not generate a heat wave.

They then explained what they had already discovered of the chemistry of the explosion. The smelter attendant had loaded not sodium chloride, but sodium nitrate. Sodium nitrate and ground aluminium is used as a military explosive. The chloride and nitrate products were from the same supplier, in similar bags with almost illegible markings due to accumulated dirt. While the nitrate bags had been stored apart from the chloride, there was not a great distance between them and no one had told the smelter attendant not to use the 'other' bags. It took perhaps one hour for the first group on the scene and another half an hour for my enquiries for the essential facts of the Occurrence and Consequence process to be understood.

This example illustrates the essential simplicity of accident investigation, assuming that those doing it have some relevant knowledge of the process which was host to the Occurrence. When an accident has occurred, what we see is the aftermath – the most immediate Consequences are evident to us. If the Outcome process leaves a trail of evidence, as in this case, we will also see that. Sometimes, the Outcome itself or some aspects of it have to be deduced from the appearance of the Consequence. Together these should be sufficient to identify the energy source, if that was ever in doubt. It is then necessary to use deduction and inference to determine the nature of the Mechanism or possible Mechanisms. The possible Mechanisms relevant to any given energy source are easily determined from first principles. The investigation of transport accidents may be (and often is) complicated by the need to determine from a mass of twisted metal whether any mechanical or control system failures had occurred.

It is when we delve into the Prerequisite Circumstances and Conditions of relevance to the Occurrence Mechanism that the complexity of the investigation escalates. There are two reasons to do this. A very common reason for a detailed analysis of Time Zone 1 in the TSM is the search for blame and evidence of negligence. The more serious the Consequence, the more likely the urge to press legal charges for breach of statutory duty or common law duty of care. There is an increasing willingness of jurisdictions to invoke criminal charges against the company, people or person seen to be at fault. In recent times this has been seen in the areas of work injury and work health, air traffic controllers, pilots, car and bus drivers, captains of ships and companies whose operations have resulted in massive environmental damage and injury to members of the public. Even a seismologist has been jailed (Davies, 2012), following widespread destruction by a volcano, for failing to adequately communicate the full expected magnitude of an eruption. This deep-seated need to blame someone (from a human to a god) leads, not surprisingly, to the suppression of the truth by those unfortunate to be involved in or witnesses to an Occurrence. Knowing that blame will be sought by the investigators, it is a very human response to seek to deflect the blame to someone else. Blame leads to punishment and truth is always the next victim. The way around this for a civilised society is to investigate without attempting to apportion blame and to seek to learn the lessons of how better to prevent such things in the future. Truth survives in this environment. Tragic victims are shown respect and those generally ordinary decent people who had the misfortune to be present at the time can be honoured for their well-intentioned efforts. Society is the better for this because we have behaved decently afterwards and because we learn more and better lessons.

The second and more sanguine reason is to understand improved controls that could be implemented in Time Zone 1 or to see what aspects of known controls failed. This is the obvious reason for those who subscribe to the energy-damage (or threat-loss) and risk view of the world and who are interested less in witch hunts or blame shifting than in practical lessons. For those who subscribe to the 'accidents are caused' philosophy, the main purpose of an investigation is to determine the cause(s) and most especially to find that elusive entity, the 'root cause'. Both types of approach (risk or accident) are actually looking at the same reality: all the philosophical difference is doing is changing the mindset of the investigator and the way in which Time Zone 1 is understood. The contention that 'cause' is not the same as 'control' has been argued in Chapters 1 and 2. However, what we think can influence our beliefs and our beliefs influence our judgements. The mindset we have may well determine the results of our investigation. This will be obvious from the two sample analyses that follow.

Retrospective Analysis

Accident investigation is simply a retrospective analysis of something that could equally have been identified and analysed prospectively. 'Accidents' are, or should be, only a surprise to those who experience them. The types of Occurrences (accidents) that are possible in any given operating environment are predictable in all respects other than when and where, as shown in Chapter 9. The goal of all control measures is to catch the process as it unfolds at the particular place and time if it has not been possible to remove the Threat. The existence of an Occurrence, whether complete to the point of Damage or Loss or not, is an opportunity to determine the adequacy of existing control measures and the absence of needed ones. It has been argued in Chapter 11 that a sensible basis of a risk management system is a collection of Occurrence analyses known to be possible given the technology and functions of the organisation. Such a collection will guide all post hoc analyses of Occurrences ('accident investigations'). Effectively, a set of standards has been created against which failures can be objectively rather than subjectively recognised. This means that failure can be uncovered also by inspections and self-audits. A lack of predictive effort and a lack of monitoring are very often uncovered in accident investigations indicating the lack of a properly preventive approach to risk management.

The post hoc analysis of Time Zone 1 necessarily depends on understanding the Mechanism: the what happened, how and why. This analysis is only as helpful as the understanding that exists of how the real world of today and now can be understood and described. In Chapter 3, the explanation and description of Time Zone 1 is relevant. The categories used to describe the features of Time Zone 1 will encourage the analyst to uncover and record all relevant nuances. From this, an understanding of the subtle progress of support for the Mechanism will be found and ideas for the introduction of new control measures and the improvement of existing ones will arise.

Example 1

As an example, Tables A1.1 and A1.2 show how the smelter explosion could be analysed. Table A1.1 shows how Consequence and Outcome observations lead to deductions about the possible energy source. In this case the option of thermal energy has been discounted as the Outcomes do not accord with that – an expanding vapour explosion would not have generated the significant heat and blast waves. Mechanism possibilities become evident once the energy source is known. These are of two main types – purposeful and unintentional as incidental (see Chapter 9) is clearly inappropriate. Further enquiry results in the unintentional Mechanism being selected and the reasons for this become evident. In Table A1.2, the results of the further enquiry are noted in the Time Zone 1 worksheet. Time Zone 1 is understood in this analysis using categories introduced in Chapter 3. Of possible interest is the ease with which the Prerequisites of this possible Mechanism might have been recognised as such prior to the Mechanism being set in progress. This depends on the frequency and nature of any routine inspections. Nonspecific 'housekeeping' inspections may well have just noted the nitrate bags were being stored nearby. The most important missing control measure is the management of chemicals according to a chemical hazard management standard. In this case, an exemplary one was put in place within a couple of weeks – after months of refusal to attend to chemical management.

Table A1.1 Backwards (investigation) analysis of Aluminium smelter explosion

Pre-requisites	Mechanism	EVENT	Outcome	Consequence
	Why?	How?	What?	What then?	(Observations)
Possible unforeseen storage of explosive materials on site	*Sabotage? Inadvertent act?*	*Introduced explosive?*	Chemical explosion	Heat wave	1. People working in the smelter — People close to source burned more. Surface burns mainly
Unforeseen storage of an additive capable of forming an explosive mixture with Aluminium and heat.	Inadvertent act?	Explosive mixture created in smelter?		Blast	2. Smelter building and equipment blown apart — Some people thrown bodily
				Aluminium splatter around the building	3. Loss of smelter load

Plain text - possibilities chosen. *Italicised text - possibilities considered.*

Example 2

During the construction of a large manufacturing facility, assembly work was done making use of an oxyacetylene set inside a steel vessel. Over a work break, the set leaked sufficient gas into the confined space to support an explosion if an ignition source had been provided and this led to an investigation. This is a partly developed Occurrence, which resulted in a Null Outcome as the gas was detected and the space cleared before work began after the break. In this case, Enabling Conditions and Circumstances are identified and assessed using a different structure of Time Zone 1, based on possible risk control points as described in Table 3.8. The tabulation shows the results of the analysis, the summary and conclusions of which are listed below. Obviously, the specific conclusions may well be different from these in a particular organisation.

1. Are contractors required to engage suitably skilled people for the work required? Is this specific to the equipment to be used?
2. Are there statements of required equipment condition contained in contracts?
3. Are shift in charge people adequately trained to understand how to effectively complete Permits to Work (PTWs), i.e. after a suitable hazard analysis of the work?
4. What practices exist to periodically provide independent inspection of equipment, skills and actual practices of contractors, of confined-space work and of work under PTWs?
5. Does the confined-space work procedure require atmosphere monitoring to be carried out before the start or recommencement of work?
6. Would the contractor have been expected to provide atmospheric monitoring equipment or should this have been a site owner obligation?
7. What training is provided to contractors with respect to confined space work?

The result is a number of questions requiring answers, from which conclusions may be drawn. It is evident and not surprising that these are likely to involve contractor management, supervision and confined-space management practices.

Table A1.2   Time Zone 1 analysis of Aluminium smelter explosion

ENABLING CONDITIONS AND CIRCUMSTANCES					PRE-REQUISITES
Physical	**Procedures**	**People**	**Organisation**	**Environment**	**Why?**
Sodium Nitrate bags hard to distinguish from Sodium Nitrate bags. Same supplier, same bags, bag markings, obscured by dust.	Informal work and communication practices	Fork lift truck driver who chose the Nitrate bags had no knowledge of the assumption that he should only take bags from one location in the same shed in which the Sodium Nitrate bags were stored.	Sodium Nitrate stored on site for trading benefit.	Nil	Sodium Nitrate used instead of Sodium Chloride, in error.
Bags of different materials stored in the same shed.			No form of chemical management programme		
Sodium Nitrate bags stored away from the Chloride bags, but in the same or adjacent shed.			No purchasing controls		

Table A1.3   Enabling Conditions and Circumstances and their control points

Event: LPG leaks into confined space over a period of time

Mechanism: Unintentional release of gas from oxyacetylene set used within the confined space

CONTROL POINTS ASSOCIATED WITH THE EQUIPMENT AND FACILITY DESIGN	
Design practices	—
Installation/commissioning practices	—
Change management	—
Purchase/contracting practices	Was the expected standard of the contractor's equipment specified? Was the contractor expected to have a safety programme, and if so, what specifically was expected of them?
Inspection/maintenance practices	Was there a process for sampling the standards of the contractor's equipment?
Equipment renewal practices	Does the contractor appear to have rundown equipment as a result of years of bidding for contracts based on lowest price? How might minimum standards of equipment be specified in contracts?
Design risk control reviews	What analysis was done of construction risks prior to letting contracts?
CONTROL POINTS ASSOCIATED WITH WORK METHODS/PROCEDURES	
Work practices	Does the contractor have any defined work practices or are there any common practices of people authorised to use this equipment? Was a Permit to Work process in place and if there was would it actually have ensured that the work was done outside the confined space?
General and task-specific training practices	Were workers skilled in correct use of this equipment? Were any checks ever made of their skills and knowledge?
Inspection/maintenance practices	Did the contractor have any routine process for checking the condition of equipment in use? What expectations for this were placed on the supervisor of the contractor?
CONTROL POINTS ASSOCIATED WITH PEOPLE	
Skill and experience standards	What skill levels were required of people who do this work?
Selection and induction practices, new and transferring employees	What are the contractor's practices? Does the contract specification communicate any expectations in this respect?
ORGANISATIONAL SUPPORT FOR CONTROL POINTS	
Risk register	Does the principal have a risk register or has one been given to the contractor?
Hazard and Threat management standards (Risk control standards)	Are there any standards which the contractor could be required to maintain?
Managing organisational failures	In what way will the lessons of the case influence the practices of the principal and the contractor?
Managing action failures	What efforts will be made to improve the skills and knowledge of associated workers?
Managing risk control improvement opportunities	How are the specific improvements suggested by this analysis to be implemented by both the principal and the contractor?

Appendix 2:
The Role of the Risk Adviser

It is perhaps obvious, but worth saying, that the complex role of the risk adviser is one that requires a mature understanding of risk theory and practice as well as of organisational psychology. All the risk knowledge in the world will not be of much value if blocks in the organisation oppose any improvement in the management of risk. Also, an organisation open to improvement and with the capability to manage it will not achieve much if its efforts at risk management are misdirected. In the absence of strong leadership in risk, the organisation will drift into a mediocre approach probably founded on prevalent accident prevention ideas and subject to the rising and waning influences of whatever fashionable commercial product and service offerings are available.

What is actually needed in an organisation depends very much on the nature of its risks and the existing standard of risk controls. Few, well-controlled risks in a simple environment that changes little, require little risk management effort. Even one significant risk in a complex environment subject to change and deterioration can require much carefully directed risk management effort, and that effort will be quite specific to the nature of the risk. Getting the need understood and the resources to make the effort requires a deep understanding of the character (culture) of the organisation. As noted ealier, there are only two aspects of culture that matter:

1. preparedness to understand the need, and
2. the ability to make the necessary changes.

It is the culture at the highest level in the organisation that will determine what is possible. It is not uncommon to find safety officers who seek any and every opportunity for a 10 second 'grab' at the attention of the Chief Executive Officer, hoping that over time the message will be heard. Without preparedness at this level to understand the need, to engage in a detailed dialogue with the risk adviser, no useful risk management will occur; risk management activity will be spasmodic and incomplete. There may be an appearance of risk management, perhaps even a policy statement on the wall of the reception office and a risk register. The responsibility for doing it poorly or well lies with the top level of management, possibly also the board of management, as well as with the risk adviser. The former need to open both their doors and their minds, and the latter needs to have insight based on a rigorous understanding of risk and be able to conduct the conversation in such a way as to gain the manager's confidence.

Intent and Structure

There is an ethical component to risk management that derives from the fact that, very commonly, adverse Consequences or the potential for them are experienced by one group (employees, customers, other departments, the environment) but decisions about risk control are made by another. Where damage to people or the environment is possible, the law makes the moral dimensions of decision-making evident. Those deciding what degree of risk control to implement may also realise that business opportunities may be diminished as a result of improved risk controls.

If managers at the most senior levels do not explicitly understand this simple fact, the underlying conflict of interest may be the origin of the first cultural problem – being unprepared to understand the need. Senior management leadership of risk management needs to make the intent of the organisation in this respect very clear. Typically, a risk management policy statement can be used for this purpose.

Evidently, the risk adviser needs access at the highest level of management to make and explain the ethical point in the context of the organisation. Given the sensitive nature of the values that a proper risk management approach brings to decision-making, it is necessary for the risk adviser to have this access as of right. It is inappropriate for the access to depend on the understanding of a manager within whose department the risk adviser is located for administrative convenience. This free access requires the risk adviser to use the right effectively.

Where a detailed technical knowledge is required before judgements can be made as to the adequacy of risk controls, the risk adviser either needs to have that level of knowledge or a productive relationship with those who do. There must be a preparedness to facilitate the communication upwards of detailed technical knowledge about the state of risk controls. It is very common for the origin of significant adverse Consequences to lie in small technical details, the significance of which may or may not be known to those aware of them but which have either not been recognised as such or have not been successfully communicated upwards in the organisation. The risk adviser must understand this level of detail, actively convey its meaning upwards in the organisation and promote any necessary changes or management practices.

Committees (risk management or health and safety) can play an important role in allowing for the routine handling of this 'down–up' direction of communication and for bringing together the decision-makers with those who suffer the effects of adverse Consequences. To achieve this potential, the committee needs to be appropriately constituted and managed by the risk adviser. These committees have an important role in the ethical and moral dimensions of risk management.

The board of management can have a significant influence on the culture of an organisation and particularly in those two aspects that are relevant to risk management. However, board members commonly have an overly simple view of risk management gained from experience rather than study as well as an overly confident assessment of their own understanding of the subject. To avoid this being counterproductive, it is very desirable that the risk adviser be present whenever risk management is on the agenda of board meetings. Achieving this should be simple where a board risk management committee exists.

Appropriately Directed Effort

Effective effort is needed in two areas. First, creating and maintaining a suitable prevention-oriented culture (the two points in the introduction above) and secondly, suitably directed at the real needs of the organisation.

Culture change is not normally rapid, unless a disaster shocks the organisation. In an organisation with a management style unsuited to the management of risk it is management capability that needs to be developed before any useful effort can be made to improve risk management ability. As risk management requires the implementation and maintenance of risk control measures over a long period, the development of written processes and practices and the use of an Opportunity for Improvement process may suffice to begin the development of useful management practices.

Specific risk management needs depend on the risks inherent in the organisation (in the risk inventory). Few, simple risks with well-designed and simple control measures make few demands on management interest or capability. Complex risks with poorly defined technical control measures place a high demand on both the risk adviser and managers, as do essentially simple risks involving large energy sources (especially with untried technology or in poorly managed organisations). To be effective, the risk adviser needs to be knowledgeable about the technology and methods employed by the organisation. For example, the operational (Table 5.4) risks at deep mines include explosives, conveyor systems and rock falls, so the risk adviser needs to be thoroughly conversant with the science and technology associated with these even if they are neither a chemist, engineer nor geologist. The nature of the effort required to manage risks depends on whether risk factors (Chapter 5) indicate high or low risk for each type of risk.

Table A2.1 is a summary of the process of diagnosing the needs of an organisation. In unpublished work for the Department of Labour in Victoria, Australia (Department of Labour, 1998), we found that the character of an organisation's capability in managing health and safety risks at least could conveniently be described under headings such as these:

1. Management style and communication.
2. Consultation and involvement of the workforce.
3. Resources made available.
4. Risk management practices.
5. Risk control efforts.
6. The management of injury.

It was found that what an organisation needed to be successful in the control of these risks could be summarised as in Table A2.1.

Table A2.1   Diagnosing the needs of the organisation

1. Management style and communication is important if:
    a) industrial relations are confrontational;
    b) consultation is needed (see below);
    c) risks are capable of being recognised by the workforce (common-sense matters and easy control measures).
2. Consultation and involvement of the workforce is necessary if:
    a) poor design and purchasing risk controls are evident;
    b) the risks in work processes are associated with high risk factors;
    c) the work is labour intensive, in that there is much exposure to risks;
    d) work facilities are old and/or crowded.
3. Resources to assist with the management of risk control become significant if:
    a) risks are not common sense;
    b) a trial and error approach to risk control is not possible;
    c) risk control measures at the point of purchase and design have not been used;
    d) work facilities are old.
4. Risk management practices of the organisation require the attention of senior managers if:
    a) there is seen to be a direct relationship between the costs of incidents and the costs of the risk management programme;
    b) costs have threatened or do threaten financial viability.
(Effective manager engagement is assisted by providing education in and knowledge of risk factors.)

5. Risk control efforts ...

... are simple if:

a) risk control resources are available;

b) The work of the organisation is labour intensive;

c) risks are of the common-sense type;

d) risks are amenable to trial and error solutions;

e) the company has a good financial performance.

... are more difficult if:

a) existing risk factors indicate high risk;

b) risks are of the high frequency and short latency period (i.e. 'accidents') type.

6. Practices for the management of injury outcomes ...

... are less important if:

a) the workplace is capital intensive and well designed;

b) communication pathways (especially vertical communication) are good;

c) industrial relations are not confrontational.

... otherwise:

a) a good claim management agent is needed;

b) an effective programme for the organisational management of rehabilitation is a necessity;

c) active involvement of line managers in rehabilitation is essential.

Common-sense risks refer to those amenable to understanding without any special knowledge, for example the potential to be run over by fork-lift trucks, to fall from high places or to be electrocuted. Examples of risks or risk factors not in this category include exposure to radioactive particles, noise, heat, chemicals, manual work in various forms, the use of control panels, powered machinery, confined spaces, management of construction risks and similar.

It will be evident that the diagnosis of need in any one organisation will depend on the risks being considered: probably operational risks do not fit into the common-sense category and many, but not all, of the general risks will. It is usually entirely inappropriate to manage operational risks in the same way as general risks. The wise risk adviser needs a mature understanding of how the general intentions indicated in Table A2.1 actually apply, probably with modification, to their own organisation.

Skilful Implementation

One of the most significant aspects of a prevention-oriented risk management programme is the handling of situations in which risk control measures could or should be improved. To managers accustomed to the common reactive approach (only fix it when something goes wrong), the need to decide on improvements before a problem (an adverse Consequence) has arisen may well be counterintuitive. It will be beneficial to make every effort to provide managers with a coherent and practically useful understanding of risk and its preventive rather than reactive management. Given a receptive and understanding audience, the risk adviser is responsible for providing managers with well-developed arguments for improvements and ensuring that these are formally presented and discussed.

An example of an unskilful approach to this occurred in a water supply authority. The risk adviser was concerned with the standard of the very old rung ladders used to inspect water supply towers in various locations and put forward a proposal to bring these up to the current standard for such ladders and go beyond that in recognition of the particular situation of these ladders and the ageing workforce. A proposal was prepared for one solution to the problem and in the absence of any formal means of bringing this to the attention of the organisation a few sheets of paper were given to the relevant manager during an ad hoc conversation, which occurred in the corridor. The manager's response was that the amount of money required was simply not in the current budget for discretionary expenditure and the idea was shelved, only to be immediately accepted some few months later immediately after one of the ageing workforce fell off a ladder and died. This is an example of reactive risk management at its worst.

The case makes evident what is needed for prevention to have a chance of success, see Chapter 11:

1. A process for submitting improvement proposals to the organisation, not to an individual manager.
2. A process for the evaluation of proposals which considers first if the proposal is in itself justifiable and secondly the matter of affordability, funding and scheduling of work. Inherently justifiable proposals remain on the list for periodic reconsideration if they cannot be afforded. Those evaluating proposals need to understand how to incorporate moral and ethical considerations in the appraisal of the financial justification for both capital investment decisions and the operating cost implications of proposals.
3. A guideline for writing proposals that ensures ideas are well researched and options provided for both short term and long term and ideal and less than ideal improvements.

The second significant aspect of a prevention-oriented risk management programme is the active involvement of the risk adviser in each and every way in which risks can be imported into the organisation, whether by the purchase of consumables and equipment or by new ventures and projects.

In both of these aspects of the adviser's job, the adviser benefits greatly from access to the advice and guidance of specialists, whatever that might mean: ladder specialists, technology specialists, scientists, engineers, tradespeople, accountants and so on – anyone who can contribute to a comprehensive and competent contribution to the role.

Bibliography

American Institute of Chemical Engineers (1989) *Guidelines for Process Equipment Reliability Data with Data Tables*. New York: Center for Chemical Process Safety.

American Society of Mechanical Engineers (2005) *Standard for Probabilistic Risk Assessment for Nuclear Power Plant Applications, ASME RA-S-2002 as Amended with ASME RA-Sa-2003 and ASME RA-Sb-2005*. New York: ASME.

American Society of Safety Engineers (2002) *White Paper on Return on Safety Investment*. Available at: http://www.asse.org/practicespecialties/bosc/bosc_article_6.php [accessed 22 June 2014].

Bahr, Nicholas, J. (1997) *System Safety Engineering and Risk Assessment: A Practical Approach*. Philadelphia, USA: Taylor and Francis.

Baig, A., Ruzli, R. and Buang, A. (2013) Reliability Analysis Using Fault Tree Analysis – A Review. *International Journal of Chemical Engineering and Applications*, 4(3), 169–73.

Bartley, W.H. (2003) *Analysis of Transformer Failures, Proc.* International Association of Engineering Insurers, 36th Annual Conference, Stockholm.

Bird, F.E. and Germain, G.L. (1986) *Loss Control Management: Practical Loss Control Leadership*, revised edition. Katy, TX: Det Norske Veritas (USA) Inc.

Blomback, J., Buchermann, R. and Schubert, B. (2004) The Centralised Component Reliability Database for PSA Purposes ZEBD – Status, Evaluation 2002, Trends. In: *Probabilistic Safety Assessment and Management 2004*, PSAM7 – ESREL'04. London: Springer-Verlag.

Borys, D. (2012) The Role of Safe Work Method Statements in the Australian Construction Industry. *Safety Science*, 50(2), 210–20.

Braithwaite, J. (1985) *To Punish or Persuade: Enforcement of Coal Mine Safety*. Albany, NY: State University of New York Press.

Brown, A. (1988) Accident Prevention in the LPG Industry. *Health and Safety at Work*, October, 14–15.

Browning, R.L. (1980) *The Loss Rate Concept in Safety Engineering*. New York: Marcel Dekker.

Buehner, M.J. (2005) Contiguity and Covariation in Human Causal Inference. *Learning & Behaviour*, 33(2), 230–38.

Bunn, W.B., Pikelny, D.B., Slavin, T.J. and Paralkar, S. (2001) Health, Safety and Productivity in a Manufacturing Environment. *Journal of Occupational and Environmental Medicine*, 43(1), 47–55.

Cartwright, N. (2004) Causation: One Word, Many Things. *Philosophy of Science*, 71(5), 805–19.

Cepin, M. and Mavko, B. (2002) A Dynamic Fault Tree. *Reliability Engineering & System Safety*, 75(1), 83–91.

Clark, W.C. (1980) Witches, Floods and Wonder Drugs: Historical Perspectives on Risk Management. In: Schwing, R.C. and Albers, W.A. (eds), *Risk Assessment*. New York: Plenum Press.

Cohen, A. (1977) Factors in Successful Occupational Safety Programs. *Journal of Safety Research*, 9, 168–78.

Collingwood, R.G. (1938) On the So-Called Idea of Causation. *Proceedings of the Aristotelian Society*, 38, 85–112.

Cowing, M.M., Pate-Cornell, M.E. and Glynn, P.W. (2004) Dynamic Modelling of the Tradeoff Between Productivity and Safety in Critical Engineering Systems. *Reliability Engineering & System Safety*, 86(3), 269–84.

Dahl, Ø. (2013) Safety Compliance in a Highly Regulated Environment: A Case Study of Workers' Knowledge of Rules and Procedures within the Petroleum Industry. *Safety Science*, 60, 185–95.

Daino, C. (1998) *Edward John Smith, Captain*. Available at: http://www.titanic-lore.info/Capt-Smith.htm [accessed 22 June 2014].

Davies, L. (2012) Jailing of Italian Seismologists Leaves Scientific Community in Shock. *The Guardian*, London, 23 October. Available at: http://www.theguardian.com/world/2012/oct/23/jailing-italian-seismologists-scientific-community [accessed 19 June 2014].

DeLuca, D.R., Stolwijk, J.A. and Horowitz, W. (1986) Public Perceptions of Technological Risks. In: Covello, V.T., Menkes, J. and Mumpower, J. (eds), *Risk Evaluation and Management*. New York: Plenum Press.

Deming, W.E. (1986) *Out of the Crisis*. Cambridge, MA: MIT Press.

Department of Labour (1998) *Time for Change: OHS Prevention Strategies for the 1990s*. Melbourne, Australia.

Eddington, I. (2006) *An Historical Explanation of the Development of Occupational Health and Safety and the Important Position it Now Occupies in Society*. Australian Graduate School of Business, University of Southern Queensland, Australia. Available at: https://eprints.usq.edu.au/1556/1/Eddington_USQ_Queensland_Safety_Forum_2006.pdf [accessed 7 November 2014].

Edmondson, A. (1996). Learning from Mistakes is Easier Said Than Done: Group and Organizational Influences on the Detection and Correction of Human Error. *Journal of Applied Behavioral Science*, 32(1), 5–28.

Eisner, H.S. and Leger, J.P. (1988) The International Safety Rating System in South African Mining. *Journal of Occupational Accidents*, 10(2), 141–60.

Ericson, C. (1999) *Fault Tree Analysis – A History*. Proc. 17th International System Safety Conference. Available at: http://www.fault-tree.net/papers/ericson-fta-history.pdf [accessed 22 June 2014].

Ferdous, R., Khan, F., Sadiq, R., Amyotte, P. and Veitch, B. (2009) Handling Data Uncertainties in Event Tree Analysis. *Process Safety and Environmental Protection*, 87, 283–92.

Ferguson, S. (2003) Other High-Risk Factors for Young Drivers – How Graduated Licensing Does, Doesn't, or Could Address Them. *Journal of Safety Research*, 34(1), 71–7.

Geller, S. (2002) Psychology of Safety: The Myth of the Root Cause. *Industrial Safety and Hygiene News*, 36(7), 18–19.

Gertman, D. and Blackman, H. (1994) *Human Reliability and Safety Analysis Data Handbook*. New York: Wiley InterScience.

Gibson, J.J. (1961) The Contribution of Experimental Psychology to the Formulation of the Problem of Safety – A Brief for Basic Research. In: Jacobs, H.H. et al., *Behavioral Approaches to Accident Research*. New York: Association for the Aid of Crippled Children.

Glaser, R. (1978) *Bathtub and Related Failure Rate Characterizations, TR-78-1440*. Washington, DC: Air Force Office of Scientific Research.

Haddon, W. (1973) Energy Damage and the Ten Countermeasure Strategies. *Journal of Trauma*, 13(4), 321–31.

Haddon, W. (1987) Injury as Disease. *Accident Analysis & Prevention*, 19(1), 13–20.

Haddon, W., Suchman, E.A. and Klein, D. (1964) *Accident Research, Methods and Approaches*. New York: Harper and Row.

Hannaman, G.W., Spurgin, A.J. and Lukic, Y.D. (1984) *Human Cognitive Reliability Model for PRA Analysis. Draft Report NUS-4531, EPRI Project RP2170-3*. Palo Alto, CA: Electric Power and Research Institute.

Haviland, A., Burns, R., Gray, W., Ruder, T. and Mendeloff, J. (2012) A New Estimate of the Impact of OSHA Inspections on Manufacturing Injury Rates, 1998–2005. *American Journal of Industrial Medicine*, 55(11), 964–75.

Haynes, S.N., Huland Spain, E. and Oliveira, J. (1993) Identifying Causal Relationships in Clinical Assessment, *Psychological Assessment*, 5(3), 281–91.

Health and Safety Executive (n.d.) *HID's Approach to ALARP Decisions*, SPC/Permissioning/39.

Heinrich, H.W. (1959) *Industrial Accident Prevention, A Scientific Approach*. New York: McGraw Hill.

Hollnagel, E. (1998) *Cognitive Reliability and Error Analysis Method*. Oxford: Elsevier Science Ltd.

Hollnagel, E. (2012) *FRAM: The Functional Resonance Analysis Method*. Farnham: Ashgate.

Hollnagel, E., Woods, D. and Leveson, N. (2012) *Resilience Engineering: Concepts and Precepts*. Farnham: Ashgate.

Hopkins, A. (1994) Is Productivity Related to Safety? The Case of Coal Mining. *Journal of Occupational Health and Safety – Australia and New Zealand*, 10(5), 431–8.

Hopkins, A. (2008) *Failure to Learn: The BP Texas City Refinery Disaster.* North Ryde, NSW, Australia: CCH Australia.

HSE (n.d.) *The History of HSE.* Available at: http://www.hse.gov.uk/aboutus/timeline/ [accessed 22 June 2014].

Hudson, P.T.W., Parker, D., Lawton, R., Verschuur, W.L.G., van der Graaf, G.C. and Kalff, J. (2000) *The Hearts and Minds Project: Creating Intrinsic Motivation for HSE.* Proc. 5th Society for Petroleum Engineering International Conference on Health, Safety and Environment in Oil and Gas Production and Exploration. CD-ROM. Richardson, TX: SPE.

Institute of Electrical and Electronic Engineers (1984) *IEEE Guide to the Collection and Presentation of Electrical, Electronic, Sensing Component, and Mechanical Equipment Reliability Data for Nuclear-Power Generating Stations.* IEEE Std 500-1984.

International Atomic Energy Agency (1988) *Component Probability Data for Use in Probabilistic Safety Assessment.* Available at: http://www-pub.iaea.org/MTCD/publications/PDF/te_478_web.pdf [accessed October 2013].

International Electrochemical Commission (2012) *Safety of Machinery: Functional Safety of Electrical, Electronic and Programmable Electronic Control Systems.* IEC/EN 62061. Geneva: IEC.

Ishikawa, K. (1968) *Ishikawa Diagram.* Available at: http://en.wikipedia.org/wiki/Ishikawa_diagram [accessed 22 June 2014].

Johnson, W.G. (1973) *The Management Oversight and Risk Tree – MORT.* Washington, DC: US Atomic Energy Commission Division of Operational Safety.

Kahnerman, D., Slovic, P. and Tversky, A. (eds) (1982) *Judgement Under Uncertainty: Heuristics and Biases.* Cambridge: Cambridge University Press.

Kinney, G.F. and Wiruth, A.D. (1976) *Practical Risk Analysis for Safety Management.* California, USA: Naval Weapons Center.

Kletz, T. (2001) *An Engineer's View of Human Error.* Rugby: Institution of Chemical Engineers.

Laurence, D. (2005) Safety Rules and Regulations on Mine Sites – The Problem and a Solution. *Journal of Safety Research,* 36(1), 39–50.

Levine, D., Toffel, M. and Johnson, M. (2012) Randomized Government Safety Inspections Reduce Worker Injuries with No Detectable Job Loss. *Science,* 336(6083), 907–11.

Linh, T.T., Dinh, H., Pasman, X., Gao, M. and Mannam, S. (2012) Resilience Engineering of Industrial Processes: Principles and Contributing Factors. *Journal of Loss Prevention in the Process Industries,* 25(2012), 233–41.

MacKenzie, C., Holmstrom, D. and Kaszniak, M. (2007) *Human Factors Analysis of the BP Texas City Refinery Explosion.* Proc. Human Factors and Ergonomics Society Annual Meeting, 1 October, 1444–8.

Madsen, P. (2013) Perils and Profits: A Reexamination of the Link Between Profitability and Safety in U.S. Aviation. *Journal of Management.* Available at: http://jom.sagepub.com/content/early/2011/04/05/0149206310396374 [accessed 22 June 2014].

Marsden, P. and Green, M. (1996) Optimising Procedures in Manufacturing Systems. *International Journal of Industrial Ergonomics,* 17(1), 43–51.

Mayr, E. (1961) Cause and Effect in Biology. *Science,* 134(3489), 1501–6.

Millican, P. (ed.) (2007) *David Hume – An Enquiry Concerning Human Understanding.* Oxford: Oxford University Press.

National Society for the Study of Education (1926) *The Present Status of Safety Education, 25th Yearbook,* Part 1. Bloomington, IL: Public School Publishing Company, p. 3.

New Scientist (1986) Dust to Dust. *New Scientist,* 110(1514), 26 June, 29.

Nohl, J. (1926) *The Black Death, A Chronicle of the Plague.* London: George Allen & Unwin Ltd.

NPR (2011) *Early Space Shuttle Flights Riskier than Estimated.* Available at: http://www.npr.org/2011/03/04/134265291/early-space-shuttle-flights-riskier-than-estimated [accessed 19 June 2014].

OSHA (2012) *OSHA Law & Regulation.* Available at: https://www.osha.gov/law-regs.html [accessed April 2012].

Oxenburg, M., Marlow, P. and Owenberg, A. (2004) *Increasing Productivity and Profit through Health and Safety: The Financial Returns from a Safe Work Environment.* Boca Raton, FL: CRC Press.

Pickering, A. and Cowley, S. (2010) Risk Matrices: Implied Accuracy and False Assumptions. *Journal of Health & Safety, Research & Practice*, 2(1), 9–16.

Procaccia, H., Arsenis, S.P. and Aufort, P. (1998) *European Industry Reliability Data Bank EIReDA 1998*. Crete, Greece: Crete University Press.

Quigley, J. and Revie, M. (2011) Estimating the Probability of Rare Events: Addressing Zero Failure Data. *Risk Analysis*, 31(7), 1120–32.

Reason, J. (1997) *Managing the Risks of Organisational Accidents*. Farnham: Ashgate.

Robens, A. (1972) *Safety and Health at Work: Report of the Committee*. London: Her Majesty's Stationery Office.

Rowe, W.D. (1977) *An Anatomy of Risk*. New York: John Wiley and Sons.

Russo, J. and Kolzow, K. (1994) Where is the Fault in Fault Trees? *Journal of Experimental Psychology: Human Perception and Performance*, 20(1), 17–32.

Samuel, H. (2012) Paris, *The Daily Telegraph*, London, 29th November.

Shannon, H.S., Robson, L.S. and Sale, J.E.M. (2001) Creating Safer and Healthier Workplaces: Role of Organizational Factors and Job Characteristics. *American Journal of Industrial Medicine*, 40(3), 319–34.

Slovic, P. (1987) Perception of Risk, *Science*, 24(17), 280–85.

Slovic, P., Fischhoff, B. and Lichtenstein, S. (1981) Perceived Risk: Psychological Factors and Social Implications. In: Warner, F. and Slater, D.H. (eds), *The Assessment and Perception of Risk*. London: The Royal Society.

Slovic, P., Fischhoff, B. and Lichtenstein, S. (1986) The Psychometric Study of Risk Perception. In: Covello, V.T., Menkes, J. and Mumpower, J. (eds), *Risk Evaluation and Management*. New York: Plenum Press.

Steel, C. (1990) Risk Estimation. *The Safety and Health Practitioner*, June, 20–21.

Sutton, I. (2007) *Fault Tree Analysis*. Houston, TX: Sutton Technical Books.

Swain, A.D. and Guttman, H.E. (1985) *Handbook of Human Reliability Analysis with Emphasis on Nuclear Power Plant Applications, NUREG/CR-1278*. Washington, DC: US Nuclear Regulatory Commission.

Tanaka, H. (1983) Fault-Tree Analysis by Fuzzy Probability. *Reliability*, 32(5), 453–7.

Taylor, Right Hon. Lord Justice (1990) *The Hillsborough Stadium Disaster*. London: Home Office.

The Times (2014) *The Times*, 16 May, p. 34.

US Atomic Energy Commission (1975) *Reactor Safety Study: An Assessment of Accident Risks in U.S. Commercial Nuclear Power Plants*, WASH-1400 (NUREG-75/014).

US Nuclear Regulatory Commission (1984) *Probabilistic Safety Analysis Procedures Guide*, NUREG/CR 2815.

US Nuclear Regulatory Commission (2003) *Handbook of Parameter Estimation for Probabilistic Risk Assessment*, NUREG/CR-6823 (SAND2003-3348P).

US Nuclear Regulatory Commission (2004) *An Approach for Determining the Technical Adequacy of Probabilistic Risk Assessment Results for Risk-Informed Activities*, Regulatory Guide 1.200 (for trial use), February 2004.

Vasey, S. (1998) *Set Phasers on Stun and Other True Tales of Design, Technology and Human Error*. Aegean Publishing Company, Santa Barbara, USA.

Veltri, A., Pagell, M., Behm, M. and Das, A. (2007) A Data-Based Evaluation of the Relationship between Occupational Safety and Operation Performance. *The Journal of SH&E Research*, 4(1), 2–22.

Veltri, A., Pagell, M., Johnston, D., Tompa, E., Robson, L., Amick, B.C., Johnson, S.H. and Macdonald, S. (2013) Understanding Safety in the Context of Business Operations: An Exploratory Study Using Case Studies. *Safety Science*, 55, 119–34.

Viner, D. (1991) *Accident Analysis and Risk Control*. Victoria, Australia: Derek Viner Pty Ltd.

Viner, D., Harvey, J. and Borys, D. (2001) An Evaluation of Risk Assessment Methods (unpublished).

Waller, J. and Klein, D. (1973) Society, Energy and Injury, Inevitable Triad? In: *Research Directions Towards the Reduction of Injury*, DHEW Publication No. (NIH) 73-124. Bethesda, MD: US Department of Health, Education and Welfare, pp. 1–37.

Weick, K. (1999) Organizing for High Reliability: Processes of Collective Mindfulness. In Sutton, R.S. and Staw, B.M. (eds), *Research in Organizational Behavior*, Volume 1. Stanford, CA: Jai Press, pp. 81–123.

Weindling, P. (ed.) (1985) *The Social History of Occupational Health*. Beckenham: Croom Helm.

Western Australian Fisheries and Marine Research Laboratories (2012) A Correlation Study of the Potential Risk Factors Associated with White Shark Attacks in Western Australian Waters. *Fisheries Occasional Publication* No. 109, Fisheries Research Division.

White, P.A. (1990) Ideas about Causation in Philosophy and Psychology. *Psychological Bulletin*, 108(1), 3–18.

Wigglesworth, E.C. (1972) A Teaching Model of Injury Causation and a Guide for Selecting Countermeasures. *Occupational Psychology*, 46, 69–78.

Wigglesworth, E.C. (1978) The Fault Doctrine and Injury Control. *Journal of Trauma*, 18(12), 789–94.

Yakovleva, P., Sobelb, R. and Russell, S. (2010) Occupational Safety and Profit Maximization: Friends or Foes? *The Journal of Socio-Economics*, 39(3), 429–35.

Index

continuous improvement 10, 190
control
    active 38–9
    design 226
    interlock 211, 215, 217, 219
    modes 218
    passive 39
    stereotypes 219
    system 188, 191, 196
controlling function 41, 155
corrosion 172, 225
Costa Concordia 100
criticality 222, 225
    see also risk type
cumulative sum (CUSUM) 178

Daino, C. 58
damage 30–43, 49, 54–6, 57, 76, 93, 143
    threshold 33–7, 109
damages 93, 204
damaging energy space 33–4, 39, 104, 106, 109
    see also energy damage model
danger
    ecology of 12
    money 136
    tag 70
dangerous 133
Davies, L. 230
decision making 122–7, 140
demand 157, 160, 173–4
Deming, W.E. 10
Department of Labor, USA 5
detection 109, 112–13, 156
discounting in time 169
domino model 7, 9, 17, 22, 29
dread factor 137
duty of care 5, 121–3, 127–9, 133–4, 230

Edmondson, A. 159
Eisner, H.S. and Leger, J.P. 202
electrical transformer 91–3
embrittlement 53, 153, 172
employment law 2, 3
enabling (condition or circumstance) 46–9, 104, 110, 169, 233–5
    see also energy damage model
energy 1, 11–14, 24, 29–46, 71–9, 91
    damage 13–14, 31, 33–4, 42, 45–6, 56, 104, 106, 146, 230
    damage duration 42
    damage model 31–4, 104
    intensity 1, 13, 33–5, 90, 106, 108–9, 122
    stored 215, 219

equitable 135–6
ergonomics 51, 153, 219
Ericson, C. 143
erosion 36, 112, 153, 225
error types 1 and 2 155, 223
event 46–60
    analysis 14, 144, 161, 163, 164, 167, 170
    see also fault tree analysis
exclusion, positive 216
exposure 59–60

Factories Act 3, 4
    inspectors 3
failure
    action 52, 144, 157–61, 171–7, 194–5, 223–6, 235
    burn-in, infant mortality 158, 172
    command 41, 153–4
    common mode 158
    functional 14, 152, 166
    latent 194
    mode 14, 158, 221
    primary and secondary 153
    random 158, 169, 173–4
    secondary 153
    systemic 192
    wear-out 158, 172, 221–2
fault tree analysis 14, 144–5, 151–2, 156–9, 174
Ferguson, S. 77
FN or fN curve 66, 124
frequency 59–61
    relative 59, 93
    see also risk

Gertman, D. and Blackman, H. 21, 159
Gibson, J.J. 11–12, 15, 17, 31–3
Glaser, R. 172
guard (machine) 3, 39, 213–15

Haddon, W. 12–14, 17, 31, 33, 104
haul truck 71–3, 76, 219
hazard 7, 34–7
    and operability study 14
    control 41, 46, 105, 147
    control failure mechanism 40–41, 147
    management standard 10–11, 49, 53, 231
    see also energy damage model
Health and Safety at Work Act 5
Health and Safety Executive (UK) 124
Heinrich, H.W. 6–9, 18–23, 29, 41, 60
hierarchy of control 128, 186
Hillsborough stadium 192
Hollnagel, E. 15, 51, 108, 223